www.studyforfe.com

Study Guide for Fundamentals of Engineering (FE) Electrical & Computer CBT Exam

- Third Edition -

Practice over 700 solved problems with detailed solutions based on NCEES® FE Reference Handbook Version 10.0.1

Wasim Asghar

PE, P. Eng, M. Eng

DISCLAIMER

This book is developed to assist reader in FE Electrical and Computer exam preparation. It has gone through multiple review cycles to produce a high-quality text. However, there are no representations or warranties, express or implied, about the completeness, accuracy, reliability, suitability, or availability with respect to the information, products or related graphics contained in this book for any purpose. The author does not accept any legal responsibility for the content within. By using this book, the reader agrees to indemnify and hold harmless the author and publisher from any damages claimed because of the content of this book.

NCEES® is a registered trademark of National Council of Examiners for Engineering and Surveying. NCEES® did not partake in the development of this publication. NCEES® does not endorse or otherwise sponsor this publication and makes no warranty, guarantee, or representation, express or implied, as to its accuracy or content.

Printed by KDP, An Amazon.com Company

Independently published

ISBN: 9798670880909

Table of Contents

Chapter # 17 – Software Engineering 159

Solutions 169

Preface

'Practice makes perfect' is as applicable to passing NCEES® FE exam as it is to anything else.

The biggest challenge involved in FE exam preparation is the breadth of knowledge and the range of topics involved. However, the silver lining is that exam questions may not be very complex. Therefore, it is important to gain fundamental understanding of all topics (more on exam taking strategy later). The intended audience of this book includes final year students, new graduates and seasoned professionals who have been out of school for a while.

What is new in the 3rd edition?

Study Guide for Fundamentals of Engineering (FE) Electrical and Computer CBT Exam has been well reviewed by students and received a lot of positive feedback. The author has made continued efforts to add challenging practice problems, introduce new concepts, offer detailed solutions, and update the content based on the latest exam format. FE Electrical and Computer exam specification was updated by NCEES® in January 2020 and exams are being conducted based on specification outlined in NCEES® FE Reference Handbook Version 10.0.1 since July 1st, 2020. To address these changes, this latest edition of Study Guide for Fundamentals of Engineering (FE) Electrical and Computer exam includes:

- 200+ brand new practice problems.
- Addition of new topics as per latest specification.
- Step-by-step solution of problems with detailed explanations.
- Free access to additional resources – exam planner, webinar and course preview.

Best way to use this book

This book covers all 17 sections of NCEES® FE Electrical and Computer CBT exam. It is centered on the idea of 'problem-based learning'. It is important to note that NCEES® FE Reference Handbook will be the only reference material available to examinees during examination. As such, this book is designed to improve reader's familiarity with the reference manual.

Students are suggested to conduct multiple reviews of applicable NCEES® FE Reference Handbook sections and understand theory behind relevant concepts and formulas using all available resources. It is recommended to attempt problems from each chapter right after studying relevant concepts. You may not be able to solve all problems in the first attempt. Therefore, it is suggested to make note of concepts requiring further review. Once the underlying theory is understood, you should revisit the problems and attempt them again. After solving the problems, you are encouraged to review solutions at the end of this book to reconfirm answers and methodology. In certain cases, there can be more than one way of solving same question, but an effort has been made to present the most efficient solving techniques. Whenever students encounter unfamiliar concepts and theories, it is recommended to research those topics to gain necessary understanding. In fact, as part of exam preparation effort, students should always think about ways in which questions can be asked.

Organization of this book

Every chapter starts with a reference to applicable sections and page numbers of NCEES® FE Reference Handbook, comments regarding difficulty level of the section and topic specific tips and formulas for effective exam preparation. Solutions are grouped at the end for ease of review. As noted earlier, this book is especially designed to develop reader's familiarity with the reference manual. Hopefully, after solving all problems and reviewing relevant solutions, students will be able to comfortably navigate NCEES® FE Reference Handbook and recall applicable formulas quickly during exam. Doing so will allow them to save precious time on exam and help improve their performance.

Errata and Error Reporting

This book has undergone multiple review cycles and significant effort has been made to produce a high-quality text. However, it is conceivable that certain errors might have gone unnoticed. Feel free to report any errors, improvements, or questions at **comments@studyforfe.com**. Please visit the website **www.studyforfe.com** to view confirmed errata online.

About the author

Wasim Asghar is a licensed Professional Engineer in Texas (PE), Florida (PE) and Ontario (P. Eng) with consulting experience in power system design, commissioning, and plant engineering for leading clients in various industries including energy, mining, and manufacturing.

He holds Bachelor of Engineering – Electrical with distinction from McMaster University, Hamilton, Canada (2010) and Master of Engineering – Power Systems from University of Toronto (2013) which was completed with full-time work.

In 2014, he undertook a two-year international work assignment for a major project in Florida and decided to pursue PE licensure in the United States. The road to licensure was challenging primarily due to a lack of useful study material for FE and PE exams.

Wasim passed both exams in first attempts. The lessons learned during exam preparation process inspired him to write this book which is designed to help aspiring professional engineers better prepare for FE Electrical and Computer exam.

Acknowledgements

I am truly thankful to the support offered by my family.

Dedication

This book is dedicated to my loving wife.

Additional resources that you may find helpful......

FREE 'FE Electrical and Computer Exam Preparation Planner'

Visit **www.studyforfe.com/free-planner-studyguide30/** to download exam planner and learn about:

- Benefits of professional licensure for electrical engineers
- Challenges involved in preparing for FE Electrical and Computer exam
- FE-style sample problems
- Warm-up exercises to for exam planning
- 4-month exam preparation schedule
- Exam taking strategies

By going through this 40-page PDF, students will be able to get a better appreciation of FE Electrical & Computer exam preparation requirements and how they should realistically allocate their time to successfully pass this exam in first attempt. Although, exam preparation timelines can vary depending on individual circumstances, schedules, and commitment levels, but one thing is certain that properly planning and executing an effective exam preparation strategy with focused effort can go a long way in increasing your chances of passing.

FREE '1-hour Webinar on 3-step framework for exam preparation'

Visit **https://resources.studyforfe.com/webinar-studyguide30/** to register and learn about:

- 3-step framework for FE Electrical and Computer exam preparation.
- Discussion on importance of maintaining momentum, developing right mind set and planning.
- Brief comparison between the FE and PE exams.
- Overview of latest exam specification including various exam section changes.
- 4-month study plan for FE Electrical and Computer exam preparation.

Chapter # 1 – Mathematics

Key Knowledge Areas*

Concepts	NCEES® FE Reference Handbook Version 10.0.1	
	Section	**Page #**
Algebra and trigonometry	Mathematics	34 – 62
Complex numbers		
Discrete mathematics		
Analytic geometry		
Calculus		
Ordinary differential equations		
Linear algebra		
Vector analysis		

Facts about this section

- 11 - 17 questions can be expected on the exam according to the latest NCEES® FE specification.
- Mathematics is the most heavily weighted exam section.
- Difficulty level of this section is rated 'Medium' by the author.

Tips for preparing this section

- Understand the concepts related to Mathematics found in NCEES® FE Reference Handbook.
- Some of the most important concepts and equations of this section include:
    - Algebra - Equations of straight line, quadratic equation/surface, logarithmic identities.
    - Complex Numbers – Rectangular form, polar form, conversions between rectangular and polar forms, addition, subtraction, multiplication and division, Euler's identity.
    - Trigonometry – Trigonometric functions/identities, law of sines and law of cosines.
    - Discrete Math – Set theory, functions, and mapping methods, directed graphs.
    - Analytic geometry – Mensuration of areas and volumes, conic sections.
    - Calculus – Differential calculus, function max/min and derivatives, L' Hospital's rule, integral calculus, definite and indefinite integrals.
    - Differential equations – 1st order differential equation solutions – separation of variables and integrating factor methods, 2nd order differential equation solutions.
    - Matrix and vector analysis – Matrix operations - addition, subtraction, multiplication, determinant, transpose, inverse, Vector operations – dot product, cross product.
- Solve the problem sets of this chapter and review solutions at the end of this book.

BONUS: Unlock a free 'Mathematics' lecture by signing-up for the On-demand FE Electrical and Computer exam preparation <u>course preview</u> at: **www.studyforfe.com/fe-course-preview**

* Exam specification details can be found on pages 479 - 481 of NCEES® FE Reference Handbook.

Problem Set # 1.1 – Algebra and Trigonometry

Consult NCEES® FE Reference Handbook – Pages 34 - 38 while solving these questions

Problem 1.1 a) Solve the following logarithmic equation for x:

$$\log_3(12x - 12) - \log_3(x) = 2$$

(A) 2

(B) 4

(C) 3

(D) 0

Problem 1.1 b) _____ logarithm(s) do not exist and cannot be calculated.

(A) $\log(0.001)$

(B) $\log(0)$

(C) $\log(-10)$

(D) $\log(10)$

Problem 1.1 c) Solve the following logarithmic equation for x:

$$\log_3(x + 1) + \log_3(x - 1) = 1$$

(A) 0

(B) 2

(C) -2

(D) 12

Problem 1.1 d) Solve the following logarithmic equation for x:

$$\ln(x^2 - 7x + 11) = 0$$

(A) 4

(B) 2

(C) 5

(D) 3

Problem 1.1 e) Find the domain of logarithmic function $\log(x^2 - 7x + 10)$.

(A) $(-\infty, 2)$

(B) $(-\infty, 5)$

(C) $(5, \infty)$

(D) $(-\infty, 2) \cup (5, \infty)$

Problem 1.1 f) $\log_5 7$ can be expressed as _____ in $\log_{10}$.

Problem 1.1 g) Simplify the following trigonometric expression:

$$\sin^2 x \, (\cot^2 x + 1)$$

(A) $\csc^2 x$

(B) 1

(C) 0

(D) $\tan^2 x$

Problem 1.1 h) Simplify the following trigonometric expression:

$$\frac{\cot^2 x}{\cot^2 x + 1}$$

(A) $\sin^2 x$ (B) $\cos^2 x$

(C) $\tan^2 x$ (D) 1

Problem 1.1 i) Simplify the following trigonometric expression:

$$(\sin x + \cos x)^2 - 1$$

(A) 0   (B) 2

(C) $\sin 2x$ (D) $\sin x \, \cos x$

Problem 1.1 j) Simplify the following trigonometric expression:

$$\csc^2 x \cot^2 x + \csc^2 x$$

(A) $\sin^2 x$ (B) $\sec^2 x$

(C) $\csc^2 x$ (D) $\csc^4 x$

Problem 1.1 k) Calculate the length of side 'a' for the triangle shown below.

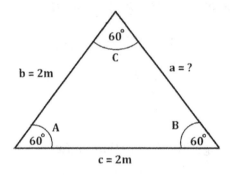

Problem 1.1 l) Calculate the unknown angles A, B and C of a triangle if the lengths of its corresponding sides are $a = 2m$, $b = 3.46m$ and $c = 4m$ respectively.

(A) $A = 30°, B = 60°, C = 90°$ (B) $A = 60°, B = 30°, C = 90°$

(C) $A = 30°, B = 90°, C = 60°$ (D) $A = 90°, B = 30°, C = 60°$

Problem Set # 1.2 – Complex Numbers

Consult NCEES® FE Reference Handbook – Pages 36 - 37 while solving these questions

Problem 1.2 a) _____ is a polar representation of $(8 + 4j) - (5 + 0j)$.

(A) $3 + 4j$

(B) $5\underline{/53°}$

(C) $5\underline{/37°}$

(D) $8\underline{/7°}$

Problem 1.2 b) _____ is a polar representation of $(4 + 4j)/(2 + 3j)$.

(A) $3 + 4j$

(B) $5\underline{/53°}$

(C) $1.5\underline{/-11°}$

(D) $8\underline{/7°}$

Problem 1.2 c) _____ is a rectangular representation of $2\underline{/30°} \times 4\underline{/15°}$.

(A) $8\underline{/45°}$

(B) $8 + \sqrt{2}j$

(C) $5.7 + 5.7j$

(D) 8

Problem 1.2 d) _____ is a rectangular representation of $4\underline{/30°} + 6\underline{/30°}$.

(A) $10\underline{/60°}$

(B) $24\underline{/90°}$

(C) $8.6 + 5j$

(D) $5.4 + 3.8j$

Problem 1.2 e) $3 + 4j$ can be expressed as _____.

(A) $5(\cos 53° + j \sin 53°)$

(B) $5e^{j53}$

(C) $5\underline{/53°}$

(D) All of the above

Problem 1.2 f) The complex conjugate of $Z = (2 + 6j) \times (3 + 3j)$ is _____.

Problem 1.2 g) $2 \cos \theta + j4 \sin \theta$ can be expressed as _____ using Euler's identity.

(A) $e^{j\theta} + e^{-j\theta}$

(B) $e^{j\theta} - 3e^{-j\theta}$

(C) $3e^{j\theta} - e^{-j\theta}$

(D) $3e^{j\theta} + e^{-j\theta}$

Problem Set # 1.3 – Discrete Mathematics and Progressions
Consult NCEES® FE Reference Handbook – Pages 34 – 35, 50 while solving these questions

Problem 1.3 a) _____ is a proper subset of set {2, 4, 6, 8, 10, 12}.

(A) {2, 3, 4, 5}   (B) {2, 4, 6, 8, 10, 12, 14}

(C) {2, 4, 6}   (D) {2, 4, 6, 8, 10, 12}

Problem 1.3 b) _____ is a subset of set {a, b, c, d, e}.

(A) {x, y, z}   (B) {a, b, c, d, e}

(C) {a, f, h, e}   (D) None of the above

Problem 1.3 c) {1, 2, 3, 4, 5} and {a, b, c, d, e} are examples of _____ sets.

(A) Disjoint   (B) Proper

(C) Sub   (D) Overlapping

Problem 1.3 d) _____ is a cartesian product of {1, 2} x {a, b, c, d}.

(A) {(1,a),(1,b),(2,a),(2,b)}

(B) {(1,a),(1,b),(1,c),(1,d),(2,a),(2,b),(2,c),(2,d)}

(C) {(a,1),(b,1),(c,1),(d,1),(a,2),(b,2),(c,2),(d,2)}

(D) None of the above

Problem 1.3 e) Which one of the following relation(s) is not an example of a function?

(A) {(1,b),(1,c),(1,d) }   (B) {(1,a),(2,a),(3,a) }

(C) {(1,a),(2,b),(3,c) }   (D) None of the above

Problem 1.3 f) {(a,1),(b,1),(c,2),(d,2)} is an example of _____ function.

(A) Injective   (B) Surjective

(C) Bijective   (D) It's not a function

Problem 1.3 g) The 35th term of progression given below is _____.

$$2, 4, 6, 8, 10, 12 \cdots$$

Problem 1.3 h) _____ is the sum of an arithmetic progression with 120 terms for which first term is 1 and last term is 259.

Problem 1.3 i) The 12th term of progression given below is _____.

$$3, 9, 27, 81 \cdots$$

Problem 1.3 j) _____ is the sum of a geometric progression for which first term is 1, last term is 19683 and common ratio is 3.

Problem 1.3 k) Select appropriate region(s) representing $A \cap B$.

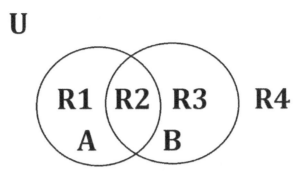

Problem 1.3 l) _____ correctly represents the set of vertices for following directed graph?

(A) {A, B, C, D}   (B) {A, B, C, D, E}

(C) {A, B, C, D, E, E}   (D) None of the above

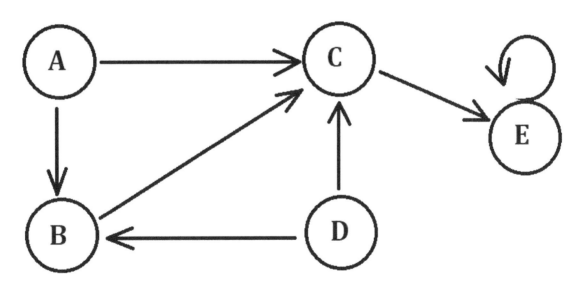

Problem 1.3 m) _____ correctly represents the set of edges for above given directed graph?

(A) {(A,C),(A,B),(B,C),(D,B),(D,C),(C,E),(E,E)}

(B) {(A,C),(B,A),(C,B),(D,B),(D,C),(C,E),(E,E)}

(C) {(A,C),(A,B),(B,C),(B,D),(C,D),(C,E),(E,E)}

(D) {(A,C),(A,B),(B,C),(D,B),(C,D),(E,C),(E,E)}

Problem Set # 1.4 – Analytic Geometry

Consult NCEES® FE Reference Handbook – Pages 35, 39 - 45 while solving these questions

Problem 1.4 a) Calculate the angle between two lines given by following equation.

$$y_1 = x_1 + 4 \quad y_2 = 5x_2 + 6$$

(A) 78.6°   (B) 11.3°

(C) 38.6°   (D) 33.7°

Problem 1.4 b) Find the equation of a straight line passing through points (2, 10) and (3, 12).

(A) $y = 3x + 12$ (B) $y = 2x + 10$

(C) $y = 2x + 6$ (D) $y = 3x + 10$

Problem 1.4 c) Equation of a straight line with slope = 2 and intercept = -5 is _____.

Problem 1.4 d) Equation of a straight line passing through a point (3,6) with slope = 4 is _____.

Problem 1.4 e) Select the option(s) that represent a straight line perpendicular to the line given below.

$$y = 4x + 4$$

(A) $y = -x/4$ (B) $y = -x/4 + 4$

(C) $y = -4x$ (D) $y = -4x + 4$

Problem 1.4 f) _____ represents a parabola with an opening on the positive y-axis.

(A) $(x - 4)^2 = 2(y - 2)$ (B) $(x - 4)^2 = -2(y - 2)$

(C) $(y - 2)^2 = -4(x - 4)$ (D) $(y - 2)^2 = 4(x - 4)$

Problem 1.4 g) _____ represents an ellipse with a vertical major axis.

(A) $\dfrac{(x-2)^2}{144} + \dfrac{(y-4)^2}{100} = 1$ (B) $\dfrac{(x-2)^2}{100} + \dfrac{(y-4)^2}{144} = 1$

(C) $\dfrac{(x-2)^2}{144} - \dfrac{(y-4)^2}{100} = 1$ (D) $\dfrac{(y-4)^2}{100} - \dfrac{(x-2)^2}{144} = 1$

Problem 1.4 h) _____ represents a hyperbola with upward/downward openings.

(A) $\dfrac{(x-2)^2}{144} + \dfrac{(y-4)^2}{100} = 1$ (B) $\dfrac{(x-2)^2}{100} + \dfrac{(y-4)^2}{144} = 1$

(C) $\dfrac{(x-2)^2}{144} - \dfrac{(y-4)^2}{100} = 1$ (D) $\dfrac{(y-4)^2}{100} - \dfrac{(x-2)^2}{144} = 1$

Problem 1.4 i) Calculate the eccentricity, directrix and focus of conic section given by following equation: $(x - 4)^2 = 12(y - 3)$.

Problem 1.4 j) Calculate the eccentricity, directrix and focus of conic section given by following equation: $(y - 8)^2 = 4(x - 2)$

Problem 1.4 k) Calculate the eccentricity, directrix and focus of conic section given by following equation: $2(x - 10)^2 + 8(y - 6)^2 = 200$.

Problem 1.4 l) Calculate the eccentricity, directrix and focus of conic section given by following equation: $2(x - 10)^2 - 8(y - 6)^2 = 200$

Problem 1.4 m) The volume of a right circular cylinder with radius = 1m and height = 2m is _____.

(A) 2.1 m^3

(B) 4.2 m^3

(C) 6.3 m^3

(D) 3.7 m^3

Problem 1.4 n) The area of a right circular cone with radius = 2m and height = 4m is _____.

(A) 40 m^2

(B) 10 m^2

(C) 20 m^2

(D) 8 m^2

Problem 1.4 o) _____ geometric shape will hold largest volume of liquid. Assume that all these shapes have the same radius and height.

(A) Right circular cone

(B) Right circular cylinder

(C) Paraboloid of Revolution

(D) All of them will hold same volume

Problem Set # 1.5 – Calculus

Consult NCEES® FE Reference Handbook – Pages 45 - 49 while solving these questions

Problem 1.5 a) Calculate the derivative of following function:

$$f(x) = 2\tan^2 x + \sin^2 x$$

(A) $4\tan x + 2\sin x$

(B) $2\sec^2 x + \cos^2 x$

(C) $4\tan x \sec^2 x + 2\sin x \cos x$

(D) 0

Problem 1.5 b) Calculate the derivative of following function:

$$f(x) = 4x^2 + 6x + 2y^2$$

(A) $8x + 6$

(B) $8x + 6 + 4y$

(C) $4x + 6 + 2y$

(D) 0

Problem 1.5 c) Calculate the derivative of following function:

$$f(x) = 2\tan x \sec x$$

(A) $2\sin x / \cos^2 x$

(B) $2(\tan^2 x \sec x + \sec^3 x)$

(C) $2\tan x \sec^3 x$

(D) 0

Problem 1.5 d) Calculate the derivative of following function:

$$f(x) = 2\sin^{-1} x + 2\cos^{-1} x$$

(A) $2/\sqrt{1 - x^2}$

(B) $-2/\sqrt{1 - x^2}$

(C) $4\sin x \cos x$

(D) 0

Problem 1.5 e) Calculate the derivative of following function:

$$f(x) = \frac{3x^3 + 2x}{2x + 4}$$

(A) $(9x^2 + 2)/2$

(B) $(12x^3 + 36x^2 + 8)/(2x + 4)^2$

(C) $(9x^2 + 2)/(2x + 4)^2$

(D) 0

Problem 1.5 f) Calculate the local minimum and maximum points of function given below.

$$f(x) = 4x^3 + x^2 - 2x + 8 \quad -1 \leq x \leq 1$$

(A) There is no minimum/maximum

(B) $x = \frac{1}{3}$ (min), $x = -\frac{1}{2}$ (max)

(C) $x = \frac{1}{3}$ (max), $x = -\frac{1}{2}$ (min)

(D) $x = \frac{1}{3}$ (min), no max

Problem 1.5 g) Calculate the local minimum and maximum points of function given below.

$$f(x) = 3x^3 + 3x^2 - 3x + 3 \quad -2 \leq x \leq 1$$

(A) There is no minimum/maximum

(B) $x = \frac{1}{3}$ (min), $x = -1$ (max)

(C) $x = \frac{1}{3}$ (max), $x = -1$ (min)

(D) $x = \frac{1}{3}$ (min), no max

Problem 1.5 h) The point of inflection for function given in problem 1.5 g) exists at $x =$ _____.

Problem 1.5 i) Evaluate the following limit:

$$\lim_{x \to 1} \frac{3x^2 - 2x - 1}{4x^2 + 6x - 10}$$

(A) 0

(B) ∞

(C) 2/7

(D) 4

Problem 1.5 j) Evaluate the following limit:

$$\lim_{x \to \pi/2} \frac{4 \cos x}{2 - 2 \sin x}$$

(A) π

(B) 0

(C) ∞

(D) $3\pi/2$

Problem 1.5 k) Evaluate the following indefinite integral:

$$\int \frac{4}{x + 3} dx$$

(A) $\frac{1}{\sqrt{4}} \tan^{-1}\left(x \sqrt{\frac{1}{3}} \right) + C$

(B) $2 \ln |2x + 6| + C$

(C) $4\sqrt{x + 3} + C$

(D) $4 \ln |x + 3| + C$

Problem 1.5 l) Evaluate the following indefinite integral:

$$\int (\sin^2 x + \cos^2 x)\,dx$$

(A) $1 + C$

(B) $x/2 - \sin 2x /4 + C$

(C) $x + C$

(D) $x/2 + \sin 2x /4 + C$

Problem 1.5 m) Evaluate the following indefinite integral:

$$\int 4x \ln x \, dx$$

(A) $2x^2 \ln x - x^2 + C$

(B) $4x^2 \ln x + x^2 + C$

(C) $2x^2 \ln x + x^2 + C$

(D) $x^2 \ln x + x^2 + C$

Problem 1.5 n) The definite integral of function given below is _____.

$$\int_0^1 xe^{2x}\,dx$$

Problem 1.5 o) Select the point on graph at which derivative of given function is <u>highest</u>.

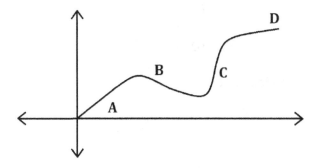

Problem 1.5 p) Select the point on graph at which derivative of given function is <u>lowest</u>.

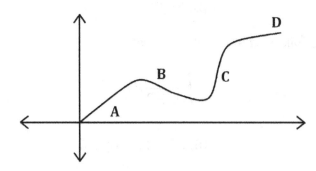

Problem Set # 1.6 – Differential Equations

Consult NCEES® FE Reference Handbook – Pages 51 - 52 while solving these questions

Problem 1.6 a) Solve the following 1st order linear differential equation with given initial values.

$$2y' + 4y = 0 \qquad y(0) = 6$$

(A) $y = 3e^{-4t}$

(B) $y = 6e^{-4t}$

(C) $y = 3e^{-2t}$

(D) $y = 6e^{-2t}$

Problem 1.6 b) Solve the following 1st order linear differential equation.

$$y' + 2x^2y = x^2$$

Problem 1.6 c) Solve the following 1st order linear differential equation.

$$2y' = 8y + 2x$$

Problem 1.6 d) Solve the following 2nd order linear differential equation.

$$y'' + 6y' + 9y = 0$$

Problem 1.6 e) Solve the following 2nd order linear differential equation with initial conditions.

$$y'' + 2y' - 8y = 0 \qquad y(0) = 6, \qquad y'(0) = 0$$

Problem 1.6 f) The 2nd order linear differential equation given below is _____.

$$2y'' + 4y' + 8y = 0$$

(A) Underdamped

(B) Overdamped

(C) Critically damped

(D) None of the above

Problem 1.6 g) Match the given differential equation with correct type.

| 1st order linear non-homogeneous differential equation |

$y'' + 8y' + 12y = 0$

| 1st order linear homogeneous differential equation |

| 2nd order linear homogeneous differential equation |

Problem Set # 1.7 – Matrix and Vector analysis
Consult NCEES® FE Reference Handbook – Pages 57 - 60 while solving these questions

Problem 1.7 a) Calculate the sum of matrices A and B given below.

$$A = \begin{bmatrix} 1 & 0 & 0 \\ 0 & 1 & 0 \\ 0 & 0 & 1 \end{bmatrix} \quad B = \begin{bmatrix} 0 & 0 & 2 \\ 0 & 2 & 0 \\ 2 & 0 & 0 \end{bmatrix}$$

(A) $\begin{bmatrix} 1 & 0 & 0 \\ 0 & 1 & 0 \\ 0 & 0 & 1 \end{bmatrix}$

(B) $\begin{bmatrix} 0 & 0 & 2 \\ 0 & 2 & 0 \\ 2 & 0 & 1 \end{bmatrix}$

(C) $\begin{bmatrix} 1 & 0 & 2 \\ 0 & 3 & 0 \\ 2 & 0 & 1 \end{bmatrix}$

(D) **A** and **B** cannot be added

Problem 1.7 b) Calculate the sum of matrices A and B given below.

$$A = \begin{bmatrix} 1 & 0 & 0 \\ 0 & 1 & 0 \\ 0 & 0 & 1 \end{bmatrix} \quad B = \begin{bmatrix} 1 & 0 \\ 0 & 1 \end{bmatrix}$$

(A) $\begin{bmatrix} 2 & 0 & 0 \\ 0 & 1 & 0 \\ 0 & 0 & 2 \end{bmatrix}$

(B) $\begin{bmatrix} 2 & 0 & 0 \\ 0 & 2 & 0 \\ 0 & 0 & 2 \end{bmatrix}$

(C) $\begin{bmatrix} 2 & 0 & 0 \\ 0 & 2 & 0 \\ 0 & 0 & 1 \end{bmatrix}$

(D) **A** and **B** cannot be added

Problem 1.7 c) Calculate the product $A \times B$ of matrices A and B given below.

$$A = \begin{bmatrix} 2 & 1 \\ 4 & 2 \\ 6 & 3 \end{bmatrix} \quad B = \begin{bmatrix} 1 & 0 \\ 2 & 1 \end{bmatrix}$$

(A) $\begin{bmatrix} 4 & 1 \\ 8 & 2 \\ 12 & 3 \end{bmatrix}$

(B) $\begin{bmatrix} 2 & 2 \\ 4 & 4 \\ 6 & 6 \end{bmatrix}$

(C) $\begin{bmatrix} 2 & 0 \\ 8 & 2 \end{bmatrix}$

(D) **A** and **B** cannot be multiplied

Problem 1.7 d) The determinant of matrix given below is _____.

$$\begin{bmatrix} 4 & 5 \\ 2 & 6 \end{bmatrix}$$

Problem 1.7 e) The inverse of matrix given in problem 1.7 d) is _____.

Problem 1.7 f) Calculate the product $A \times B$ of matrices A and B given below.

$$A = \begin{bmatrix} 2 & 1 \\ 4 & 2 \\ 6 & 3 \end{bmatrix} \qquad B = \begin{bmatrix} 7 & 10 \\ 8 & 11 \\ 9 & 12 \end{bmatrix}$$

(A) $\begin{bmatrix} 14 & 20 \\ 32 & 22 \\ 54 & 36 \end{bmatrix}$

(B) $\begin{bmatrix} 7 & 20 \\ 16 & 44 \\ 27 & 72 \end{bmatrix}$

(C) $\begin{bmatrix} 14 & 20 \\ 32 & 22 \end{bmatrix}$

(D) **A** and **B** cannot be multiplied

Problem 1.7 g) _____ option is <u>NOT</u> true for all matrices.

(A) $A \times B = B \times A$

(B) $A + B = B + A$

(C) $[A][A]^{-1} = [A]^{-1}[A]$

(D) $A^{-1} = adj(A)/\det(A)$

Problem 1.7 h) The determinant of matrix given below is _____.

$$\begin{bmatrix} 2 & 4 & 6 \\ 8 & 10 & 12 \\ 1 & 3 & 5 \end{bmatrix}$$

Problem 1.7 i) The dot product of vectors $\vec{A}$ and $\vec{B}$ is _____

$$\vec{A} = 2i + j + 3k$$

$$\vec{B} = i + 2j + 4k$$

Problem 1.7 j) The cross product of vectors $\vec{A}$ and $\vec{B}$ is _____.

$$\vec{A} = 3i + 2j + k$$

$$\vec{B} = i + 4j + 0k$$

Problem 1.7 k) Select the correct resultant vector from the options given below.

$\vec{X} = $ ↗ $\vec{Y} = $ →

$\vec{X} + \vec{Y} = $ _____

Option - A →   Option - B ↗   Option - C ←   Option - D ↙

Chapter # 2 – Probability and Statistics

Key Knowledge Areas*

Concepts	NCEES® FE Reference Handbook Version 10.0.1	
	Section	Page #
Measures of central tendencies and dispersions		
Probability distributions	Probability and Statistics	63 – 84
Expected value in decision making		

Facts about this section

- 4 – 6 questions can be expected on the exam according to the latest NCEES® FE specification.
- Probability and Statistics is one of the most lightly weighted exam sections.
- Difficulty level of this section is rated 'Medium' by the author.

Tips for preparing this section

- Understand the concepts related to this section found in NCEES® FE Reference Handbook.
- Some of the most important concepts and equations of this section include:
    - Measures of central tendencies and dispersion – Calculation of mean, mode, median, standard deviation, sample range and sample variance.
    - Probability distributions – Normal distribution, binomial distribution, continuous distribution, discrete distribution.
    - Laws of probability – Probability definition, law of total probability, law of joint probability, Bayes' Theorem.
    - Expected value– Probability density functions, probability mass functions, cumulative distribution function.
- Solve the problem sets of this chapter and review the solutions at the end of this book.

BONUS: Unlock a free 'Probability and Statistics' lecture by signing-up for the On-demand FE Electrical and Computer exam preparation course preview: **www.studyforfe.com/fe-course-preview**

* Exam specification details can be found on pages 479 - 481 of NCEES® FE Reference Handbook.

Problem Set # 2.1 – Measures of central tendencies
Consult NCEES® FE Reference Handbook – Page 63 while solving these questions

Problem 2.1 a) Arithmetic mean of the observations given below is _____.

$$2, 4, 10, 8, 4, 8$$

Problem 2.1 b) The average annual summer temperature of a small town is recorded as follows.

$$2017(90°F) \quad 2016(84°F) \quad 2015(88°F) \quad 2014(92°F)$$

What is the weighted average of summer temperature if 50% weight is assigned to 2017, 30% weight to 2016, 10% to 2015 and 10% to 2014?

Problem 2.1 c) Sample standard deviation value of the data set given below is _____.

$$2, 4, 6, 8$$

Problem 2.1 d) Sample geometric mean value of the data set given below is _____.

$$1, 2, 3, 4$$

Problem 2.1 e) Sample root mean square value of the data set given below is _____.

$$3, 5, 6, 11$$

Problem 2.1 f) Median value of the data set given below is _____.

$$2, 3, 7, 1, 4, 9, 0$$

Problem 2.1 g) Median value of the data set given below is _____.

$$90, 60, 70, 110, 50, 40, 200, 210$$

Problem 2.1 h) Mode of the data set given below is _____.

$$1, 3, 3, 4, 9, 7, 3, 4$$

Problem 2.1 i) Sample range of data set given below is _____.

$$50, 20, 10, 50, 70, 80, 100, 120$$

Problem 2.1 j) Select the option that correctly describes an important feature of 'mean'.

Mean _____

| Influenced by outliers |

| Not a measure of central tendency |

| Marginally influenced by outlier |

Problem Set # 2.2 – Permutation/Combination & Laws of Probability

Consult NCEES® FE Reference Handbook – Pages 64 - 65 while solving these questions

Following scenario applies to problems 2.2 a) to 2.2 d). Assume that you are the captain of a local basketball team. Your team roster comprises of 12 players.

Problem 2.2 a) How many ways can you select 5 team members from the given roster of 12 players if order of selection is important?

(A) 479×10^6

(B) 95040

(C) 792

(D) 1

Problem 2.2 b) How many ways can you select 5 team members from the given roster of 12 players if order of selection is not important?

(A) 479×10^6

(B) 95040

(C) 792

(D) 1

Problem 2.2 c) How many ways can you select 12 team members from the given roster of 12 players if order of selection is important?

(A) 479×10^6

(B) 95040

(C) 792

(D) 1

Problem 2.2 d) How many ways can you select 12 team members from the given roster of 12 players if order of selection is not important?

(A) 479×10^6

(B) 95040

(C) 792

(D) 1

Following scenario applies to problems 2.2 e) to 2.2 i).

Consider a sample space of $S = \{1,2,3,4,5,6,7,8,9,10\}$, events $A = \{1,3,5,7,10\}$ and $B = \{1,2,4,6,10\}$.

Problem 2.2 e) The probability of event A = _____ and the probability of event B = _____.

Problem 2.2 f) The probability that both A and B will occur simultaneously = _____.

Problem 2.2 g) The probability that either A or B will occur alone, or both will occur together = _____.

Problem 2.2 h) The probability that B occurs given that A has already occurred = _____.

Problem 2.2 i) The probability that A occurs given that B has already occurred = _____.

Problem 2.2 j) According to latest weather forecast, the probability that weekend will be sunny is 0.25, cloudy is 0.35 and both sunny and cloudy is 0.15. What is the probability that weekend will be sunny, cloudy or both?

(A) 0.25

(B) 0.30

(C) 0.45

(D) 0.75

Problem 2.2 k) The total probability of events A and B based on Venn diagram given below is _____.

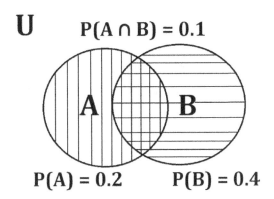

Problem Set # 2.3 – Probability Distributions
Consult NCEES® FE Reference Handbook – Pages 65 - 67 while solving these questions

Problem 2.3 a) According to a study, 8% of all adults will experience major depression at same point in their lives. Assume that 90% of diagnostic tests for major depression detect it correctly (true positive) whereas 10% of the tests are false positive. Calculate the probability of someone suffering from major depression given that this person has already tested positive.

(A) 10%

(B) 44%

(C) 56%

(D) 90%

Problem 2.3 b) According to the data collected by a superstore chain, 20% of customers prefer online shopping whereas remaining customers prefer in-store shopping. 50% of the customers preferring online shopping are under 30 years of age and 40% of the customers preferring in-store shopping are under 30 years of age.

What is the probability of randomly selecting a customer with preference for online shopping given that person is under 30 years of age?

Problem 2.3 c) The probability of an engineering firm hiring a new graduate after an on-campus interview is 0.10. The probability of hiring 2 new graduates after 30 on-campus interviews is _____.

Problem 2.3 d) A top-seed tennis player is confident that she has 40% chance of winning each of the four grand slam tournaments next year. What is the probability that she will win 2 to 4 grand slams?

Problem 2.3 e) The average GMAT® score of successful applicants at a well-reputed business school is 740 with a standard deviation of 20. Calculate the probability of admission for students with scores less than 700. Assume that acceptance based on GMAT® score follows normal distribution.

Problem 2.3 f) The average useful life of a typical dishwasher is 10 years with standard deviation of 2 years. Calculate the probability of this dishwasher lasting between 12 to 14 years. Assume that useful life of dishwasher follows normal distribution.

Following scenario applies to problems 2.3 g) to 2.3 i). Assume that a typical buyer of a new car replaces the car after every 8 years (on average) with a standard deviation of 2 years. Moreover, it can be further assumed that replacement timeline of a new car follows the normal distribution.

Problem 2.3 g) The probability that new car will be replaced in less than 2 years = _____.

Problem 2.3 h) The probability that new car will be replaced after 10 years = _____.

Problem 2.3 i) The probability that new car will be replaced between 4 - 6 years = _____.

Problem Set # 2.4 – Expected values
Consult NCEES® FE Reference Handbook – Pages 65 – 66 while solving these questions

Problem 2.4 a) The expected value of a discrete random variable X with probability mass function $f(x_k)$ given below is _____ .

$$f(x_k) = \frac{1}{33}(3x_k + 2) \quad x_1 = 2, \quad x_2 = 3, \quad x_3 = 4$$

Problem 2.4 b) The variance of X in problem 2.4 a) is _____ .

Problem 2.4 c) According to the guidance provided by a fund manager at an investment bank, the fund is forecasted to perform in accordance with following probability distribution.

Gain	-5%	0%	5%	10%	15%
Probability	0.10	0.20	0.30	0.30	0.10

Investors can expect fund performance to be approximately _____%.

Problem 2.4 d) A typical college student spends X portion of study time on completing assignments. Probability density function of X is given as follows:

$$f(x) = 4x - 1 \quad 0 \leq x \leq 1$$

$$f(x) = 0 \qquad otherwise$$

The expected value of study time spent by student in doing assignments is _____ .

Problem 2.4 e) According to the data collected by an automobile insurance company, the probability distribution function of number of traffic violations per driver (denoted by X) can be given as follows:

$$f(x) = 2x^{-3} \qquad x \geq 1$$

$$f(x) = 0 \qquad otherwise$$

The expected number of traffic violations per driver is _____ .

Problem 2.4 f) The total area under probability density function and probability mass function is always equal to _____ .

Chapter # 3 – Ethics and Professional Practice

Key Knowledge Areas*

Concepts	NCEES® FE Reference Handbook Version 10.0.1	
	Section	Page #
Code of Ethics	Ethics and Professional Practice	4 – 12
Intellectual property		
Safety	Safety	13 – 33

Facts about this section

- 4 – 6 questions can be expected on the exam according to the latest NCEES® FE specification.
- Ethics and Professional Practice is one of the most lightly weighted exam sections.
- Difficulty level of this section is rated 'Easy' by the author.

Tips for preparing this section

- Understand the concepts related to this section found it NCEES® FE Reference Handbook.
- Some of the most important concepts of this section include:
    - Code of ethics – Background and definitions.
    - NCEES Model Law and Model Rules – Rules of professional conduct, licensee's obligation to the public, licensee's obligation to the employer and client, licensee's obligation to other licensees, general requirements for licensure, grounds for disciplinary action, general requirements for certificate of authorization, exemption clause.
    - Intellectual property – Trademark, copyright, patent, industrial design, trade secret.
    - Safety – General understanding of safety with a focus on electrical safety, grounding, material safety data sheets, personal protective equipment.
- Solve problem sets on next pages and review solutions at the end of this book.

* Exam specification details can be found on pages 479 - 481 of NCEES® FE Reference Handbook.

Problem Set # 3.1 – Code of Ethics & NCEES® Model Law and Rules

Consult NCEES® FE Reference Handbook – Pages 4 - 11 while solving these questions

Problem 3.1 a) A recently licensed professional engineer is working under the supervision of a senior engineer. The junior engineer brings a potential design deficiency to senior engineer's attention which can result in a safety hazard. The senior engineer tells her that design is based on standard industry practice, construction is underway and the probability of safety incident occurring is practically zero.

What should be junior engineer's response after learning these facts?

(A) Junior engineer is not required to do anything further because senior engineer is competent.

(B) Junior engineer is not required to do anything further because she's already expressed concern.

(C) Junior engineer shall escalate her concerns to a higher level because she's still worried about safety.

(D) Junior engineer shall escalate her concerns to a higher level because it will raise her profile.

Problem 3.1 b) John is a well-respected engineer with a specialization in power systems and some experience in control systems. John has an excellent track record of delivering successful projects on time and under budget. He is asked by his new supervisor to take an assignment involving control systems scope. John's new supervisor does not know his past work experience very well, but he has heard wonderful things about John from other managers.

Is it ethically acceptable for John to accept this assignment?

(A) Yes, accepting the assignment will give him an opportunity to enhance skills in control systems.

(B) Yes, it is his professional obligation to work diligently for the employer.

(C) No, John is a power systems specialist and should only work in that area.

(D) John should review assignment requirements and his expertise with his supervisor and then decide.

Problem 3.1 c) Sarah is a professional engineer and she is brought on a project as a discipline lead. The project is in its final design stages. Project manager has asked her to quickly review near complete engineering documents and seal them. These documents were prepared by other engineers who are not licensed. However, she knows that all of them are competent based on her experience.

Should Sarah sign and seal these documents?

(A) Yes, she is familiar with quality of team.

(B) Yes, she is the new lead and can review documents even though timeline is tight.

(C) No, documents were not developed by licensed engineers.

(D) No, documents were not developed under her supervision and review time may be insufficient.

Problem 3.1 d) A professional engineer is reviewing equipment drawings for compliance on behalf of a client. The engineer notices that vendor is providing a technically acceptable alternative to one of the specification requirements listed in the original bid. Upon further research, the engineer finds that proposed alternative is cheaper than the one required by client's specification.

What should be included in the engineer's recommendation report to the client?

(A) Rejection, because proposed alternative is cheaper than original requirement

(B) Rejection, because proposed alternative is not the same as one required by specification

(C) Acceptance, because proposed alternative is technically acceptable.

(D) Acceptance, because proposed alternative is acceptable but negotiate a price credit from supplier.

Problem 3.1 e) Mark is a licensed professional engineer who independently provides engineering consultancy services to various clients. He recently came across a proprietary solution while working for one of his regular clients which can be deployed in similar scenarios faced by many other clients.

Can Mark use this unique solution in similar applications for other clients?

(A) Yes, Mark is obligated to provide solutions to his clients to the best of his knowledge

(B) Yes, Mark's clients hire him because of his wide experience and expect innovative solutions

(C) No, Mark cannot use confidential details without obtaining consent from relevant clients

(D) No, Mark is obligated to produce innovative solutions for each client.

Problem 3.1 f) Drag and drop correct NCEES® Model Rules, Section 240.15, Rule of Professional Conduct reference in front of given description.

Respect of fellow licensees _____.

A-4   A-1   C-3   C-4   B-1   B-4

Problem 3.1 g) Which one of the following statements is correct?

(A) Only licensed engineers are expected to conduct themselves professionally.

(B) Ethical problems are always straight forward.

(C) Engineers possess special knowledge which is not common in public domain.

(D) Engineer is not liable for violating an ethical principle if he/she was not aware of it.

Problem 3.1 h) _____ is/are not necessarily duly licensed as professional engineer by the board.

(A) Engineer

(B) Professional Engineer

(C) Professional Engineer, Retired

(D) Engineering Intern

Problem 3.1 i) According to Model Law's 'General Requirements for Licensure' if an applicant has a PhD. in engineering acceptable to the board and has passed the FE exam requires only _____ years of progressive engineering experience to meet experience requirements for PE licensure.

(A) 1

(B) 2

(C) 3

(D) 4

Problem 3.1 j) Boards have the power to take disciplinary actions on valid grounds against _____.

(A) Licensed engineers and interns

(B) Unlicensed individuals

(C) Firms holding certificate of authorization

(D) All of the above

Problem Set # 3.2 – Intellectual Property
Consult NCEES® FE Reference Handbook – Pages 11 - 12 while solving these questions

Problem 3.2 a) An advertising agency interested in protecting creative marketing slogans for its clients should consider _____ registration.

(A) Trademark

(B) Copyright

(C) Patent

(D) Industrial design

Problem 3.2 b) A manufacturing plant interested in protecting its innovative processing techniques should consider _____ registration.

(A) Trademark

(B) Copyright

(C) Patent

(D) Industrial design

Problem 3.2 c) A publishing company interested in protecting content of its publications should consider _____ registration.

(A) Trademark

(B) Copyright

(C) Patent

(D) Industrial design

Problem 3.2 d) A toy manufacturer interested in preventing competitors from copying its packaging styles should consider _____ registration.

(A) Trademark

(B) Copyright

(C) Patent

(D) Industrial design

Problem 3.2 e) Drag and drop correct symbol against given intellectual property registration products.

1 - Trademark _____

2 - Copyright _____

3 - Registered Trademark _____

$$A=\text{©} \qquad B=\text{®} \qquad C=\text{я} \qquad D=\text{T} \qquad E=\text{Ɠ} \qquad F=\text{™}$$

Problem 3.2 f) _____ qualifies as an example of intellectual property.

(A) Stocks

(B) Bonds

(C) Software program

(D) Real estate

Problem Set # 3.3 – Safety
Consult NCEES® FE Reference Handbook – Pages 13 - 33 while solving these questions

Problem 3.3 a) National Electrical Code NEC® is developed and maintained by _____ and it is adopted across the U.S. as a benchmark for safe electrical design, installation, and inspection.

(A) ANSI®

(B) CSA®

(C) NFPA®

(D) OSHA®

Problem 3.3 b) _____ is the 'Standard for Electrical Safety in the Workplace'.

(A) NEC®

(B) NFPA 70E®

(C) NFPA 77®

(D) NFPA 80®

Problem 3.3 c) _____ scenario presents greatest risk to safety.

(A) High hazard and low probability

(B) High hazard and high probability

(C) Low hazard and low probability

(D) Low hazard and high probability

Problem 3.3 d) Equipment/system grounding improves overall safety by means of _____.

(A) Reducing magnitude of transient over-voltages

(B) Protecting personnel by offering a low resistance path to current

(C) Allowing faster operation of protective devices and isolation of faulty equipment

(D) All of the above

Problem 3.3 e) Electrical current as low as _____ can cause death due to extreme pain, respiratory arrest, severe muscular contractions, and inability of the victim to break electrical contact.

Problem 3.3 f) NFPA 70E® 'Standard for Electrical Safety in the Workplace' classifies arc flash PPE into a total of _____ categories based on arc flash incident energy levels.

Problem 3.3 g) Safety data sheets (SDS) of hazardous chemical products must include following information about the product in addition to other applicable details.

(A) Name/Address/Phone Number of the manufacturer

(B) Chemical ingredients of the product

(C) Emergency procedures, PPE requirements, containment, and cleanup methods

(D) All of the above

Chapter # 4 – Engineering Economics

Key Knowledge Areas*

Concepts	NCEES® FE Reference Handbook Version 10.0.1	
	Section	Page #
Time value of money	Engineering Economics	230 – 237
Cost estimation		
Risk identification		
Analysis		

Facts about this section

- 5 – 8 questions can be expected on the exam according to the latest NCEES® FE specification.
- Engineering Economics is one of the most lightly weighted exam sections.
- Difficulty level of this section is rated 'Easy' by the author.

Tips for preparing this section

- Understand the concepts related to this section found in NCEES® FE Reference Handbook.
- Some of the most important concepts and equations of this section include:
    - Time value of money – Single payment compound amount, single payment present worth, uniform series sinking fund, capital recovery, uniform series compound amount, uniform series present worth, uniform gradient worth, uniform gradient future worth, uniform gradient uniform series.
    - Cost estimation – Inflation, depreciation, book value, capitalized costs.
    - Risk identification – Definition, rate-of-return, decision tree.
    - Analysis – Break-even analysis, benefit-cost analysis.
- Learn how to use interest rate tables given in NCEES® FE Reference Handbook.
- Solve the problem sets of this chapter and review solutions at the end of this book.

BONUS: Unlock a free 'Engineering Economics' lecture by signing-up for the On-demand FE Electrical and Computer exam preparation course preview: **www.studyforfe.com/fe-course-preview**

*Exam specification details can be found on pages 479 - 481 of NCEES® FE Reference Handbook.

Problem Set # 4.1 – Time value of money
Consult NCEES® FE Reference Handbook – Page 230 while solving these questions

Problem 4.1 a) Calculate the future worth of $25,000 investment, 20 years from now. 12% annual interest rate can be assumed for this calculation.

Problem 4.1 b) Calculate the present worth of a retirement fund if it is expected to be $750,000 approximately 30 years from now. 4% annual interest rate can be assumed for this calculation.

Problem 4.1 c) _____ converts an annuity into a future amount.

(A) Capital Recovery   (B) Uniform Series Compound Amount

(C) Uniform Series Present Worth   (D) Uniform Series Sinking Fund

Problem 4.1 d) _____ converts a present value into an annuity.

(A) Capital Recovery   (B) Uniform Series Compound Amount

(C) Uniform Series Present Worth   (D) Uniform Series Sinking Fund

Problem 4.1 e) A retired couple is considering a 20-year term annuity with their $200,000 cash savings at 6% annual interest rate. The yearly annuity amount they can expect to receive is _____.

Problem 4.1 f) Amanda needs to have $_____ saved today if she plans to get a 20-year term annuity that will pay her $40,000 annually for the duration of its term? 8% annual interest rate can be assumed for this calculation.

Problem 4.1 g) Calculate the future worth of an investment plan in which $15,000 are invested each year for 30 years. Assume that investments earn interest annually at a rate of 8%.

Problem 4.1 h) A nominal interest rate of 10% compounded monthly will result in an annual effective interest rate of _____ %.

Problem 4.1 i) Sam is considering enrollment into a 6-year degree program at a college that combines undergraduate and graduate course work. He can expect to pay $40,000 in tuition for 1st year, $42,000 for 2nd year, $44,000 for 3rd year and so on (i.e. tuition will increase by $2,000 each year).

Assuming 2% annual interest rate, Sam's total tuition in today's dollars will be _____.

Problem 4.1 j) John just bought a brand-new car which he plans on keeping for 6 years. First year maintenance cost will only include a routine oil changes that will cost him $600 each year. However, due to regular wear and tear, maintenance cost will increase by $200 each year as shown below.

M_{year-1} = $600, M_{year-2} = $800, M_{year-3} = $1000, M_{year-4} = $1200, M_{year-5} = $1400, M_{year-6} = $1600

Assuming 8% annual interest rate, car's total maintenance cost in today's dollars will be _____.

Problem Set # 4.2 – Cost estimation

Consult NCEES® FE Reference Handbook – Pages 231 - 232 while solving these questions

Problem 4.2 a) Calculate the annual inflation adjusted interest rate if annual inflation rate is 4% and annual interest rate over the same period is 6%.

(A) 6.5%   (B) 24%

(C) 12.7%   (D) 10.2%

Problem 4.2 b) _____ depreciation method results in same value decline each year.

Problem 4.2 c) The capitalized cost of operating a restaurant with an annual operating expense of $20,000 at 8% interest rate is _____.

Problem 4.2 d) What is the accumulated depreciation of a car at the end of year 4 if its useful life is 30 years. The initial cost was $32,000 and the end of life salvage value will be $2,000.

Problem 4.2 e) Calculate the accumulated depreciation of office printer in year 3 using MACRS factors table if it has a useful life of 10 years. The initial cost was $7,000 and salvage value will be $500.

Consider the following scenario for problems 4.2 f) to 4.2 h). A transport truck is purchased for an initial cost of $50,000. It has a useful life of 5 years and its salvage value is expected to be $2000.

Problem 4.2 f) As per MACRS factors table, accumulated depreciation of this truck after 2 years is ___.

Problem 4.2 g) As per MACRS factors table, book value of this truck after 2 years is _____.

Problem 4.2 h) Complete the following MACRS depreciation schedule for the given transport truck.

Year	Current Depreciation	Accumulated Depreciation	Book Value
0			$50,000
1	$50,000 x 20% = $10000	$10,000	$50,000 - $10,000 = $40,000
2	$50,000 x 32% = $16000	$26,000	$50,000 - $26000 = $24,000
3	?	?	?
4	?	?	?
5	?	?	?
6	?	?	$0

Problem Set # 4.3 – Risk Identification and Analysis

Problem 4.3 a) Two production lines have very different cost structures for manufacturing same item. Production line A has a fixed cost = $100,000 and variable cost = $5 per item. Production line B does not have any fixed costs, but it has a higher variable cost = $10 per item. The break-even point of both production lines is _____.

Problem 4.3 b) _____ statement(s) correctly describe the scenario in the previous problem.

(A) Line A performs better below break-even point   (B) Line B performs better below break-even point

(C) Both perform equally at break even point   (D) None of the above

Problem 4.3 c) It costs a chair manufacturing company $50,000 in fixed cost and $2 per chair in variable cost to manufacture a chair. How many chairs need to be sold to break-even if selling price of each chair is $27?

Problem 4.3 d) A logistics company has short-listed two contractors for a multi-year project involving upgrade of its warehouse. Assuming identical scope of work, service quality and annual interest rate of 8%, which one of the following contractors is offering the most competitive quote?

Contactor A – Down payment of $20,000 and final payment of $40,000 in year 6.

Contractor B – $10,000 payment each year for six years.

Problem 4.3 e) Perform a cost-benefit analysis to determine which one of the following investment options is more profitable (assume 10% annual interest rate)?

Option A - $100,000 purchase of stocks, expected to sell for $200,000 in year 10.

Option B - $100,000 real estate investment that pays $5000 in rent each year and is expected to sell for $160,000 in year 10.

Option C - $100,000 deposit in a savings account earning 10% annual interest for 10 years.

Problem 4.3 f) Based on the decision tree given below, project _____ looks most promising.

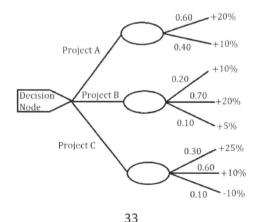

Chapter # 5 – Properties of Electrical Materials

Key Knowledge Areas*

Concepts	NCEES® FE Reference Handbook Version 10.0.1	
	Section	Page #
Semiconductor Materials		
Tunneling	Electrical and Computer Engineering	382 - 383
Diffusion/Drift current		
Energy bands/Doping bands		
P-N Theory		
Note: Semiconductor materials are covered in Chapter 9 of this Study Guide.		
Electrical Properties		
Capacitance	Electrical and Computer Engineering	355 - 359
Conductivity		
Resistivity		
Permittivity		
Magnetic Permeability		
Note: Electrical Properties are also discussed on page 95 of NCEES® FE Reference Handbook		
Thermal Properties		
Expansion, Specific Heat	Material Science/Structure of Matter	104 -105
Conductivity		

Facts about this section

- 4-6 questions can be expected on the exam according to the latest NCEES® FE specification.
- Properties of Electrical Materials is one of the most lightly weighted exam sections.
- Difficulty level of this section is rated 'Easy' by the author.

Tips for preparing this section

- Understand the concepts related to this section found in NCEES® FE Reference Handbook.
- It is important to handle the units of measurement carefully because of complicated quantities.
- Some of the most important equations of this section relate to resistivity, resistance, capacitance, magnetic field strength, inductance, and temperature coefficient.
- Solve the problem sets of this chapter and review solutions at the end of this book.

Note – Semiconductor materials are covered in Chapter 9 of this Study Guide.

* Exam specification details can be found on pages 479 - 481 of NCEES® FE Reference Handbook.

Problem Set # 5.1 – Electrical Properties
Consult NCEES® FE Reference Handbook – Pages 95, 355 - 357 while solving these questions

Problem 5.1 a) Calculate the resistivity of a 100m long wire with a cross-sectional diameter = 2mm and resistance = 5Ω at 30°C.

(A) 3.14×10^{-7} Ωm

(B) 1.57×10^{-3} Ωm

(C) 3.14×10^{-3} Ωm

(D) 1.57×10^{-7} Ωm

Problem 5.1 b) The resistivity of cable 'A' is four times that of cable 'B'. Both cables can offer same resistance under a given temperature if _____.

(A) Area is same and A is twice as long as B

(B) Area of B is four times that of A

(C) Area of B is one-fourth of A and same length

(D) Resistance of A and B cannot be same

Problem 5.1 c) Capacitance of a parallel plate capacitor can be increased by _____

(A) Decreasing the cross-sectional area of plates

(B) Decreasing the distance between plates

(C) Inserting an insulating material with a higher dielectric constant

(D) Options B & C are correct

Problem 5.1 d) Materials with high electrical conductivity typically have _____.

(A) High resistivity

(B) High heat conductivity

(C) Low elasticity

(D) Low ductility

Problem 5.1 e) Calculate the magnetic permeability of a medium in which an infinitely long wire carrying 100A current produces 0.5T magnetic field at a distance of 50cm perpendicular to the wire.

Problem 5.1 f) Photoelectric effect can take place in _____ under suitable conditions.

(A) Metals

(B) Non-metals

(C) Liquids and gases

(D) All of the above

Problem 5.1 g) How many electrons pass through a point on conductor if it carries 1mA current for 5s?

(A) 1.56×10^{16}

(B) 3.12×10^{16}

(C) 6.24×10^{12}

(D) 3.12×10^{12}

Problem 5.1 h) Calculate the energy stored in the electric field of a parallel plate capacitor that has potential difference of 200V if the distance between two plates is 0.1m and area of each plate is 1m² (assume that $\varepsilon = 8.85 \times 10^{-12}\ Fm^{-1}$).

(A) 8.85 x 10⁻¹¹ J   (B) 1.33 x 10⁻³ J

(C) 3.54 x 10⁻⁶ J   (D) 1.77 x 10⁻⁶ J

Problem 5.1 i) Calculate the voltage applied across a parallel plate capacitor carrying 400µC charge with a 0.02m² plate surface area and 0.01m plate spacing (assume that $\varepsilon = 8.85 \times 10^{-12}\ Fm^{-1}$).

(A) 22.6 x 10⁶ V   (B) 2.2 x 10⁻¹⁴ V

(C) 0 V   (D) 1.5 x 10⁻¹⁰ V

Problem 5.1 j) The capacitance of parallel plate capacitor is 100µF. Initial voltage across capacitor was 5V. Calculate constant charging current if voltage across capacitor is recorded as 10V after 3 minutes.

(A) 5.4µA   (B) 2.7µA

(C) 16.6mA   (D) 8mA

Problem 5.1 k) A 200µF capacitor has voltage $v(t) = 240 \sin(377t)\ V$ across it. Calculate the energy stored in this capacitor as a function of time.

(A) 0J   (B) $5.76 \sin^2(377t)\ J$

(C) $5.76 \sin(142129t)\ J$ (D) $1.36 \sin^2(377t)\ J$

Problem 5.1 l) Calculate the capacitive charging current if voltage across a 100µF capacitor increases by 10V in 5s.

(A) 1mA   (B) 0.2mA

(C) 2A   (D) 4A

Problem 5.1 m) The equivalent capacitance of circuit shown below is _____.

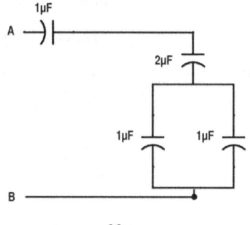

Problem 5.1 n) What is the inductance of a 1m long coil with 100 turns and a cross-sectional area of 0.1m² (assume $\mu = 4\pi10^{-7}\ H/m$)?

(A) 1.25mH

(B) 1000H

(C) 0.625mH

(D) 2.5mH

Problem 5.1 o) Calculate the voltage induced in a 5mH inductor if current in the inductor is increased from 0 to 100mA in 2ms.

(A) 5V

(B) 0.25V

(C) 1V

(D) 0V

Problem 5.1 p) _____ energy is stored in a 100mH inductor carrying current $i(t) = t^2$ at $t = 10s$.

(A) 100J

(B) 10J

(C) 2.5J

(D) 500J

Problem 5.1 q) Energy storage capacity of an inductor can be increased by _____.

(A) Decreasing voltage across it

(B) Increasing number of turns

(C) Increasing its length

(D) Options A, B, C are correct

Problem 5.1 r) The equivalent inductance of circuit shown below is _____.

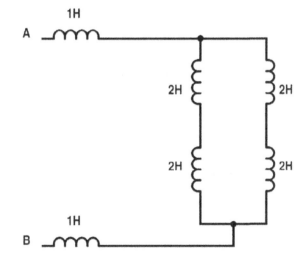

Problem Set # 5.2 – Thermal Properties
Consult NCEES® FE Reference Handbook – Pages 104 - 105 while solving these questions

Problem 5.2 a) Bi-metallic strip of a thermostat should be made of materials with _____

(A) Different lengths

(B) Different coefficients of thermal expansion

(C) Same resistivity

(D) Same density

Problem 5.2 b) A material of 1m length is kept at room temperature (296 K) and constant pressure. It is observed that a 7K temperature rise results in an engineering strain of 3×10^{-3}. Calculate the temperature required to cause 6×10^{-3} engineering strain for this material.

(A) 319 K

(B) 307 K

(C) 310 K

(D) 303 K

Problem 5.2 c) A design engineer is calculating space allowance required for railway steel track expansion. Thermal expansion coefficient of steel being used is $1.2 \times 10^{-5}\,^{\circ}C^{-1}$. Temperature is expected to increase from an average of 20 °C to a peak of 45 °C. Calculate the strain that can be experienced by rail tracks due to thermal expansion.

(A) 3×10^{-2}

(B) 30×10^{-5}

(C) 50×10^{-5}

(D) 75×10^{-6}

Problem 5.2 d) What is the temperature coefficient of a given metal specimen if its resistance doubles with a 25K temperature rise?

Problem 5.2 e) Resistivity of a material is completely independent of _____.

(A) Resistance

(B) Volume

(C) Temperature

(D) Depends on resistance, temperature & volume

Problem 5.2 f) Students are measuring heat capacities of three different samples of same liquid. Sample 1 = 1kg, sample 2 = 2kg and sample 3 = 3kg.

_____ option correctly describes the heat capacities of given samples.

(A) Sample 1 > Sample 2 > Sample 3

(B) Sample 1 < Sample 2 < Sample 3

(C) Sample 1 = Sample 2 = Sample 3

(D) It cannot be determined

Chapter # 6 – Circuit Analysis

Key Knowledge Areas*

Concepts	NCEES® FE Reference Handbook Version 10.0.1	
	Section	Page #
Kirchhoff's Laws - KCL, KVL	Electrical and Computer Engineering	357 – 361
Series/parallel equivalent circuits		
Thevenin and Norton theorems		
Node and loop analysis		
Waveform analysis		
Phasors		
Impedance		

Facts about this section

- 11 – 17 questions can be expected on the exam according to NCEES® FE specification.
- Circuit Analysis is one of the most heavily weighted exam sections.
- Difficulty level of this section is rated 'Medium' by the author.

Tips for preparing this section

- Understand the concepts related to Circuit Analysis found in NCEES® FE Reference Handbook.
- Some of the important equations relevant to this section include Ohm's Law, KCL, KVL, voltage divider, current divider, Thevenin, Norton, source transformation, average value, effective value, and RMS value.
- Revisit basic circuit theory using your university/college electrical textbook.
- Circuits can be solved using different methods such as KCL, KVL, Thevenin, Norton, superposition but certain techniques may be better suited for a given problem.
- Maximum power transfer occurs when $Z_l = Z_{Th}^*$.
- Equivalent resistance in series $R_s = R_1 + R_2 + R_3 \ldots .. + R_n$
- Equivalent resistance in parallel $R_p = 1/(1/R_1 + 1/R_2 + 1/R_3 \ldots .. + 1/R_n)$
- Equivalent inductance in series $L_s = L_1 + L_2 + L_3 \ldots .. + L_n$
- Equivalent inductance in parallel $L_p = 1/(1/L_1 + 1/L_2 + 1/L_3 \ldots .. + 1/L_n)$
- Equivalent capacitance in parallel $C_p = C_1 + C_2 + C_3 \ldots .. + C_n$
- Equivalent capacitance in series $C_s = 1/(1/C_1 + 1/C_2 + 1/C_3 \ldots .. + 1/C_n)$
- Sinusoidal signals require conversion to a standard form (cosine) for phasor representation.

BONUS: Unlock a free 'Circuit Analysis' lecture by signing-up for the On-demand FE Electrical and Computer exam preparation course preview at: **www.studyforfe.com/fe-course-preview**

*Exam specification details can be found on pages 479 - 481 of NCEES® FE Reference Handbook.

Problem Set # 6.1 - Kirchhoff's Laws – KCL, KVL

Consult NCEES® FE Reference Handbook – Page 357 while solving these questions

Problem 6.1 a) Calculate the voltage across 10kΩ resistor in the circuit shown below using KCL.

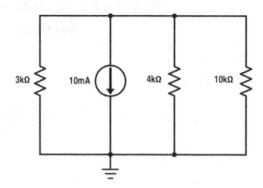

(A) 70.5V

(B) -14.6V

(C) 1.46mV

(D) 5V

Problem 6.1 b) Calculate the current passing through 2kΩ resistor in following circuit using KCL.

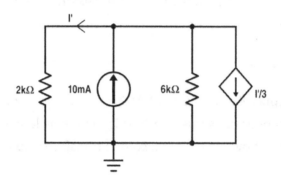

(A) 4mA

(B) 3mA

(C) 2mA

(D) 6mA

Problem 6.1 c) Calculate the voltage across 3Ω resistor in the circuit shown below.

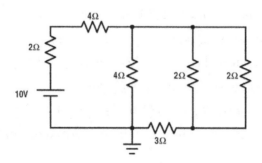

(A) 2.5V

(B) 1.87V

(C) 7.5V

(D) 3.75V

Problem 6.1 d) Calculate the current I_x in the circuit shown below.

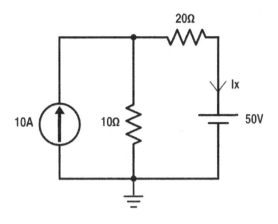

(A) 4A

(B) 3.5A

(C) 7A

(D) 1.7A

Problem 6.1 e) Calculate the current passing through the 1kΩ resistor in the circuit shown below.

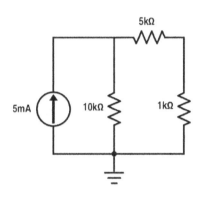

(A) 3.1mA

(B) 5mA

(C) 2.5mA

(D) 1.5mA

Problem 6.1 f) Calculate the current passing through the 5kΩ resistor in the circuit shown below.

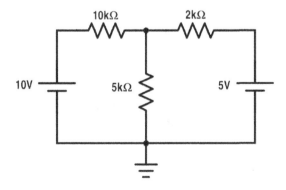

Problem Set # 6.2 - Series / Parallel Equivalent Circuits
Consult NCEES® FE Reference Handbook – Page 357 while solving these questions

Problem 6.2 a) Find the equivalent resistance between terminals A-B of the circuit shown below.

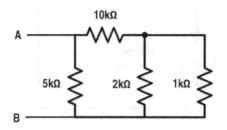

(A) 5kΩ   (B) 7.5kΩ

(C) 2kΩ   (D) 3.4kΩ

Problem 6.2 b) Find the equivalent resistance between terminals A-B of the circuit shown below.

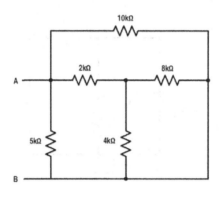

(A) 2kΩ   (B) 3kΩ

(C) 1kΩ   (D) 5kΩ

Problem 6.2 c) Find the equivalent resistance between terminals A-B of the circuit shown below.

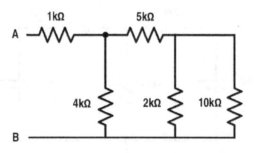

(A) 7kΩ   (B) 3.5kΩ

(C) 1.5kΩ   (D) 5kΩ

Problem 6.2 d) Find the equivalent resistance between terminals A-B of the circuit shown below.

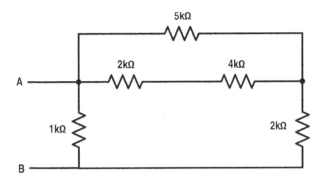

(A) 3.0kΩ

(B) 2.75kΩ

(C) 0.825kΩ

(D) 5.50kΩ

Problem 6.2 e) The equivalent resistance between terminals A-B of the circuit shown below is _____.

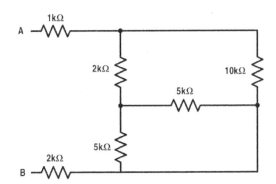

Problem Set # 6.3 - Thevenin and Norton Theorems

Consult NCEES® FE Reference Handbook – Pages 357 - 358 while solving these questions

Problem 6.3 a) Thevenin equivalent voltage V_{oc} between terminals a-b of following circuit is _____.

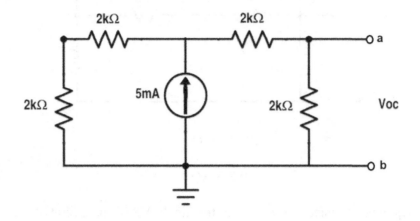

(A) 10V   (B) 5V

(C) 37V   (D) 100V

Problem 6.3 b) Thevenin equivalent resistance R_{eq} of the circuit given in problem 6.3 a) is _____.

Problem 6.3 c) Thevenin equivalent resistance R_{eq} of the circuit given below is _____.

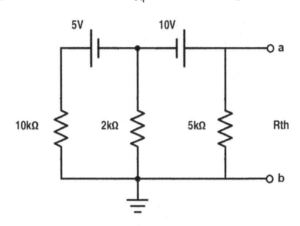

(A) 1.25kΩ   (B) 5kΩ

(C) 2.5kΩ   (D) 3kΩ

Problem 6.3 d) Norton source current I_{sc} between load terminals a-b of given circuit is _____.

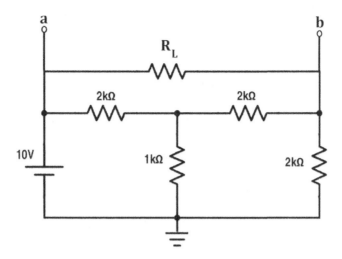

Problem 6.3 e) Norton equivalent resistance R_{eq} of the circuit given in problem 6.3 d) is _____.

Problem 6.3 f) Norton source current I_{sc} between load terminals a-b of the following circuit is _____.

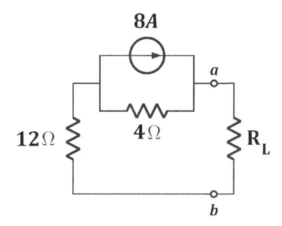

Problem 6.3 g) Norton equivalent resistance R_{eq} of the circuit given in problem 6.3 f) is _____.

Problem 6.3 h) In the problem 6.3 f), use source transformation to calculate the Thevenin equivalent voltage $V_{th} =$_____.

Problem Set # 6.4 - Waveform Analysis

Consult NCEES® FE Reference Handbook – Pages 359 - 360 while solving these questions

Problem 6.4 a) _____ is the maximum voltage of a full-wave rectified sinusoid with $V_{eff} = 10V$.

(A) 20.5V

(B) 5V

(C) 14.1V

(D) 10V

Problem 6.4 b) Calculate the sum of following sinusoids:

$$V_1 = 10 \cos(500t) \qquad V_2 = 15 \cos(100t + 45^0)$$

(A) $25 \cos(600t + 45^0)$

(B) $10 \cos(500t) - 10.6 \cos(100t) + 10.6 \sin(100t)$

(C) $150 \cos(500t) \cos(100t + 45^0)$

(D) $10 \cos(500t) + 10.6 \cos(100t) - 10.6 \sin(100t)$

Problem 6.4 c) _____ is the frequency of sinusoidal signal given by $100 \cos(500t + 50^0)$.

(A) 500Hz

(B) 250Hz

(C) 79.5Hz

(D) 50Hz

Problem 6.4 d) _____ is the average value of a half-wave rectified signal given by $15 \cos(100t + 50^0)$.

(A) 7.5

(B) 4.77

(C) 9.54

(D) 10.6

Problem 6.4 e) The average value of periodic current waveform shown below is _____.

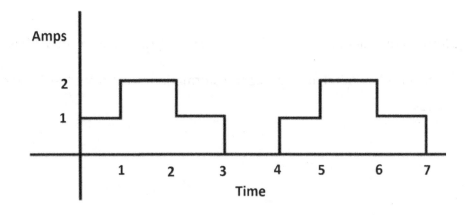

Problem 6.4 f) Calculate the time-period of a single-phase voltage waveform given below.

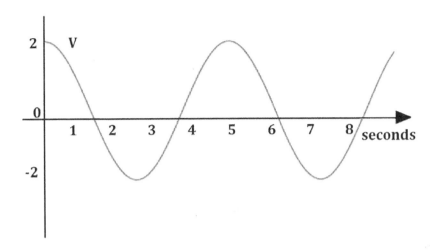

(A) 3s

(B) 5s

(C) 7s

(D) 10s

Problem 6.4 g) In problem 6.4 f), calculate the frequency of voltage waveform.

(A) 0.1Hz

(B) 0.2Hz

(C) 0.5Hz

(D) 1Hz

Consider the following scenario for problems 6.4 h) to 6.4 j). A single-phase alternating current source is given by following equation: $i(t) = 40\sqrt{2}\cos(377t + 30°) \, A$

Problem 6.4 h) The peak waveform value of given single-phase current is _____.

(A) 40 A

(B) $40\sqrt{2}$ A

(C) 20 A

(D) $40/\sqrt{2}$ A

Problem 6.4 i) System frequency of given single-phase network is _____ Hz.

(A) 30

(B) 50

(C) 60

(D) 377

Problem 6.4 j) Calculate the RMS value of current $i(t)$ if it is full-wave rectified.

(A) 40 A

(B) $40\sqrt{2}$ A

(C) 20 A

(D) $40/\sqrt{2}$ A

Problem Set # 6.5 - Phasors
Consult NCEES® FE Reference Handbook – Pages 360 - 361 while solving these questions

Problem 6.5 a) Calculate the phasor current of circuit shown below where $V_{max} = 100V$.

(A) $100\underline{/60^\circ}$ A

(B) $12.5\underline{/-30^\circ}$ A

(C) $70.7\underline{/-30^\circ}$ A

(D) $1.8\underline{/-120^\circ}$ A

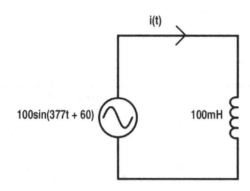

Problem 6.5 b) Express $v(t) = 212\cos(\omega t + 50^\circ)\, V$ in phasor form.

(A) $150\underline{/-40^\circ}$ V   (B) $212\underline{/50^\circ}$ V

(C) $150\underline{/50^\circ}$ V   (D) $212\underline{/-40^\circ}$ V

Problem 6.5 c) Express $v(t) = 212\sin(\omega t + 50^\circ)\, V$ in phasor form.

(A) $150\underline{/-40^\circ}$ V   (B) $212\underline{/50^\circ}$ V

(C) $150\underline{/50^\circ}$ V   (D) $212\underline{/-40^\circ}$ V

Problem 6.5 d) Calculate the phasor current of circuit shown below where $V_{max} = 100V$.

(A) $0.14\underline{/349^\circ}$ A

(B) $0.14\underline{/11.3^\circ}$ A

(C) $0.5\underline{/0^\circ}$ A

(D) $1.75\underline{/50^\circ}$ A

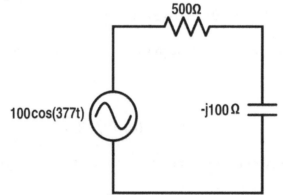

Problem 6.5 e) Calculate the phasor current of circuit shown below where $V_{max} = 100V$.

(A) $70\underline{/10^\circ}$ A

(B) $1000\underline{/-80^\circ}$ A

(C) $2665\underline{/100^\circ}$ A

(D) $550\underline{/-10^\circ}$ A

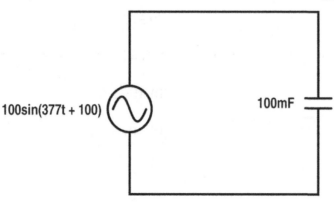

Problem Set # 6.6 - Impedance

Consult NCEES® FE Reference Handbook – Page 361 while solving these questions

Problem 6.6 a) Determine the equivalent impedance of the circuit shown below.

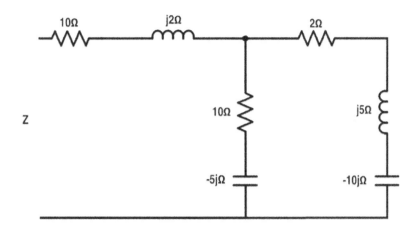

(A) $12 - j \ \Omega$

(B) $5 + 2j \ \Omega$

(C) $2 - 3j \ \Omega$

(D) $0j \ \Omega$

Problem 6.6 b) Determine the equivalent impedance of the circuit shown below.

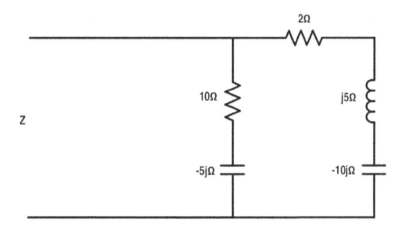

(A) $5 - 3j \ \Omega$

(B) $2 - 3j \ \Omega$

(C) $1 + 2j \ \Omega$

(D) $10j \ \Omega$

Problem 6.6 c) Determine the equivalent impedance of the circuit shown below if frequency is 60Hz.

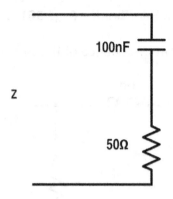

(A) $50 + j26525 \ \Omega$ (B) $50 - j26525 \ \Omega$

(C) $50 + j535 \ \Omega$ (D) $50 - j535 \ \Omega$

Problem 6.6 d) Determine the equivalent impedance of the circuit shown below if frequency is 60Hz.

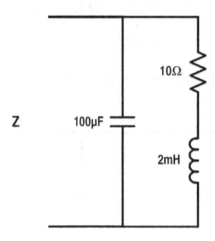

(A) $(10 + j2 \ \Omega)||(-j100 \ \Omega)$ (B) $(10 + j0.5 \ \Omega)||(-j100 \ \Omega)$

(C) $(10 + j0.75 \ \Omega)||(-j26.5 \ \Omega)$ (D) $10 \ \Omega$

Problem 6.6 e) The equivalent impedance of circuit given below is _____ if system frequency is 60Hz.

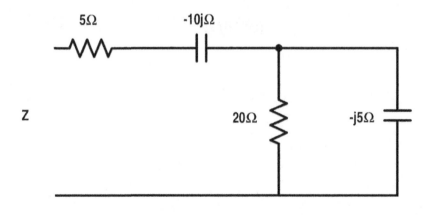

Problem 6.6 f) Determine the load impedance 'Z' required for maximum power transfer.

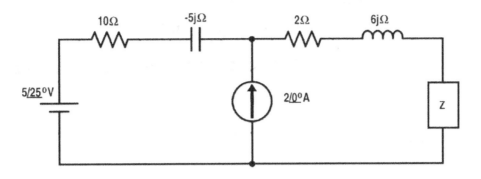

(A) 10Ω   (B) 12Ω

(C) −jΩ   (D) 12 − jΩ

Problem 6.6 g) Determine the load impedance 'Z' required for maximum power transfer.

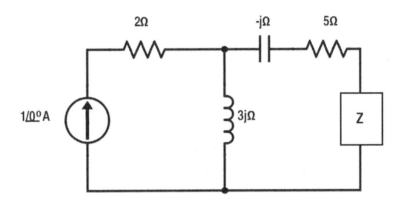

(A) 5 - 2j Ω   (B) 5 + 0.6j Ω

(C) 5 Ω   (D) 1.66j Ω

Chapter # 7 – Linear Systems

Key Knowledge Areas*

Concepts	NCEES® FE Reference Handbook Version 10.0.1	
	Section	Page #
Frequency / transient response	Electrical and Computer Engineering	361 – 362
Resonance		
Transfer functions		
Laplace transforms	Mathematics	56

Facts about this section

- 5 – 8 questions can be expected on the exam according to NCEES® FE specification.
- Linear Systems is an average weighted exam section.
- Difficulty level of this section is rated 'Easy' by the author.

Tips for preparing this section

- Understand the concepts related to Linear Systems found in NCEES® FE Reference Handbook.
- Some of the important equations relevant to this section include RC and RL transient circuits, RLC series and parallel resonance circuits and Laplace transform pairs.
- RLC series and parallel resonance circuits are very similar therefore students need to be careful.
- Carefully use correct quality factor equations after determining whether given circuit is RLC series or parallel resonance circuit.
- Initial conditions of RC and RL transient circuit shall be established carefully.
- Transfer functions shall be converted to a standard form to calculate gain, poles, and zeros.
- Develop familiarity with Laplace transform pairs.
- Learn how to perform partial fraction expansion while calculating inverse Laplace transforms.
- Solve the problem sets of this chapter and review solutions at the end of this book.

* Exam specification details can be found on pages 479 - 481 of NCEES® FE Reference Handbook.

Problem Set # 7.1 - Frequency / transient response

Consult NCEES® FE Reference Handbook – Pages 361 - 362 while solving these questions

Problem 7.1 a) Assume that the switch shown in the circuit below has been in indicated position for a long time. Calculate voltage across capacitor $v_c(t)$ 5 minutes after switch changes position at t = 0 s.

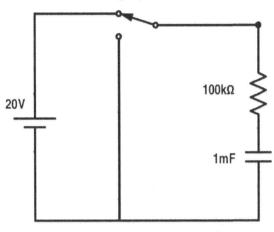

Switch changes position at t = 0s

20V

100kΩ

1mF

(A) 15V   (B) 10V

(C) 1V   (D) 3V

Problem 7.1 b) Calculate the voltage across the capacitor $v_c(t)$ for $t > 0$ in the circuit shown below.

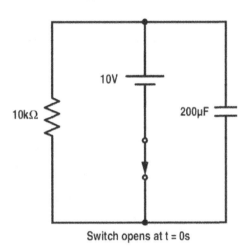

10V

10kΩ

200μF

Switch opens at t = 0s

(A) $e^{-t/2}V$ (B) $10e^{-t/2}V$

(C) $10e^{-t/4}V$ (D) $5e^{-t/2}V$

Problem 7.1 c) Calculate the current $i(t)$ in the following circuit if the switch closes at t = 0 s.

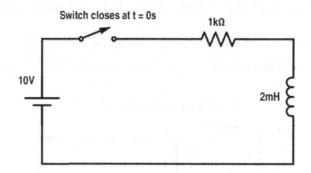

(A) $10(1 - e^{-\frac{t}{2}})A$

(B) $1 - e^{-500000t}A$

(C) $e^{-500000t} + 0.01(1 - e^{-500000t})$ A

(D) $0.01 (1 - e^{-500000t})$ A

Problem 7.1 d) Assume that the switch has been in the indicated position for a long time. Calculate the current $i(t)$ after 10 time constants of opening the switch.

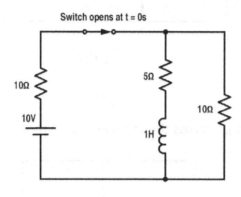

(A) 0.5A

(B) 22.6µA

(C) 1A

(D) 0.18A

Problem 7.1 e) Assume that the switch has been in the indicated position for a long time. Calculate the voltage across capacitor $v_c(t)$ after 5 time constants of changing switch position at t = 0 s.

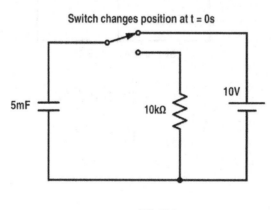

(A) 9.99V

(B) 2V

(C) 67mV

(D) 35mV

54

Problem Set # 7.2 - Resonance
Consult NCEES® FE Reference Handbook – Page 362 while solving these questions

Problem 7.2 a) Calculate the resonant frequency of RLC circuit shown below.

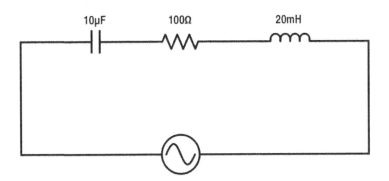

10µF   100Ω   20mH

(A) 1414 rad/s   (B) 250 rad/s

(C) 500 rad/s   (D) 2236 rad/s

Problem 7.2 b) The bandwidth (BW) of the circuit given in problem 7.2 a) is _____.

Problem 7.2 c) Calculate the maximum current of RLC circuit shown below (voltage source is 120VAC).

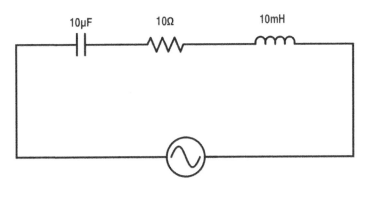

10µF   10Ω   10mH

(A) 4 A   (B) 12 A

(C) 5 A   (D) 7.5 A

Problem 7.2 d) The frequency at which maximum current occurs in problem 7.2 c) is _____.

Problem 7.2 e) A parallel resonant circuit has $R = 10k\Omega$, $C = 100\mu F$, $L = 100mH$. Calculate the quality factor and bandwidth of this resonant circuit.

Problem 7.2 f) In the previous problem, recalculate quality factor and bandwidth of the resonant circuit if the resistor, capacitor, and inductor are now arranged in series configuration.

Problem 7.2 g) Calculate the quality factor of the parallel RLC circuit shown below.

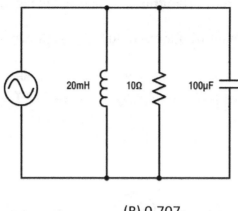

(A) 250   (B) 0.707

(C) 500   (D) 707

Problem 7.2 h) The bandwidth (BW) of circuit shown in problem 7.2 g) is _____.

Problem Set # 7.3 - Laplace Transform
Consult NCEES® FE Reference Handbook – Page 56 while solving these questions

Problem 7.3 a) Find the Laplace transform of function: $f(t) = e^{-bt}$ $(b > 0)$

(A) $\dfrac{1}{s+b}$

(B) $\dfrac{1}{s-b}$

(C) $\dfrac{s}{s+b}$

(D) $\dfrac{s}{s-b}$

Problem 7.3 b) Find the Laplace transform of function: $f(t) = e^{-at}u(t-1)$

(A) $\dfrac{1}{s+a}$

(B) $\dfrac{e^{-(s+a)}}{s+a}$

(C) $\dfrac{s^2}{s-a}$

(D) $\dfrac{e^{-(s-a)}}{s-a}$

Problem 7.3 c) Find the Laplace transform of function: $f(t) = te^{-at}u(t-1)$

(A) $\dfrac{s+a}{(s+a)^2+1}$

(B) $\dfrac{e^{-(s+a)}}{(s-a)^2}$

(C) $e^{-(s+a)}\left(\dfrac{1}{(s+a)^2} + \dfrac{1}{(s+a)}\right)$

(D) $\dfrac{s}{(s+a)^2}$

Problem 7.3 d) Find the Laplace transform of function: $f(t) = \left(e^{-(t-3)} - e^{-3(t-3)}\right)u(t-3)$

(A) $e^{3s}\left(\dfrac{1}{s+1} + \dfrac{1}{s+3}\right)$

(B) $\dfrac{s}{(s+1)(s+3)}$

(C) $\dfrac{1}{(s+3)(s-3)}$

(D) $e^{-3s}\left(\dfrac{1}{s+1} - \dfrac{1}{s+3}\right)$

Problem 7.3 e) Find the Laplace transform of function: $f(t) = te^{-at}\delta(t-2)$

(A) $2e^{-2(s+a)}$

(B) $\dfrac{1}{(s+a)^2}$

(C) $e^{-(s+a)}$

(D) $\dfrac{e^{-(s+a)}}{s+a}$

Problem 7.3 f) Find the Laplace transform of function: $f(t) = tu(t) * \sin 4t$

(A) $4/(s^2 + 16)$

(B) $4/[s^2(s^2 + 16)]$

(C) $4/s^2$

(D) $1/(s^2 + 16)$

Problem 7.3 g) Find the inverse Laplace transform of following function:

$$F(s) = \frac{5}{(s+3) + (s+5)}$$

(A) $3e^{-3t} + 5e^{-5t}$ (B) e^{-4t}

(C) $2e^{-8t}$ (D) $\frac{5}{2}e^{-4t}$

Problem 7.3 h) Find the inverse Laplace transform of following function:

$$F(s) = \frac{s+8}{(s+1)(s+7)}$$

(A) $e^{-8t} + e^{-t} - e^{-7t}$ (B) $e^{-t} + e^{-7t}$

(C) $\frac{1}{6}(7e^{-t} - e^{-7t})$ (D) $5e^{-7t} - 8e^{-t}$

Problem 7.3 i) Find the inverse Laplace transform of following function:

$$F(s) = \frac{s^2 + 2s + 1}{(s+2)(s)(s+3)}$$

(A) $\frac{u(t)}{6} - \frac{1}{2}e^{-2t} + \frac{4}{3}e^{-3t}$ (B) $e^{-2t} + e^{-3t} + \frac{2}{3}$

(C) $te^{-2t}e^{-3t}$ (D) $\delta(t)(e^{-2t} + e^{-3t})$

Problem 7.3 j) Find the inverse Laplace transform of following function:

$$F(s) = \frac{s+4}{(s^2)(s+5)}$$

(A) $5e^{-5t} + \frac{1}{4} + \frac{t^2}{5}$ (B) $\frac{4}{5}e^{-5t} + \frac{1}{4}t$

(C) $\frac{1}{25}u(t) + \frac{4}{5}t - \frac{1}{25}e^{-5t}$ (D) $25u(t) - e^{-5t}$

Problem Set # 7.4 - Transfer functions

Consult NCEES® FE Reference Handbook – Pages 56, 361 - 362 while solving these questions

Problem 7.4 a) _____ statements regarding transfer function are INCORRECT.

(A) Transfer function is the ratio of LTI system's output to input in Laplace domain

(B) Transfer function is the ratio of LTI system's output to input in time domain

(C) Initial conditions of LTI system are must be set to zero.

(D) Initial conditions of LTI system can be non-zero.

Problem 7.4 b) Transfer function of the LTI system given below is _____.

$$y(t) = 2\frac{d}{dt}x(t) + \int_0^t x(t)dt - x(t-2)u(t-2)$$

Problem 7.4 c) Determine the impulse response of the transfer function given below:

$$H(s) = \frac{s+4}{s^2 + 3s + 2}$$

Problem 7.4 d) Calculate the transfer function V_o/V_i for the circuit shown below.

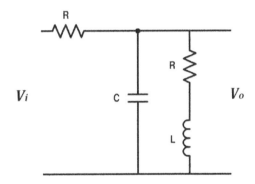

(A) $(R||sL)/[(R+sL)||\left(\frac{1}{sC}\right)]$

(B) $(R||sL)/[R+(R+sL)||\left(\frac{1}{sC}\right)]$

(C) $(R+sL)/[(R+sL)||\left(\frac{1}{sC}\right)]$

(D)$[(R+sL)||\left(\frac{1}{sC}\right)]/[R+(R+sL)||\left(\frac{1}{sC}\right)]$

Problem 7.4 e) Calculate the transfer function V_o/V_i for the circuit shown below.

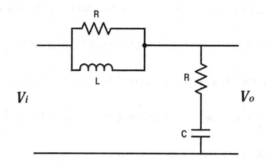

(A) $R/(R||sL)$

(B) $\left[R + \left(R + \frac{1}{sC}\right)\right]/(R||sL)$

(C) $\left(R + \frac{1}{sC}\right)/\left[(R||sL) + \left(R + \frac{1}{sC}\right)\right]$

(D) $\left[R + \frac{1}{sC} + \left(R + \frac{1}{sC}\right)\right]/\left[(R||sL) + \left(R + \frac{1}{sC}\right)\right]$

Problem 7.4 f) Calculate the transfer function V_o/V_i for the circuit shown below.

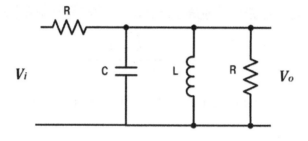

(A) $R + \frac{1}{sC}||(R + sL||R)$

(B) $R + \frac{1}{sC}||sL||R$

(C) $\frac{1}{sC}||sL||R$

(D) $(R||sL||1/sC)/[R + (R||sL||1/sC)]$

Chapter # 8 – Signal Processing

Key Knowledge Areas*

Concepts	NCEES® FE Reference Handbook Version 10.0.1	
	Section	Page #
Sampling, Aliasing, Nyquist Theorem	Electrical and Computer Engineering	376
Analog Filters		379 – 380
Digital Filters, Z-Transform, Difference Equations		369 – 371
Convolution		370

Facts about this section

- 5 – 8 questions can be expected on the exam according to NCEES® FE specification.
- Signal Processing is an average weighted exam section.
- Difficulty level of this section is rated 'Medium' by the author.
- Students with a major in telecommunication engineering may find this section easier.

Tips for preparing this section

- Understand the concepts related to Signal Processing found in NCEES® FE Reference Handbook.
- Some of the important equations relevant to this section include continuous time convolution, discrete time convolution, z-transform, and Nyquist theorem.
- Graphical convolution of continuous time functions involves flipping simpler function about y-axis, determining regions of overlap, identifying limits of integration, and correctly calculating integrals.
- Graphical convolution of discrete time functions involves flipping simpler function about y-axis, determining regions of overlap, and calculating integrals.
- Develop familiarity with Z transform table and its application in difference equation.
- Identify signal with highest frequency to correctly apply Nyquist theorem.
- Calculate transfer functions of analog filter circuits given in NCEES® FE Reference Handbook to develop understanding through derivation.
- Solve the problem sets of this chapter and review the solutions at the end of this book.

Note – Although convolution has been removed as a line item from FE Electrical and Computer exam specification in the latest NCEES® FE Reference Handbook, it is still present in the Electrical and Computer Engineering section of NCEES® FE Reference Handbook.

BONUS: Unlock a free 'Signal Processing' lecture by signing-up for the On-demand FE Electrical and Computer exam preparation course preview at: **www.studyforfe.com/fe-course-preview**

* Exam specification details can be found on pages 479 - 481 of NCEES® FE Reference Handbook.

Problem Set # 8.1 - Sampling

Consult NCEES® FE Reference Handbook – Pages 225 and 376 while solving these questions

Problem 8.1 a) For perfect reconstruction of a band limited signal, it must be _____

(A) Sampled at or above Nyquist rate

(B) Passed through ideal low pass filter

(C) Modulated with high frequency signal

(D) Options A and B are correct

Problem 8.1 b) The minimum sampling frequency required for perfect reconstruction of the message signal $\text{sinc}(1000\pi t) + \text{sinc}(2000\pi t)$ is _____.

Problem 8.1 c) Sampling continuous time signal $\cos(3000\pi t + \theta)$ at 2000 Hz will result in _____

(A) Nyquist sampling

(B) Critical sampling

(C) Aliasing

(D) Oversampling

Problem 8.1 d) In the previous problem, recovered signal will be _____ if sampling rate is 2000Hz.

(A) $\cos(3000\pi t + \theta)$

(B) $\cos(3000\pi t - \theta)$

(C) $\cos(1000\pi t + \theta)$

(D) $\cos(1000\pi t - \theta)$

Problem 8.1 e) Determine the aliased frequency of $x(t) = \cos(500\pi t + \theta)$ if it is sample at 500 Hz.

(A) 500 Hz

(B) 250 Hz

(C) 0 Hz

(D) There will be no aliasing

Problem 8.1 f) In the previous problem, recovered signal will be _____ if sampling rate is 200Hz.

(A) $\cos(500\pi t + \theta)$

(B) $\cos(500\pi t - \theta)$

(C) $\cos(100\pi t + \theta)$

(D) $\cos(100\pi t - \theta)$

Problem 8.1 g) Determine the aliased frequency of $x(t) = \cos(400\pi t + \theta)$ if it is sampled at 300 Hz.

(A) 200 Hz

(B) 300 Hz

(C) 100 Hz

(D) 400 Hz

Problem 8.1 h) In the previous problem, recovered signal will be _____ if it is sampled at 150 Hz.

(A) $\cos(400\pi t + \theta)$

(B) $\cos(400\pi t - \theta)$

(C) $\cos(100\pi t + \theta)$

(D) $\cos(100\pi t - \theta)$

Problem Set # 8.2 – Analog Filters

Consult NCEES® FE Reference Handbook – Pages 379 - 380 while solving these questions

Problem 8.2 a) Identify the filter type given by following transfer function of an analog filter.

$$H(j\omega) = \frac{300\left((j\omega)^2 + \frac{1}{50}\right)}{(j\omega)^2 + 100j\omega + \frac{1}{50}}$$

(A) High-Pass Filter   (B) Low-Pass Filter

(C) Band-Pass Filter   (D) Band-Reject Filter

Problem 8.2 b) _____ is the -3 dB (cut-off) frequency of a series RL circuit with $R_S = 2k\Omega$ and $L = 2H$.

(A) $10\ rad/s$ (B) $500\ rad/s$

(C) $1000\ rad/s$ (D) $1500\ rad/s$

Problem 8.2 c) The series RL circuit mentioned in previous problem can be used as a _____.

(A) High-Pass Filter   (B) Low-Pass Filter

(C) Band-Pass Filter   (D) Band-Reject Filter

Problem 8.2 d) _____ is the -3 dB frequency of a series RC circuit with $R_S = 2k\Omega$ and $C = 50\mu F$.

(A) $10\ rad/s$ (B) $500\ rad/s$

(C) $1000\ rad/s$ (D) $1500\ rad/s$

Problem 8.2 e) The series RC circuit mentioned in previous problem can be used as a _____.

(A) High-Pass Filter   (B) Low-Pass Filter

(C) Band-Pass Filter   (D) Band-Reject Filter

Consider a series RLC circuit with $R_S = 2k\Omega, C = 50\mu F$ and $L = 2H$ for problems 8.2 f) to 8.2 h).

Problem 8.2 f) The bandwidth of this series RLC circuit is _____.

Problem 8.2 g) This series RLC circuit can be used as a _____.

Problem 8.2 h) Calculate the lower cut-off frequency ω_L of this filter if its upper cut-off frequency ω_U is found to be $1500\ rad/s$.

(A) $10\ rad/s$ (B) $500\ rad/s$

(C) $1000\ rad/s$ (D) $1500\ rad/s$

Problem Set # 8.3 – Digital Filters, Z-transforms, Difference Equation

Consult NCEES® FE Reference Handbook – Pages 369 - 371 while solving these questions

Problem 8.3 a) _____ is used to solve a difference equation that models a discrete time system.

(A) Laplace Transform

(B) Discrete Convolution

(C) Z-Transform

(D) Integration

Problem 8.3 b) Find the z-transform of $x[n] = u[n] - u[n-5]$.

(A) $z^{-1} + z^{-2} + z^{-3} + z^{-4}$

(B) $1 + z^{-1} + z^{-2} + z^{-3} + z^{-4}$

(C) $5z^{-5}$

(D) $1 + z^{-1} + z^{-2} + z^{-3} + z^{-4} + z^{-5}$

Problem 8.3 c) Find the z-transform of $x[n] = 0.2^n u[n]$.

(A) $(0.2\, z^{-1})^n$

(B) $0.2^n z^{-1}$

(C) $0.2/(1 - z^{-1})$

(D) $1/(1 - 0.2z^{-1})$

Problem 8.3 d) Find the z-transform of $x[n] = [2\ 3\ 1\ 0\ 5]$.

(A) $2 + 3z^{-1} + z^{-2} + 5z^{-4}$

(B) $1/(2 + 3z^{-1} + z^{-2} + 5z^{-4})$

(C) $5(1 - 0.75^n z^{-1})$

(D) $2 + 3z$

Problem 8.3 e) Find the z-transform of $x[n] = [2\ 3\ \check{1}\ 0\ 5]$ (arrow indicates location of $x[0]$).

(A) $2 + 3z^{-1} + z^{-2} + 5z^{-4}$

(B) $2z^2 + 3z + 1 + 5z^{-2}$

(C) $5(1 - 0.75^n z^{-1})$

(D) $2 + 3z$

Problem 8.3 f) Find the z-transform of $x[n] = 5(0.75^n)u[n]$.

(A) $5/(1 - 0.75z^{-1})$

(B) $5(0.75^n z^{-n})$

(C) $5(1 - 0.75^n z^{-1})$

(D) $0.5^n z^{-n}$

Problem 8.3 g) Find the inverse z-transform of $X(z) = 4 + 2z^{-1} + 3z^{-3} + z^{-5}$.

(A) {4,2,3,1}

(B) {4,2,0,3,0,1}

(C) {0,4,2,0,3,1}

(D) {4,2,3,1,0}

Problem 8.3 h) Find the inverse z-transform of $X(z) = z/(z - 0.5)$

(A) $1/(1 - 0.5z^{-1})$

(B) $0.5^{n-1}u[n]$

(C) $0.5^n u[n]$

(D) $1 - 0.5^n$

Problem 8.3 i) Find the inverse z-transform of $X(z) = (5z + 2)/[(z - 1)(z - 4)]$

(A) $\frac{1}{5}(4^n u[n] - 1^n u[n] + \delta[n])$

(B) $\cos[n] - 4^n u[n]$

(C) $\frac{1}{2}4^n u[n] + \frac{1}{5}u[n]$

(D) $\frac{1}{2}\delta[n] - \frac{7}{3}u[n] + \frac{11}{6}4^n u[n]$

Problem 8.3 j) Find the inverse z-transform of $X(z) = [(z - 2)(z + 1)]/[(z - 0.1)(z - 0.2)]$

(A) $\frac{1}{2}0.1^n - 2(0.2)^n u[n]$

(B) $-100\delta[n] + 209(0.1)^n u[n] - 108(0.2)^n u[n]$

(C) $\frac{1}{3}\delta(n) + 0.1^n u[n] + 0.3^n u[n]$

(D) $0.5\delta[n] + 2(0.1)^n u[n]$

Problem 8.3 k) Find the inverse z-transform of $X(z) = (z + 0.5)/[(z - 0.1)(z + 0.4)]$

(A) $-\frac{25}{2}\delta[n] + 12(0.1)^n u[n] + \frac{1}{2}(-0.4)^n u[n]$

(B) $\frac{3}{4}0.1^n u[n] + \frac{1}{2}(-0.4)^n u[n]$

(C) $2\delta[n] + 6(0.1)^n u[n] - \frac{3}{4}(0.4)^n u[n]$

(D) $\frac{1}{2}(0.1)^n u[n] + \frac{5}{2}0.4^n u[n]$

Problem 8.3 l) Solve the following difference equation to determine $y[n]$.

$y[n] + y[n - 1] + 2y[n - 2] = x[n] + x[n - 1] + 2x[n - 2]$ where $x[n] = 4^n$

Problem 8.3 m) A digital filter based on a discrete-time, linear, time-invariant system is given by the difference equation: $y[n] + 2y[n - 1] = x[n] + 3x[n - 1]$. Determine the transfer function $H(s)$ if all initial conditions are equal to zero.

Problem 8.3 n) _____ is a type of non-recursive digital filter.

(A) Finite Impulse Response Filter

(B) Infinite Impulse Response Filter

(C) Options A and B are correct

(D) Non-recursive filters don't exist

Problem 8.3 o) _____ is a type of recursive digital filter.

(A) Finite Impulse Response Filter

(B) Infinite Impulse Response Filter

(C) Options A and B are correct

(D) Non-recursive filters don't exist

Problem 8.3 p) Digital filtering does not involve _____.

(A) Sampling

(B) A/D conversion

(C) D/A conversion

(D) Phase modulation

Problem Set # 8.4 - Continuous Time Convolution

Consult NCEES® FE Reference Handbook – Page 370 while solving these questions

Problem 8.4 a) _____ option correctly represents the convolved output of $x(t)$ and $h(t)$.

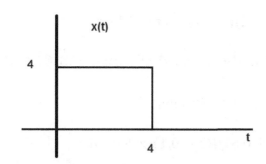

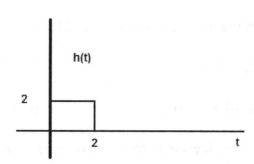

$$x(t) = 4\big(u(t) - u(t-4)\big)$$

$$y(t) = 2\big(u(t) - u(t-2)\big)$$

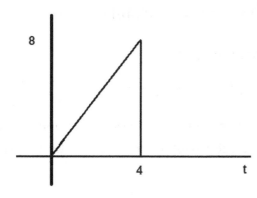

(A)

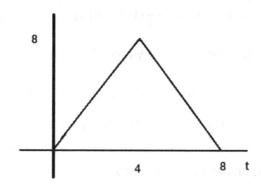

(B)

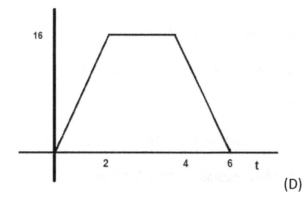

(C)

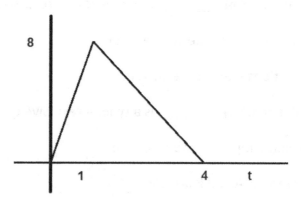

(D)

Problem 8.4 b) _____ option correctly represents the convolved output of $f(t)$ and $h(t)$.

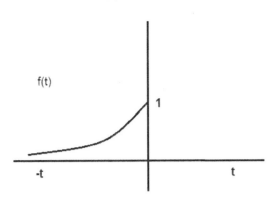

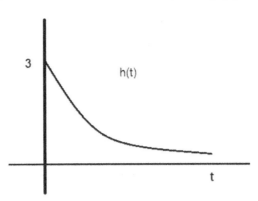

$$f(t) = e^t u(-t)$$

$$h(t) = 3e^{-t}u(t)$$

(A) $\frac{3}{2}e^t$ for $t < 0, \frac{3}{2}e^{-t}$ for $t \geq 0$

(B) $\frac{1}{2}e^{2t}$ for $t < 0, -\frac{1}{2}e^{-2t}$ for $t \geq 0$

(C) $\frac{3}{2}e^{-t}$ for $t < 0, \frac{3}{2}e^t$ for $t \geq 0$

(D) 0 for $t < 0, 3e^t$ for $t \geq 0$

Problem 8.4 c) _____ option correctly represents the convolved output of $x(t)$ and $y(t)$.

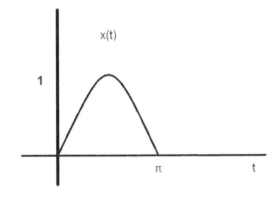

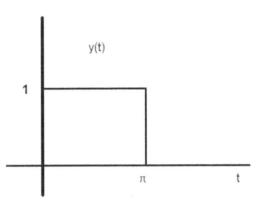

$$x(t) = \sin(t)\left(u(t) - u(t - \pi)\right)$$

$$y(t) = u(t) - u(t - \pi)$$

(A) $\cos(t)\ 0 < t \leq \pi, -\cos(t)\ \pi < t \leq 2\pi$

(B) $\sin(t)\ 0 < t \leq \pi, 1 - \sin(t)\ \pi < t \leq 2\pi$

(C) $\cos(t) - 1\ 0 < t \leq \pi,\ 1 - \cos(t)\ \pi < t \leq 2\pi$

(D) $1 - \cos(t)\ 0 < t \leq \pi,\ 1 - \cos(t)\ \pi < t \leq 2\pi$

Problem 8.4 d) _____ option correctly represents the convolved output of $x(t)$ and $y(t)$.

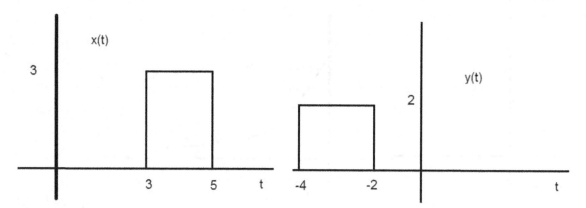

$$x(t) = 3(u(t-3) - u(t-5))$$

$$y(t) = 2(u(t+4) - u(t+2))$$

(A) $6(1+t)$ for $-1 \leq t < 1$, $6(1-t)$ for $1 \leq t < 3$

(B) $1 + 6t$ for $-1 \leq t < 1$, $1 - 6t$ for $1 \leq t < 3$

(C) $6(1+t)$ for $-1 \leq t < 1$, $6(3-t)$ for $1 \leq t < 3$

(D) $6(t)$ for $-1 \leq t < 1$, $3 - t$ for $1 \leq t < 3$

Problem 8.4 e) Find the convolved output of following functions for $t \geq 2$.

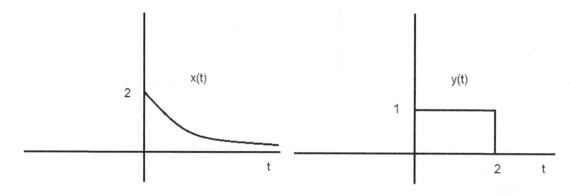

$$x(t) = 2e^{-t}$$

$$y(t) = u(t) - u(t-2)$$

(A) 0

(B) $2(e^t - e^{-t})$

(C) $2(e^{-t+2} - e^{-t})$

(D) $e^t - e^{-t-2}$

Problem Set # 8.5 - Discrete Time Convolution

Consult NCEES® FE Reference Handbook – **Page 370 while solving these questions**

Problem 8.5 a) Find the convolved output of discrete time functions $x[n]$ and $y[n]$ shown below.

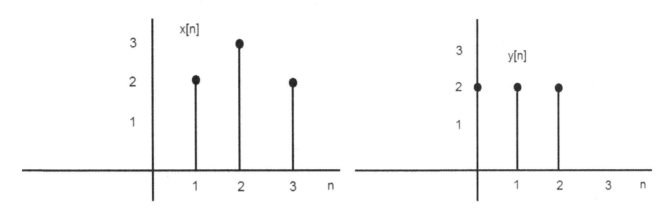

(A) [0 4 10 4 0]

(B) [0 4 10 14 10 4 0]

(C) [0 2 4 8 4 2 0]

(D) [0 2 6 2 0]

Problem 8.5 b) Find the convolved output of discrete time functions $x[n]$ and $y[n]$ shown below.

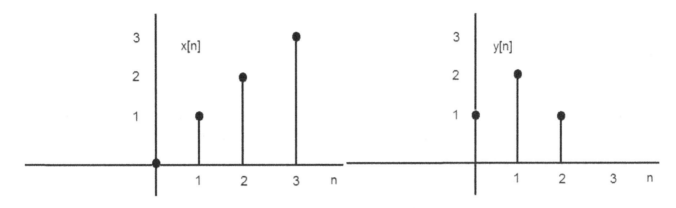

(A) [0 1 4 6 4 1 0]

(B) [0 1 4 1 0]

(C) [0 1 4 8 8 3 0]

(D) [0 1 8 8 1 0]

Problem 8.5 c) Discrete time convolution is used to find _____

(A) Zero input solution

(B) Zero state solution

(C) Product of signals

(D) Modulation index

Problem 8.5 d) The convolved output of $x[n] = u[n] - u[n-5]$ and $y[n] = 0.2^n u[n]$ is _____.

Problem 8.5 e) The convolved output of $x[n] = u[n-2]$ and $y[n] = 0.4^n u[n]$ is _____.

Chapter # 9 – Electronics

Key Knowledge Areas*

Concepts	NCEES® FE Reference Handbook Version 10.0.1	
	Section	Page #
Semiconductor materials*	Electrical and Computer Engineering	381 – 388
Discrete devices		
Amplifiers		
Operational Amplifiers		
Power Electronics		
Instrumentation	Instrumentation, Measurement and Control	220 - 225
Note: Semiconductor materials belong to Properties of Electrical Materials but are discussed here.		

Facts about this section

- 7 – 11 questions can be expected on the exam according to the latest NCEES® FE specification.
- Electronics is one of the most heavily weighted exam sections.
- Difficulty level of this section is rated 'Hard' by the author.
- Students with a major in electronics engineering may find this section easier.

Tips for preparing this section

- Understand the concepts related to 'Electronics' found in NCEES® FE Reference Handbook.
- Some of the most important equations relevant to this section include conductivity of semi-conductors, contact potential, Shockley's equation, BJT's mathematical relationships, JFETs and MOSFETs mathematical relationships.
- Learn how to calculate the Q-point of diodes, BJTs, JFETs and MOSFETs.
- BJT amplification takes place in the 'active region'.
- JFET/MOSFET amplification takes place in the 'saturation region'.
- Derive equations for two-source configuration of an ideal Operational Amplifier and CMRR given in NCEES® FE Reference Handbook.
- Familiarize yourself with workings of measurement devices such as RTDs, thermocouples, Wheatstone bridge, ammeters, voltmeters etc.
- Review basic concepts related to power electronics and understand equations related to choppers and rectifiers.
- Solve the problem sets of this chapter and review solutions at the end of this book.

BONUS: Unlock a free 'Electronics' lecture by signing-up for the On-demand FE Electrical and Computer exam preparation course preview at: **www.studyforfe.com/fe-course-preview**

* Exam specification can be found on pages 479 - 481 of NCEES® FE Reference Handbook.

Problem Set # 9.1 - Semiconductor materials
Consult NCEES® FE Reference Handbook – Pages 382 - 383 while solving these questions

Problem 9.1 a) _____ is typically used as n-type doping material.

(A) Antimony   (B) Silicon

(C) Germanium   (D) Boron

Problem 9.1 b) _____ is typically used as p-type doping material.

(A) Antimony   (B) Silicon

(C) Germanium   (D) Boron

Problem 9.1 c) Electron and hole concentrations of a semi-conductor wafer at equilibrium are found to be $n = p = 2 \times 10^{10} m^{-3}$. Mobilities of electrons and holes can be assumed as $\mu_n = 0.20 \ m^2V^{-1}s^{-1}$ and $\mu_p = 0.10 m^2V^{-1}s^{-1}$ respectively. Calculate the conductivity of this semi-conductor wafer.

(A) 4.8 x 10^{-10} S/m   (B) 9.6 x 10^{-10} S/m

(C) 1.4 x 10^{-9} S/m   (D) 7.2 x 10^{-10} S/m

Problem 9.1 d) A p-n junction has acceptor concentration $= 2 \times 10^{15} m^{-3}$, donor concentration $= 2 \times 10^{15} m^{-3}$ and intrinsic concentration $= 1 \times 10^{10} m^{-3}$. Calculate the contact potential of this p-n junction at 300 K.

Problem 9.1 e) _____ material class has the largest energy gap between valence and conduction bands.

(A) Semi-conductors   (B) Conductors

(C) Insulators   (D) All materials have same energy gaps

Problem 9.1 f) Drift current in semi-conductors (at constant temperature) can be increased by _____.

(A) Increasing applied potential   (B) Decreasing applied potential

(C) Increasing surface area   (D) Decreasing surface area

Problem 9.1 g) Diffusion current is caused by difference in _____ between different regions.

(A) Electric potential   (B) Temperature

(C) Charge concentration   (D) All of the above

Problem 9.1 h) Group _____ elements of periodic table are typically used as p-type doping materials.

Problem Set # 9.2 – Diodes and Thyristors

Consult NCEES® FE Reference Handbook – Page 385 while solving these questions

Problem 9.2 a) Find the operating states of diodes D_1 and D_2 in following circuit assuming ideal model.

(A) D_1 On, D_2 Off

(B) D_1 On, D_2 On

(C) D_1 Off, D_2 On

(D) D_1 Off, D_2 Off

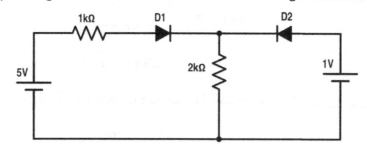

Problem 9.2 b) Calculate the current passing through diode shown below assuming ideal diode model.

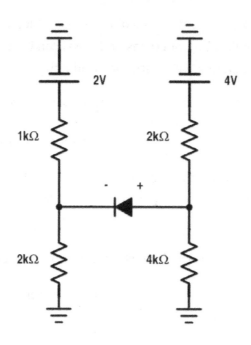

Problem 9.2 c) Calculate the diode current in given circuit assuming constant voltage drop $V_{on} = 0.7V$.

Problem 9.2 d) Calculate the diode currents in given circuit assuming constant voltage drop $V_{on} = 0.7$ V.

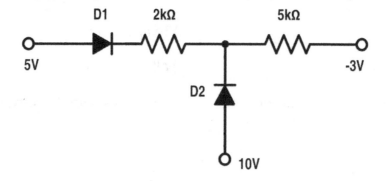

Problem 9.2 e) Calculate the minimum value of resistance for resistor R which is required for maintaining Zener voltage $V_z = 2V$ across the resistor R. I_z represents Zener knee current which is the minimum current that must flow through the diode in reverse breakdown region.

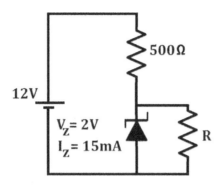

Problem 9.2 f) The current flowing through the Zener diode circuit given below is _____.

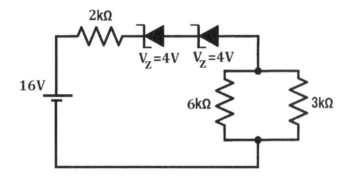

Problem 9.2 g) A diode circuit has saturation current $I_S = 10^{-16}A$, emission coefficient $\eta = 2$ and diode current $= 50\mu A$. Calculate the voltage applied across this diode if it is operating at $T = 300K$.

Problem 9.2 h) Calculate the average output voltage of a thyristor-based single phase half-wave controlled rectifier with a purely resistive load if input voltage $V_{max} = 480V$ @ $60Hz$ and thyristor is fired at $60°$ in every positive half cycle of the input voltage.

Problem 9.2 i) In the previous problem, recalculate the average output DC voltage if a full-wave center-tap thyristor-based single-phase rectifier with an RL inductive load is used.

Problem 9.2 j) Match the semiconductor devices with correct controllability features.

Semiconductor Devices	Controllability
1 – Thyristor (SCR)	A – Fully controllable
2 – Diode	B – Semi-controllable
3 – BJT	C - Uncontrollable
4 – MOSFET	

Problem 9.2 k) A thyristor-based single-phase half-wave controlled rectifier is powered by a 110 VAC, 60Hz power source and it is connected to a 5Ω load resistor.

Select the graph that most accurately represents the voltage across resistor if firing angle is 45°

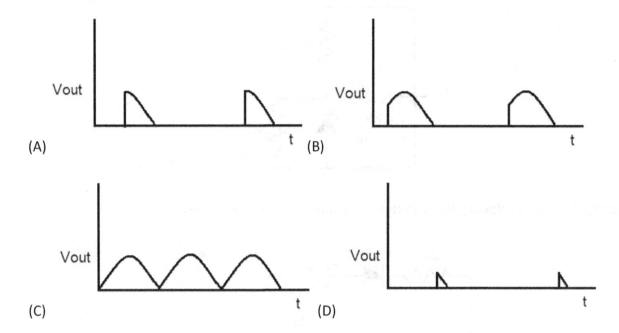

(A)

(B)

(C)

(D)

Problem Set # 9.3 – Bipolar Junction Transistors (BJTs)

Consult NCEES® FE Reference Handbook – Page 386 while solving these questions

Problem 9.3 a) Calculate the emitter current I_E and the voltage V_{CE} for the BJT shown below.

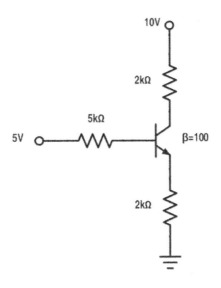

(A) $I_E = 0$, $V_{CE} = 0.5$ V

(B) $I_E = 0$, $V_{CE} = 1.75$ V

(C) $I_E = 2.09$ mA, $V_{CE} = 1.68$ V

(D) $I_E = 1.5$ mA, $V_{CE} = 2.5$ V

Problem 9.3 b) Calculate the collector current I_C and the voltage V_{CE} for the BJT shown below.

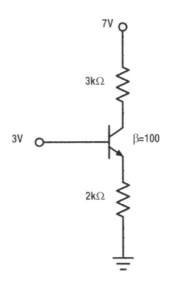

(A) $I_C = 0$ mA, $V_{CE} = 0.5$ V

(B) $I_C = 1.5$ mA, $V_{CE} = 2$ V

(C) $I_C = 0.75$ mA, $V_{CE} = 0.1$ V

(D) $I_C = 1.13$ mA, $V_{CE} = 1.3$ V

Problem 9.3 c) Determine the operating region of the transistor shown in the circuit given below.

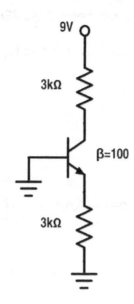

9V

3kΩ

β=100

3kΩ

Problem 9.3 d) Calculate the emitter current I_E and the voltage V_{CE} for the BJT shown below.

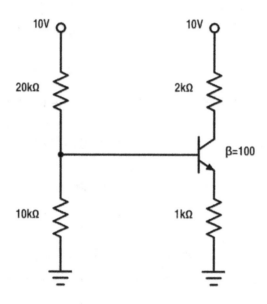

10V   10V

20kΩ   2kΩ

β=100

10kΩ   1kΩ

(A) I_E = 2.4 mA, V_{CE}= 2.7V

(B) I_E =0 mA, V_{CE} = 0.2V

(C) I_E =0 mA, V_{CE}= 10V

(D) I_E = 5 mA, V_{CE} = 4.5V

Problem 9.3 e) Calculate the emitter current I_E and the voltage V_{EC} for the BJT shown below.

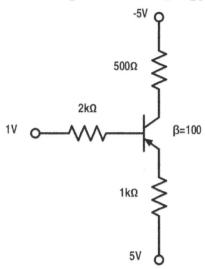

Problem 9.3 f) Calculate the emitter current I_E and the voltage V_{EC} for the BJT shown below.

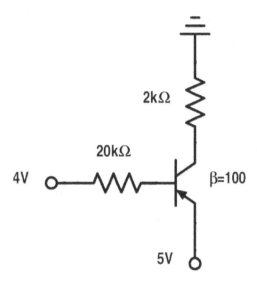

Problem 9.3 g) Calculate the emitter current I_E and the voltage V_{EC} for the BJT shown below.

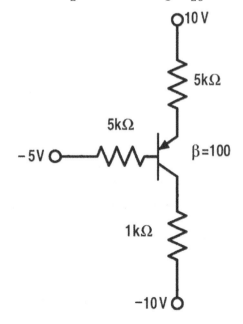

Problem Set # 9.4 – Junction Field Effect Transistors (JFETs)

Consult NCEES® FE Reference Handbook – Page 387 while solving these questions

Problem 9.4 a) Consider the JFET circuit shown below for which $I_{DSS} = 7.5mA$ and pinch-off voltage $V_p = -3V$. Calculate the value of source resistance R_s that will result in drain current $i_D = 5mA$.

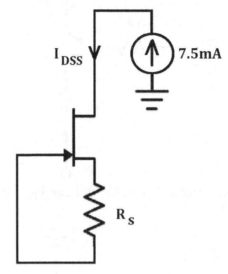

Problem 9.4 b) Calculate the maximum transconductance g_m of an N-channel JFET which has $I_{DSS} = 2mA$ and pinch-off voltage $V_p = -4V$.

Problem 9.4 c) The JFET given below is operating in _____ region ($V_p = -5V$, $I_{DSS} = 10mA$).

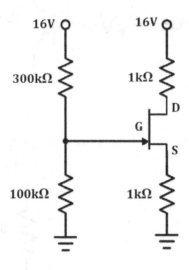

(A) Cut-off   (B) Saturation

(C) Triode   (D) None of the above

Problem 9.4 d) In the previous problem, transconductance g_m of given JFET is _____.

Problem Set # 9.5 – Metal-Oxide Semiconductor Field Effect Transistors (MOSFETs)

Consult NCEES® FE Reference Handbook – Page 388 while solving these questions

Problem 9.5 a) Calculate the drain current i_D for the following transistor ($K = 0.5mA/V^2$, $V_t = 1V$).

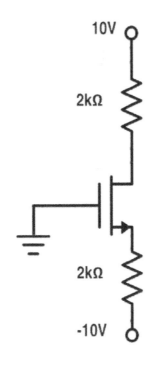

(A) 0mA   (B) 1.5mA

(C) 2.5mA   (D) 3.2mA

Problem 9.5 b) Find the operating region of the transistor shown below ($K = 0.5mA/V^2$, $V_t = 1V$).

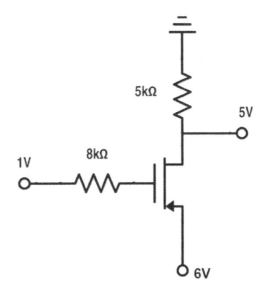

Problem 9.5 c) Calculate the V_{DS} for the MOSFET circuit shown below ($K = 0.2mA/V^2$, $V_t = 1V$).

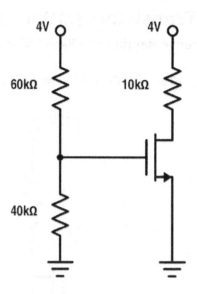

(A) 0. 5V   (B) 3.28V

(C) 0V   (D) 1.75V

Problem 9.5 d) Calculate the drain current i_D for the following transistor ($K = 0.1mA/V^2$, $V_t = -1V$).

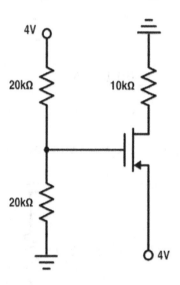

(A) 5mA   (B) 0.3mA

(C) 0.1mA   (D) 0

Problem 9.5 e) Calculate the drain current i_D for following transistor ($K = 0.1mA/V^2$, $V_t = 1V$).

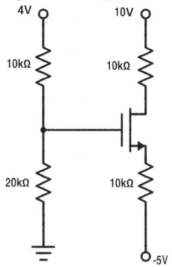

Problem 9.5 f) Determine the operating region of MOSFET shown in the circuit shown below if threshold voltage $V_t = 1V$ and conductivity factor $K = 0.25mA/V^2$.

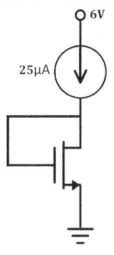

Problem 9.5 g) Calculate the value of drain resistor R_1 and source resistor R_2 if drain current $i_D = 1mA$, drain voltage $V_D = 1.2V$, threshold voltage $V_t = 1V$ and conductivity factor $K = 0.25mA/V^2$.

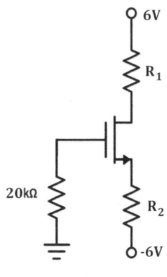

Problem Set # 9.6 - Operational Amplifiers

Consult NCEES® FE Reference Handbook – Pages 381 - 382 while solving these questions

Problem 9.6 a) Find the output voltage V_o in the circuit shown below.

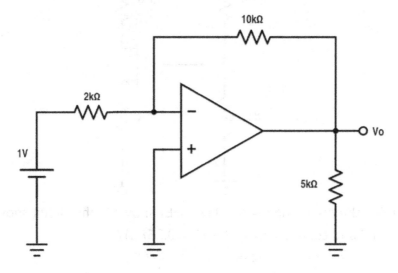

Problem 9.6 b) Find the value of resistance $'R'$ in the circuit shown below if $V_o = 12V$.

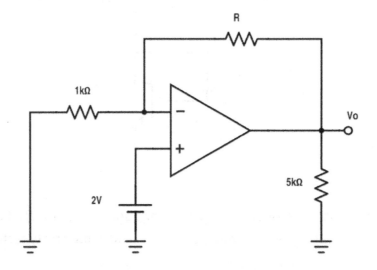

Problem 9.6 c) Find the output voltage V_o in the circuit shown below.

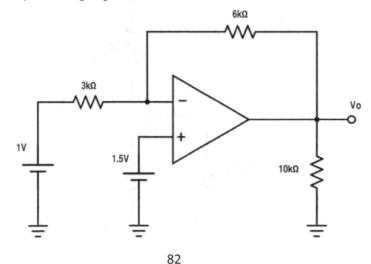

Problem 9.6 d) Find the output voltage V_o in the circuit shown below.

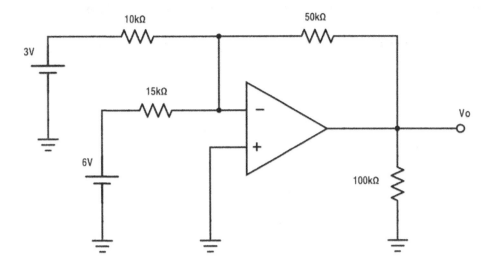

Problem 9.6 e) Find the output voltage V_o in the circuit shown below.

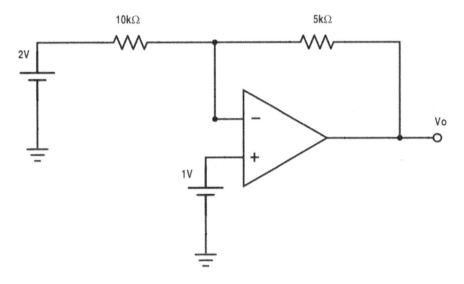

Problem 9.6 f) Consider the basic BJT differential amplifier circuit shown below. Determine the value of V_{B2} for which $I_{E1} = 2I_{E2}$ if threshold voltage $V_t = 1V$.

Problem 9.6 g) In the previous problem, $I_{E1} =$ ___ and $I_{E2} =$ ___ if current source $I_{E-total} = 6mA$.

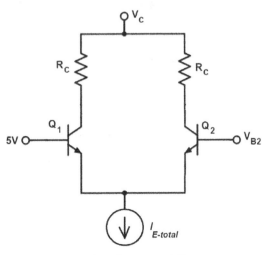

Problem Set # 9.7 - Power Electronics
Consult NCEES® FE Reference Handbook – Page 384 while solving these questions

Problem 9.7 a) Power electronics converter that changes DC to DC is called _____

(A) Inverter   (B) Chopper

(C) Rectifier   (D) Cycloconverter

Problem 9.7 b) A boost converter is to be used to feed a load at 600VDC from a 150VDC source. Calculate the switching frequency of this chopper if its ON time is $10\mu s$.

(A) $25kHz$ (B) $50kHz$

(C) $75kHz$ (D) $100kHz$

Problem 9.7 c) A buck converter with input voltage source of 60VDC feeds a resistive load of 5Ω. Calculate the output current if chopper frequency is 500Hz and its ON time is 1.5ms.

(A) 3A   (B) 6A

(C) 9A   (D) 12A

Problem 9.7 d) In the previous problem, recalculate the value of output voltage if Buck-Boost converter is used instead of Buck converter.

(A) 120VDC   (B) -120VDC

(C) 180VDC   (D) -180VDC

Problem 9.7 e) Calculate the average DC output voltage of a 6-pulse rectifier with a line-line RMS voltage of 600V @ 60Hz and no output filter.

(A) 790V   (B) 810V

(C) 839V   (D) 862V

Problem 9.7 f) In the previous problem, recalculate the average DC output voltage if 12-pulse rectifier is used instead of the 6-pulse rectifier.

(A) 790V   (B) 810V

(C) 839V   (D) 862V

Problem 9.7 g) Calculate the line-line RMS fundamental output voltage of a 3-phase voltage-source inverter if it is used with an input voltage of 600VDC and sine-triangle pulse width modulation with a peak modulation index of 0.5.

Problem Set # 9.8 – Instrumentation
Consult NCEES® FE Reference Handbook – Pages 220 - 224 while solving these questions

Problem 9.8 a) _____ is not an example of a transducer.

(A) Microphone

(B) Thermocouple

(C) Vernier Calliper

(D) Photo diode

Problem 9.8 b) A 200Ω RTD has a temperature coefficient = 0.0039 °C⁻¹ at room temperature (20°C). Find the new resistance of this RTD if it is placed in a 35°C environment.

(A) 188 Ω

(B) 211 Ω

(C) 200 Ω

(D) 255 Ω

Problem 9.8 c) Determine R_x if Wheatstone bridge is balanced and $R_1 = 100Ω$, $R_2 = 1000Ω$, $R_3 = 500Ω$.

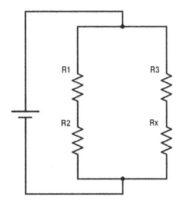

Problem 9.8 d) Calculate the incremental resistance R if the voltage difference in the circuit is 0.5V.

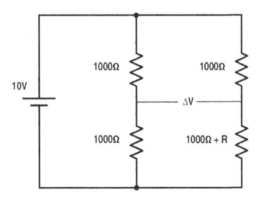

Problem 9.8 e) The gauge factor for a metallic strain gauge is found to be 1.5. Calculate the change in resistance of this metal if its original resistance was 100Ω and a strain of 0.10 was recorded.

(A) 5Ω

(B) 10Ω

(C) 15Ω

(D) 20Ω

Problem 9.8 f) Calculate voltage across 10kΩ resistor measured by a voltmeter with 100 kΩ resistance.

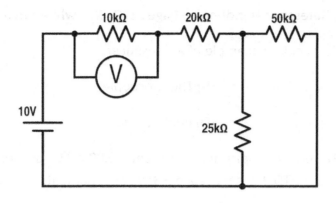

(A) 2.5V   (B) 1.98V

(C) 1V   (D) 5.5V

Problem 9.8 g) Recalculate the voltage across 10kΩ resistor of the previous problem if 500kΩ voltmeter is used instead of the 100kΩ voltmeter.

(A) 2.1V   (B) 1.98V

(C) 1V   (D) 5.5V

Problem 9.8 h) The percentage error in calculating current using 50 Ω ammeter shown in the circuit given below is _____.

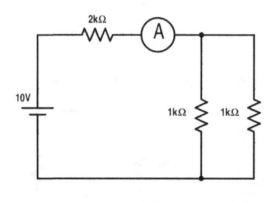

(A) 1%   (B) 2%

(C) 2.5%   (D) 5%

Chapter # 10 – Power Systems

Key Knowledge Areas*

Concepts	NCEES® FE Reference Handbook Version 10.0.1	
	Section	Pages
Power theory – power factor, single/three phase, voltage regulation, voltage drop	Electrical and Computer Engineering	363 - 368
Transmission and distribution – real/reactive losses, efficiency, delta/wye		
Transformers – connections, impedance		
Motors and generators – synchronous, induction, dc, servomotors, generators		

Facts about this section

- 8 – 12 questions can be expected on the exam according to the latest NCEES® FE specification.
- Power Systems is one of the most heavily weighted exam sections.
- Difficulty level of this section is rated 'Medium' by the author.
- Students with a major in power engineering may find this section easier.

Tips for preparing this section

- Understand the concepts related to Power Systems found in NCEES® FE Reference Handbook.
- Some of the most important equations relevant to this section include single-phase power, three-phase power, conversion between line and phase quantities, conversion between Δ - Y quantities, transformer turns ratio, power factor, voltage regulation, voltage drop, efficiency, losses, power, torque and synchronous speed.
- Reactive power required to bring power factor angle from ϑ_1 to ϑ_2 is given by:
$$Q = P(tan\,\vartheta_1 - tan\,\vartheta_2) \qquad Q = \omega C V^2$$
- Transformer impedance varies depending on viewpoint (primary or secondary).
- Understand the difference between leading/lagging power factor and real/reactive power.
- Review basic power related concepts using your college/university textbooks.
- Solve the problem sets of this chapter and review solutions at the end of this book.

BONUS: Unlock a free 'Power Systems' lecture by signing-up for the On-demand FE Electrical and Computer exam preparation course preview at: **www.studyforfe.com/fe-course-preview**

* Exam specification can be found on pages 479 - 481 of NCEES® FE Reference Handbook.

Problem Set # 10.1 – Power Theory/Single Phase Power

Consult NCEES® FE Reference Handbook – Pages 363 - 368 while solving these questions

Problem 10.1 a) _____ W real power is supplied by a generator to a single-phase load of $20 + 5j$ Ω operating at 120V if line impedance is $2 + 2j$ Ω.

Problem 10.1 b) Calculate the current passing through the circuit shown below.

(A) $2\underline{/80^{\circ}}$ A

(B) $1.96\underline{/68.7^{\circ}}$ A

(C) $2\underline{/11.3^{\circ}}$ A

(D) $10\underline{/-10^{\circ}}$ A

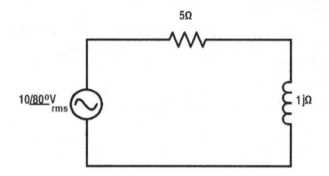

Problem 10.1 c) Calculate the apparent power supplied by current source to the circuit shown below.

(A) $20\underline{/90^{\circ}}$ VA

(B) $100\underline{/0^{\circ}}$ VA

(C) $200\underline{/-67.3^{\circ}}$ VA

(D) $50\underline{/0^{\circ}}$ VA

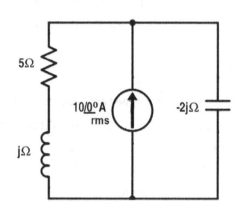

Problem 10.1 d) Calculate the total power (in Watts) absorbed by the circuit shown below.

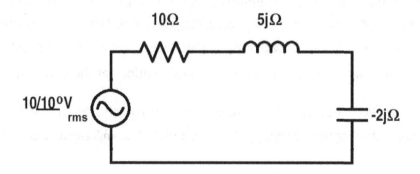

Problem 10.1 e) Calculate the average power absorbed by 5Ω resistor shown in circuit given below.

(A) 1W

(B) 5W

(C) 25W

(D) 0W

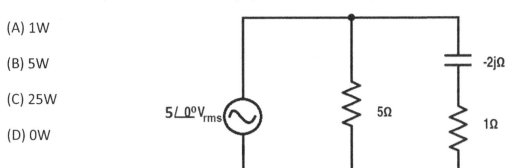

Problem 10.1 f) Calculate the real power delivered by a single-phase voltage source $v(t) = 120\sqrt{2}\cos(377t)$ V to a purely resistive load as shown in the circuit given below.

(A) 0W

(B) 120W

(C) 720W

(D) 2400W

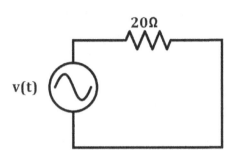

Problem 10.1 g) Calculate the real power delivered by a single-phase voltage source $v(t) = 120\sqrt{2}\cos(377t)$ V to a purely inductive load as shown in the circuit given below.

(A) 0W

(B) 120W

(C) 720W

(D) 2400W

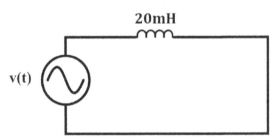

Problem 10.1 h) Calculate real power delivered by a single-phase voltage source $v(t) = 120\sqrt{2}\cos(377t)$ V to a purely capacitive load as shown in the circuit given below.

(A) 0W

(B) 120W

(C) 720W

(D) 2400W

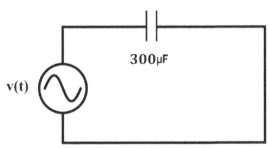

Problem Set # 10.2 - Transmission and Distribution / 3-Phase Power

Consult NCEES® FE Reference Handbook – Pages 363 - 368 while solving these questions

Problem 10.2 a) Calculate the line voltages of a balanced 3-ϕ Y- connected system if $V_{an} = 120\underline{/30^0}$ V.

(A) $120\underline{/30^0}$ V, $120\underline{/-30^0}$ V, $120\underline{/150^0}$ V

(B) $208\underline{/30^0}$ V, $120\underline{/-30^0}$ V, $120\underline{/150^0}$ V

(C) $208\underline{/60^0}$ V, $208\underline{/-60^0}$ V, $208\underline{/180^0}$ V

(D) $120\underline{/60^0}$ V, $120\underline{/-60^0}$ V, $120\underline{/180^0}$ V

Problem 10.2 b) A balanced 3-ϕ Y- connected load with $Z_{\varphi} = 20 + 5j\Omega$ is connected to a positive-sequence balanced 3-ϕ Y- connected source $V_{an} = 120\underline{/30^0}$ V. Calculate the phase current I_{an}.

(A) $5.8\underline{/-104^0}$ A

(B) $5.8\underline{/16^0}$ A

(C) $22\underline{/30^0}$ A

(D) $22\underline{/-120^0}$ A

Problem 10.2 c) Calculate line current I_L supplied by a balanced positive-sequence 3-ϕ Y- connected source $V_{an} = 277\underline{/0^0}$ V to a balanced 3 ϕ Y network with $Z_{\varphi} = 5 + 5j\Omega$ and $Z_{line} = 1 + 1j\Omega$.

(A) $15\underline{/0^0}$ A

(B) $195\underline{/-15^0}$ A

(C) $33\underline{/-45^0}$ A

(D) $3.3\underline{/-45^0}$ A

Problem 10.2 d) Calculate the load voltage of a positive sequence balanced 3-ϕ Y-Y network consisting of $V_{an} = 120\underline{/60^0}$ V source with $Z_{line} = 2 + 1j\Omega$ and $Z_{load} = 10 + 10j\Omega$.

(A) $104\underline{/63^0}$ V

(B) $120\underline{/30^0}$ V

(C) $16.5\underline{/44.5^0}$ V

(D) $110\underline{/53^0}$ V

Problem 10.2 e) Calculate the load impedance of a positive sequence balanced 3-ϕ Y-Y system with source voltage $V_{an} = 120\underline{/0^0}$ V, line current $I_{an} = 5\underline{/-5^0}$A and $Z_{line} = 0.5 + 0.25j\Omega$.

(A) $10.5\underline{/55^0}$ Ω

(B) $23.5\underline{/4.5^0}$ Ω

(C) $7.8\underline{/9^0}$ Ω

(D) $13\underline{/50^0}$ Ω

Problem 10.2 f) Calculate the line current I_a in a network comprising of Δ source $V_{ab} = 208\underline{/30^0}$ V powering a 3-ϕ balanced Y-connected load bank with $Z_Y = 10 + 5j\Omega$ (assume lossless line).

(A) $18.5\underline{/30^0}$ A

(B) $10.7\underline{/-26.6^0}$ A

(C) $18.5\underline{/-26.5^0}$ A

(D) $10.7\underline{/30^0}$ A

Problem 10.2 g) Calculate the line current I_a provided by a balanced 3-ϕ Y-connected source with $V_{an} = 120\underline{/0^\circ}$ V to a balanced 3 ϕ Δ connected load having per phase $Z_{phase} = 10 + 2j\Omega$.

(A) $20\underline{/12^\circ}$ A

(B) $15\underline{/45^\circ}$ A

(C) $25.8\underline{/-25^\circ}$ A

(D) $35.3\underline{/-11.3^\circ}$ A

Problem 10.2 h) Calculate the equivalent Wye load for a load network consisting of balanced 3 ϕ Y-loads in parallel with balanced 3 ϕ Δ loads if $Z_{phase-Y} = 10 + 5j\Omega$ and $Z_{phase-\Delta} = 6 + 9j\Omega$.

(A) 2.8 Ω

(B) 4.2 Ω

(C) 8.4 Ω

(D) 12.6 Ω

Problem 10.2 i) Calculate the equivalent Δ load in the previous problem.

(A) 2.8 Ω

(B) 4.2 Ω

(C) 8.4 Ω

(D) 12.6 Ω

Problem 10.2 j) A positive sequence balanced 3- ϕ Y-Y network has source voltage $V_{an} = 120\underline{/0^\circ}$ V feeding load impedance $20\underline{/0^\circ}$ Ω. Calculate the power generated by source if $Z_{line} = 0\Omega$.

(A) 720 VA

(B) 2400 VA

(C) 360 VA

(D) 2160 VA

Problem 10.2 k) A food processing plant consumes 200 kW at 0.83 pf lagging. It is serviced by a 1-ϕ distribution line carrying 400 A current. What is the voltage across load?

(A) 500 V

(B) 200 V

(C) 600 V

(D) 0.5 V

Problem 10.2 l) Calculate the losses of a 1-ϕ distribution line if it provides 200 A to a small municipality that consumes 100 kW at 600 V and 0.85 pf lagging.

(A) 2 kW

(B) 20 kW

(C) 10 kW

(D) 0 kW

Problem 10.2 m) Calculate phase voltage at service entrance of a hospital (consuming 125 kW) which is being fed by a lossless 3-ϕ balanced Y network providing 300 A line current at 0.694 power factor.

(A) 416 V

(B) 200 V

(C) 289 V

(D) 600 V

Problem 10.2 n) The diagram given below shows secondary winding of a three phase 480V/208V Delta-Wye transformer. Calculate the voltage between terminals A and B.

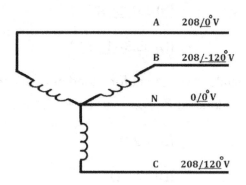

(A) 480V   (B) 120V

(C) 208V   (D) 360V

Problem 10.2 o) In the previous problem, calculate the voltage between terminals C and N.

(A) 480V   (B) 120V

(C) 208V   (D) 360V

Problem Set # 10.3 - Power Factor

Consult NCEES® FE Reference Handbook – Pages 363 - 368 while solving these questions

Problem 10.3 a) Calculate the size of a capacitor bank for 600V/60Hz system required for increasing the power factor of an industrial facility from 0.75 pf lagging to 0.9 lagging. The real power consumption of this industrial facility is 200 kW.

(A) 400µF

(B) 293µF

(C) 703µF

(D) 586µF

Problem 10.3 b) An automotive plant contains a 480V MCC that feeds several induction motors. The total real power demand of this MCC is 100kW and the overall power factor at this MCC is found to be 0.60. Calculate the magnitude of reactive power that must be provided locally to this MCC by a capacitor bank to improve its power factor from 0.60 lagging to unity.

(A) 33kVAR

(B) 133kVAR

(C) 15kVAR

(D) 0kVAR

Problem 10.3 c) A 750 µF capacitor bank operating at $V_{rms} = 400V, 60Hz$ is to be connected in parallel to an industrial load consuming 75 kW at 0.80 power factor lagging. The power factor after connecting this capacitor bank will be _____.

Problem 10.3 d) An electrical utility is providing 3-phase 75 kVA power supply at 0.85 lagging power factor and another 3-phase 35 kVA power supply at 0.75 lagging power factor to a customer operating a 600V, 60 Hz system. The overall power factor at customer's end is _____.

Problem 10.3 e) A balanced 3-phase positive sequence source $V_{an} = 120V\underline{/0°}$V, 60Hz is connected to a 3-phase phase Y-connected load that consumes 375 kW at 0.85 power factor lagging. A balanced 3-phase Y-connected capacitor will be installed in parallel with this load. Calculate the per-phase capacitance of this capacitor bank if power factor needs to be improved to 0.95 lagging.

(A) 10µF

(B) 8µF

(C) 15mF

(D) 7mF

Problem Set # 10.4 - Voltage Regulation/ Voltage Drop

Consult NCEES® FE Reference Handbook – Pages 363 - 368 while solving these questions

Problem 10.4 a) A power transformer is rated 2.5 MVA 13.8 kV/600 V with no-load secondary voltage of 650V. Calculate the voltage regulation of this transformer.

(A) -5%   (B) 2.5%

(C) 8.3%   (D) 4.7%

Problem 10.4 b) For an ideal transformer, voltage regulation is always _____.

(A) > 1   (B) > 2.5

(C) = 0   (D) ≠ 0

Problem 10.4 c) A distribution transformer is rated 10 kVA 4000 V/400 V with equivalent series impedance = $1 + 0.5j$ Ω. Calculate the voltage regulation at 0.85 lagging power factor.

Problem 10.4 d) A power transformer is rated 5MVA 12000V/240V with voltage regulation of 5%. Calculate the no-load voltage rating of this power transformer.

(A) 276 V   (B) 252 V

(C) 360 V   (D) 240 V

Problem 10.4 e) A leading power factor will result in _____ voltage regulation.

(A) > 0   (B) < 0

(C) = 0   (D) > 1

Problem 10.4 f) Voltage drop occurs due to _____ of a line.

(A) Resistance   (B) Reactance

(C) Both resistance and reactance   (D) None of the above

Problem 10.4 g) A single-phase 240V power source is feeding a 20A, unity power factor load with #10 AWG copper conductor in a steel conduit having resistance $R = 1.2Ω/1000ft$ (circuit reactance X_L can be ignored). One-way circuit length is 500 ft. Calculate the circuit's total voltage drop.

(A) 9.3V   (B) 17V

(C) 19V   (D) 24V

Problem Set # 10.5 - Transformers

Consult NCEES® FE Reference Handbook – Pages 363 - 368 while solving these questions

Problem 10.5 a) A distribution transformer has 50:1 turns ratio. Calculate the primary voltage if 1A current flows through a 12Ω load connected on transformer secondary.

(A) 50 V

(B) 600 V

(C) 12 V

(D) 1 V

Problem 10.5 b) The rated secondary current of a 1-phase 15kVA 600V/ 120V transformer is _____.

(A) 125 A

(B) 7.2 A

(C) 2.5 A

(D) 15 A

Problem 10.5 c) A 5kVA distribution transformer has 10:1 turns ratio. Calculate the primary current if rated secondary voltage of this transformer is 120V.

Problem 10.5 d) _____ Ω impedance Z_p is seen by the transformer primary in the figure shown below.

50:1

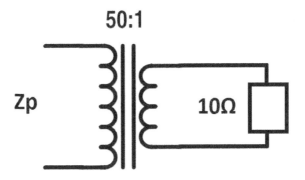

Problem 10.5 e) _____ Ω impedance Z_s is seen by the transformer secondary in the figure shown below.

10:1

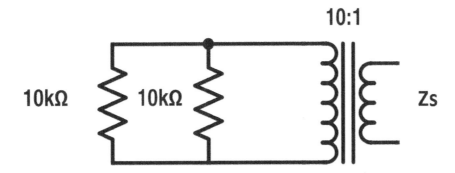

Problem 10.5 f) Select the option that best describes transformer connections shown below.

(A) Delta-Delta

(B) Delta-Wye

(C) Wye-Delta

(D) Wye-Wye

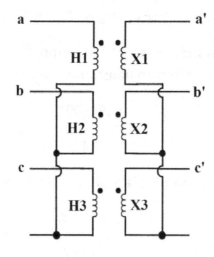

Problem 10.5 g) Select the option that best describes transformer connections shown below.

(A) Delta-Delta

(B) Delta-Wye

(C) Wye-Delta

(D) Wye-Wye

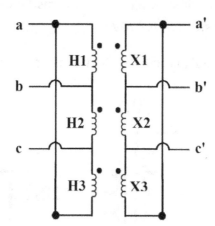

Problem 10.5 h) Select the option that best describes transformer connections shown below.

(A) Delta-Delta

(B) Delta-Wye

(C) Wye-Delta

(D) Wye-Wye

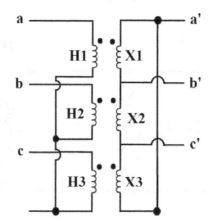

Problem Set # 10.6 - Motors & Generators
Consult NCEES® FE Reference Handbook – Pages 363 - 368 while solving these questions

Problem 10.6 a) Calculate the number of poles present in a 3-ϕ 480 V induction motor with synchronous speed of 1800 rpm (system frequency is 60 Hz).

(A) 1

(B) 2

(C) 4

(D) 8

Problem 10.6 b) Find the synchronous speed of a 3-ϕ 600V 2-pole induction motor operating at 60Hz.

(A) 7200 rpm

(B) 1800 rpm

(C) 3600 rpm

(D) 1200 rpm

Problem 10.6 c) An existing synchronous motor is retrofitted from 50Hz, 4-pole construction to a 60Hz 2-pole construction. Calculate the change in its synchronous speed.

(A) 1500 rpm

(B) 2100 rpm

(C) 3600 rpm

(D) 0 rpm

Problem 10.6 d) Calculate the slip of a 2-pole 600V induction motor operating at 60Hz with a rotational speed of 3400 rpm.

Problem 10.6 e) Calculate the rotational speed of a 60Hz, 4-pole 3-phase induction motor operating at 2.3kV and full-load slip of 0.1.

(A) 1800 rpm

(B) 1980 rpm

(C) 1720 rpm

(D) 1620 rpm

Following scenario applies to problems 10.6 f) and 10.6 g). A three-phase induction motor is rated as 480V, 50hp, 60Hz and has two poles.

Problem 10.6 f) Identify the operating state of this induction motor if it has a slip of value 1.5.

(A) Stationary

(B) Braking

(C) Motoring

(D) Generating

Problem 10.6 g) Identify the operating state of this induction motor if it has a slip of value -0.5.

(A) Stationary

(B) Braking

(C) Motoring

(D) Generating

Problem 10.6 h) An induction motor acts as a generator when _____.

(A) Rotor speed is less than synchronous speed

(B) Rotor speed is equal to synchronous speed

(C) Rotor speed is greater than synchronous speed

(D) Only synchronous motor can be run as a generator

Problem 10.6 i) Calculate the per phase armature voltage (E_a) of a 3-phase, Y-connected, 100kVA, 480V, 60Hz synchronous generator if it has a synchronous reactance of 1Ω/phase with a terminal voltage of 480V (line-line). Assume that load power factor is 0.90 lagging and armature resistance is negligible.

(A) 277V   (B) 347V

(C) 480V   (D) None of the above

Problem 10.6 j) Select the statement that best describes the effect of increasing load current I_a on synchronous generator's armature voltage E_a if constant power factor is maintained.

(A) E_a will increase by increasing I_a (B) E_a will decrease by increasing I_a

(C) E_a will remain constant   (D) None of the above

Consider following scenario for next problems 10.6 k) to 10.6 o). A 240VDC separately excited DC motor delivers 50hp mechanical power to the connected load at 1200rpm with 90% efficiency.

Problem 10.6 k) The total input power supplied to this DC motor is _____kW.

Problem 10.6 l) Mechanical torque developed by this DC motor is _____Nm.

Problem 10.6 m) The armature current I_a of this DC motor is _____A.

Problem 10.6 n) The internal voltage V_a of this DC motor is _____V.

Problem 10.6 o) The armature resistance R_a of this DC motor is _____Ω (ignore armature inductance).

Chapter # 11 – Electromagnetics

Key Knowledge Areas*

Concepts	NCEES® FE Reference Handbook Version 10.0.1	
	Section	Page #
Electrostatics/Magnetostatics	Electrical and Computer Engineering	355 – 356
Electrodynamics – Maxwell's equations, Wave propagation		59 - 60, 368
Transmission Lines		369

Facts about this section

- 4 – 6 questions can be expected on the exam according to the latest NCEES® FE specification.
- Electromagnetics is one of the most lightly weighted exam sections.
- Difficulty level of this section is rated 'Easy' by the author.

Tips for preparing this section

- Understand the concepts related to Electromagnetics found in NCEES® FE Reference Handbook.
- Some of the important equations relevant to this section include Maxwell's equations, transmission line reflection coefficient equation, standing wave ratio equation, wave equation.
- Review vector calculus and learn how to calculate divergence and curl of a given vector.
- Divergence of a magnetic field is zero.
- $\nabla \times \vec{E} = -\partial \vec{B}/\partial t$ is the vector form of Faraday's Law.
- $\nabla \times \vec{H} = \vec{J} + \partial \vec{D}/\partial t$ is the vector form of Ampere's Law.
- $\nabla . \vec{D} = \rho$ is the vector form of Gauss' Law for electric field.
- $\nabla . \vec{B} = 0$ is the vector form of Gauss' Law for magnetic field.
- Read transmission line questions carefully to distinguish between characteristic impedance and load impedance.
- Solve the problem sets of this chapter and review solutions at the end of this book.

* Exam specification can be found on pages 479 - 481 of NCEES® FE Reference Handbook.

Problem Set # 11.1 - Electrostatics

Consult NCEES® FE Reference Handbook – Pages 355 - 356 while solving these questions

Problem 11.1 a) Calculate the magnitude of force on charge $Q_1 = 5nC$ located at $P_1(0,1,0)$ due to another charge $Q_2 = 10nC$ located at $P_2(0,0,2)$.

(A) 50 x 10⁻⁶ N

(B) 10 x 10⁻⁹ N

(C) 20 x 10⁻⁶ N

(D) 90 x 10⁻⁹ N

Problem 11.1 b) Calculate the magnitude of force between point charges $Q_1 = 10\mu C$ and $Q_2 = 100\mu C$ that are separated by 1cm distance.

(A) 90kN

(B) 450kN

(C) 225kN

(D) 4.5kN

Problem 11.1 c) Calculate the electric field intensity at origin due to point charges $Q_1 = 50nC$ located at (0, 1, 0) and $Q_1 = -50nC$ located at (0, -1, 0).

(A) 0 V/m

(B) 100 V/m

(C) 900 V/m

(D) 50 V/m

Problem 11.1 d) Calculate the electric field at a point P between two infinitely large parallel plates located in the x-y plane having charge densities ρ_s and $-\rho_s$ respectively.

(A) 0

(B) ρ_s/ε

(C) $2\rho_s/\varepsilon$

(D) $\rho_s\varepsilon$

Problem 11.1 e) Two infinitely long parallel wires (having line charge densities of + 2 C/m and -1 C/m respectively) located along z axis have 1m space between them. Calculate the electric field mid-way between the two wires.

(A) 3 V/m

(B) 0 V/m

(C) 2 x 10¹⁰ V/m

(D) 1 x 10¹¹ V/m

Problem 11.1 f) Calculate the amount of work required to bring a charge $Q_1 = 10^{-6}C$ from infinity to P_1 (0, 0, 0) in the presence of another charge $Q_2 = 2 \times 10^{-6}C$ located at P_2 (2, 0, 0).

(A) 4.5 x 10⁻¹² J

(B) 4.5 x 10⁻³ J

(C) 9 x 10⁻¹² J

(D) 9 x 10⁻³ J

Problem 11.1 g) Calculate potential energy stored by system of two charges $Q_1 = 5 \times 10^{-6}C$ and $Q_2 = 10^{-6}C$ located at P_1 (1, 0, 0) and P_2 (0, 1, 0) respectively.

(A) 63.6mJ

(B) 31.9mJ

(C) 15.9mJ

(D) 5mJ

Problem 11.1 h) System A contains charges $Q_1 = 50 \times 10^{-6}C$ and $Q_2 = 100 \times 10^{-6}C$ that are 1m apart. System B contains charges $Q_3 = 5 \times 10^{-6}C$ and $Q_4 = 10 \times 10^{-6}C$ that are 1cm apart. Select the option that accurately represents potential energies of System A and System B.

(A) System A = System B = 45J

(B) System A = 4.5 x 10^{13} J, System B = 45 J

(C) System A = 45J, System B = 4.5 x 10^{13} J

(D) System A = 4.5 J, System B = 45 J

Problem 11.1 i) Calculate the amount of work that needs to be done to decrease the space between $Q_1 = 9 \times 10^{-9}C$ and $Q_2 = 15 \times 10^{-9}C$ from 1m to 1cm.

(A) 1.215 x 10^{-6} J

(B) 15 x 10^{-4} J

(C) 1.202 x 10^{-6} J

(D) 1.202 x 10^{-4} J

Problem 11.1 j) Calculate the amount of work done in moving a charge $Q_1 = 10 \times 10^{-9}C$ through a distance of 2cm along y-axis in a 200 V/m a_x electric field.

(A) 4 x 10^{-8} J

(B) 0 J

(C) 4 x 10^{-9} J

(D) 2 x 10^{-9} J

Problem 11.1 k) Calculate the potential difference between two parallel plates that are 1m apart and have an electric field strength of 2000 V/m.

(A) 2000 V

(B) 2 V

(C) 0 V

(D) 100 V

Problem 11.1 l) A point charge $Q_1 = 100 \times 10^{-9}C$ is accelerated 200m between two parallel plates in a constant electric field strength of 1kV/m. Calculate the potential difference between these plates.

(A) 22.5 mV

(B) 100 kV

(C) 200 kV

(D) 1 kV

Problem Set # 11.2 - Magnetostatics
Consult NCEES® FE Reference Handbook – Pages 355 - 356 while solving these questions

Problem 11.2 a) Calculate the force on a 2A current-carrying conductor of length 2m in a uniform magnetic field = 0.5T (assume that angle between conductor and field is 30°).

(A) 2 N   (B) 4 N

(C) 0 N   (D) 1 N

Problem 11.2 b) Calculate the energy stored in a magnetic field that has a strength of 2A/m in a 2m^3 volume (assume $\mu = 4\pi$ x 10^{-7} H/m).

Problem 11.2 c) Consider a 0.1m long conductor carrying 5A in a 10μT magnetic field. If the force resulting on this conductor is 1 μN, the angle between conductor and magnetic field is _____.

Problem 11.2 d) Calculate the voltage induced in a coil with 20 turns if flux passing through it changes from 0.1Wb to 1.5Wb in 2s.

(A) -28 V   (B) -14 V

(C) -1.4 V   (D) -10 V

Problem 11.2 e) A coil of length 20cm has 50 turns and a cross-sectional area of 2cm^2. Calculate the induced voltage if current is increased from 50mA to 100mA in 1s (assume $\mu = \mu = 4\pi \times 10^{-7} \ H/m$).

Problem 11.2 f) Calculate the magnetic flux density inside a torus of radius 2cm having 50 turns if 1A current is passing through it.

Problem 11.2 g) Two infinitely long parallel wires are placed as shown below. The magnetic flux density at point 'A' due to these wires (assume $\mu = 4\pi \times 10^{-7} \ H/m$) is _____.

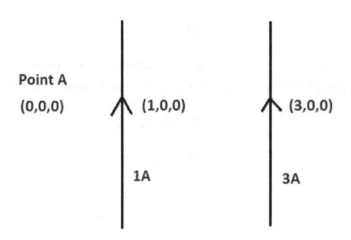

Point A
(0,0,0)   (1,0,0)   (3,0,0)

1A   3A

Problem 11.2 h) A current carrying wire in air is generating 0.1T magnetic flux density at a radial distance of 20cm. The total current passing through this wire is _____.

Problem Set # 11.3 – Electrodynamics - Maxwell's Equations
Consult NCEES® FE Reference Handbook – Pages 59 - 60, 368 while solving these questions

Problem 11.3 a) Calculate the divergence of electric field $\vec{E}$ given by following equation:

$$\vec{E} = 3xi + 2y^2j + xk$$

(A) $3x + 2y^2 + x$

(B) $3 + 4y^2 + 1$

(C) 0

(D) $3 + 4y$

Problem 11.3 b) Calculate the divergence of a vector field $\vec{D}$ given by following equation:

$$\vec{D} = xyi + yzj + xz^2k$$

(A) $xy + yz + xz^2$

(B) $y + z + 2xz$

(C) $x + z + 2x$

(D) 0

Problem 11.3 c) Calculate the net electric flux from a hollow sphere which contains the point charges $Q_a = +1nC$, $Q_b = +3nC$, $Q_c = +1nC$ and $Q_d = -2nC$.

(A) 0Vm

(B) 1017Vm

(C) 339Vm

(D) 678Vm

Problem 11.3 d) Calculate the net flux from a hollow sphere of radius 5cm which contains two concentric spheres. Inner sphere has a radius = 1cm with surface charge density = $3\mu C/m^2$ and the outer sphere has radius = 3cm with surface charge density = $-5\mu C/m^2$.

(A) 1250Vm

(B) -5963Vm

(C) 3750Vm

(D) 410Vm

Problem 11.3 e) Calculate the value of "a" given that $\vec{B}$ is a magnetic field.

$$\vec{B} = 3axi + 2yj - 2zk$$

(A) 3

(B) 1

(C) 0

(D) -1

Problem 11.3 f) Which of the following vector fields can be magnetic in nature?

$$\vec{A} = 2x^2i + yj + 3z^2k \qquad\qquad \vec{B} = 2y^2i + 3xj - 2xyk$$

(A) $\vec{A}$

(B) $\vec{B}$

(C) Both $\vec{A}$ and $\vec{B}$

(D) Neither $\vec{A}$ nor $\vec{B}$

Problem 11.3 g) A changing magnetic field is inducing an electric field $\vec{E}$ given by equation below

$\vec{E} = 2yz\mathbf{i} + 3x^2y\mathbf{j} + x^2y^2\mathbf{k}$. Calculate the time rate of change of the magnetic field.

(A) $-2yz\,\mathbf{i} + 3x^2y\mathbf{j} + x^2\mathbf{k}$

(B) $-2x^2y\mathbf{i} - (2y - 2xy^2)\mathbf{j} - (6xy - 2z)\mathbf{k}$

(C) $3x^2\mathbf{j}$

(D) 0

Problem 11.3 h) Calculate the curl of an induced electric field produced by a changing magnetic field B given by $\vec{B} = -\cos^2(3t)\mathbf{k}$.

(A) $-2\cos(3t)\mathbf{i}$

(B) $\sin^2(3t)\mathbf{k}$

(C) $-6\cos(3t)\sin(3t)\mathbf{k}$

(D) $5\sin(3t)\mathbf{j}$

Problem 11.3 i) Match the entries in Column A with the correct entries in Column B.

Column A	Column B
Gauss' Law for Electric Fields	$\oint E.dl = -\iint_S \frac{\partial B}{\partial t}.dS$
Gauss' Law for Magnetic Fields	$\oint H.dl = I_{enc} + \iint_S \frac{\partial D}{\partial t}.dS$
Faraday's Law	$\oiint_{SV} D.dS = \iiint_V \rho dv$
Ampere's Law	$\oiint_{SV} B.dS = 0$

Problem 11.3 j) The total magnetic flux emitting from a closed surface **S** containing magnetic field **B** within its boundaries is equal to _____.

(A) dB/dS

(B) $B.S$

(C) $B \times S$

(D) 0

Problem Set # 11.4 – Electrodynamics - Wave Propagation
Consult NCEES® FE Reference Handbook – Page 369 while solving these questions

Problem 11.4 a) The characteristic impedance of a transmission line is 100Ω and its wavelength is 20m. has. Find the expression for voltage on this transmission line at 100m distance.

(A) $V^+e^{j2\pi} + V^-e^{-j2\pi}$

(B) $V^+e^{j10\pi} + V^-e^{-j10\pi}$

(C) $V^+e^{j200\pi} + V^-e^{-j200\pi}$

(D) $\frac{1}{100}(V^+e^{j2\pi} + V^-e^{-j2\pi})$

Problem 11.4 b) In the previous problem, find an expression for current at 100 m.

(A) $V^+e^{j10\pi} + V^-e^{-j10\pi}$

(B) $\frac{1}{100}(V^+e^{j10\pi} + V^-e^{-j10\pi})$

(C) $\frac{1}{100}(V^+e^{j10\pi} - V^-e^{-j10\pi})$

(D) None of the above

Consider the following scenario for next problems 11.4 c) and 11.4 d). Magnetic field intensity of an electromagnetic wave is given by $H = 10\cos(10^8t - 4z)\hat{a}_x\ A/m$.

Problem 11.4 c) Calculate the frequency (Hz) of this electromagnetic wave.

(A) 2×10^8

(B) 10^8

(C) $10^8/\pi$

(D) $10^8/2\pi$

Problem 11.4 d) Calculate the wavelength (metres) of this electromagnetic wave.

(A) π

(B) $\pi/2$

(C) $\pi/4$

(D) $\pi/6$

Consider the following scenario for problems 11.4 e) and 11.4 f). Electric field intensity of an electromagnetic wave is given by $E = 12\cos(2 \times 10^9t - \beta z)\hat{a}_x\ A/m$. Assume that wave is travelling at the speed of light $(3 \times 10^8 m/s)$.

Problem 11.4 e) Calculate the time taken by this wave to cover a distance equal to 50% of wavelength.

(A) $2\pi/10^9\ s$

(B) $2/10^9\ s$

(C) $\pi/10^9\ s$

(D) $\pi/(2 \times 10^9)\ s$

Problem 11.4 f) Calculate the wavelength (metres) of this electromagnetic wave.

(A) 0.3π

(B) 3π

(C) 30π

(D) None of the above

Problem Set # 11.5 - Transmission Lines

Consult NCEES® FE Reference Handbook – Page 369 while solving these questions

Problem 11.5 a) A transmission line with 100 Ω characteristic impedance is connected to a 300 + 50jΩ load. The reflection coefficient Γ at the load is _____.

Problem 11.5 b) Calculate the standing wave ratio of a transmission line having characteristic impedance = 50Ω and load impedance = 500 + 25jΩ.

(A) 1   (B) 2

(C) 10   (D) 5

Problem 11.5 c) A transmission line has per unit length inductance = 100mH per unit and capacitance = 10μF per unit. Calculate magnitude of load impedance that will allow a reflection coefficient Γ = 0.5.

(A) 100Ω   (B) 300Ω

(C) 200Ω   (D) 500Ω

Problem 11.5 d) The wavelength of a transmission line with characteristic impedance = 200Ω is 10m. Calculate the input impedance at 100m if the line is connected to a purely resistive load of 500Ω.

(A) 1000Ω   (B) 3500Ω

(C) 200Ω   (D) 500Ω

Problem 11.5 e) Calculate the load connected at the end of a transmission line (250Ω characteristic impedance) if its standing wave ratio is 2.

(A) 100Ω   (B) 300Ω

(C) 1000Ω   (D) 500Ω

Problem 11.5 f) A lossless transmission line has maximum current magnitude of 10A and minimum current magnitude of 2A. Calculate the reflection co-efficient of this transmission line.

(A) 1/2   (B) 2/3

(C) 3/4   (D) 1

Chapter # 12 – Control Systems

Key Knowledge Areas*

Concepts	NCEES® FE Reference Handbook Version 10.0.1	
	Section	Page #
Block diagrams	Instrumentation, Measurement and Control	226 - 229
Closed-loop/Open-loop response, Stability		
Controller performance – Steady-state error, settling time, overshoot		
Bode Plots	Electrical and Computer Engineering	373 – 374

Facts about this section

- 6 – 9 questions can be expected on the exam according to the latest NCEES® FE specification.
- Control Systems is an average weighted exam section.
- Difficulty level of this section is rated as 'Medium' by the author.
- Students with a major in controls engineering may find this section easier.

Tips for preparing this section

- Understand the concepts related to Control Systems found in NCEES® FE Reference Handbook.
- Some of the important equations relevant to this section include steady-state error – final value theorem, stability, and Bode Plot.
- Derive transfer function of classical negative feedback control system model block diagram given in NCEES® Reference Handbook to gain understanding of block diagrams, closed-loop and open-loop response.
- Review the formulas related to controller performance – steady-state gain, damping ratio, 2% settling time, percent overshoot etc.
- Solve the problem sets of this chapter and review solutions at the end of this book.

BONUS: Unlock a free 'Control Systems' lecture by signing-up for the On-demand FE Electrical and Computer exam preparation course preview at: **www.studyforfe.com/fe-course-preview**

---

* Exam specification can be found on pages 479 - 481 of NCEES® FE Reference Handbook.

Problem Set # 12.1 - Block Diagrams/Closed-loop response/Open-loop response

Consult NCEES® FE Reference Handbook – Pages 226 - 227 while solving these questions

Consider the feedback control system shown below for problems 12.1 a) and 12.1 b).

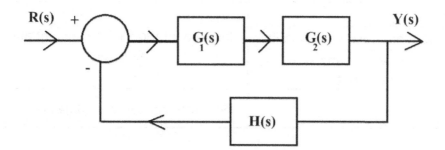

Problem 12.1 a) The closed-loop transfer function of this control system is _____.

Problem 12.1 b) The open-loop transfer function of this control system is _____.

Consider the following control blocks for problems 12.1 c) and 12.1 d).

$$G_1(s) = \frac{1}{s} \quad G_2(s) = \frac{s+3}{s+4}$$

Problem 12.1 c) Determine the equivalent transfer function if above given control blocks are connected in parallel with each other.

Problem 12.1 d) Determine the equivalent transfer function if above given control blocks are connected in series with each other.

Problem 12.1 e) Find the closed loop transfer function for following system.

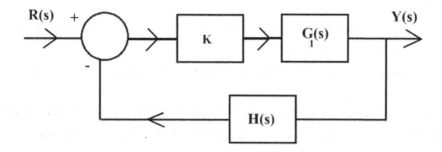

(A) $\dfrac{kG_1(s)}{1+kG_1(s)H(s)}$

(B) $\dfrac{kG_1(s)}{1+H(s)}$

(C) $\dfrac{1}{1+kG_1(s)H(s)}$

(D) $\dfrac{kG_1(s)+H(s)}{1+kG_1(s)H(s)}$

Problem 12.1 f) Find the relationship between $Y(s), R(s), N(s)$ and $L(s)$ for following control system.

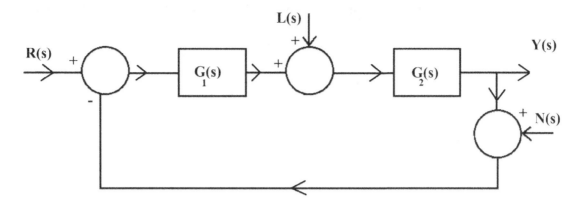

Problem 12.1 g) Determine the closed-loop transfer function of the following control system.

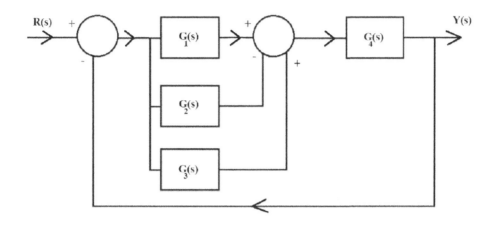

Problem 12.1 h) Determine the closed-loop transfer function of the following control system.

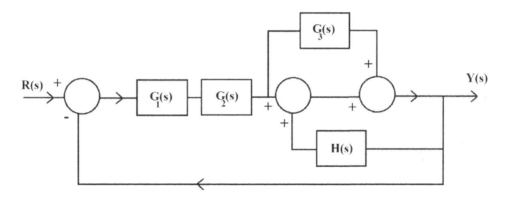

Problem Set # 12.2 - Bode Plots

Consult NCEES® FE Reference Handbook – Pages 373 - 374 while solving these questions

Problem 12.2 a) Select the option that best represents the open-loop transfer function $G(s)$ for the Bode Plot given below.

(A) $50/(s + 10)$

(B) $50/(s + 10)(s + 100)$

(C) $14/(s + 10)$

(D) $14/(s + 10)(s + 100)$

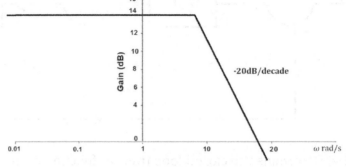

Problem 12.2 b) Select the option that best represents the open-loop transfer function $G(s)$ for the Bode Plot given below.

(A) $20/(s + 10)$

(B) $20/(s + 1)(s + 10)$

(C) $10/(s + 10)$

(D) $10/s^2$

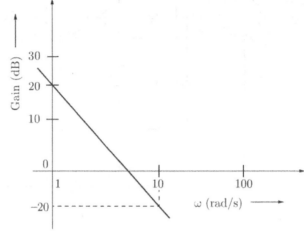

Problem 12.2 c) Select the option that best represents the open-loop transfer function $G(s)$ for the Bode Plot given below.

(A) $20/(s + 10)$

(B) $20/(s + 10)(s + 100)$

(C) $10(s + 10)/(s + 100)$

(D) $10(s + 100)/(s + 10)$

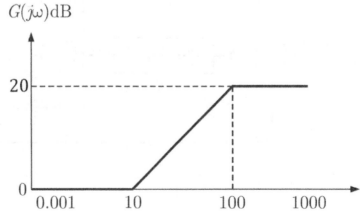

Problem 12.2 d) The open-loop transfer function $G(s)$ for the Bode Plot given below is _____.

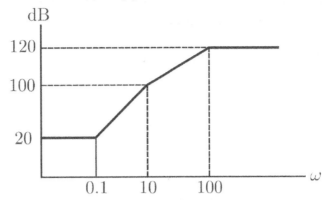

Problem 12.2 e) Select the option that correctly describes the Bode log phase angle plot of following open-loop transfer function:

$$G(s) = \frac{1}{(4s + 100)}$$

(A) $\angle G(j2.5) = 0^0, \angle G(j25) = 0^0, \angle G(j250) = 0^0$

(B) $\angle G(j2.5) = 0^0, \angle G(j25) = 90^0, \angle G(j250) = 0^0$

(C) $\angle G(j2.5) = 0^0, \angle G(j25) = -45^0, \angle G(j250) = 90^0$

(D) $\angle G(j2.5) = 0^0, \angle G(j25) = -45^0, \angle G(j25) = -90^0$

Problem 12.2 f) The magnitude gain of following open-loop transfer function is _____.

$$G(s) = \frac{(50)(s + 2)}{(s + 100)(s + 1000)}$$

Problem 12.2 g) The magnitude gain of following open-loop transfer function is _____.

$$G(s) = \frac{100(s + 1)}{s(s + 10)}$$

Problem 12.2 h) The magnitude gain of following open-loop transfer function is _____.

$$G(s) = \frac{100s}{s^2 + 150s + 5000}$$

Problem Set # 12.3 – System stability/Frequency response

Consult NCEES® FE Reference Handbook – Pages 226 - 227 while solving these questions

Problem 12.3 a) Stability of a control system depends on _____.

(A) Location of zeros
(B) Location of poles

(C) Phase angle
(D) None of the above

Problem 12.3 b) Options _____ and _____ represent stable control systems.

(A) Bounded input results in bounded output

(B) Bounded input results in unbounded output

(C) Poles are located in the left half of s-plane

(D) Poles are located in the right half of s-plane

Problem 12.3 c) A control system with non-repeated poles on imaginary axis is considered _____.

(A) Stable
(B) Unstable

(C) Marginally stable
(D) None of the above

Problem 12.3 d) A control system with repeated poles on imaginary axis is considered _____.

(A) Stable
(B) Unstable

(C) Marginally stable
(D) None of the above

Problem 12.3 e) Determine the phase margin (PM) of a unity gain feedback control system for which the open-loop transfer function is $G(s) = \frac{1}{(s+1)^2}$

(A) 0^0
(B) 60^0

(C) 90^0
(D) 180^0

Problem 12.3 f) Determine the gain margin (GM) of a unity gain feedback control system for which the open-loop transfer function is $G(s) = \frac{1}{(s+1)^4}$

(A) 10dB
(B) 12dB

(C) 20dB
(D) 40dB

Problem 12.3 g) The closed-loop characteristic equation of following control system is _____.

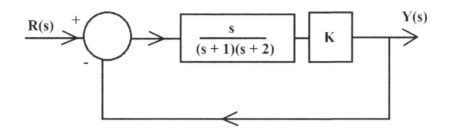

Problem 12.3 h) Compute the entry b_1 in Routh Array table of following closed-loop transfer function

$$T(s) = \frac{s+1}{2s^5 + 2s^3 + 3s^4 + 7s^2 + s + 10}$$

s^5	2	2	1
s^4	3	7	10
s^3	b_1 =?		

Problem 12.3 i) Determine the stability of system given by the following closed-loop transfer function using Routh Hurwitz criteria of system stability.

$$T(s) = \frac{s}{2s^4 + 3s^3 + s^2 + s + 1}$$

(A) Stable   (B) Unstable

(C) Depends on K   (D) Cannot be determined

Problem 12.3 j) Determine the range of k for which the system given by following closed loop transfer function is stable.

$$T(s) = \frac{(k)(s+10)}{3s^3 + 5s^2 + (k+10)s + 5k}$$

113

Copyrighted Material © 2020

Problem Set # 12.4 – Controller performance
Consult NCEES® FE Reference Handbook – Page 227 - 229 while solving these questions

Problem 12.4 a) Transfer function of a first-order control system is given as follows:

$$\frac{Y(s)}{R(s)} = \frac{4}{2s + 1}$$

Determine the time domain representation of output $y(t)$ if $y_0 = 0$ and $r(t) = 5u(t)$

Problem 12.4 b) In the previous problem, determine the time domain representation $y(t)$ if there is a time delay $\theta = 3$ in the control system as shown below:

$$\frac{Y(s)}{R(s)} = \frac{4e^{-3s}}{2s + 1}$$

Initial condition $y_0 = 0$ and input $r(t) = u(t)$.

Consider a control system with following transfer function for problems 12.4 c) to 12.4 l).

$$\frac{Y(s)}{R(s)} = \frac{32}{s^2 + 4s + 16}$$

Unit-step input is provided to this control system. Calculate the following parameters for this system.

Problem 12.4 c) The steady-state gain K is _____.

Problem 12.4 d) The damping ratio ζ is _____.

Problem 12.4 e) The given control system is _____ damped.

(A) Under   (B) Critically

(C) Over   (D) None of the above

Problem 12.4 f) The time t_p required to reach the peak output value M_p is _____.

Problem 12.4 g) The peak output value M_p is _____.

Problem 12.4 h) The percent overshoot (%OS) of the response is _____.

Problem 12.4 i) The damped natural frequency ω_d is _____.

Problem 12.4 j) The damped resonant frequency ω_r is _____.

Problem 12.4 k) The logarithmic decrement δ is _____.

Problem 12.4 l) The 2% settling time T_s is _____.

Problem 12.4 m) Calculate the steady-state error of following system if input is $10u(t)$.

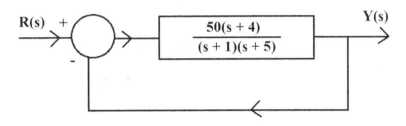

Problem 12.4 n) Calculate the steady-state error of following system if input is $5tu(t)$.

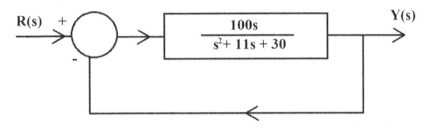

Problem 12.4 o) Calculate the steady-state error of following system if input is $10t^2u(t)$.

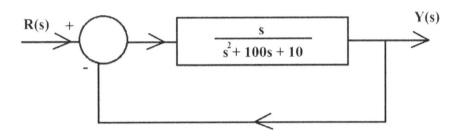

Problem 12.4 p) Calculate the steady-state error of following system if input is $2tu(t)$.

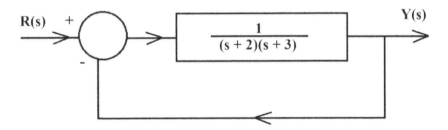

Problem 12.4 q) Calculate the steady-state error of following system if input is $3u(t)$.

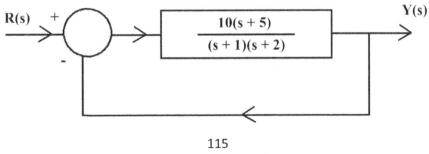

Chapter # 13 – Communications
Key Knowledge Areas*

Concepts	NCEES® FE Reference Handbook Version 10.0.1	
	Section	Page #
Modulation / Demodulation	Electrical and Computer Engineering	372 - 377
Digital Communications		
Fourier transforms / Fourier Series	Mathematics	52 – 55
Multiplexing	Note: Specific details on this topic are not available in NCEES® FE Reference Handbook.	

Facts about this section

- 5 – 8 questions can be expected on the exam according to the latest NCEES® FE specification.
- Communications is an average weighted exam section.
- Difficulty level of this section is rated 'Medium' by the author.
- Students with a major in communications engineering may find this section easier.

Tips for preparing this section

- Understand the concepts related to Communications found in NCEES® FE Reference Handbook.
- Some of the important equations relevant to this section include efficiency of amplitude modulation, power transmitted in a message, modulation index, 98% bandwidth power of FM signal, PCM, PAM, Fourier transform pairs, parity bit coding, cyclical redundancy code.
- Learn how to differentiate between graphical illustrations of AM, FM and PM signals.
- Frequency and Phase Modulated signals appear very similar.
- Understand the steps involved in digital signal processing.
- Learn how to calculate Fourier transform/series using table.
- Develop understanding of the two main multiplexing techniques
  - Time Division Multiplexing
  - Frequency Division Multiplexing
- Review the error coding process especially parity-bit coding and cyclical redundancy coding.
- Solve problem sets of this chapter and review solutions at the end of this book.

* Exam specification can be found on pages 479 - 481 of NCEES® FE Reference Handbook.

Problem Set # 13.1 – Communication Theory
Consult NCEES® FE Reference Handbook – Page 372 while solving these questions

Problem 13.1 a) _____ is a unit step function that starts at $t = 4$ and has a magnitude of 2.

(A) $2u(t - 2)$

(B) $4u(t - 2)$

(C) $2u(t - 4)$

(D) $2u(t)e^{-4t}$

Problem 13.1 b) Unit step function $u(3t - 9)$ is equal to _____.

Problem 13.1 c) ____ is a rectangular pulse with center at $t = 4$, amplitude = 2 and time-period = 1/3.

(A) $2\Pi\left(\frac{t}{3}\right)$

(B) $2\Pi\left(\frac{t-4}{3}\right)$

(C) $4\Pi\left(\frac{t-2}{3}\right)$

(D) $2\Pi(3(t - 4))$

Problem 13.1 d) _____ is a triangular pulse with center at $t = -1$, amplitude = 5 and $\tau = 2$.

(A) $5\Lambda\left(\frac{t-1}{2}\right)$

(B) $5\Lambda\left(\frac{t+1}{2}\right)$

(C) $5\Lambda(2(t - 1))$

(D) $5\Lambda(2(t + 1))$

Problem 13.1 e) Unit impulse function $\delta(-3t)$ is equal to _____.

Problem 13.1 f) Consider a time-domain signal $f(t)$. Which one of the following options correctly describe the impact of $f(4t)$?

(A) $f(4t) = 4f(t)$

(B) $f(4t) = f(t)/4$

(C) Time period of $f(4t)$ increases by 4

(D) Time period of $f(4t)$ decreases by 4

Problem 13.1 g) _____ is an example of an even function.

(A) $f(t) = t^5 \sin 3t$

(B) $f(t) = \sin 3t$

(C) $f(t) = t^2 + \sin 3t$

(D) None of the above

Problem 13.1 h) _____ is an example of an odd function.

(A) $f(t) = t^5 \sin 3t$

(B) $f(t) = \sin 3t$

(C) $f(t) = t^2 + \sin 3t$

(D) None of the above

Problem 13.1 i) Calculate the total energy (Joules) contained in a finite energy signal given below:

$$x(t) = 3\Pi\left(\frac{t - 2}{2}\right)$$

Problem Set # 13.2 - Amplitude Modulation
Consult NCEES® FE Reference Handbook – Page 375 while solving these questions

Consider the following scenario for problems 13.2 a) to 13.2 c).

The maximum amplitude of an amplitude-modulated (AM) wave is 12V and minimum amplitude is 2V.

Problem 13.2 a) The amplitude of carrier signal is _____.

Problem 13.2 b) The amplitude of message/modulating signal is _____.

Problem 13.2 c) The modulation index of this AM wave is _____.

Consider the following amplitude modulated (AM) wave for problems 13.1 d) to 13.1 f).

$$x(t) = 50(1 + 0.8 \cos 400\pi t) \cos(100000\pi t)$$

Problem 13.2 d) The modulation index of this AM wave is _____.

Problem 13.2 e) The frequency of message/modulating signal is _____ Hz.

Problem 13.2 f) The frequency of carrier signal is _____ Hz.

Problem 13.2 g) Costas-loop is used for detecting a signal modulated with _____ modulation technique.

(A) Single-Sideband Amplitude Modulation   (B) Angle Modulation

(C) Frequency Modulation   (D) Double Sideband Amplitude Modulation

Problem 13.2 h) The modulation index of an amplitude modulated wave with message signal $5 \sin 2\pi(1000t)$ and carrier signal $50 \sin 2\pi(4000t)$ is _____.

(A) 20%   (B) 100%

(C) 10%   (D) 50%

Consider the following scenario for problems 13.2 i) and 13.2 j).

An amplitude modulated (AM) wave is double-sideband modulated with a monotone message signal $m(t) = A \cos \omega t$. The normalized average power for this message is $< m_n^2(t) > = 1/2$.

Problem 13.2 i) Calculate the efficiency of this AM wave if modulation index is 0.60.

Problem 13.2 j) What percentage of the total power is contained in carrier wave?

Problem 13.2 k) _____ option represents an amplitude modulated wave.

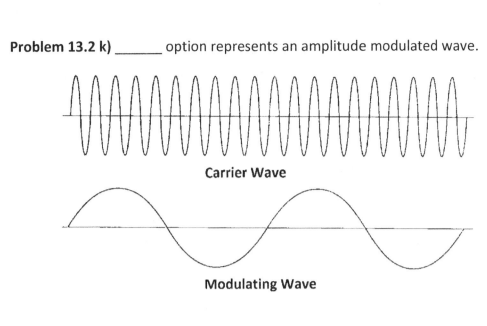

Carrier Wave

Modulating Wave

Modulated Wave

(A)

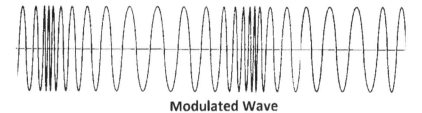

Modulated Wave

(B)

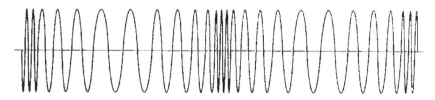

Modulated Wave

(C)

(D) None of the above

Problem Set # 13.3 - Angle Modulation
Consult NCEES® FE Reference Handbook – Pages 375 - 376 while solving these questions

Consider the following scenario for problems 13.3 a) and 13.3 b). A frequency-modulated wave has a maximum frequency deviation value = 100kHz and the bandwidth of its modulating signal is 5kHz.

Problem 13.3 a) The frequency-deviation ratio of given FM wave is _____.

Problem 13.3 b) 98% bandwidth of given FM wave is _____.

Consider the following equation of an analog modulated wave for problems 13.3 c) to 13.3 d).

$$x(t) = 20 \cos(2000\pi t + 5 \sin(20\pi t))$$

Original message/modulating signal is $100\pi \cos(20\pi t)$.

Problem 13.3 c) The given wave $x(t)$ has been _____ modulated.

(A) Amplitude   (B) Frequency

(C) Phase   (D) Pulse-code

Problem 13.3 d) Carrier frequency is _____ and message frequency is _____.

Consider the following equation of an analog modulated wave for problems 13.3 e) to 13.3 h).

$$x(t) = 20 \cos(2000\pi t + 10\pi \cos(20\pi t))$$

Original message/modulating signal is $10\pi \cos(20\pi t)$.

Problem 13.3 e) The given wave modulated wave $x(t)$ has been _____ modulated.

(A) Amplitude   (B) Frequency

(C) Phase   (D) Pulse-code

Problem 13.3 f) The instantaneous phase of modulated wave $x(t)$ is _____.

Problem 13.3 g) The instantaneous frequency of modulated wave $x(t)$ is _____.

Problem 13.3 h) The frequency deviation of modulated wave $x(t)$ is _____.

Problem 13.3 i) Calculate the 98% power bandwidth of a frequency modulated signal if the signal has frequency deviation ratio = 1.25 and its message bandwidth = 10 kHz.

(A) 20000Hz   (B) 10000Hz

(C) 125000Hz   (D) 45000Hz

Problem 13.3 j) Angle modulated signals can be demodulated using _____

(A) Costas loop   (B) Phase-lock loop

(C) Envelope detection   (D) Sampling

Problem 13.3 k) In the problem 13.2 k) which option represents a frequency-modulated wave?

(A) Option A   (B) Option B

(C) Option C   (D) None

Problem 13.3 l) In the problem 13.2 k) which option represents a phase-modulated wave?

(A) Option A   (B) Option B

(C) Option C   (D) None

Problem 13.3 m) Calculate 98% power bandwidth of a frequency modulated signal with frequency deviation ratio of 0.1 and message bandwidth of 10 kHz.

(A) 10000Hz   (B) 5000Hz

(C) 1000Hz   (D) 20000Hz

Problem Set # 13.4 - Fourier Transforms

Consult NCEES® FE Reference Handbook – Pages 52 – 55, 372 - 373 while solving these questions

Problem 13.4 a) Fourier transform of the function shown in the figure given below is _____.

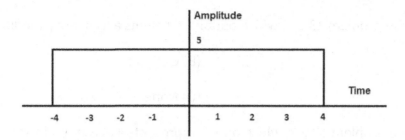

Problem 13.4 b) Fourier transform of the function shown in the figure given below is _____.

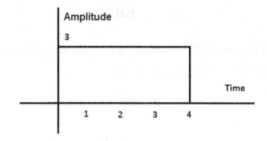

Problem 13.4 c) Calculate the Fourier transform of the function given below:

$$x(t) = \cos(2\pi(300)t) \, \Pi\left(\frac{t}{6}\right)$$

(A) $6 \, \text{sinc}(6f)$

(B) $6 \, \text{sinc}\left(6(f - 300)\right)$

(C) $3 \, \text{sinc}\left(6(f - 300)\right) + 3 \, \text{sinc}\left(6(f + 300)\right)$

(D) $6 \, \text{sinc}(6f)e^{-2\pi f 300}$

Problem 13.4 d) Calculate the Fourier transform of the function given below

$$x(t) = e^{-5t} \cos(2\pi(20)t) \, u(t)$$

(A) $\dfrac{1}{j2\pi f + 5}$

(B) $\dfrac{1}{j2\pi(f-20)+5} + \dfrac{1}{j2\pi(f+20)+5}$

(C) $\dfrac{1}{j2\pi f + 5}e^{-40\pi j f}$

(D) $\dfrac{1}{2}\left(\dfrac{1}{j2\pi(f-20)+5} + \dfrac{1}{j2\pi(f+20)+5}\right)$

Problem 13.4 e) Fourier transform of the function given below is _____.

$$x(t) = 4\Pi\left(\frac{t - 2}{2}\right)$$

Problem Set # 13.5 – Digital Communications
Consult NCEES® FE Reference Handbook – Pages 377 and 379 while solving these questions

Problem 13.5 a) _____ quantization levels can be represented by a binary word of length 7 bits.

Problem 13.5 b) The minimum bandwidth required to transmit a pulse code modulated message $m(t)$, with $M(f) = 0$ for $f \geq 100Hz$ using 256 quantization levels is _____.

Problem 13.5 c) A PAM system modulates 15 kHz signal and uses a clock to sample the signal at equal time intervals. The minimum clock frequency required for this PAM system is _____.

(A) 15 kHz   (B) 30 kHz

(C) 7.5 kHz   (D) 150 kHz

Problem 13.5 d) In the previous problem, calculate the time spacing between adjacent samples of the pulse-amplitude modulated wave form is _____ μs.

Problem 13.5 e) Calculate the channel capacity (bits/sec) of a digital communication system that has signal-to-noise ratio S/N = 10dB and available bandwidth = 10kHz.

Problem 13.5 f) Calculate the minimum signal-to-noise ratio S/N (in dB) required to transmit 100,000 bits/sec if available bandwidth is 25kHz.

Consider the following scenario for problems 13.5 g) and 13.5 h).

A digital communication system is using cyclical redundancy code for multiple error detection such that data frame $T = 101011$ and generator code $G = 111$.

Problem 13.5 g) The remainder E for this scheme is _____.

Problem 13.5 h) The transmitted code for this scheme is _____.

Problem 13.5 i) Complete the following table by adding odd-parity bits for error detection.

Data Frame	Odd-Parity Bit (0/1)
0000	
1000	
0111	

Problem 13.5 j) Complete the following table by adding even parity bits for error detection.

Data Frame	Even-Parity Bit (0/1)
0000	
1000	
0111	

Problem Set # 13.6 - Multiplexing

Problem 13.6 a) _____ is an example of digital multiplexing.

(A) Time-division multiplexing

(B) Frequency-division

(C) Wavelength division

(D) Options A, B and C are examples of digital multiplexing

Problem 13.6 b) Three channels are to be frequency multiplexed together as shown below:

Channel 1 has a Band Width of 50kHz

Channel 2 has a Band Width of 100kHz

Channel 3 has a Band Width of 50kHz

Calculate the minimum link bandwidth if a guard band of 5kHz is required between channels.

(A) 200kHz

(B) 215kHz

(C) 210kHz

(D) 220kHz

Problem 13.6 c) Five channels are multiplexed using time division multiplexing. Every channel sends 10 bytes/second. Calculate the frame size if this system can multiplex 1 byte/channel.

(A) 10 bytes

(B) 1 bytes

(C) 5 bytes

(D) 50 bytes

Problem 13.6 d) The bit rate in previous problem is _____ bps.

Problem 13.6 e) Calculate the bit duration of a time-division multiplexer that multiplexes three 50 kbps channels using 1-bit time slots.

(A) $5\mu s$

(B) $6.66\mu s$

(C) $10\mu s$

(D) $20\mu s$

Problem 13.6 f) The frame duration in problem previous problem is _____.

Problem 13.6 g) Four bandlimited signals $x_1(t), x_2(t), x_3(t)$ and $x_4(t)$ with bandwidths $BW_1 = 4kHz, BW_2 = 2kHz, BW_3 = 1kHz$ and $BW_4 = 500Hz$ (respectively) are transmitted over a communication channel using time-division multiplexing.

The overall sampling rate required for perfect reconstruction of message is _____.

Chapter # 14 – Computer Networks

Key Knowledge Areas*

Concepts	NCEES® FE Reference Handbook Version 10.0.1	
	Section	Page #
Routing and Switching	Electrical and Computer Engineering	392 – 407
Network topologies		
Network types		
Network models		
Network intrusion detection/prevention		413 – 416
Network security		

Facts about this section

- 4 – 6 questions can be expected on the exam according to the latest NCEES® FE specification.
- Computer Networks is one of the most lightly weighted exam sections.
- Difficulty level of this section is rated 'Easy' by the author.
- Students with a major in computer network engineering may find this section easier.

Tips for preparing this section

- Understand the computer networking concepts found in NCEES® FE Reference Handbook.
- Learn routing/switching process including data forwarding, routing tables etc.
- Review the differences between major network topologies (bus, ring, star etc.).
- Understand differences and similarities between OSI and TCP/IP model.
- Review computer network protocols such as IPv4, IPv6, TCP, UDP and ICMP.
- Familiarize yourself with fundamentals of network security such as firewalls, port scanning, web vulnerability testing, penetration testing and basics of encryption.
- Understand the algorithm of Diffie-Hellman key-exchange protocol, RSA public-key cryptosystem and McCabe' cyclomatic complexity.
- Solve problem sets on next pages and review solutions at the end of this book.

BONUS: Unlock a free 'Computer Networks' lecture by signing-up for the On-demand FE Electrical and Computer exam preparation course preview at: **www.studyforfe.com/fe-course-preview**

* Exam specification can be found on pages 479 - 481 of NCEES® FE Reference Handbook.

Problem Set # 14.1 - Routing and Switching

Consult NCEES® FE Reference Handbook – Page 392 – 407 while solving these questions

Problem 14.1 a) The process of finding efficient paths between nodes based on address is called_____.

Problem 14.1 b) Which of the following table(s) is maintained by a router?

(A) Time table

(B) Forwarding table

(C) Routing table

(D) Options C & B are correct

Problem 14.1 c) Routing takes place in OSI Model's _____ layer.

Problem 14.1 d) Switching takes place in OSI Model's _____ layer.

Problem 14.1 e) _____ establishes computer's unique hardware media access control (MAC) address.

(A) Router

(B) Switch

(C) Network Interface Card

(D) Hub

Problem 14.1 f) _____ has access to IP datagram and can use IP address for determining optimal paths.

(A) Router

(B) Switch

(C) Network Interface Card

(D) Hub

Problem 14.1 g) Complete the routing table given below. Assume that you are starting at node A.

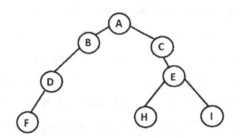

Destination Node	Next Hop
B	
C	
D	
E	
F	

Problem Set # 14.2 - Network Topologies / Types / Models
Consult NCEES® FE Reference Handbook – Pages 392 – 407 while solving these questions

Problem 14.2 a) http and email will run in _____ OSI model layer.

Problem 14.2 b) Session layer is not responsible for _____.

(A) Modulation/Demodulation

(B) Relation between two end users

(C) Identifying users

(D) Controlling data exchanged by users

Problem 14.2 c) Breaking a single connection can disrupt an entire network in _____ implementation.

(A) Bus

(B) Star

(C) Ring

(D) All of the above

Problem 14.2 d) LAN can be implemented using _____ topology.

(A) Ring

(B) Star

(C) Bus

(D) All of the above

Problem 14.2 e) ATM LAN is an example of _____.

(A) Star topology

(B) Bus topology

(C) Ring topology

(D) Mesh topology

Problem 14.2 f) _____ network type serves the largest geographical region.

(A) LAN

(B) WAN

(C) MAN

(D) PAN

Problem 14.2 g) _____ links are required to connect 29 nodes in a fully connected mesh network.

Problem 14.2 h) In the previous problem, _____ input/output ports are required on each node to construct a fully connected mesh network with 29 nodes.

Problem 14.2 i) Tree topology can be considered a hybrid of _____ and _____.

(A) Bus, Ring

(B) Ring, Star

(C) Bus, Star

(D) Bus, Mesh

Problem 14.2 j) Select the option that correctly ranks network topologies based on cabling cost.

(A) Bus > Star > Mesh

(B) Mesh > Bus > Star

(C) Star > Bus > Mesh

(D) Mesh > Star > Bus

Problem 14.2 k) Ring topology is generally used to create a _____ network.

(A) LAN

(B) WAN

(C) MAN

(D) PAN

Problem 14.2 l) OSI Model's presentation layer is responsible for performing _____ function(s).

(A) Encryption/Decryption

(B) Compression/Decompression

(C) Translation

(D) All of the above

Problem 14.2 m) Physical addressing is performed in _____ layer of OSI model.

(A) Network

(B) Transport

(C) Data Link

(D) Session

Problem 14.2 n) As data packet moves from an upper layer to a lower layer, headers are _____ and the process is called _____.

(A) Added, Decapsulation

(B) Removed, Encapsulation

(C) Added, Encapsulation

(D) Removed, Decapsulation

Problem Set # 14.3 – Internet Protocol Addressing: IPv4/IPv6

Consult NCEES® FE Reference Handbook – Pages 394 – 400 while solving these questions

Problem 14.3 a) _____ header field(s) handle fragmentation in IPv4 addressing.

(A) Identification

(B) Fragment Offset

(C) Flags

(D) All of the above

Problem 14.3 b) Select the scenario in which the least significant bit of 'Flags' field is set (=1) for a fragmented IPv4 datagram?

(A) First fragment

(B) Last fragment

(C) All fragments except first

(D) All fragments except last

Problem 14.3 c) How many routers can be visited by an IPv4 datagram before being dropped if its 'Time To Live' field is 20?

(A) 0

(B) 2

(C) 19

(D) 20

Problem 14.3 d) Calculate the header length of an IPv4 datagram if its Internet Header Length 'IHL' field contains 1000.

(A) 8 bits

(B) 32 bits

(C) 8 bytes

(D) 32 bytes

Problem 14.3 e) Select the statement that correctly describes IPv4 datagram based on IHL value calculated in the previous question.

(A) IPv4 header is of minimum size

(B) IPv4 header is of maximum size

(C) IPv4 header uses 'Options' field

(D) IPv4 header does not use 'Options' field

Problem 14.3 f) Fragment offset field of an IPv4 header is equal to 200_{10}. Which one of the following statements correctly describe the fragmentation order of this fragment?

(A) 200 bytes of data has already arrived ahead of this fragment

(B) 200 bytes of data is expected t to arrive after this fragment

(C) 1600 bytes of data has already arrived ahead of this fragment

(D) 1600 bytes of data is expected to arrive after this fragment

Problem 14.3 g) Select the correct statement regarding IPv6 datagram header from following options.

(A) Header length is at least 20 bytes

(B) Header length has a fixed size of 20 bytes

(C) Header length is at least 40 bytes

(D) Header length has a fixed size of 40 bytes

Problem 14.3 h) _____ field determines the lifetime of an IPv6 datagram.

(A) Flow label   (B) Time to live

(C) Hop limit   (D) Payload length

Problem 14.3 i) Select the option that represents the most abbreviated form of following IPv6 address:

2A1F:0000:0000:0011:0000:0000:0000:2100

(A) 2A1F::11::2100

(B) 2A1F:0:0:11:0:0:0:2100

(C) 2A1F:0:0:11::2100

(D) 2A1F::11:0::2100

Problem 14.3 j) Select the option that represents the expanded form of following IPv6 address:

B:C8::15:0:AC

(A) B:C8:0:0:0:15:0:AC

(B) B000:C8:0:0:0:15:0:AC

(C) 000B:00C8:0000:0000:0000:0015:0000:00AC

(D) B000:C800:0000:0000:0000:0015:0000:00AC

Problem Set # 14.4 – Protocols: TCP/UDP/ICMP
Consult NCEES® FE Reference Handbook – Pages 400 – 404 while solving these questions

Problem 14.4 a) Protocol data unit (PDU) in TCP is called _____.

(A) Frame

(B) Segment

(C) Datagram

(D) Bits

Problem 14.4 b) Select the INCORRECT statement(s) from given options.

(A) TCP is a connection-oriented protocol

(B) TCP uses acknowledgment mechanism

(C) UDP is a connectionless protocol

(D) UDP uses acknowledgment mechanism

Problem 14.4 c) TCP header can have a maximum and minimum size of _____ and _____ respectively.

(A) 65535, 0

(B) 40, 16

(C) 60, 20

(D) 160, 20

Problem 14.4 d) TCP establishes connection between client and server by means of _____.

(A) Two-way handshake

(B) Three-way handshake

(C) Four-way handshake

(D) None of the above

Problem 14.4 e) _____ application layer protocol(s) use TCP protocol in transport layer.

(A) Telnet

(B) SMTP

(C) http

(D) All of the above

Problem 14.4 f) _____ messages can be broadly categorized as error-reporting and query messages.

(A) TCP

(B) UDP

(C) IP

(D) ICMP

Problem 14.4 g) ICMP error messages are reported to _____.

(A) Destination only

(B) Source and destination

(C) Source only

(D) All network nodes

Problem 14.4 h) Suppose that an IPv4 datagram arrives at a router and requires fragmentation but Don't Fragment (DF) flag is set. In this case, type and code field of ICMP message will be _____ and ___.

(A) 11, 1

(B) 3, 1

(C) 5, 2

(D) 3, 4

Problem Set # 14.5 – Network Security: Intrusion Detection/Prevention and Encryption

Consult NCEES® FE Reference Handbook – Pages 413 – 416 while solving these questions

Problem 14.5 a) Which one of the following statement(s) INCORRECTLY describes firewall capabilities?

(A) Firewall is not required if communication is encrypted

(B) Firewalls can prevent traffic from specific IP addresses

(C) Firewall acts as a security checkpoint between networks

(D) Firewall controls incoming/outgoing traffic based on predefined rules

Problem 14.5 b) _____ firewall provides network security by inspecting IP header and TCP header using a list of pre-established rules.

(A) Packet filtering   (B) Application level gateway

(C) Circuit level gateway   (D) Dynamic

Problem 14.5 c) Which one of the following statements is NOT true regarding signature-based intrusion detection systems?

(A) They are helpful against previously unknown threats

(B) They compare current user patterns (signatures) with a list of known malicious patterns

(C) They require frequent updates of signatures to remain effective

(D) None of the above

Problem 14.5 d) _____ parameter(s) can be used as part of anomaly-based intrusion detection systems?

(A) Time-of-day use   (B) Computer power consumption

(C) User profiles   (D) All of the above

Problem 14.5 e) _____ information is revealed by the following command: nmap 192.1.2.3

(A) Open ports   (B) Open services

(C) Domain name   (D) All of the above

Problem 14.5 f) _____ type of scan is performed by the following command: nmap-F 192.1.2.3

(A) Full   (B) Fast

(C) Forward   (D) Final

Problem 14.5 g) Alpha digitally signs a message using RSA public-key cryptosystem and sends it to Beta. In order to verify this signature, Beta will require _____.

(A) Alpha's private key   (B) Alpha's public key

(C) Beta's private key   (D) Beta's public key

Problem 14.5 h) Alpha and Beta are using RSA public-key cryptosystem for encrypting confidential data. Alpha chooses two prime numbers p = 7 and q = 9 to generate public and private keys. Determine Alpha's private key if Alpha's public key is 11.

(A) 9   (B) 10

(C) 11   (D) 12

Problem 14.5 i) In the previous problem, calculate the value of cyphertext if plain text is 8.

Problem 14.5 j) Public key is known to _____ and private key is known to _____ in public-key encryption.

(A) Everyone, Sender   (B) Everyone, Receiver

(C) Everyone, Sender   (D) Sender, Receiver

Problem 14.5 k) Alpha and Beta are using Diffie-Hellman key-exchange protocol to exchange a secret key between themselves without transmitting it. They publicly select 5 as prime modulo (p) and 3 as base generator (g). Alpha and Beta then select 1 and 2 as their private keys, respectively.

Calculate the value of their Diffie-Hellman secret key.

Problem 14.5 l) Create a control flow graph of given code to determine number of nodes and edges.

```
int sumCalculator (int x) {

int count = 0;

int sum = 0;

while (count < x) {

sum = sum + count;

count++; }

return sum;}
```

Problem 14.5 m) In the previous problem, calculate McCabe's cyclomatic complexity.

(A) 0   (B) 2

(C) 4   (D) 6

Chapter # 15 – Digital Systems

Key Knowledge Areas*

Concepts	NCEES® FE Reference Handbook Version 10.0.1	
	Section	Page #
Number systems	Electrical and Computer Engineering	389 – 392
Boolean logic		
Logic gates and circuits		
Logic minimization (K-Maps, SOP, POS)		
Flip-flops and counters		
State machine design	Mathematics	34
Programmable logic devices	Note: NCEES® FE Reference Handbook does not contain specific details on these topics.	
Timing		

Facts about this section

- 8 – 12 questions can be expected on the exam according to the latest NCEES® FE specification.
- Digital Systems is one of the most heavily weighted exam sections.
- Difficulty level of this section is rated 'Hard' by the author.
- Students with a major in computer engineering may find this section easier.

Tips for preparing this section

- Understand digital system concepts found in NCEES® FE Reference Handbook.
- Learn how to use calculator for converting numbers between different bases.
- Study the truth tables of all logic operators especially XOR and XNOR.
- Understand the difference between 1's complement and 2's complement calculations.
- Review graphical symbols of logic gates, combinational and sequential logic devices.
- Understand the rules regarding grouping of K-map terms for function minimization.
- Gain understanding of how different flip-flops and counters work.
- Learn how to navigate between state diagram and state table.
- Develop familiarity with programmable logic devices, controllers, and timing diagrams.
- Review relevant concepts using college/university textbooks.
- Solve the problem sets of this chapter and review solutions at the end of this book.

BONUS: Unlock a free 'Digital Systems' lecture by signing-up for the On-demand FE Electrical and Computer exam preparation course preview at: **www.studyforfe.com/fe-course-preview**

* Exam specification can be found on pages 479 - 481 of NCEES® FE Reference Handbook.

Problem Set # 15.1 – Number Systems
Consult NCEES® FE Reference Handbook – Page 389 while solving these questions

Problem 15.1 a) $8AD_{HEX}$ is equal to _____ in binary number system.

Problem 15.1 b) 963_{10} is equal to _____ in binary number system.

Problem 15.1 c) Select the option(s) that correctly represent 101010_2 in respective number systems.

(A) $2A_{16}$ (B) 42_{10}

(C) 52_8 (D) All of the above

Problem 15.1 d) 1's complement sum of 0010_2 and 0011_2 is equal to _____.

Problem 15.1 e) 1's complement sum of 1101_2 and 1011_2 is equal to _____.

Problem 15.1 f) 2's complement sum of 1011_2 and 0101_2 is equal to _____.

Problem 15.1 g) 2's complement sum of 1110_2 and 0101_2 is equal to _____.

Problem 15.1 h) 1010_2 and 111010_2 are 2's complement representation of _____ and _____ respectively.

(A) 5, 6   (B) -5, -6

(C) 6, 6   (D) -6, -6

Problem 15.1 i) Select the option that represents INCORRECT pairing of decimal number with its 2's complement representation in binary number system.

(A) -20, 101100   (B) -16, 110000

(C) -30, 100010   (D) -11, 101111

Problem 15.1 j) Select the option that represents INCORRECT pairing of decimal number with its 1's complement representation in binary number system.

(A) -20, 101011   (B) -16, 110010

(C) -30, 100001   (D) -17, 101110

Problem Set # 15.2 – Boolean Logic
Consult NCEES® FE Reference Handbook – Page 390 while solving these questions

Problem 15.2 a) Apply De Morgan's Theorem to following function: $\overline{[A + BC\overline{D} + (\overline{E} + \overline{F})]}$

(A) $(B + C + D)(\overline{E})(\overline{F})\,(A)$

(B) $(\overline{A})(\overline{B}\,\overline{C}D)(E\overline{F})$

(C) $\overline{A} + \overline{B}\,\overline{C}D + (E + \overline{F})$

(D) $(\overline{A})(\overline{B} + \overline{C} + D)(E)(F)$

Problem 15.2 b) Apply De Morgan's Theorem to following function: $\overline{[(ABC)(D + E\overline{F})]}$

(A) $\overline{A} + \overline{B} + \overline{C} + \overline{D}(\overline{E} + F)$

(B) $(\overline{A}\,\overline{B}\,\overline{C})(\overline{D})(\overline{E}F)$

(C) $A + B + C + DE$

(D) $\overline{A}\,\overline{B} + \overline{D}EF$

Problem 15.2 c) Simplify following function using Boolean logic: $A\overline{B} + A\overline{(BC)} + B\overline{(A + C)}$

(A) $A\overline{B} + A(\overline{B} + \overline{C}) + B(\overline{A}\,\overline{C})$

(B) $A\overline{B} + \overline{C}(A + B)$

(C) $A\overline{B} + \overline{A}\,\overline{B}\,\overline{C}$

(D) $A\overline{B} + A(\overline{B}\,\overline{C})$

Problem 15.2 d) Simplify following function using Boolean logic: $AB + B(A + C) + C(A + B)$

(A) $AB + AB + BC + AC + BC$

(B) $AB + BC + AC$

(C) $AB + BC$

(D) ABC

Problem 15.2 e) Convert following function to 'Sum of Product' form: $(A + B)(A + B + C)$

(A) $A + AB + BC$

(B) $A + B + C$

(C) $A + B$

(D) $AB + BC$

Problem 15.2 f) Simplify $A\overline{C} + \overline{A}C$ using Boolean logic if $C = A\overline{B} + \overline{A}B$.

(A) A

(B) B

(C) $\overline{A}$

(D) $\overline{B}$

Problem Set # 15.3 – Logic gates and circuits

Consult NCEES® FE Reference Handbook – Page 390 while solving these questions

Problem 15.3 a) Find the output expression for logic circuit shown below.

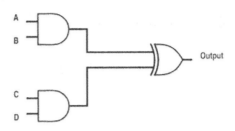

(A) $AB + CD$

(B) $AB(\overline{C} + \overline{D}) + (\overline{A} + \overline{B})CD$

(C) $AB(C + D)$

(D) $AB(\overline{C} + \overline{D})$

Problem 15.3 b) Find the output expression for logic circuit shown below.

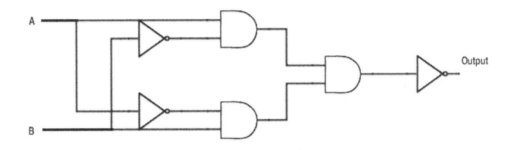

(A) 0

(B) $\overline{A} + \overline{B}$

(C) 1

(D) $A + B$

Problem 15.3 c) Find the output expression for logic circuit shown below.

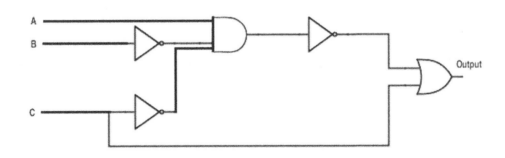

(A) $\overline{A} + B + C$

(B) $AB + C$

(C) $A + BC$

(D) $AB + BC$

Problem 15.3 d) Find the output expression for logic circuit shown below.

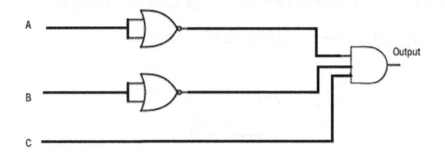

(A) $A\overline{B} + C$ (B) $AB\overline{C}$

(C) $\overline{A}\,\overline{B}\,C$ (D) $A + B + \overline{C}$

Problem 15.3 e) Find the output expression for logic circuit shown below.

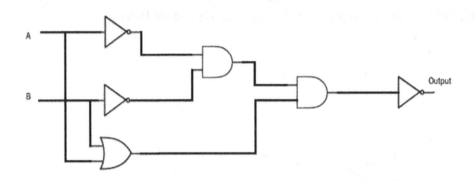

(A) 0   (B) 1

(C) $A\overline{B}$ (D) $\overline{A} + B$

Problem 15.3 f) _____ logical function can be used to detect odd number of 1s in a given input.

(A) AND   (B) OR

(C) XOR   (D) XNOR

Problem Set # 15.4 – Logic minimization - K-Maps/SOP/POS

Consult NCEES® FE Reference Handbook – Pages 391 - 392 while solving these questions

Problem 15.4 a) Determine minimized 'Sum of Product' expression for logic function given by K-Map.

C

	0	1
00		
01	1	1
11	1	
10		1

AB

(A) $C + \overline{A}B + B\overline{C}$

(B) $A\overline{B}C + \overline{A}B + B\overline{C}$

(C) $B\overline{C} + AB + \overline{A}\,\overline{B}\,C$

(D) $\overline{A}B\overline{C} + A\overline{B} + \overline{B}C$

Problem 15.4 b) Determine minimized 'Sum of Product' expression for logic function given by K-Map.

C

	0	1
00	1	1
01	1	1
11		
10		

AB

(A) $\overline{A}B + \overline{A}\,\overline{B}$

(B) $\overline{A}B\overline{C} + \overline{A}\,\overline{B}C$

(C) A

(D) $\overline{A}$

Problem 15.4 c) Determine minimized 'Sum of Product' expression for logic function given by K-Map.

CD

	00	01	11	10
00	1	1	1	1
01				
11				
10	1	1	1	1

AB

(A) $\overline{A}\,\overline{B} + A\overline{B}$

(B) B

(C) $\overline{B}$

(D) $AB + \overline{A}\,\overline{B}$

Problem 15.4 d) Determine minimized 'Sum of Product' expression for logic function given by K-Map.

	CD 00	01	11	10
00		1	1	
01				
11	1	1	1	1
10			1	1

(AB rows on left)

(A) $AC + AB + \overline{A}\,\overline{B}D$

(B) $A + AB + BCD$

(C) $AC + AB\overline{C} + \overline{A}\,\overline{B}D$

(D) $AB + A\overline{B}C + \overline{A}\,\overline{B}D$

Problem 15.4 e) Determine minimized 'Sum of Product' expression for logic function given by K-Map.

	CD 00	01	11	10
00	1			1
01	1		1	1
11	1		1	1
10	1			1

(AB rows on left)

(A) $\overline{A}\,\overline{B} + \overline{C}\,\overline{D}$

(B) $\overline{C}\,\overline{D} + C\overline{D} + BC$

(C) $\overline{D} + BC$

(D) $AB\overline{C} + \overline{D}$

Problem 15.4 f) Determine minimized 'Sum of Product' expression for logic function given by K-Map.

	C 0	1
00	1	
01		
11		1
10		1

(AB rows on left)

(A) $\overline{B} + AC$

(B) $\overline{A}\,\overline{C} + ABC$

(C) $\overline{A}\,\overline{B}\,\overline{C} + AC$

(D) $C + \overline{A}\,\overline{C}$

Problem Set # 15.5 – Sequential Circuits – Flip-Flops and Counters

Consult NCEES® FE Reference Handbook – Page 391 while solving these questions

Problem 15.5 a) Determine the output sequence of flip-flop # 2 shown in the circuit given below.

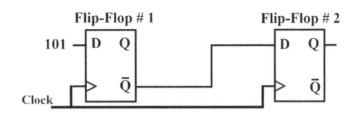

(A) 101   (B) 111

(C) 010   (D) 000

Problem 15.5 b) The logical circuit shown below represents a _____.

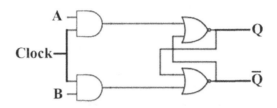

(A) JK Flip-Flop   (B) SR Flip-Flop

(C) D Flip-Flop   (D) Multiplexer

Problem 15.5 c) The logical circuit shown below represents a _____.

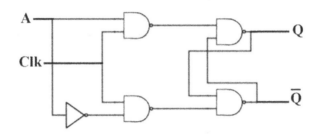

(A) JK Flip-Flop   (B) SR Flip-Flop

(C) D Flip-Flop   (D) Multiplexer

Problem 15.5 d) The logical circuit shown below represents a _____.

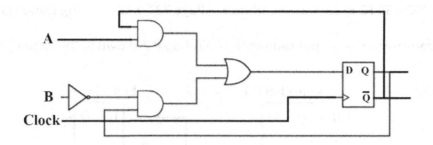

(A) JK Flip-Flop   (B) SR Flip-Flop

(C) T Flip-Flop   (D) Multiplexer

Problem 15.5 e) Determine the output sequence Q_2 of SR flip-flop shown in the circuit given below.

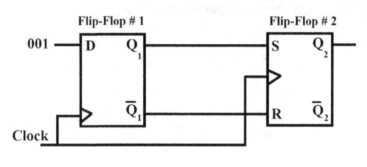

(A) 100   (B) 001

(C) 111   (D) 110

Problem 15.5 f) Determine the output state $Q_3 Q_2 Q_1$ of the counter shown below after application of three clock cycles. Assume that initially output states are $Q_3 = Q_2 = Q_1 = 0$.

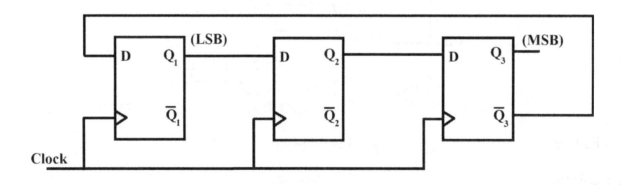

(A) 000   (B) 111

(C) 001   (D) 011

Problem 15.5 g) Determine the output state $Q_3Q_2Q_1Q_0$ of the counter shown below after application of three clock cycles. Assume that initially output states are $Q_3 = Q_2 = Q_1 = Q_0 = 1$.

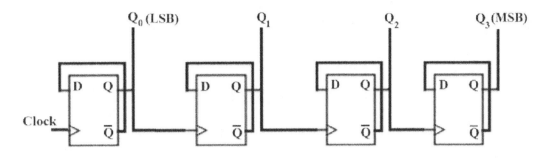

(A) 1000   (B) 0000

(C) 1010   (D) 1100

Problem 15.5 h) Determine the output sequence of the counter shown below. Assume that initially output states are $Q_1 = Q_0 = 0$.

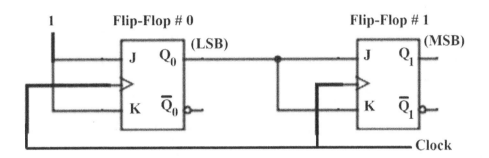

(A) $(0\ 0)$ initial state, $(0\ 1)$ cycle 1, $(1\ 0)$ cycle 2, $(1\ 1)$ cycle 3

(B) $(0\ 0)$ initial state, $(1\ 0)$ cycle 1, $(0\ 1)$ cycle 2, $(1\ 1)$ cycle 3

(C) $(1\ 1)$ initial state, $(0\ 1)$ cycle 1, $(1\ 0)$ cycle 2, $(0\ 0)$ cycle 3

(D) $(1\ 1)$ initial state, $(0\ 1)$ cycle 1, $(1\ 0)$ cycle 2, $(0\ 0)$ cycle 3

Problem Set # 15.6 – Combinational circuits

Consult NCEES® FE Reference Handbook – Page 391 while solving these questions

Problem 15.6 a) _____ is not an example of a combinational circuit.

(A) Decoder

(B) Encoder

(C) Multiplexer

(D) Flip-flop

Problem 15.6 b) A decoder with n inputs will have _____ outputs.

(A) n

(B) $n - 1$

(C) 2^n

(D) $2^n - 1$

Consider the following 2-to-4 decoder for problems 15.6 c) and 15.6 d).

Problem 15.6 c) Complete the truth table of 2-to-4 decoder given below where 'E' represents enable.

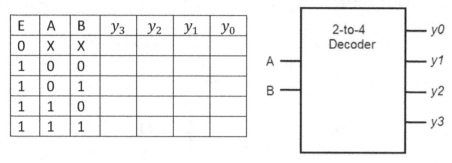

E	A	B	y_3	y_2	y_1	y_0
0	X	X				
1	0	0				
1	0	1				
1	1	0				
1	1	1				

Problem 15.6 d) Match the output in Column A with correct combination of logical inputs in Column B.

Column A	Column B
y_0	ABE
y_1	$A\bar{B}E$
y_2	$\bar{A}BE$
y_3	$\bar{A}\bar{B}E$

Consider the following 3-to-8 decoder for problems 15.6 e) and 15.6 f).

Problem 15.6 e) Complete the truth table of a 3-to-8 decoder given below where 'E' represents enable.

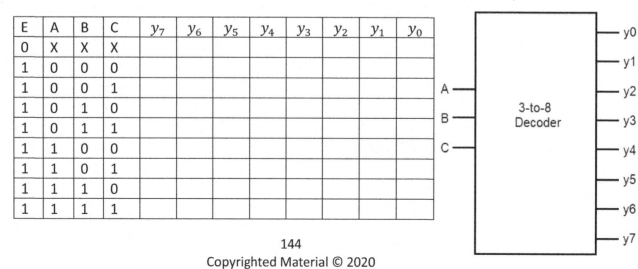

E	A	B	C	y_7	y_6	y_5	y_4	y_3	y_2	y_1	y_0
0	X	X	X								
1	0	0	0								
1	0	0	1								
1	0	1	0								
1	0	1	1								
1	1	0	0								
1	1	0	1								
1	1	1	0								
1	1	1	1								

Problem 15.6 f) Match the output in Column A with correct combination of logical inputs in Column B.

Column A	Column B
y_0	$ABCE$
y_1	$\bar{A}B\bar{C}E$
y_2	$\bar{A}\bar{B}\bar{C}E$
y_7	$\bar{A}\bar{B}CE$

Consider the following combinational circuit for problems 15.6 g) and 15.6 h).

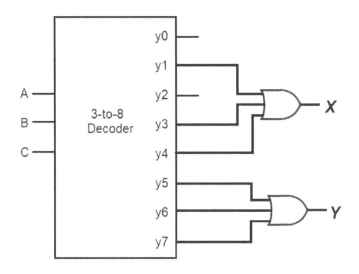

Problem 15.6 g) The output X can be expressed as _____.

Problem 15.6 h) The output Y can be expressed as _____.

Problem 15.6 i) A multiplexer with n selection lines will have _____ outputs and _____ inputs.

(A) 2^n outputs, 1 input

(B) 1 output, 2^n inputs

(C) n outputs, 1 input

(D) 1 output, n inputs

Problem 15.6 j) $[2^4 \times 1]$ Multiplexer will have _____ inputs and _____ selection lines.

(A) 16 inputs, 4 selection lines

(B) 16 inputs, 1 selection line

(C) 4 inputs, 16 selection lines

(D) None of the above

Consider the following [4 × 1] Multiplexer for problems 15.6 k) and 15.6 l).

Problem 15.6 k) Complete the truth table of the [4 × 1] multiplexer given below.

E	S_1	S_0	X
0	X	X	
1	0	0	
1	0	1	
1	1	0	
1	1	1	

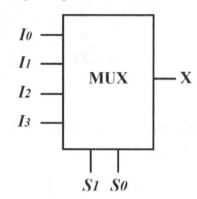

Problem 15.6 l) The output X can be expressed in terms of input, selection lines and enable E as ____.

(A) $E[S_1\bar{S_0}I_0 + S_1S_0I_1 + S_1S_0I_2 + S_1S_0I_3]$

(B) $E[\bar{S_1}S_0I_0 + \bar{S_1}S_0I_1 + S_1S_0I_2 + \bar{S_1}S_0I_3]$

(C) $E[\bar{S_1}\bar{S_0}I_0 + \bar{S_1}S_0I_1 + S_1\bar{S_0}I_2 + S_1S_0I_3]$

(D) None of the above

Problem 15.6 m) Complete the truth table of [8 × 1] multiplexer given below.

E	S_2	S_1	S_0	X
0	X	X	X	
1	0	0	0	
1	0	0	1	
1	0	1	0	
1	0	1	1	
1	1	0	0	
1	1	0	1	
1	1	1	0	
1	1	1	1	

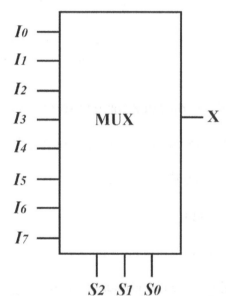

Problem 15.6 n) The output function of following [4 × 1] multiplexer is _____ (assume $E = 1$).

(A) 0

(B) XYZ

(C) $X + Y + Z$

(D) $\bar{X} + \bar{Y} + \bar{Z}$

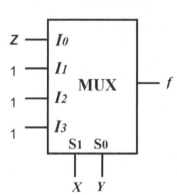

Problem Set # 15.7 – Programmable Logic Devices/Gate Array

Problem 15.7 a) Match the programmable logic devices in Column A with the correct combination of AND-OR plane in Column B.

Column A	Column B
PAL	AND-plane programmable, OR-plane programmable
PLA	AND-plane programmable, OR-plane fixed
ROM	AND-plane fixed, OR-plane programmable
	AND-plane fixed, OR-plane fixed

Consider the following programmable logic device for problems 15.7 b) to 15.7 e).

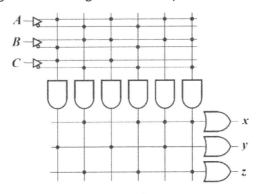

Problem 15.7 b) The given programmable logic device is an example of a _____.

(A) PAL   (B) PLA

(C) ROM   (D) FPGA

Problem 15.7 c) The output x can be expressed as _____.

(A) $\bar{A}B\bar{C} + \bar{A}\bar{B}\bar{C} + AB\bar{C}$ (B) $A\bar{B}C + ABC + AB$

(C) $\bar{A}B\bar{C} + \bar{A}\bar{B}\bar{C} + AB + AB\bar{C}$ (D) None of the above

Problem 15.7 d) The output y can be expressed as _____.

(A) $\bar{A}B\bar{C} + \bar{A}\bar{B}\bar{C} + AB\bar{C}$ (B) $A\bar{B}C + ABC + AB$

(C) $\bar{A}B\bar{C} + \bar{A}\bar{B}\bar{C} + AB + AB\bar{C}$ (D) None of the above

Problem 15.7 e) The output z can be expressed as _____.

(A) $\bar{A}B\bar{C} + \bar{A}\bar{B}\bar{C} + AB\bar{C}$ (B) $A\bar{B}C + ABC + AB$

(C) $\bar{A}B\bar{C} + \bar{A}\bar{B}\bar{C} + AB + AB\bar{C}$ (D) None of the above

Consider the following programmable logic device for problems 15.7 f) to 15.7 i).

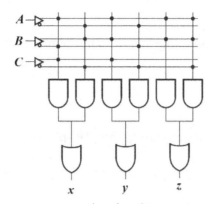

Problem 15.7 f) The given programmable logic device is an example of a _____.

(A) PAL   (B) PLA

(C) ROM   (D) FPGA

Problem 15.7 g) The output x can be expressed as _____.

(A) $AB + AB\bar{C}$ (B) $ABC + \bar{A}\bar{B}\bar{C}$

(C) $A\bar{B}C + \bar{A}B\bar{C}$ (D) None of the above

Problem 15.7 h) The output y can be expressed as _____.

(A) $AB + AB\bar{C}$ (B) $ABC + \bar{A}\bar{B}\bar{C}$

(C) $A\bar{B}C + \bar{A}B\bar{C}$ (D) None of the above

Problem 15.7 i) The output z can be expressed as _____.

(A) $AB + AB\bar{C}$ (B) $ABC + \bar{A}\bar{B}\bar{C}$

(C) $A\bar{B}C + \bar{A}B\bar{C}$ (D) None of the above

Problem Set # 15.8 – State Machine Design

Consult NCEES® FE Reference Handbook – Page 34 while solving these questions

Problem 15.8 a) Complete the state table for the 'Finite State Machine' shown below.

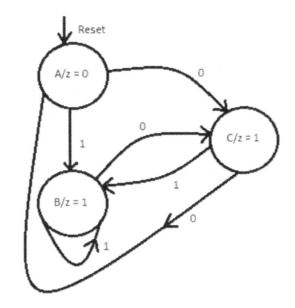

Present State	Next State		Output z
	$w = 0$	$w = 1$	
A	C	B	0
B	C	B	1
C	?	?	?

(A) $w = 0$ (B), $w = 1$ (A), z = 1   (B) $w = 0$ (A), $w = 1$ (B), z = 0

(C) $w = 0$ (A), $w = 1$ (B), z = 1   (D) $w = 0$ (C), $w = 1$ (A), z = 0

Problem 15.8 b) In problem 15.8 a) an input sequence $w = 111$ is applied to the 'Finite State Machine'. Calculate the output sequence if machine is initially in state A.

(A) 111   (B) 010

(C) 000   (D) 011

Problem 15.8 c) In problem 15.8 a) an input sequence $w = 000$ is applied to the 'Finite State Machine'. Calculate the output sequence if machine is initially in state A.

(A) 101   (B) 000

(C) 010   (D) 111

Problem 15.8 d) Complete the state table for the 'Finite State Machine' shown below.

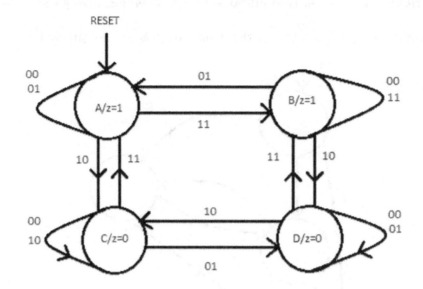

Present State	Next State				Output z
	$ab = 00$	01	10	11	
A	A	A	C	B	1
B	B	A	D	B	1
C	?	?	C	A	0
D	D	D	C	B	0

(A) 00 – C, 01 – D

(B) 00 – C, 01 - C

(C) 00 – D, 01 – C

(D) 00 – A, 01 - D

Problem 15.8 e) States A, B, C and D of problem 15.8 d) are represented by $y_2 y_1$ – 00, 01, 10, 11 respectively in the table given below.

Select the simplified output expression for 'z' as a function of present state.

Present State $y_2 y_1$	Next State				Output 'z'
	$ab = 00$	01	10	11	
00	00	00	10	01	1
01	01	00	10	01	1
10	10	11	10	00	0
11	11	11	10	01	0

(A) $z = \overline{y_2}\, y_1$

(B) $z = y_1$

(C) $z = \overline{y_2}\, \overline{y_1}$

(D) $z = \overline{y_2}$

Problem Set # 15.9 – Timing

Problem 15.9 a) Calculate the propagation delay of a logical circuit for which timing diagram is given below. This circuit has a positive edge triggered clock. Q represents the output of this logical circuit which changes its state at positive clock edge as shown below.

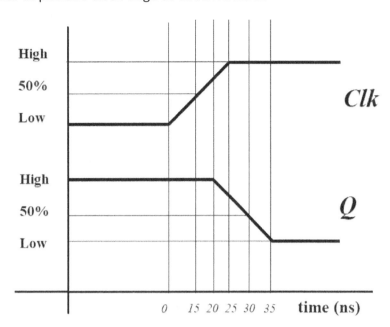

(A) 10ns   (B) 15ns

(C) 20ns   (D) 35ns

Problem 15.9 b) An input change that causes the output to unintentionally change from 1 to 0 to 1 when the output was originally expected to stay constant as 1, is called a _____.

(A) Dynamic hazard   (B) Static-1 hazard

(C) Static-0 hazard   (D) Propagation delay

Problem 15.9 c) An input change that causes the output to unintentionally change from 0 to 1 to 0 when the output was originally expected to stay constant as 0, is called a _____.

(A) Dynamic hazard   (B) Static-1 hazard

(C) Static-0 hazard   (D) Propagation delay

Problem 15.9 d) An input change that causes the output to unintentionally change from 0 to 1 to 0 to 1 or 1 to 0 to 1 to 0 when the output was expected to change just once as 0 to 1 or 1 to 0 is called a ___.

(A) Dynamic hazard   (B) Static-1 hazard

(C) Static-0 hazard   (D) Propagation delay

Problem 15.9 e) Racing condition can be observed in a JK Flip-Flop when the clock signal is high and input values for J and K are _____ respectively.

(A) 0 and 0

(B) 0 and 1

(C) 1 and 0

(D) 1 and 1

Problem 15.9 f) Racing condition of JK Flip-Flop can be addressed by implementing _____.

(A) PLA

(B) PAL

(C) Master-Slave JK Flip-Flop

(D) None of the above

Chapter # 16 – Computer Systems

Key Knowledge Areas*

Concepts	NCEES® FE Reference Handbook Version 10.0.1	
	Section	Page #
Microprocessors	Electrical and Computer Engineering	408 – 410
Memory technology and Systems		
Interfacing		

Facts about this section

- 5 – 8 questions can be expected on the exam according to the latest NCEES® FE specification.
- Computer Systems is one of the most lightly weighted exam sections.
- Difficulty level of this section is rated 'Easy' by the author.
- Students with a major in computer engineering may find this section easier.

Tips for preparing this section

- Understand the computer systems concepts found in NCEES® FE Reference Handbook.
- Review computer architecture and the role of functional units such as ALU, I/O, CU etc.
- Learn the fundamental concepts related to microprocessors.
- Familiarize yourself with different memory technologies (RAM, ROM, EROM etc.).
- Learn how different components of computer system interface with each other.
- Understand the difference between direct-mapped cache, fully associative cache and n-way set associative cache.
- Learn how to calculate tag bits, index bits, block offset bits and address bits of cache memory.
- Review cache replacement policy and write policy.
- Solve the problem sets of chapter and review solutions at the end of this book.

BONUS: Unlock a free 'Computer Systems' lecture by signing-up for the On-demand FE Electrical and Computer exam preparation course preview at: **www.studyforfe.com/fe-course-preview**

* Exam specification can be found on pages 479 – 481 of NCEES® FE Reference Handbook.

Problem Set # 16.1- Microprocessor
Consult NCEES® FE Reference Handbook – Page 409 while solving these questions

Problem 16.1 a) A microprocessor register that stores address of the most recently requested program in a buffer register is called _____.

(A) Program counter

(B) Stack pointer

(C) Instruction pointer

(D) Accumulator

Problem 16.1 b) A microprocessor register that stores address of current or next instructions in a buffer register is called _____.

(A) Program counter

(B) Stack pointer

(C) Accumulator

(D) Options A and B are correct

Problem 16.1 c) A single integrated circuit that accepts and executes coded instructions for data processing and controlling associated circuitry in a computer system is called a _____.

(A) Microprocessor

(B) Microcomputer

(C) Microcontroller

(D) Personal computer

Problem 16.1 d) _____ microprocessor has a hard-wired control unit with a simple instruction set.

(A) Single-core

(B) RISC

(C) Multi-core

(D) CISC

Problem 16.1 e) ADD R5, #6 is an example of instruction in which _____ addressing mode is being used.

(A) Direct

(B) Immediate

(C) Register Direct

(D) Register Indirect

Problem 16.1 f) _____ option correctly describes the result of instruction given in previous problem.

(A) Content of R5 is added to memory location 6

(B) Content of memory location 6 is added to R5

(C) Constant 6 is added to R5

(D) None of the above

Problem 16.1 g) LOAD R4, (R5) is an example of an instruction using _____ addressing mode.

(A) Direct

(B) Immediate

(C) Register Direct

(D) Register Indirect

Problem 16.1 h) _____ option correctly describes the result of instruction given in previous problem.

(A) Content of R4 is loaded to R5

(B) Content of R4 is loaded to memory location pointed by R5

(C) Content of R5 is loaded to R4

(D) Content stored at memory location pointed by R5 will be loaded to R4

Problem 16.1 i) Match the addressing mode in Column A with correct application in Column B.

Column A	Column B
Indirect addressing	Static data
Immediate addressing	Loops
Direct addressing	Constants
Auto-indexed addressing	Pointers
	Registers

Problem 16.1 j) Select the INCORRECT statement(s) regarding multithreading from given options.

(A) Multithreading allows execution of multiple processes simultaneously

(B) Single-core processors use frequency-division multiplexing to provide multithreading

(C) Multicore processors use time-division multiplexing to provide multithreading

(D) All of the above options are incorrect

Problem Set # 16.2 - Memory Technology and Systems
Consult NCEES® FE Reference Handbook – Page 409 while solving these questions

Problem 16.2 a) _____ storage device uses random access methods for accessing memory.

(A) Cassette tape

(B) CD

(C) Hard disk

(D) Flash memory

Problem 16.2 b) A Giga Byte contains _____ bits.

Problem 16.2 c) A memory that acts as a buffer between CPU and main memory to speed up processing is called _____.

(A) DRAM (Dynamic Random Access Memory)

(B) ROM

(C) Cache Memory

(D) EPROM

Problem 16.2 d) _____ is an example of a secondary memory.

(A) Cache memory

(B) RAM (Random Access Memory)

(C) DVD

(D) DRAM (Dynamic Random Access Memory)

Problem 16.2 e) _____ ROM can be programmed only once and it is non-erasable.

(A) PROM

(B) EPROM

(C) EEPROM

(D) DRAM

Problem 16.2 f) _____ is a memory unit which varies in size between different computer systems.

(A) Nibble

(B) Word

(C) Bit

(D) Byte

Consider the following scenario for problems 16.2 g) to 16.2 j).

A direct-mapped cache memory is 32KB with a block size of 512 bytes. Main memory size is 256KB.

Problem 16.2 g) A total of _____ address bits are required for cache memory address.

Problem 16.2 h) _____ bits are required in the block offset field of cache memory address.

Problem 16.2 i) _____ bits are required in the index field of cache memory address.

Problem 16.2 j) _____ bits are required in the tag field of cache memory address.

Problem 16.2 k) Replacement policy is not required for _____ mapping.

(A) Direct

(B) N-way set associative

(C) Fully set associative

(D) All of the above

Consider the following scenario for problems 16.2 l) to 16.2 o).

A fully associative cache memory is 32KB with a block size of 512 bytes. Main memory size is 256KB.

Problem 16.2 l) A total of _____ address bits are required for cache memory address.

Problem 16.2 m) _____ bits are required in the block offset field of cache memory address.

Problem 16.2 n) _____ bits are required in the index field of cache memory address.

Problem 16.2 o) _____ bits are required for the tag field of cache memory address.

Consider the following scenario for problems 16.2 p) to 16.2 s).

4-way set associative cache memory is 32KB with a block size of 512 bytes. Main memory size is 256KB.

Problem 16.2 p) _____ bits are required for block offset field of cache memory.

Problem 16.2 q) The total number of sets in this cache are equal to _____.

Problem 16.2 r) _____ bits are required in the index field of cache memory address.

Problem 16.2 s) _____ bits are required for the tag field of cache memory address.

Problem 16.2 t) What is the average memory access time of a single direct-mapped cache memory with a hit rate of 90%, a hit time of 5ns and a miss penalty of 200ns.

(A) 5ns

(B) 10ns

(C) 15ns

(D) 25ns

Problem Set # 16.3 - Architecture & Interfacing

Consult NCEES® FE Reference Handbook – Page 409 while solving these questions

Problem 16.3 a) Basic Input Output System (BIOS) is read from _____ during normal start-up routine.

(A) RAM   (B) ROM

(C) USB   (D) CD

Problem 16.3 b) _____ is the process of transforming data into different format for another system.

(A) Encryption   (B) Encoding

(C) Hashing   (D) Decoding

Problem 16.3 c) Computer architecture is primarily concerned with _____ of a computer.

(A) Logical/functional design   (B) Instruction set

(C) Addressing modes   (D) All of the above

Problem 16.3 d) Central processing unit (CPU) consists of _____.

(A) ALU   (B) Control Unit

(C) Register Array   (D) All of the above

Problem 16.3 e) A set of conductors used to transfer data, instructions, addresses and control signals between various components of a computer system is called _____.

(A) Stack pointer   (B) Register

(C) Interrupter   (D) Bus

Problem 16.3 f) The width of _____ bus directly impacts the processing speed of a microprocessor.

(A) Address   (B) Data

(C) Control   (D) All of the above

Problem 16.3 g) _____ has a shared memory storage and signal pathway for instruction and data.

(A) Harvard architecture   (B) Von Neumann/Princeton architecture

(C) MIT architecture   (D) Stanford architecture

Chapter # 17 – Software Engineering
Key Knowledge Areas*

Concepts	NCEES® FE Reference Handbook Version 10.0.1	
	Section	Page #
Algorithms	Electrical and Computer Engineering	410 – 413
Data structures		
Software implementation		

Facts about this section

- 4 – 6 questions can be expected on the exam according to the latest NCEES® FE specification.
- Software Engineering is one of the most lightly weighted exam sections.
- Difficulty level of this section is rated 'Medium' by the author.
- Students with a major in computer engineering may find this section easier.

Tips for preparing this section

- Understand software engineering concepts found in NCEES® FE Reference Handbook.
- Learn how to dry run pseudo codes and simple algorithms.
- Understand the mechanics of sorting algorithms (such as bubble sort, merge sort, heap sort, quick sort) and searching algorithms (such as binary search and hash trees).
- Review graph traversal algorithms - breadth-first search (BFS) and depth-first search (DFS).
- Review tree traversal algorithms – in-order, pre-order, and post-order tree traversal.
- Review flow chart development and its symbols.
- Gain fundamental understanding of object-oriented and structured programming including different types of data structures (static and dynamic).
- Learn key steps involved in software implementation and testing process.
- Review relevant concepts using your college/university textbooks.
- Solve problem sets on next pages and review solutions at the end of this book.

BONUS: Unlock a free 'Software Engineering' lecture by signing-up for the On-demand FE Electrical and Computer exam preparation course preview at: **www.studyforfe.com/fe-course-preview**

* Exam specification can be found on pages 479 – 481 of NCEES® FE Reference Handbook.

Problem Set # 17.1 – Algorithms – Complexity, Big-O

Consult NCEES® FE Reference Handbook – Page 412 while solving these questions

Problem 17.1 a) The value of x after execution of following pseudo-code will be _____.

int $x = 0; y = 0; z = 10$;

    do while $z > 0$

       { $y = y + 1$;

           $x = 2y - 1$;

           $z = z - 3$;   }

    end while

Problem 17.1 b) The value of $temp$ after execution of following pseudo-code will be _____.

int $temp = 0$;

    for $(int\ N = 1; N <= 100; N + +)$

    $\{N = 2^N$;

    $temp = N;\}$

Problem 17.1 c) Processing time of an algorithm for solving a problem of size n is given by expression $60 + 0.005n^3 + 0.01n$. Select the option that correctly identifies Big-O value of this algorithm.

(A) $O(1)$ (B) $O(n)$

(C) $O(n^3)$ (D) None of the above

Problem 17.1 d) Processing time of an algorithm for solving a problem of size n is given by expression $0.5n + 15n^2 + 20n \log_2 n$. Select the option that correctly identifies Big-O value of this algorithm.

(A) $O(n)$ (B) $O(n \log_2 n)$

(C) $O(n^2)$ (D) $O(\log_2 n)$

Problem 17.1 e) Select the INCORRECT statement(s) from given options.

(A) $O(x + y) = O(x) + O(y)$ (B) $O(xy) = O(x)O(y)$

(C) $O(x + y) = \max\{O(x), O(y)\}$ (D) $O(x') = O(x)$ if $x' = cx$ for all $c > 0$

Problem 17.1 f) Processing time of an algorithm X for solving a problem of size n is given as $x(n) = 0.2n^2 \log_{10} n$ (milli-seconds) and that of an algorithm Y is given as $y(n) = 10n^2$ (milli-seconds). Which algorithm has a better Big-O performance?

(A) Algorithm X

(B) Algorithm Y

(C) Performances are equal

(D) Insufficient details

Problem 17.1 g) In the previous problem, the largest problem size n_0 below which algorithm X will perform better than algorithm Y is _____.

Problem 17.1 h) Calculate the worst-case time complexity of following code fragment.

for $(int\ i = 0; i < n; i + +)\{$

    for $(int\ j = 0; j < n; j + +)\{$

        printf ("*First loop*");

        }

    for $(int\ k = 0; k < n; k + +)\{$

        printf ("*Second loop*");

    }}}

(A) $O(n)$

(B) $O(n^2)$

(C) $O(n + n)$

(D) $nO(n)$

Problem 17.1 i) _____ correctly compares Big-O complexity as a function of problem size 'n'.

(A) $O(n^3) < O(n^2)$

(B) $O(n^2) < O(2^n)$

(C) $O(n) < O(\log n)$

(D) $O(n \log n) < O(n)$

Problem Set # 17.2 – Algorithms – Sorting, Searching

Consult NCEES® FE Reference Handbook – Page 410 while solving these questions

Problem 17.2 a) _____ option correctly represents the order of $array[\ ] = \{4,0,3,1,7\}$ after it has undergone two passes of bubble sort.

(A) $\{0,3,1,4,7\}$

(B) $\{3,0,1,4,7\}$

(C) $\{0,1,3,4,7\}$

(D) $\{0,1,3,7,4\}$

Problem 17.2 b) Bubble sort requires a maximum of ___ comparisons for sorting an array with 7 items.

(A) 6

(B) 7

(C) 21

(D) 49

Problem 17.2 c) The best-case run-time complexity of bubble sort algorithm is _____.

(A) $O(\log n)$

(B) $O(n)$

(C) $O(n \log n)$

(D) $O(n^2)$

Problem 17.2 d) An unsorted array contains 8 elements. _____ passes will be required to fully sort this array using insertion sort.

Problem 17.2 e) Select the option that correctly shows intermediate steps of insertion sort algorithm on $array[\ ] = \{10,15,5,13\}$.

(A) 10,15,5,13 5,10,15,13 5,10,13,15

(B) 10,15,5,13 5,13,10,15 5,10,13,15

(C) 10,5,15,13 10,5,13,15 5,10,13,15

(D) 5,15,10,13 5,10,15,13 5,10,13,15

Problem 17.2 f) Merge sort requires _____ additional space for sorting an unsorted array of size n.

(A) $O(1)$

(B) $O(\log n)$

(C) $O(n \log n)$

(D) $O(n)$

Problem 17.2 g) Select the option that correctly describes time complexity of merge sort algorithm.

(A) Best-case time complexity = $O(n \log n)$

(B) Average-case time complexity = $O(n \log n)$

(C) Worst-case time complexity = $O(n \log n)$

(D) All of the above

Problem 17.2 h) Consider two sorted sub-arrays $a[\ ] = \{14,46,60,64\}$ and $b[\ ] = \{31,33,76,82\}$ that need to be merged into a final sorted array $c[\ ]$ using merge sort. How many comparisons will be required to place the first item within $c[\ ]$?

(A) 1   (B) 2

(C) 3   (D) 4

Problem 17.2 i) _____ pivot option will result in best Big-O performance using quick sort algorithm.

(A) First item   (B) Last item

(C) Median of three   (D) Random item

Problem 17.2 j) The median-of-three pivot for quick sort implementation on $array[\ ] = \{43,6,13,2,17,29,11,31,73\}$ will be _____.

Problem 17.2 k) Apply quick sort on $array[\ ] = \{3,9,8,10,2,11,4\}$ using the last item (4) as pivot. Select the option that best represents the array after (4) has been inserted in its correct location.

(A) $\{10,11,4,8,2,3,9\}$ (B) $\{9,2,4,8,10,3,11\}$

(C) $\{3,2,4,10,9,11,8\}$ (D) $\{2,11,4,8,9,11,3\}$

Problem 17.2 l) How many recursions are required to search 105 in $array[\ ] = \{5,10,15,25,105\}$ (sorted array) using binary search algorithm?

(A) 1   (B) 2

(C) 3   (D) 4

Problem 17.2 m) Select the option that correctly represents the hash table of size m = 8 that maps the items 20, 10, 16, 14, 15, 17 using hash function $h(x) = x\%m$. Assume that hash table is initially empty.

(A)

16	17	10		20		14	15

(B)

16	17	10		20		14	15		

(C)

15	14		20		10	17	16	

(D) None of the above

Problem Set # 17.3 Data Structures – Array/Linked List/Stack/Queue

Consult NCEES® FE Reference Handbook – Page 411 while solving these questions

Problem 17.3 a) Select the option that correctly describes the output of following code fragment.

int $array[\ ] = \{11,9,15,16,21,3\}$;

for (int $i = 0; i < 4; i + +)\{$

   printf $(\%d, array[i])$; }

(A) 0 1 2 3   (B) 11 9 15 16 21

(C) 11 9 15 16   (D) 11 9 15 16 21 3

Problem 17.3 b) Select the option that correctly describes the time complexity involved in counting the number of items in a linked list.

(A) $O(1)$ (B) $O(\log n)$

(C) $O(n)$ (D) $O(n \log n)$

Problem 17.3 c) The purpose of following code segment for a given linked list is to _____.

struct node * function (struct node * head, int data) {

struct node * temp = (struct node*) malloc (size(struct node));

temp -> data = data;

temp -> next = head;

return (temp); }

(A) Delete a node   (B) Insert a new node at the end

(C) Insert a new node in the middle   (D) Insert a new node at the start

Problem 17.3 d) Every linked list node contains _____.

(A) Data   (B) Link to next node

(C) Both A and B   (D) None of the above

Problem 17.3 e) The process of adding data to a stack is called a _____ operation.

(A) Push   (B) Pop

(C) Peek   (D) Traversal

Problem 17.3 f) The purpose of following code segment for a given stack is to _____.

void function ( ) {

struct node * temp; temp = top;

printf ("%d", temp -> data);}

(A) Push   (B) Pop

(C) Peek   (D) Traversal

Problem 17.3 g) If following operations are performed on an empty stack, the sequence of popped values will be _____.

Push(4), Push(8), Pop( ), Push(6), Push(10), Pop( ).

(A) 4, 8   (B) 8, 6, 10

(C) 4, 6   (D) 8, 10

Problem 17.3 h) In the previous problem, the final state of given stack will be _____.

(A) Top – 10, 6, 8, 4 – Bottom   (B) Top – 10, 4 – Bottom

(C) Top – 8, 4 – Bottom   (D) Top – 6, 4 – Bottom

Problem 17.3 i) The purpose of following code segment for a given queue is to _____.

void function ( ) {

printf ("%d", front -> data);}

front = front -> next;}

(A) Enqueue   (B) Dequeue

(C) Display   (D) Peek

Problem 17.3 j) Suppose that items are inserted in a queue as follow: 5(first item), 6, 3, 1, 9 (last item). What will be the order of removal from this queue?

(A) 9, 1, 3, 6, 5   (B) 5, 6, 3, 1, 9

(C) 9, 3, 5, 6, 1   (D) 5, 3, 9, 6, 1

Problem Set # 17.4 Data Structures – Tree/Graph

Consult NCEES® FE Reference Handbook – Page 411 while solving these questions

Problem 17.4 a) _____ is an example of a non-linear data structure.

(A) Array   (B) Linked List

(C) Tree   (D) Stack

Consider the following tree for problems 17.4 b) and 17.4 c).

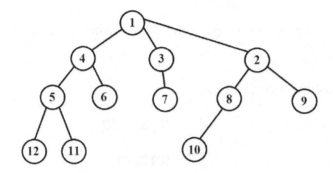

Problem 17.4 b) What is the height of this tree?

(A) 0   (B) 1

(C) 2   (D) 3

Problem 17.4 c) What is the depth of node 1 in this tree?

(A) 0   (B) 1

(C) 2   (D) 3

Consider the following tree for problems 17.4 d) to 17.4 f).

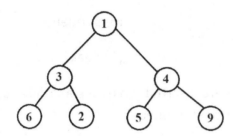

Problem 17.4 d) Select the option that correctly identifies in-order traversal for given tree.

(A) 6, 2, 3, 5, 9, 4, 1   (B) 1, 3, 6, 2, 4, 5, 9

(C) 6, 3, 2, 1, 5, 4, 9   (D) None of the above

Problem 17.4 e) Select the option that correctly identifies pre-order traversal for given tree.

(A) 6, 2, 3, 5, 9, 4, 1   (B) 1, 3, 6, 2, 4, 5, 9

(C) 6, 3, 2, 1, 5, 4, 9   (D) None of the above

Problem 17.4 f) Select the option that correctly identifies post-order traversal for given tree.

(A) 6, 2, 3, 5, 9, 4, 1   (B) 1, 3, 6, 2, 4, 5, 9

(C) 6, 3, 2, 1, 5, 4, 9   (D) None of the above

Problem 17.4 g) Graphs can be represented using _____ method(s).

(A) Adjacency matrix   (B) Incidence matrix

(C) Adjacency list   (D) All of the above

Consider the following graph for problems 17.4 h) and 17.4 i).

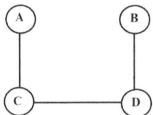

Problem 17.4 h) The size of adjacency matrix required to represent this graph is _____.

Problem 17.4 i) _____ non-zero entries exist in the adjacency matrix of given graph.

Consider the following graph for next two problems (assume 'O' as starting point).

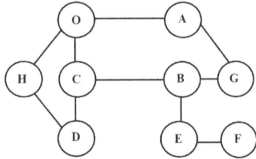

Problem 17.4 j) _____ will be the output of breadth first search (BFS) algorithm on this graph.

(A) O A G B E F C D H   (B) O A C H G B D E F

(C) O A H C D B E F G   (D) O A G B C D H E F

Problem 17.4 k) _____ will be the output of depth first search (DFS) algorithm on this graph.

(A) O A G B E F C D H   (B) O A C H G B D E F

(C) O A H C D B E F G   (D) O A G B C D H E F

Problem Set # 17.5 - Software design methods/implementation/testing

Consult NCEES® FE Reference Handbook – Pages 412 – 413 while solving these questions

Problem 17.5 a) Software with a tendency to break due to changes in unrelated segments is called ___.

Problem 17.5 b) Static software testing involves verification through _____.

(A) program code review

(B) program code execution

(C) software maintenance

(D) Options A, B and C are all correct

Problem 17.5 c) Glass box testing of a software is also known as _____ testing.

Problem 17.5 d) _____ testing is conducted at software's interface without close examination of its internal structure.

Problem 17.5 e) _____ is the process of testing individual pieces of source code before handing it over for formal execution of test cases.

(A) System testing

(B) Integration testing

(C) Unit testing

(D) User acceptance testing

Problem 17.5 f) _____ model requires sequential execution of design, integration, and testing.

(A) Iterative

(B) Spiral

(C) Waterfall

(D) Code-and-fix

Problem 17.5 g) _____ describes the functionality of algorithm implemented by following flow chart.

(A) Sum calculation

(B) Average calculation

(C) Finding the largest number

(D) Finding the smallest number

Solutions

Problem	Answer	Problem	Answer	Problem	Answer	Problem	Answer
1.1 a	B	1.3 l	B	1.5 n	See Sol.	2.1 j	See Sol.
1.1 b	B, C	1.3 m	A	1.5 o	C	2.2 a	B
1.1 c	B	1.4 a	D	1.5 p	B	2.2 b	C
1.1 d	B, C	1.4 b	C	1.6 a	D	2.2 c	A
1.1 e	D	1.4 c	y=2x -5	1.6 b	See Sol.	2.2 d	D
1.1 f	See Sol.	1.4 d	See Sol.	1.6 c	See Sol.	2.2 e	0.5,0.5
1.1 g	B	1.4 e	A, B	1.6 d	See Sol.	2.2 f	0.20
1.1 h	B	1.4 f	A	1.6 e	See Sol.	2.2 g	0.80
1.1 i	C	1.4 g	B	1.6 f	A	2.2 h	0.40
1.1 j	D	1.4 h	D	1.6 g	See Sol.	2.2 i	0.40
1.1 k	2m	1.4 i	See Sol.	1.7 a	C	2.2 j	C
1.1 l	A	1.4 j	See Sol.	1.7 b	D	2.2 k	0.50
1.2 a	B	1.4 k	See Sol.	1.7 c	A	2.3 a	B
1.2 b	C	1.4 l	See Sol.	1.7 d	14	2.3 b	0.24
1.2 c	C	1.4 m	C	1.7 e	See Sol.	2.3 c	0.228
1.2 d	C	1.4 n	A	1.7 f	D	2.3 d	0.51
1.2 e	D	1.4 o	B	1.7 g	A	2.3 e	0.0228
1.2 f	-12 -24j	1.5 a	C	1. 7 h	0	2.3 f	0.1359
1.2 g	C	1.5 b	A	1.7 i	16	2.3 g	0.0013
1.3 a	C	1.5 c	B	1.7 j	-4i+j+10k	2.3 h	0.1587
1.3 b	B	1.5 d	D	1.7 k	B	2.3 i	0.1359
1.3 c	A	1.5 e	B	2.1 a	6	2.4 a	3.18
1.3 d	B	1.5 f	B	2.1 b	88.2^0F	2.4 b	0.63
1.3 e	A	1.5 g	B	2.1 c	$\sqrt{20/3}$	2.4 c	5.5%
1.3 f	B	1.5 h	-1/3	2.1 d	2.21	2.4 d	5/6
1.3 g	70	1.5 i	C	2.1 e	6.9	2.4 e	2
1.3 h	15600	1.5 j	C	2.1 f	3	2.4 f	1
1.3 i	531441	1.5 k	D	2.1 g	80	3.1 a	C
1.3 j	29524	1.5 l	C	2.1 h	3	3.1 b	D
1.3 k	R2	1.5 m	A	2.1 i	110	3.1 c	D

Problem	Answer	Problem	Answer	Problem	Answer	Problem	Answer
3.1 d	D	4.2 d	$4000	5.2 e	D	6.5 c	A
3.1 e	C	4.2 e	$2,968	5.2 f	B	6.5 d	B
3.1 f	C3	4.2 f	$26,000	6.1 a	B	6.5 e	C
3.1 g	C	4.2 g	$24,000	6.1 b	D	6.6 a	A
3.1 h	A, D	4.2 h	See Sol.	6.1 c	B	6.6 b	B
3.1 i	B	4.3 a	20000	6.1 d	D	6.6 c	B
3.1 j	D	4.3 b	B, C	6.1 e	A	6.6 d	C
3.2 a	A	4.3 c	2000	6.1 f	$875\mu A$	6.6 e	$6.2-14j\Omega$
3.2 b	C	4.3 d	Contr. A	6.2 a	D	6.6 f	D
3.2 c	B	4.3 e	Opt. C	6.2 b	A	6.6 g	A
3.2 d	D	4.3 f	Proj. B	6.2 c	B	7.1 a	C
3.2 e	1F,2A,3B	5.1 a	D	6.2 d	C	7.1 b	B
3.2 f	C	5.1 b	C	6.2 e	$6k\Omega$	7.1 c	D
3.3 a	C	5.1 c	D	6.3 a	B	7.1 d	B
3.3 b	B	5.1 d	B	6.3 b	$1.5k\Omega$	7.1 e	C
3.3 c	B	5.1 e	.015H/m	6.3 c	A	7.2 a	D
3.3 d	D	5.1 f	D	6.3 d	7.5mA	7.2 b	$5000rads^{-1}$
3.3 e	17-99mA	5.1 g	B	6.3 e	$1k\Omega$	7.2 c	B
3.3 f	4	5.1 h	D	6.3 f	2A	7.2 d	$3162rads^{-1}$
3.3 g	D	5.1 i	A	6.3 g	16Ω	7.2 e	See sol.
4.1 a	$241,157	5.1 j	B	6.3 h	32V	7.2 f	See sol.
4.1 b	$231,225	5.1 k	B	6.4 a	C	7.2 g	B
4.1 c	B	5.1 l	B	6.4 b	D	7.2 h	$1000rads^{-1}$
4.1 d	A	5.1 m	$0.5\mu F$	6.4 c	C	7.3 a	A
4.1 e	$17,440	5.1 n	A	6.4 d	B	7.3 b	B
4.1 f	$392,724	5.1 o	B	6.4 e	1A	7.3 c	C
4.1 g	$1.69mn	5.1 p	D	6.4 f	B	7.3 d	D
4.1 h	10.47%	5.1 q	B	6.4 g	B	7.3 e	A
4.1 i	$251,416	5.1 r	4H	6.4 h	B	7.3 f	B
4.1 j	$4878	5.2 a	B	6.4 i	C	7.3 g	D
4.2 a	D	5.2 b	C	6.4 j	A	7.3 h	C
4.2 b	str. line	5.2 c	B	6.5 a	D	7.3 i	A
4.2 c	$250,000	5.2 d	$.04K^{-1}$	6.5 b	C	7.3 j	C

Problem	Answer	Problem	Answer	Problem	Answer	Problem	Answer
7.4 a	B, D	8.3 l	4^n	9.2 k	B	9.8 a	C
7.4 b	See sol.	8.3 m	See sol.	9.3 a	C	9.8 b	B
7.4 c	See sol.	8.3 n	A	9.3 b	D	9.8 c	5000Ω
7.4 d	D	8.3 o	B	9.3 c	Cut-off	9.8 d	200Ω
7.4 e	C	8.3 p	D	9.3 d	A	9.8 e	C
7.4 f	D	8.4 a	C	9.3 e	See sol.	9.8 f	B
8.1 a	A	8.4 b	A	9.3 f	See sol.	9.8 g	A
8.1 b	2kHz	8.4 c	D	9.3 g	See sol.	9.8 h	B
8.1 c	C	8.4 d	C	9.4 a	110Ω	10.1 a	592W
8.1 d	D	8.4 e	C	9.4 b	1mS	10.1 b	B
8.1 e	D	8.5 a	B	9.4 c	B	10.1 c	C
8.1 f	C	8.5 b	C	9.4 d	2.92mS	10.1 d	9.19W
8.1 g	C	8.5 c	B	9.5 a	D	10.1 e	B
8.1 h	C	8.5 d	See Sol.	9.5 b	Triode	10.1 f	C
8.2 a	D	8.5 e	See Sol.	9.5 c	B	10.1 g	A
8.2 b	C	9.1 a	A	9.5 d	C	10.1 h	A
8.2 c	B	9.1 b	D	9.5 e	0.44mA	10.2 a	C
8.2 d	A	9.1 c	B	9.5 f	Saturation	10.2 b	B
8.2 e	A	9.1 d	0.634V	9.5 g	$5k\Omega,3k\Omega$	10.2 c	C
8.2 f	1000 rad/s	9.1 e	C	9.6 a	-5V	10.2 d	A
8.2 g	Band-pass	9.1 f	A	9.6 b	$5k\Omega$	10.2 e	B
8.2 h	B	9.1 g	C	9.6 c	2.5V	10.2 f	B
8.3 a	C	9.1 h	Group III	9.6 d	-35V	10.2 g	D
8.3 b	B	9.2 a	A	9.6 e	0.5V	10.2 h	A
8.3 c	D	9.2 b	0.66mA	9.6 f	4.3V	10.2 i	C
8.3 d	A	9.2 c	0.13mA	9.6 g	See Sol.	10.2 j	D
8.3 e	B	9.2 d	See sol.	9.7 a	B	10.2 k	C
8.3 f	A	9.2 e	400Ω	9.7 b	C	10.2 l	A
8.3 g	B	9.2 f	2mA	9.7 c	C	10.2 m	B
8.3 h	C	9.2 g	1.4V	9.7 d	D	10.2 n	D
8.3 i	D	9.2 h	114V	9.7 e	B	10.2 o	C
8.3 j	B	9.2 i	152V	9.7 f	C	10.3 a	D
8.3 k	A	9.2 j	See sol.	9.7 g	183V	10.3 b	B

Problem	Answer	Problem	Answer	Problem	Answer	Problem	Answer
10.3 c	0.98 lag	11.1 a	D	11.4 d	B	12.3 i	B
10.3 d	0.82 lag	11.1 b	A	11.4 e	D	12.3 j	0<k<5
10.3 e	D	11.1 c	C	11.4 f	A	12.4 a	See sol.
10.4 a	C	11.1 d	B	11.5 a	$0.5\underline{/6.91^0}$	12.4 b	See sol.
10.4 b	C	11.1 e	D	11.5 b	C	12.4 c	2
10.4 c	7%	11.1 f	D	11.5 c	B	12.4 d	0.50
10.4 d	B	11.1 g	B	11.5 d	D	12.4 e	A
10.4 e	B	11.1 h	A	11.5 e	D	12.4 f	0.90s
10.4 f	C	11.1 i	D	11.5 f	B	12.4 g	1.16
10.4 g	D	11.1 j	B	12.1 a	See sol.	12.4 h	16.3%
10.5 a	B	11.1 k	A	12.1 b	See sol.	12.4 i	3.46rad/s
10.5 b	A	11.1 l	C	12.1 c	See sol.	12.4 j	2.82rad/s
10.5 c	4.16A	11.2 a	D	12.1 d	See sol.	12.4 k	3.62
10.5 d	25000Ω	11.2 b	5μJ	12.1 e	A	12.4 l	2s
10.5 e	50Ω	11.2 c	11.5^0	12.1 f	See sol.	12.4 m	0.24
10.5 f	D	11.2 d	B	12.1 g	See sol.	12.4 n	∞
10.5 g	A	11.2 e	0.15μV	12.1 h	See sol.	12.4 o	∞
10.5 h	C	11.2 f	500μT	12.2 a	A	12.4 p	∞
10.6 a	C	11.2 g	0.4μT	12.2 b	D	12.4 q	0.11
10.6 b	C	11.2 h	100kA	12.2 c	C	13.1 a	C
10.6 c	B	11.3 a	D	12.2 d	See sol.	13.1 b	u(t-3)
10.6 d	5.5%	11.3 b	B	12.2 e	D	13.1 c	D
10.6 e	D	11.3 c	C	12.2 f	-60dB	13.1 d	B
10.6 f	B	11.3 d	B	12.2 g	20dB	13.1 e	δ(t)/3
10.6 g	D	11.3 e	C	12.2 h	-33.9dB	13.1 f	D
10.6 h	C	11.3 f	B	12.3 a	B	13.1 g	A
10.6 i	B	11.3 g	B	12.3 b	A, C	13.1 h	B
10.6 j	C	11.3 h	C	12.3 c	C	13.1 i	18J
10.6 k	41.4kW	11.3 i	See sol.	12.3 d	B	13.2 a	7V
10.6 l	297Nm	11.3 j	D	12.3 e	D	13.2 b	5V
10.6 m	173A	11.4 a	B	12.3 f	B	13.2 c	0.71
10.6 n	215V	11.4 b	C	12.3 g	See sol.	13.2 d	0.80
10.6 o	0.14Ω	11.4 c	D	12.3 h	-8/3	13.2 e	200Hz

Problem	Answer	Problem	Answer	Problem	Answer	Problem	Answer
13.2 f	50kHz	13.5 j	See Sol.	14.3 e	C	15.1 g	0011_2
13.2 g	D	13.6 a	A	14.3 f	C	15.1 h	D
13.2 h	C	13.6 b	C	14.3 g	D	15.1 i	D
13.2 i	15.2%	13.6 c	C	14.3 h	C	15.1 j	B
13.2 j	84.7%	13.6 d	400bps	14.3 i	C	15.2 a	D
13.2 k	A	13.6 e	B	14.3 j	C	15.2 b	A
13.3 a	3.18	13.6 f	$20\mu s$	14.4 a	B	15.2 c	B
13.3 b	41.8kHz	13.6 g	15kHz	14.4 b	D	15.2 d	B
13.3 c	B	14.1 a	Routing	14.4 c	C	15.2 e	C
13.3 d	1kHz,10Hz	14.1 b	D	14.4 d	B	15.2 f	B
13.3 e	C	14.1 c	Network	14.4 e	D	15.3 a	B
13.3 f	See sol.	14.1 d	Data link	14.4 f	D	15.3 b	C
13.3 g	See sol.	14.1 e	C	14.4 g	C	15.3 c	A
13.3 h	See sol.	14.1 f	A	14.4 h	D	15.3 d	C
13.3 i	D	14.1 g	See Sol.	14.5 a	A	15.3 e	B
13.3 j	B	14.2 a	App. Lyr	14.5 b	A	15.3 f	C
13.3 k	B	14.2 b	A	14.5 c	A	15.4 a	B
13.3 l	C	14.2 c	C	14.5 d	D	15.4 b	D
13.3 m	D	14.2 d	D	14.5 e	D	15.4 c	C
13.4 a	40sinc(8f)	14.2 e	A	14.5 f	B	15.4 d	A
13.4 b	See sol.	14.2 f	B	14.5 g	B	15.4 e	C
13.4 c	C	14.2 g	406	14.5 h	C	15.4 f	C
13.4 d	D	14.2 h	28	14.5 i	8	15.5 a	C
13.4 e	See Sol.	14.2 i	C	14.5 j	B	15.5 b	B
13.5 a	128	14.2 j	D	14.5 k	4	15.5 c	C
13.5 b	D	14.2 k	B	14.5 l	See Sol.	15.5 d	A
13.5 c	B	14.2 l	D	14.5 m	B	15.5 e	B
13.5 d	C	14.2 m	C	15.1 a	See Sol.	15.5 f	B
13.5 e	34.5kbps	14.2 n	C	15.1 b	See Sol.	15.5 g	D
13.5 f	11.7dB	14.3 a	D	15.1 c	D	15.5 h	A
13.5 g	11	14.3 b	D	15.1 d	0101_2	15.6 a	D
13.5 h	10101111	14.3 c	D	15.1 e	1001_2	15.6 b	C
13.5 i	See Sol.	14.3 d	D	15.1 f	0000_2	15.6 c	See Sol.

Problem	Answer	Problem	Answer	Problem	Answer	Problem	Answer
15.6 d	See Sol.	16.1 c	A	16.3 f	B	17.3 j	B
15.6 e	See Sol.	16.1 d	B	16.3 g	B	17.4 a	C
15.6 f	See Sol.	16.1 e	B	17.1 a	7	17.4 b	D
15.6 g	See Sol.	16.1 f	C	17.1 b	2^9	17.4 c	A
15.6 h	See Sol.	16.1 g	D	17.1 c	C	17.4 d	C
15.6 i	B	16.1 h	D	17.1 d	C	17.4 e	B
15.6 j	A	16.1 i	See Sol.	17.1 e	A	17.4 f	A
15.6 k	See Sol.	16.1 j	D	17.1 f	B	17.4 g	D
15.6 l	C	16.2 a	D	17.1 g	10^{50}	17.4 h	4 x 4
15.6 m	See Sol.	16.2 b	8×2^{30} bits	17.1 h	B	17.4 i	6
15.6 n	C	16.2 c	C	17.1 i	B	17.4 j	B
15.7 a	See Sol.	16.2 d	C	17.2 a	C	17.4 k	A, D
15.7 b	B	16.2 e	A	17.2 b	C	17.5 a	Fragile
15.7 c	C	16.2 f	B	17.2 c	B	17.5 b	A
15.7 d	B	16.2 g	18	17.2 d	7	17.5 c	White box
15.7 e	A	16.2 h	9	17.2 e	A	17.5 d	Black box
15.7 f	A	16.2 i	6	17.2 f	D	17.5 e	C
15.7 g	C	16.2 j	3	17.2 g	D	17.5 f	C
15.7 h	B	16.2 k	A	17.2 h	A	17.5 g	B
15.7 i	A	16.2 l	18	17.2 i	D		
15.8 a	C	16.2 m	9	17.2 j	43		
15.8 b	D	16.2 n	0	17.2 k	C		
15.8 c	C	16.2 o	9	17.2 l	C		
15.8 d	A	16.2 p	9	17.2 m	A		
15.8 e	D	16.2 q	16	17.3 a	C		
15.9 a	B	16.2 r	4	17.3 b	C		
15.9 b	B	16.2 s	5	17.3 c	D		
15.9 c	C	16.2 t	D	17.3 d	C		
15.9 d	A	16.3 a	B	17.3 e	A		
15.9 e	D	16.3 b	B	17.3 f	C		
15.9 f	C	16.3 c	D	17.3 g	D		
16.1 a	B	16.3 d	D	17.3 h	D		
16.1 b	A	16.3 e	D	17.3 i	B		

Chapter # 1 – Mathematics

1.1 Algebra and Trigonometry

Consult NCEES® FE Reference Handbook – Pages 34 - 38 for reference

1.1 a) CORRECT ANSWER – B

$$\log_3(12x - 12) - \log_3(x) = 2$$

According to the logarithmic identities given in NCEES® FE Reference Handbook:

$$\log x - \log y = \log\frac{x}{y} \rightarrow \log_3(12x - 12) - \log_3(x) = \log_3\frac{(12x - 12)}{(x)}$$

The given logarithmic function can be rearranged as follows:

$$\log_3\frac{(12x - 12)}{(x)} = 2$$

$$\frac{(12x - 12)}{(x)} = 3^2 \rightarrow 12x - 12 = 9x \rightarrow 3x = 12 \rightarrow x = 4$$

1.1 b) CORRECT ANSWERS – B, C

Logarithm can only be calculated for positive real numbers.

Logarithms of 0 and negative real numbers are undefined.

1.1 c) CORRECT ANSWER – B

$$\log_3(x + 1) + \log_3(x - 1) = 1$$

According to the logarithmic identities given in NCEES® FE Reference Handbook:

$$\log x + \log y = \log xy \rightarrow \log_3(x + 1) + \log_3(x - 1) = \log_3[(x + 1)(x - 1)] = \log_3(x^2 - 1)$$

The given logarithmic function can be rearranged as follows:

$$\log_3(x^2 - 1) = 1$$

Taking anti-log on both sides of the equation results in following:

$$x^2 - 1 = 3^1 = 3$$

$$x^2 = 4 \rightarrow x = 2, -2$$

It is important to validate these results by substitution to see if values of x are acceptable solutions.

$$\log_3(2 + 1) + \log_3(2 - 1) = 1 + 0 = 1 \text{ Therefore, } x = 2 \text{ is a valid solution.}$$

$$\log_3(-2 + 1) + \log_3(-2 - 1) = \log_3(-1) + \log_3(-3) \quad x = -2 \text{ is an invalid solution because logarithm}$$
of negative real number is undefined.

1.1 d) CORRECT ANSWER – B, C

$\ln(x^2 - 7x + 11) = 0$

$x^2 - 7x + 11 = e^0 = 1 \rightarrow x^2 - 7x + 10 = 0$

$x = 5, 2$ can be obtained by solving above given quadratic equation.

Helpful tip – Verify that $x = 5, 2$ are valid solutions.

1.1 e) CORRECT ANSWER – D

Domain represents the set of valid input x values for which logarithmic function can be calculated.

$\log(x^2 - 7x + 10)$ can be calculated if $x^2 - 7x + 10 > 0 \rightarrow (x - 5)(x - 2) > 0$

$x = 5$ and $x = 2$ are the two critical points that need to be considered on the number line to evaluate the range of inputs for which $x^2 - 7x + 10 > 0$

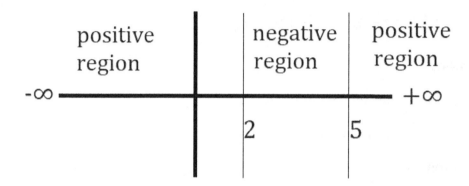

It can be observed that $x^2 - 7x + 10 > 0$ can be guaranteed for $(-\infty, 2)$ and $(5, \infty)$.

Helpful tip – Verify that $2 < x < 5$ will result in $x^2 - 7x + 10 < 0$

1.1 f) CORRECT ANSWER: $\log_{10} 7 / \log_{10} 5$

According to the logarithmic details given in NCEES® FE Reference Handbook:

$\log_b x = \log_a x / \log_a b$

In our case, $b = 5$, $a = 10$ and $x = 7$.

Therefore, $\log_5 7$ can be expressed in log-base 10 as follows:

$\log_5 7 = \log_{10} 7 / \log_{10} 5$

1.1 g) CORRECT ANSWER – B

This problem falls under the category of 'Trigonometry'.

According to the trigonometric identities given in NCEES® FE Reference Handbook:

$$\cot^2 x = \frac{1}{\tan^2 x} = \frac{\cos^2 x}{\sin^2 x} \qquad \sin^2 x + \cos^2 x = 1$$

Substituting this identity into the given trigonometric expression results in:

$$\sin^2 x \,(\cot^2 x + 1) = \sin^2 x \left(\frac{\cos^2 x}{\sin^2 x} + 1\right) = \sin^2 x + \cos^2 x = 1$$

1.1 h) CORRECT ANSWER – B

This problem falls under the category of 'Trigonometry'.

According to the trigonometric identities given in NCEES® FE Reference Handbook:

$$\cot^2 x = \frac{1}{\tan^2 x} = \frac{\cos^2 x}{\sin^2 x} \qquad \sin^2 x + \cos^2 x = 1$$

Substituting this identity into the given trigonometric expression results in:

$$\frac{\cot^2 x}{(\cot^2 x + 1)} = \frac{\frac{\cos^2 x}{\sin^2 x}}{\left(\frac{\cos^2 x}{\sin^2 x} + 1\right)} = \frac{\frac{\cos^2 x}{\sin^2 x}}{\left(\frac{\cos^2 x + \sin^2 x}{\sin^2 x}\right)} = \frac{\cos^2 x}{1} = \cos^2 x$$

1.1 i) CORRECT ANSWER – C

This problem falls under the category of 'Trigonometry'.

$$(\sin x + \cos x)^2 - 1 = (\sin^2 x + \cos^2 x + 2 \sin x \cos x) - 1$$

According to the trigonometric identities given in NCEES® FE Reference Handbook:

$$\sin^2 x + \cos^2 x = 1 \qquad \sin 2x = 2 \sin x \cos x$$

Therefore, $(\sin x + \cos x)^2 - 1 = (1) + (\sin 2x) - 1 = \sin 2x$

1.1 j) CORRECT ANSWER – D

This problem falls under the category of 'Trigonometry'.

$$\csc^2 x \cot^2 x + \csc^2 x = \csc^2 x \,(\cot^2 x + 1)$$

According to the trigonometric identities given in NCEES® FE Reference Handbook:

$$\cot^2 x + 1 = \csc^2 x$$

Therefore, $\csc^2 x \,(\cot^2 x + 1) = \csc^2 x \,(\csc^2 x) = \csc^4 x$

1.1 k) CORRECT ANSWER: 2m

According to the 'Law of Sines' given in NCEES® FE Reference Handbook:

$$\frac{a}{\sin A} = \frac{b}{\sin B} = \frac{c}{\sin C}$$

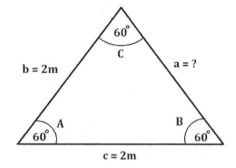

$$\frac{a}{\sin 60°} = \frac{2m}{\sin 60°}$$

$$a = \frac{(2m)\cancel{(\sin 60°)}}{\cancel{\sin 60°}} = 2m$$

Note – Equilateral triangle has equal sides and equal angles.

1.1 l) CORRECT ANSWER – A

According to the 'Law of Cosines' given in NCEES® FE Reference Handbook:

$$a^2 = b^2 + c^2 - 2bc \cos A$$

$$A = \cos^{-1}\frac{b^2 + c^2 - a^2}{2bc}$$

$$A = \cos^{-1}\frac{3.46^2 + 4^2 - 2^2}{2(3.46)(4)} = 30°$$

$$b^2 = a^2 + c^2 - 2ac \cos B$$

$$B = \cos^{-1}\frac{a^2 + c^2 - b^2}{2ac}$$

$$B = \cos^{-1}\frac{2^2 + 4^2 - 3.46^2}{2(2)(4)} = 60°$$

The sum of angles in a triangle = 180°.

Therefore, $A + B + C = 180°$

$C = 180° - A - B = 90°$

1.2 Complex Numbers - Solutions

Consult NCEES® FE Reference Handbook – Pages 36 - 37 for reference

1.2 a) CORRECT ANSWER - B

This problem falls under the category of 'Algebra of Complex Numbers'.

$$a = 8 + 4j \qquad b = 5 + 0j$$

$$a - b = (8 + 4j) - (5 + 0j)$$

$$a - b = 3 + 4j$$

Polar representation of given complex number can be found as shown below:

$$r = |3 + 4j| = \sqrt{3^2 + 4^2} = 5$$

$$\theta = \tan^{-1}\left(\frac{4}{3}\right) = 53°$$

Therefore, $a - b = 5\underline{/53^0}$ in polar format.

Helpful tip – Complex number arithmetic can be performed quickly using calculators.

1.2 b) CORRECT ANSWER - C

This problem falls under the category of 'Algebra of Complex Numbers'.

$a = 4 + 4j = 5.66\underline{/45^0}$ in polar format.

$b = 2 + 3j = 3.61\underline{/56.3^0}$ in polar format.

$a/b = (5.66\underline{/45^0})/(3.61\underline{/56.3^0})$

$a/b = (1.56\underline{/45^0\text{-}56.3^0}) = (1.56\underline{/\text{-}11^0})$

Helpful tip – Complex number division can be performed easily in polar form.

1.2 c) CORRECT ANSWER - C

This problem falls under the category of 'Algebra of Complex Numbers'.

$$a = 2\underline{/30^0} \qquad b = 4\underline{/15^0}$$

$$a \times b = (2\underline{/30^0})\,(4\underline{/15^0}) = 8\underline{/45^0}$$

$$a \times b = 8\cos 45° + j8\sin 45° = 5.7 + 5.7j$$

Helpful tip – Complex number multiplication can be easily performed in polar form.

1.2 d) CORRECT ANSWER - C

This problem falls under the category of 'Algebra of Complex Numbers'.

$a = 4\underline{/30^0} = 4\cos 30° + j4\sin 30° = 3.46 + 2j$

$b = 6\underline{/30^0} = 6\cos 30° + j6\sin 30° = 5.2 + 3j$

$a + b = (3.46 + 2j) + (5.2 + 3j) = 8.66 + 5j$

$a + b = 8.66 + 5j$

Helpful tip –Addition/subtraction of complex number can be easily performed in rectangular form.

1.2 e) CORRECT ANSWER - D

This problem falls under the category of 'Algebra of Complex Numbers'.

$5(\cos 53^0 + j\sin 53^0)$ is rectangular form of $3 + 4j$.

$5e^{j53}$ is Euler's form of $3 + 4j$.

$5\underline{/53^0}$ is polar form of $3 + 4j$.

Therefore, all options are accurate representations of $3 + 4j$.

1.2 f) CORRECT ANSWER: $-12 - 24j$

$Z = (2 + 6j) \times (3 + 3j)$

$Z = 6 + 6j + 18j + 18j^2$

$Z = 6 + 24j + 18(-1)$

$Z = 6 + 24j - 18 = -12 + 24j$

$Z^* = -12 - 24j$

1.2 g) CORRECT ANSWER - C

According to the Euler's Identity:

$$\cos\theta = \frac{e^{j\theta} + e^{-j\theta}}{2}$$

$$\sin\theta = \frac{e^{j\theta} - e^{-j\theta}}{2j}$$

$$2\cos\theta + j4\sin\theta = 2\frac{e^{j\theta} + e^{-j\theta}}{2} + j4\frac{e^{j\theta} - e^{-j\theta}}{2j}$$

$$2\cos\theta + j4\sin\theta = e^{j\theta} + e^{-j\theta} + 2(e^{j\theta} - e^{-j\theta})$$

$$2\cos\theta + j4\sin\theta = 3e^{j\theta} - e^{-j\theta}$$

1.3 Discrete Mathematics and Progressions - Solutions
Consult NCEES® FE Reference Handbook – Pages 34 – 35, 50 for reference

1.3 a) CORRECT ANSWER - C

This problem falls under the category of 'Discrete Math – Set Theory'.

'Set A' is defined as the proper subset of 'Set B' if every element in 'Set A' is also present in 'Set B', and there exists at least one element in 'Set B' which is not present in 'Set A'.

According to above given definition only {2, 4, 6} qualifies as a proper subset of {2, 4, 6, 8, 10, 12}.

1.3 b) CORRECT ANSWER - B

This problem falls under the category of 'Discrete Math – Set Theory'.

'Set A' is defined as a subset of 'Set B' if every element in 'Set A' is also present in 'Set B'.

Equal sets are also subsets. According to the definition {a, b, c, d, e} qualifies as a subset of {a, b, c, d, e}.

1.3 c) CORRECT ANSWER - A

This problem falls under the category of 'Discrete Math – Set Theory'.

{1, 2, 3, 4, 5} and {a, b, c, d, e} are examples of disjoint sets because they do not share any common element.

1.3 d) CORRECT ANSWER - B

This problem falls under the category of 'Discrete Math – Set Theory'.

Cartesian product of A x B contains ordered pairs in the format (a, b).

Therefore, {(1,a),(1,b),(1,c),(1,d),(2,a),(2,b),(2,c),(2,d)} is the cartesian product of {1,2} x {a, b, c, d}.

1.3 e) CORRECT ANSWER - A

This problem falls under the category of 'Discrete Math – Function Characteristics'.

Function is defined as a set of relations between inputs (domain – x) and outputs (range – y) such that each input is related to only one output.

According to the definition, {(1, a), (1, b), (1, c)} is not a function because input 1 is related to multiple outputs.

1.3 f) CORRECT ANSWER - B

This problem falls under the category of 'Discrete Math – Function Characteristics'.

{(a, 1), (b, 1), (c, 2), (d, 2)} is a surjective function because each output is linked to at least one input.

Helpful tip – Understand the difference between injective, surjective and bijective functions.

1.3 g) CORRECT ANSWER: 70

According to the problem statement, progression is 2, 4, 6, 8, 10, 12 ······

It can be observed that given progression is 'Arithmetic' such that:

First term value $'a' = 2$, difference between terms $'d' = 2$, # of terms $'n' = 35$, last term $'l' = ?$

According to the arithmetic progression formula given in NCEES® FE Reference Handbook:

$l = a + (n - 1)d$

$l_{35} = 2 + (35 - 1)2 = 70$

Therefore, 35th term of the given arithmetic progression is 70.

Helpful tip – Review arithmetic progression formulas given in NCEES® FE Reference Handbook.

1.3 h) CORRECT ANSWER: 15600

This problem falls under the category of 'Progressions and Series'.

According to the problem statement, we are given an arithmetic progression such that:

First term value $'a' = 1$, # of terms $'n' = 120$, last term $'l' = 259$, sum $'S' = ?$

According to the arithmetic progression formula given in NCEES® FE Reference Handbook:

$S = n(a + l)/2$

$S = \dfrac{120(1 + 259)}{2} = 15600$

Therefore, sum of given arithmetic progression is 15600.

1.3 i) CORRECT ANSWER : 531441

This problem falls under the category of 'Progressions and Series'.

According to the problem statement, progression is 3, 9, 27, 81 ······

It can be observed that given progression is geometric such that:

First term value $'a' = 3$, common ratio $'r' = 3$, # of terms $'n' = 12$, last term $'l' = ?$

According to the geometric progression formula given in NCEES® FE Reference Handbook:

$l = ar^{n-1}$

$l_{12} = (3)(3)^{12-1} = 531441$

Therefore, 12th term of the given geometric progression is 531441.

Helpful tip – Review geometric progression formulas given in NCEES® FE Reference Handbook.

1.3 j) CORRECT ANSWER : 29524

This problem falls under the category of 'Progressions and Series'.

According to the problem statement, progression is geometric such that:

First term value $'a' = 1$, common ratio $'r' = 3$, last term $'l' = 19683, 'S' = ?$

According to the geometric progression formula given in NCEES® FE Reference Handbook:

$$S = (a - rl)/(1 - r)$$

$$S = \frac{1 - (3 \times 19683)}{1 - 3} = 29524$$

Therefore, sum of given geometric progression is 29524.

1.3 k) CORRECT ANSWER – R2

$A \cap B$ is the intersection of sets A and B.

R2 represents overlapping areas of sets A and B.

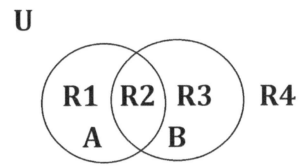

1.3 l) CORRECT ANSWER – B

It can be observed that given directed graph has 5 nodes/vertices in the form of A, B, C, D and E.

1.3 m) CORRECT ANSWER – A

The given directed graph contains following edges/arcs:

$A \rightarrow C \ (A, C)$

$A \rightarrow B \ (A, B)$

$B \rightarrow C \ (B, C)$

$D \rightarrow B \ (D, B)$

$D \rightarrow C \ (D, C)$

$C \rightarrow E \ (C, E)$

$E \rightarrow E \ (E, E)$

1.4 Analytic Geometry - Solutions
Consult NCEES® FE Reference Handbook – Pages 35, 39 - 45 for reference

1.4 a) CORRECT ANSWER - D

Angle α between two straight lines can be calculated using following equation:

$$\alpha = \tan^{-1}\frac{m_2 - m_1}{1 + m_1 m_2}$$

m_1 and m_2 are slopes of lines L_1 and L_2 respectively.

According to the problem statement:

$$y_1 = x_1 + 4 = (1)x_1 + 4 \quad m_1 = 1$$

$$y_2 = 5x_2 + 6 = (5)x_2 + 6 \quad m_2 = 5$$

$$\alpha = \tan^{-1}\frac{5 - 1}{1 + (5)(1)} = \tan^{-1}\frac{4}{6} = 33.7°$$

Helpful tip – Review straight line equations given in NCEES® FE Reference Handbook.

1.4 b) CORRECT ANSWER - C

The standard form of straight-line equation is given below.

$$y = mx + b$$

According to the problem statement, straight line passes through (2, 10) and (3, 12).

$$m = \frac{y_2 - y_1}{x_2 - x_1} = \frac{12 - 10}{3 - 2} = 2$$

$$y = 2x + b$$

Since the line passes through (2, 10), it implies that $10 = 2(2) + b$

$$b = 10 - 4 = 6$$

Therefore, equation of a straight line passing through (2, 10) and (3, 12) is $y = 2x + 6$

1.4 c) CORRECT ANSWER : $y = 2x - 5$

The standard form of straight-line equation is given below.

$$y = mx + b$$

According to the problem statement, slope is 2 and intercept is -5.

$$y = (2)x + (-5)$$

Therefore, equation of a straight line with slope 2 and intercept -5 is $y = 2x - 5$.

1.4 d) CORRECT ANSWER: $y = 4(x - 3) + 6$

Point-slope form of straight-line equation is given below:

$$y - y_1 = m(x - x_1)$$

According to the problem statement, $m = 4$ and $(x_1, y_1) = (3,6)$.

$$y - 6 = 4(x - 3)$$

$$y = 4(x - 3) + 6$$

1.4 e) CORRECT ANSWERS – A, B

The equation of straight line given in the problem statement is $y = 4x + 4$. Therefore, its slope = 4.

Perpendicular line must have a slope = $-1/4$ and its general equation will be $y = -x/4 + b$.

Straight line equations given below meet above mentioned requirements:

$$y = -\frac{x}{4}$$

$$y = -x/4 + 4$$

Note: y-intercept $'b'$ is irrelevant for this problem.

1.4 f) CORRECT ANSWER - A

Standard forms of parabola equations are given below.

$(y - k)^2 = 2p(x - h)$ Parabola opening on the positive x-axis.

$(y - k)^2 = -2p(x - h)$ Parabola opening on the negative x-axis.

$(x - h)^2 = 2p(y - k)$ Parabola opening on the positive y-axis.

$(x - h)^2 = -2p(y - k)$ Parabola opening on the negative y-axis.

It can be observed that $(x - 4)^2 = 2(y - 2)$ represents a parabola opening on the positive y-axis.

1.4 g) CORRECT ANSWER - B

Standard forms of ellipse equations are given below.

$\frac{(x-h)^2}{a^2} + \frac{(y-k)^2}{b^2} = 1 \quad a > b$ Ellipse with a horizontal major axis (wide ellipse).

$\frac{(x-h)^2}{b^2} + \frac{(y-k)^2}{a^2} = 1 \quad a > b$ Ellipse with a vertical major axis (tall ellipse).

It can be observed that $\frac{(x-2)^2}{100} + \frac{(y-4)^2}{144} = 1$ represents a tall ellipse with a vertical major axis.

1.4 h) CORRECT ANSWER - D

Standard forms of hyperbola equations are given below.

$\frac{(x-h)^2}{a^2} - \frac{(y-k)^2}{b^2} = 1$ Hyperbola opening on the x-axis (sideways).

$\frac{(y-k)^2}{a^2} - \frac{(x-h)^2}{b^2} = 1$ Hyperbola opening on the y-axis (upwards/downwards).

It can be observed that $\frac{(y-4)^2}{100} - \frac{(x-2)^2}{144} = 1$ represents a hyperbola that opens upwards/downwards.

1.4 i) CORRECT ANSWER – See Solution.

It can be observed that given conic section is a parabola with following standard equation:

$(x - h)^2 = 2p(y - k)$ Parabola opening on the positive y-axis.

According to the problem statement: $(x - 4)^2 = 12(y - 3) = 2(6)(y - 3) \rightarrow h = 4, k = 3, p = 6$

Eccentricity of a parabola is always equal to 1.

Focus $= (h, \ k + p/2) = \left(4, 3 + \frac{6}{2}\right) = (4,6)$. Directrix = $y = k - \frac{p}{2} = 3 - \frac{6}{2} = 0$.

1.4 j) CORRECT ANSWER – See Solution.

It can be observed that given conic section is a parabola with following standard equation:

$(y - k)^2 = 2p(x - h)$ Parabola opening on the positive x-axis.

According to the problem statement: $(y - 8)^2 = 4(x - 2) = 2(2)(x - 2) \rightarrow h = 2, k = 8, p = 2$

Eccentricity of a parabola is always equal to 1.

Focus $= (h + p/2, k) = \left(2 + \frac{2}{2}, 8\right) = (3,8)$. Directrix = $x = h - \frac{p}{2} = 2 - \frac{2}{2} = 1$.

1.4 k) CORRECT ANSWER – See Solution.

$2(x - 10)^2 + 8(y - 6)^2 = 200$

Let us first convert the given conic section equation into standard form as shown below:

$$\frac{2(x - 10)^2}{200} + \frac{8(y - 6)^2}{200} = \frac{200}{200} \rightarrow \frac{(x - 10)^2}{100} + \frac{(y - 6)^2}{25} = 1 \rightarrow \frac{(x - 10)^2}{(10)^2} + \frac{(y - 6)^2}{(5)^2} = 1$$

It can be observed that given conic section is an ellipse (standard form of an ellipse is given below for reference).

$$\frac{(x - h)^2}{a^2} + \frac{(y - k)^2}{b^2} = 1$$

In our case, $a = 10, b = 5, h = 10, k = 6$. This represents a wide ellipse with a horizontal major axis.

Eccentricity of an ellipse is given by following equation:

$$e = \sqrt{1 - b^2/a^2} = \sqrt{1 - 25/100} = 0.866 \qquad c = \sqrt{a^2 - b^2} = \sqrt{75}$$

Focus $= (h \pm c, k) = (10 \pm \sqrt{75}, 6)$. Directrix $= x = \left(h \pm \dfrac{a}{e}\right) = \left(10 \pm \dfrac{10}{0.866}\right) = (10 \pm 11.54)$

1.4 l) CORRECT ANSWER – See Solution.

$$2(x - 10)^2 - 8(y - 6)^2 = 200$$

Let us first convert the given conic section equation into standard form as shown below:

$$\frac{2(x-10)^2}{200} - \frac{8(y-6)^2}{200} = \frac{200}{200} \rightarrow \frac{(x-10)^2}{100} - \frac{(y-6)^2}{25} = 1 \rightarrow \frac{(x-10)^2}{(10)^2} - \frac{(y-6)^2}{(5)^2} = 1$$

It can be observed that given conic section is a hyperbola opening along x-axis.

$$\frac{(x-h)^2}{a^2} - \frac{(y-k)^2}{b^2} = 1$$

In our case, $a = 10$, $b = 5$, $h = 10$, $k = 6$.

Eccentricity of a hyperbola is given by following equation:

$$e = \sqrt{1 + b^2/a^2} = \sqrt{1 + 25/100} = 1.11 \qquad c = \sqrt{a^2 + b^2} = \sqrt{125}$$

Focus $= (h \pm c, k) = (10 \pm \sqrt{125}, 6)$. Directrix $= x = \left(h \pm \dfrac{a}{e}\right) = \left(10 \pm \dfrac{10}{1.11}\right) = (10 \pm 9)$

1.4 m) CORRECT ANSWER - C

According to the formulas given in NCEES® FE Reference Handbook, volume (V) of a right circular cylinder is:

$$V = \pi r^2 h = \pi (1m)^2 (2m) = 6.28 m^3$$

Helpful tip – Review formulas of different geometric shapes given in NCEES® FE Reference Handbook.

1.4 n) CORRECT ANSWER - A

According to the formulas given in NCEES® FE Reference Handbook, area (A) of a right circular cone is:

$$A = \pi r \left(r + \sqrt{r^2 + h^2}\right)$$

According to the problem details: $A = \pi r(r + \sqrt{r^2 + h^2}) = A = \pi(2m)\left(2m + \sqrt{(2m)^2 + (4m)^2}\right) = 40.6 m^2$

1.4 o) CORRECT ANSWER - B

$$V_{right\ circular\ cone} = \frac{\pi r^2 h}{3} \qquad V_{right\ circular\ cylinder} = \pi r^2 h \qquad V_{paraboloid\ of\ rev} = \frac{\pi d^2 h}{8} = \frac{\pi r^2 h}{32}$$

It can be observed that right circular cylinder can hold highest volume of liquid.

1.5 Calculus - Solutions

Consult NCEES® FE Reference Handbook – Pages 45 - 49 for reference

1.5 a) CORRECT ANSWER - C

This problem falls under the category of 'Differential Calculus'.

$$f(x) = 2\tan^2 x + \sin^2 x$$

$$f'(x) = 2\frac{d}{dx}\tan^2 x + \frac{d}{dx}\sin^2 x$$

$$f'(x) = 2\left(2\tan x \frac{d}{dx}\tan x\right) + 2\sin x \frac{d}{dx}\sin x$$

According to the derivatives given in NCEES® FE Reference Handbook:

$$\frac{d}{dx}\tan x = \sec^2 x \qquad \frac{d}{dx}\sin x = \cos x$$

Substituting these formulas results in:

$$f'(x) = 4\tan x \sec^2 x + 2\sin x \cos x$$

1.5 b) CORRECT ANSWER - A

This problem falls under the category of 'Differential Calculus'.

$$f(x) = 4x^2 + 6x + 2y^2$$

$$f'(x) = 4\frac{d}{dx}x^2 + 6\frac{d}{dx}x + 2\frac{d}{dx}y^2$$

According to the derivatives given in NCEES® FE Reference Handbook:

$$\frac{d}{dx}x^n = nx^{n-1}$$

$$f'(x) = 4(2x) + 6(1) + 2(0)$$

$$f'(x) = 8x + 6$$

1.5 c) CORRECT ANSWER - B

This problem falls under the category of 'Differential Calculus'.

$$f(x) = 2\tan x \sec x$$

$$f'(x) = 2\frac{d}{dx}(\tan x \sec x)$$

$$f'(x) = 2\left(\tan x \frac{d}{dx}\sec x + \sec x \frac{d}{dx}\tan x\right)$$

According to the derivatives given in NCEES® FE Reference Handbook:

$$\frac{d}{dx}\tan x = \sec^2 x \qquad \frac{d}{dx}\sec x = \sec x \, \tan x$$

Substituting these formulas results in:

$$f'(x) = 2\big(\tan x \,(\sec x \, \tan x) + \sec x \,(\sec^2 x)\big)$$

$$f'(x) = 2(\tan^2 x \sec x + \sec^3 x)$$

1.5 d) CORRECT ANSWER - D

This problem falls under the category of 'Differential Calculus'.

$$f(x) = 2\sin^{-1} x + 2\cos^{-1} x$$

$$f'(x) = 2\frac{d}{dx}(\sin^{-1} x) + 2\frac{d}{dx}(\cos^{-1} x)$$

According to the derivatives given in NCEES® FE Reference Handbook:

$$\frac{d}{dx}\sin^{-1} x = \frac{1}{\sqrt{1-x^2}} \qquad \frac{d}{dx}\cos^{-1} x = \frac{-1}{\sqrt{1-x^2}}$$

Substituting these formulas results in:

$$f'(x) = 2\left(\frac{1}{\sqrt{1-x^2}}\right) + 2\left(\frac{-1}{\sqrt{1-x^2}}\right) \rightarrow f'(x) = 0$$

1.5 e) CORRECT ANSWER - B

$$f(x) = \frac{3x^3 + 2x}{2x + 4}$$

According to the quotient rule given in NCEES® FE Reference Handbook:

$$f'(x) = \frac{(2x+4)\frac{d}{dx}(3x^3 + 2x) - (3x^3 + 2x)\frac{d}{dx}(2x+4)}{(2x+4)^2}$$

$$f'(x) = \frac{(2x+4)(9x^2 + 2) - (3x^3 + 2x)(2)}{(2x+4)^2} = \frac{18x^3 + 4x + 36x^2 + 8 - 6x^3 - 4x}{(2x+4)^2}$$

$$f'(x) = \frac{12x^3 + 36x^2 + 8}{(2x+4)^2}$$

1.5 f) CORRECT ANSWER - B

According to the problem statement:

$$f(x) = 4x^3 + x^2 - 2x + 8 \qquad -1 \le x \le 1$$

To calculate the maximum and minimum of a function, first order derivative is calculated as shown below:

$f'(x) = 12x^2 + 2x - 2$

The roots of $f'(x)$ can be calculated using factorization, quadratic equation, or a calculator.

$12x^2 + 2x - 2 \rightarrow x = \dfrac{1}{3}, x = -1/2$

Now, we need to calculate second order derivative $f''(x) = 24x + 2$

Substituting $x = -1/2$ in second derivative equation results in negative value. Therefore, it is a local maximum.

Substituting $x = 1/3$ in second derivative equation results in positive value. Therefore, it is a local minimum.

1.5 g) CORRECT ANSWER - B

According to the problem statement:

$f(x) = 3x^3 + 3x^2 - 3x + 3 \qquad -2 \leq x \leq 1$

To calculate the maximum and minimum of a function, first order derivative is calculated as shown below:

$f'(x) = 9x^2 + 6x - 3$

The roots of $f'(x)$ can be calculated using factorization, quadratic equation, or calculator.

$9x^2 + 6x - 3 = 0 \rightarrow x = \dfrac{1}{3}, x = -1$

Now, we need to calculate second order derivative $f''(x) = 18x + 6$

Substituting $x = -1$ in second derivative equation results in negative value. Therefore, it is a local maximum.

Substituting $x = 1/3$ in second derivative equation results in positive value. Therefore, it is a local minimum.

1.5 h) CORRECT ANSWER: $x = -1/3$

In the previous problem, $f''(x) = 18x + 6$

Point of inflection is calculated by taking second order derivative and setting it to zero as shown below:

$f''(x) = 18x + 6 = 0 \rightarrow x = -1/3$

The calculated value of x is a point of inflection because at this point second derivative is zero and second derivative also changes sign as x increases through it (test by substituting incremental values).

1.5 i) CORRECT ANSWER - C

This problem falls under the category of 'Differential Calculus – L'Hospital's Rule'.

According to the problem statement:

$$\lim_{x \to 1} \dfrac{3x^2 - 2x - 1}{4x^2 + 6x - 10} = \dfrac{3(1)^2 - 2(1) - 1}{4(1)^2 + 6(1) - 10} = \dfrac{0}{0}$$

0/0 is an indeterminate form (∞/∞ is the other indeterminate form).

Therefore, we need to use L'Hospital's rule to evaluate this limit.

$$\lim_{x \to 1} \frac{3x^2 - 2x - 1}{4x^2 + 6x - 10} = \lim_{x \to 1} \frac{\frac{d}{dx}(3x^2 - 2x - 1)}{\frac{d}{dx}(4x^2 + 6x - 10)} = \lim_{x \to 1} \frac{6x - 2}{8x + 6} = \frac{6(1) - 2}{8(1) + 6} = \left(\frac{4}{14}\right) = \frac{2}{7}$$

1.5 j) CORRECT ANSWER - C

This problem falls under the category of 'Differential Calculus – L'Hospital's Rule'.

According to the problem statement:

$$\lim_{x \to \pi/2} \frac{4 \cos x}{2 - 2 \sin x} = \frac{4 \cos \pi/2}{2 - 2 \sin \pi/2} = \frac{4(0)}{2 - 2(1)} = \frac{0}{0}$$

0/0 is an indeterminate form. Therefore, we need to use L'Hospital's rule to evaluate this limit.

$$\lim_{x \to \pi/2} \frac{4 \cos x}{2 - 2 \sin x} = \lim_{x \to \pi/2} \frac{\frac{d}{dx}(4 \cos x)}{\frac{d}{dx}(2 - 2 \sin x)} = \lim_{x \to \pi/2} \frac{-4 \sin x}{-2 \cos x} = 2 \tan \frac{\pi}{2} = \infty$$

1.5 k) CORRECT ANSWER - D

This problem falls under the category of 'Integral Calculus'.

$$\int \frac{4}{x + 3} dx = 4 \int \frac{1}{x + 3} dx$$

According to the indefinite integrals given in NCEES® FE Reference Handbook:

$$\int \frac{1}{ax + b} dx = \frac{1}{a} \ln |ax + b| + C$$

Substituting this formula in given indefinite integral results in:

$$4 \frac{1}{1} \ln |x + 3| = 4 \ln |x + 3| + C$$

Helpful tip – Review tables of derivatives and indefinite integrals given in NCEES® FE Reference Handbook.

1.5 l) CORRECT ANSWER - C

This problem falls under the category of 'Integral Calculus'.

$$\int (\sin^2 x + \cos^2 x) \, dx$$

According to the trigonometric identity given in NCEES® FE Reference Handbook:

$$\sin^2 x + \cos^2 x = 1$$

Substituting this formula in given indefinite integral results in: $\int (\sin^2 x + \cos^2 x) \, dx = \int 1 \, dx = x + C$

1.5 m) CORRECT ANSWER - A

According to the integration by parts formula provided in NCEES® FE Reference Handbook:

$$\int u\,dv = uv - \int v\,du$$

For the given problem, let us assume that: $u = \ln x \rightarrow du = \frac{1}{x}dx \quad dv = xdx \rightarrow v = \frac{x^2}{2}$

$$\int 4x\ln x\,dx = 4\int u\,dv = 4\left(uv - \int v\,du\right) = 4\left(\ln x\frac{x^2}{2} - \int \frac{x^2}{2}\frac{1}{x}dx\right) = 2x^2\ln x - x^2 + C$$

1.5 n) CORRECT ANSWER: $\frac{e^2}{4} + \frac{1}{4}$

According to the trigonometric identity given in NCEES® FE Reference Handbook:

$$\int xe^{ax}\,dx = \frac{e^{ax}}{a^2}(ax - 1)$$

$$\int_0^1 xe^{2x}\,dx = \left(\frac{e^{2x}}{2^2}(2x - 1)\right)_0^1 = \left(\frac{e^{2(1)}}{4}(2(1) - 1)\right) - \left(\frac{e^{2(0)}}{4}(2(0) - 1)\right) = \frac{e^2}{4} + \frac{1}{4}$$

1.5 o) CORRECT ANSWER - C

Derivative is highest when the rate of rise over run is highest. In other words, it is a measure of the steepness of a curve. It can be observed that given function is steepest at point C.

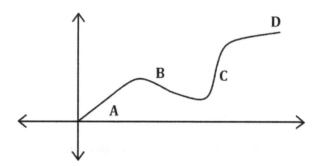

1.5 p) CORRECT ANSWER - B

Derivative is lowest when the rate of rise over run is lowest. The given function has a negative slope at point B.

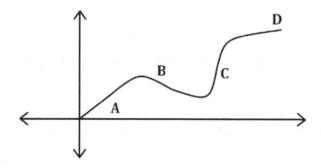

1.6 Differential Equations - Solutions
Consult NCEES® FE Reference Handbook – Pages 51 - 52 for reference

1.6 a) CORRECT ANSWER - D

This problem falls under the category of 'Differential Equations'.

$$2y' + 4y = 0 \qquad y(0) = 6$$

Standard form of 1st order differential equation with constant coefficient is given below:

$$y' + ay = 0$$

Solution of standard equation is $y = Ce^{-at}$.

Divide given equation by 2 to convert it into standard form $y' + 2y = 0$

In our case, $a = 2$. Therefore, general solution is $y = Ce^{-2t}$.

We can calculate coefficient using initial conditions as shown below:

$$y(0) = 6 \qquad 6 = Ce^{(-2)(0)} \rightarrow C = 6$$

Therefore, $y = 6e^{-2t}$

1.6 b) CORRECT ANSWER: $y = \dfrac{1 - e^{-\frac{2}{3}x^3}}{2}$

This problem falls under the category of 'Differential Equations'.

$$y' + 2x^2y = x^2$$

We can use the method of separation of variables to solve this differential equation as shown below.

$$\frac{dy}{dx} + 2x^2y = x^2 \rightarrow \frac{dy}{dx} = x^2 - 2x^2y \rightarrow \frac{dy}{dx} = x^2(1 - 2y)$$

$$\frac{1}{(1 - 2y)}dy = x^2dx$$

Taking integrals on both side of equations results in following:

$$-\frac{1}{2}\ln|1 - 2y| = \frac{x^3}{3} \rightarrow \ln|1 - 2y| = -\frac{2}{3}x^3$$

$$1 - 2y = e^{-\frac{2}{3}x^3} \rightarrow y = \frac{1 - e^{-\frac{2}{3}x^3}}{2}$$

Helpful tip – Learn separation of variables and integrating factor methods.

1.6 c) CORRECT ANSWER : $y = -\frac{x}{4} - \frac{1}{16} + Ce^{4x}$

$2y' = 8y + 2x$ needs to be converted into standard form $y' + P(x)y = Q(x)$ as shown below.

$2y' - 8y = 2x \rightarrow y' - 4y = x$

Integrating factor method will be used to solve this differential equation because variables cannot be separated.

Step # 1 – Determine the integrating factor $e^{\int P(x)dx}$.

$e^{\int P(x)dx} = e^{\int -4dx} = e^{-4x}$

Step # 2 – Multiply the entire equation by the integrating factor.

$e^{-4x}(y' - 4y) = x(e^{-4x})$

Left hand side of the equation can be expressed as $\frac{d}{dx}(e^{-4x}y)$.

$\frac{d}{dx}(e^{-4x}y) = x(e^{-4x})$

Step # 3 – Integrate both sides of the equation.

$\int \frac{d}{dx}(e^{-4x}y) = \int x(e^{-4x})$

$\int x(e^{ax}) = \frac{e^{ax}}{a^2}(ax - 1)$

$\int x(e^{-4x}) = \frac{e^{-4x}}{(-4)^2}(-4x - 1) + C = -\frac{xe^{-4x}}{4} - \frac{e^{-4x}}{16} + C$

$e^{-4x}y = -\frac{xe^{-4x}}{4} - \frac{e^{-4x}}{16} + C$

$y = -\frac{x}{4} - \frac{1}{16} + Ce^{4x}$

1.6 d) CORRECT ANSWER : $y = (C_1 + C_2x)e^{-3x}$

$y'' + 6y' + 9y = 0$

We can use the method of undetermined coefficients, as explained in NCEES® FE Reference Handbook.

The solution will be of form $y = Ce^{rx}$ with characteristic equation: $r^2 + 6r + 9 = 0$

Comparing this equation with the standard form $r^2 + ar + b = 0$ shows that $a = 6, b = 9$.

Solving $r^2 + 6r + 9 = 0$ results in $r_1 = r_2 = -3$

Since $a^2 = 4b = 36$, solution is critically-damped and it can be represented as follows.

$y = (C_1 + C_2x)e^{r_1x} \rightarrow y = (C_1 + C_2x)e^{-3x}$

194

1.6 e) CORRECT ANSWER : $y = 4e^{2x} + 2e^{-4x}$

This problem falls under the category of 'Differential Equations'.

$$y'' + 2y' - 8y = 0 \qquad y(0) = 6 \quad y'(0) = 0$$

We can use the method of undetermined coefficients, as explained in NCEES® FE Reference Handbook.

The solution will be of the form $y = Ce^{rx}$ with characteristic equation: $r^2 + 2r - 8 = 0$

Comparing this equation with standard form $r^2 + ar + b = 0$ shows that $a = 2, b = -8$.

Solving $r^2 + 2r - 8 = 0$ results in $r_1 = 2, r_2 = -4$

Since $a^2 = 4 > 4b = -32$, solution is overdamped and can be represented as shown below:

$$y = C_1 e^{r_1 x} + C_2 e^{r_2 x} \quad y' = C_1 r_1 e^{r_1 x} + C_2 r_2 e^{r_2 x}$$

We can calculate the coefficients using initial conditions as shown below:

$$y(0) = 6 \rightarrow \quad 6 = C_1 e^{(2)(0)} + C_2 e^{(-4)(0)} = C_1 + C_2 \rightarrow C_1 = 6 - C_2 \; Eq \# 1$$

$$y'(0) = 0 \rightarrow \quad 0 = C_1 2 e^{(2)(0)} + C_2(-4)e^{(-4)(0)} = 2C_1 - 4C_2 = 0 \quad Eq \# 2$$

Substituting the value of C_1 from equation # 1 into equation # 2 results in following:

$$2(6 - C_2) - 4C_2 = 0$$

$$12 - 2C_2 - 4C_2 = 0$$

Solving these equations results in $C_1 = 4$ and $C_2 = 2$. Therefore, $y = 4e^{2x} + 2e^{-4x}$

1.6 f) CORRECT ANSWER - A

This problem falls under the category of 'Differential Equations'.

$$2y'' + 4y' + 8y = 0$$

Divide the given equation by 2 to convert into standard form $y'' + 2y' + 4y = 0$

We can use the method of undetermined coefficients, as explained in NCEES® FE Reference Handbook.

The solution will be of the form $y = Ce^{rx}$ with characteristic equation: $r^2 + 2r + 4 = 0$

Comparing this equation with standard form $r^2 + ar + b = 0$ shows that $a = 2, b = 4$.

Since $a^2 = 4 < 4b = 16$, solution is underdamped.

1.6 g) CORRECT ANSWER – 2nd order linear homogeneous differential equation

$y'' + 8y' + 12y = 0$ is an example of 2nd order linear homogeneous differential equation.

Helpful tip – Review the differences between several types of differential equations.

1.7 Matrix and Vector Analysis - Solutions
Consult NCEES® FE Reference Handbook – Pages 57 - 60 for reference

1.7 a) CORRECT ANSWER - C

This problem falls under the category of 'Matrices'.

According to the problem statement:

$$A = \begin{bmatrix} 1 & 0 & 0 \\ 0 & 1 & 0 \\ 0 & 0 & 1 \end{bmatrix} \quad B = \begin{bmatrix} 0 & 0 & 2 \\ 0 & 2 & 0 \\ 2 & 0 & 0 \end{bmatrix}$$

$$A + B = \begin{bmatrix} 1+0 & 0+0 & 0+2 \\ 0+0 & 1+2 & 0+0 \\ 0+2 & 0+0 & 1+0 \end{bmatrix} = \begin{bmatrix} 1 & 0 & 2 \\ 0 & 3 & 0 \\ 2 & 0 & 1 \end{bmatrix}$$

Helpful tip – Matrix operations (addition, subtraction, multiplication, inverse) using calculator can save time and reduce chances of error. Alternatively, you may perform conversion by hand and cross-check it with calculator.

1.7 b) CORRECT ANSWER - D

This problem falls under the category of 'Matrices'.

According to the problem statement:

$$A = \begin{bmatrix} 1 & 0 & 0 \\ 0 & 1 & 0 \\ 0 & 0 & 1 \end{bmatrix} \quad B = \begin{bmatrix} 1 & 0 \\ 0 & 1 \end{bmatrix}$$

Matrix addition requires both matrices to have same number of rows and columns. In this case, the two matrices do not have same dimensions. Therefore, given matrices cannot be added.

1.7 c) CORRECT ANSWER - A

This problem falls under the category of 'Matrices'.

According to the problem statement:

$$A = \begin{bmatrix} 2 & 1 \\ 4 & 2 \\ 6 & 3 \end{bmatrix} \quad B = \begin{bmatrix} 1 & 0 \\ 2 & 1 \end{bmatrix}$$

$$A \times B = \begin{bmatrix} 2\times1+1\times2 & 2\times0+1\times1 \\ 4\times1+2\times2 & 4\times0+2\times1 \\ 6\times1+3\times2 & 6\times0+3\times1 \end{bmatrix} = \begin{bmatrix} 4 & 1 \\ 8 & 2 \\ 12 & 3 \end{bmatrix}$$

1.7 d) CORRECT ANSWER - 14

This problem falls under the category of 'Matrices'.

$$det \begin{bmatrix} 4 & 5 \\ 2 & 6 \end{bmatrix} = (4 \times 6) - (2 \times 5) = 14$$

Helpful tip – Learn how to find the determinant of a 2 x 2 matrix using calculator.

1.7 e) CORRECT ANSWER: $\begin{bmatrix} \frac{3}{7} & -\frac{5}{14} \\ -\frac{1}{7} & \frac{2}{7} \end{bmatrix}$

Matrix inverse is calculated using following equation.

$$A^{-1} = \frac{adj(A)}{|A|} = \frac{adj \begin{bmatrix} 4 & 5 \\ 2 & 6 \end{bmatrix}}{det \begin{bmatrix} 4 & 5 \\ 2 & 6 \end{bmatrix}} = \frac{\begin{bmatrix} 6 & -5 \\ -2 & 4 \end{bmatrix}}{14} = \begin{bmatrix} 6/14 & -5/14 \\ -2/14 & 4/14 \end{bmatrix} = \begin{bmatrix} \frac{3}{7} & -\frac{5}{14} \\ -\frac{1}{7} & \frac{2}{7} \end{bmatrix}$$

Helpful tip – Learn how to find the inverse of a 2 x 2 matrix using calculator.

1.7 f) CORRECT ANSWER - D

According to the problem statement:

$$A = \begin{bmatrix} 2 & 1 \\ 4 & 2 \\ 6 & 3 \end{bmatrix} \quad B = \begin{bmatrix} 7 & 10 \\ 8 & 11 \\ 9 & 12 \end{bmatrix}$$

Matrix multiplication requires the number of columns in first matrix to be equal to the number of rows in the second matrix. In this case, the two matrices do not meet this requirement.

1.7 g) CORRECT ANSWER: A

This problem falls under the category of 'Matrices'.

$A \times B$ is not always equal to $B \times A$.

1.7 h) CORRECT ANSWER: 0

This problem falls under the category of 'Matrices'.

$$det \begin{bmatrix} 2 & 4 & 6 \\ 8 & 10 & 12 \\ 1 & 3 & 5 \end{bmatrix} = 2[(10)(5) - (3)(12)] - 4[(8)(5) - (12)(1)] + 6[(8)(3) - (10)(1)]$$

$$det \begin{bmatrix} 2 & 4 & 6 \\ 8 & 10 & 12 \\ 1 & 3 & 5 \end{bmatrix} = 2(14) - 4(28) + 6(14) = 0$$

Helpful tip – Learn how to find the determinant and inverse of a 3 x 3 matrix using calculator.

1.7 i) CORRECT ANSWER: 16

$$\vec{A} = 2i + j + 3k \quad \vec{B} = i + 2j + 4k$$

$$\vec{A}.\vec{B} = (2i + j + 3k).(i + 2j + 4k)$$

$$\vec{A}.\vec{B} = 2.1 + 1.2 + 3.4 = 16$$

Helpful tip – Also learn how to calculate angle between vectors $\vec{A}$ and $\vec{B}$ using cross product. Typically, it is easier to calculate angle using dot product.

1.7 j) CORRECT ANSWER: $-4i + j + 10k$

$$\vec{A} = 3i + 2j + k \qquad \vec{B} = i + 4j + 0k$$

$$\vec{A} \times \vec{B} = (3i + 2j + k) \times (i + 4j + 0k) = \begin{vmatrix} i & j & k \\ 3 & 2 & 1 \\ 1 & 4 & 0 \end{vmatrix}$$

$$\vec{A} \times \vec{B} = (2 \times 0 - 1 \times 4)i - (3 \times 0 - 1 \times 1)j + (3 \times 4 - 2 \times 1)k$$

$$\vec{A} \times \vec{B} = -4i + j + 10k$$

Helpful tip – Learn how to use calculator to find vector product.

1.7 k) CORRECT ANSWER - B

We can use head-tail rule to confirm that resultant vector will be Option B  as shown below.

$$\vec{X} + \vec{Y} =$$

Helpful tip – Review head-tail rule for vector addition and subtraction. Try to calculate $\vec{X} - \vec{Y}$.

Chapter # 2 – Probability and Statistics
2.1 Measures of Central Tendencies and Dispersions
Consult NCEES® FE Reference Handbook – Page 63 for reference

2.1 a) CORRECT ANSWER: 6

Arithmetic mean of given data set can be calculated as shown below.

$$\bar{X} = \frac{1}{6}(2 + 4 + 10 + 8 + 4 + 8) = \frac{36}{6} = 6$$

2.1 b) CORRECT ANSWER: 88.2°F

Weighted average of given data set can be calculated as shown below.

$$\overline{X_w} = \frac{(\sum w_i X_i)}{\sum w_i} = \frac{(0.50 \times 90°F) + (0.30 \times 84°F) + (0.10 \times 88°F) + (0.10 \times 92°F)}{0.50 + 0.30 + 0.10 + 0.10} = 88.2°F$$

Helpful tip – Arithmetic mean $\bar{X}$ is a special case of weighted average in which all weights are equal.

2.1 c) CORRECT ANSWER: $\sqrt{20/3}$

Sample standard deviation is calculated by using the equation given below:

$$s = \sqrt{\frac{\sum_{i=1}^{n}(X_i - \bar{X})^2}{n - 1}}$$

$$\bar{X} = \frac{1}{4}(2 + 4 + 6 + 8) = 5, \quad n = 4$$

$$s = \sqrt{\frac{(2 - 5)^2 + (4 - 5)^2 + (6 - 5)^2 + (8 - 5)^2}{4 - 1}} = \sqrt{\frac{(3)^2 + (1)^2 + (1)^2 + (3)^2}{3}}$$

$$s = \sqrt{20/3}$$

Helpful tip – It is important to understand the difference between 'sample' and 'population' because formulas are different for sample and population.

2.1 d) CORRECT ANSWER: 2.21

Sample geometric mean is calculated by using the equation given below:

$$s = \sqrt[n]{X_1 X_2 X_3 \cdots X_n}$$

$$s = \sqrt[4]{(1)(2)(3)(4)}$$

$$s = \sqrt[4]{24} = 2.21$$

Helpful tip – Review measure of central tendency/dispersion formulas given in NCEES® FE Reference Handbook.

2.1 e) CORRECT ANSWER : 6.9

Sample root mean square is calculated by using the equation given below:

$$s = \sqrt{\frac{1}{n} \sum X_1^2}$$

$$s = \sqrt{\frac{1}{4}(3^2 + 5^2 + 6^2 + 11^2)}$$

$$s = \sqrt{\frac{1}{4}(9 + 25 + 36 + 121)} = 6.9$$

2.1 f) CORRECT ANSWER : 3

Let us first arrange the given data set in ascending order.

$$2, 3, 7, 1, 4, 9, 0 \rightarrow 0, 1, 2, 3, 4, 7, 9$$

It can be observed that the median of given data set is 3 because it bisects the data set.

2.1 g) CORRECT ANSWER : 80

Let us first arrange the given data set in ascending order.

$$90, 60, 70, 110, 50, 40, 200, 210 \rightarrow 40, 50, 60, 70, 90, 110, 200, 210$$

It can be observed that we have even number of terms (n = 8) due to which median will be average of $\left(\frac{n}{2}\right)^{th}$ and $\left(\frac{n}{2}+1\right)^{th}$ terms. Therefore, median = $(70 + 90)/2 = 80$

2.1 h) CORRECT ANSWER : 3

Mode of a given data set is the value that occurs with greatest frequency. It can be observed that in the given data set 1, 3, 3, 4, 9, 7, 3, 4, the value 3 occurs with highest frequency.

Helpful tip – There can be more than one modes in a data set. For instance, in this example if we replace 9 with 4, then it becomes a bimodal data set with two modes i.e. 3 and 4.

2.1 i) CORRECT ANSWER : 110

According to the definition given NCEES® FE Reference Handbook, sample range is the difference between largest and smallest sample value.

In our case, largest and smallest sample values are 120 and 10 respectively. Sample range = 120 – 10 = 110.

2.1 j) CORRECT ANSWER – Influenced by outliers

Mean is highly influenced by outliers. Standard deviation is a measure of dispersion. Median is marginally influenced by outliers.

2.2 Permutation/Combination & Laws of Probability - Solutions

Consult NCEES® FE Reference Handbook – Pages 64 – 65 for reference

2.2 a) CORRECT ANSWER: B

Since the order of selection is important, we need to calculate permutation $P(n,r)$ where $n = 12, r = 5$.

$$P(n,r) = P(12,5) = 95040$$

2.2 b) CORRECT ANSWER: C

Since the order of selection is not important, we need to calculate combination $C(n,r)$ where $n = 12, r = 5$.

$$C(n,r) = C(12,5) = 792$$

2.2 c) CORRECT ANSWER: A

Since the order of selection is important, we need to calculate permutation $P(n,r)$ where $n = 12, r = n = 12$.

$$P(n,r) = P(n,n) = P(12,12) = 12! = 479001600$$

2.2 d) CORRECT ANSWER: D

Since the order of selection isn't important, we need to calculate combination $C(n,r)$ with $n = 12, r = n = 12$.

$$C(n,r) = C(n,n) = C(12,12) = 1$$

2.2 e) CORRECT ANSWER : 0.5, 0.5

$$P(A) = \frac{N(A)}{N(S)} \qquad P(B) = \frac{N(B)}{N(S)}$$

$N(A)$ and $N(B)$ represent the total number of possible outcomes belonging to events A and B respectively.

$N(S)$ represents the total number of possible outcomes belonging to sample space S.

$$P(A) = \frac{N(A)}{N(S)} = \frac{5}{10} = 0.5$$

$$P(B) = \frac{N(B)}{N(S)} = \frac{5}{10} = 0.5$$

2.2 f) CORRECT ANSWER : 0.20

Probability of both A and B occurring simultaneously = $P(A,B)$

$$P(A,B) = \frac{N(A \cap B)}{N(S)}$$

$N(A \cap B)$ represents the total number of possible outcomes that are common between events A and B.

$$P(A,B) = \frac{N(A \cap B)}{N(S)} = \frac{2}{10} = 0.20$$

2.2 g) CORRECT ANSWER : 0.80

Probability that either A or B will occur alone or that both events will occur together can be calculated as:

$$P(A + B) = P(A) + P(B) - P(A, B)$$

$$P(A + B) = 0.50 + 0.50 - 0.20 = 0.80$$

2.2 h) CORRECT ANSWER : 0.40

Probability that B occurs given that A has already occurred is given by following equation:

$$P(B|A) = \frac{P(A, B)}{P(A)} = \frac{0.20}{0.50} = 0.40$$

2.2 i) CORRECT ANSWER : 0.40

Probability that A occurs given that B has already occurred is given by following equation:

$$P(A|B) = \frac{P(A, B)}{P(B)} = \frac{0.20}{0.50} = 0.40$$

2.2 j) CORRECT ANSWER - C

This problem falls under the category of 'Law of Total Probability' which is given by equation below:

$$P(A + B) = P(A) + P(B) - P(A, B)$$

Probability of sunny weather = $P(A) = 0.25$

Probability of cloudy weather = $P(B) = 0.35$

Probability of both sunny and cloudy weather = $P(A, B) = 0.15$

Probability of sunny weather, cloudy weather or both = $P(A + B) = 0.25 + 0.35 - 0.15 = 0.45$

2.2 k) CORRECT ANSWER: 0.50

This problem falls under the category of 'Law of Total Probability' which is given by equation below:

$$P(A + B) = P(A) + P(B) - P(A, B) = 0.20 + 0.40 - 0.10 = 0.50$$

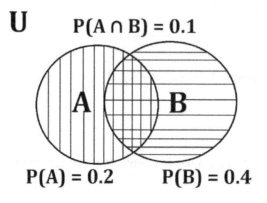

2.3 Probability Distributions - Solutions

Consult NCEES® FE Reference Handbook – Pages 65 – 67 for reference

2.3 a) CORRECT ANSWER – B

This problem falls under the category of 'Bayes' Theorem'.

According to NCEES® FE Reference Handbook, Bayes' Theorem is given by equation shown below:

$$P(B_j|A) = \frac{P(B_j)P(A|B_j)}{\sum_{i=1}^{n} P(A|B_i)\, P(B_i)}$$

$P(A_j)$ is the probability of event A_j in population of A.

$P(B_j)$ is the probability of event B_j in population of B.

Probability of an adult suffering major depression at some point in life = P(D) = 8% = 0.08

Probability of an adult not suffering major depression at some point in life = P(D') =1 – P(D) = 92%

Probability of a positive result given that person has depression (true positive) = P(+|D) = 90% = 0.90

Probability of a positive result given that person doesn't have depression (false positive) = P(+|D') = 10% = 0.1

Probability of having depression given positive result = P(D|+) = ?

$$P(D|+) = \frac{P(D)P(+|D)}{P(+|D)P(D) + P(+|D')P(D')}$$

$$P(D|+) = \frac{(0.08)(0.90)}{(0.08)(0.90) + (0.92)(0.10)} = 43.9\% \cong 44\%$$

2.3 b) CORRECT ANSWER: 0.24

Probability of a customer preferring online shopping = P(Online) = 0.20

Probability of a customer preferring in-store shopping = P(Store) = 0.80

Probability of a customer under 30 years of age given he/she prefers online shopping = P(30|Online) = 0.50

Probability of a customer under 30 years of age given he/she prefers in-store shopping = P(30|Store) = 0.40

Probability of a customer preferring online shopping given that customer is less than 30 years old = ?

$$P(Online|30) = \frac{P(Online)P(30|Online)}{P(30|Online)P(Online) + P(30|Store)P(Store)}$$

$$P(Online|30) = \frac{(0.20)(0.50)}{(0.50)(0.20) + (0.40)(0.80)} = 0.238 \cong 0.24$$

2.3 c) CORRECT ANSWER: 0.228

This problem falls under the category of 'Binomial Distribution' which is given by equation below:

$$P_n(x) = C(n,x)p^x q^{n-x}$$

n = # of on-campus interviews.

x = # of hiring.

q = Failure/rejection probability.

p = Success/hiring probability.

According to the given scenario:

$n = 30$ $x = 2$ $p = 0.10$ $q = 0.90$

$$P_{30}(2) = C(30,2)0.1^2 0.9^{30-2} = 0.228 = 22.8\%$$

Therefore, the engineering firm has 22.8% chance of hiring 2 new graduates after 30 interviews.

Helpful tip – Binomial distribution involves binary outcomes such as yes/no, pass/fail, head/tail etc. To gain better understanding, it is recommended to review Binomial distribution examples and practice problems.

2.3 d) CORRECT ANSWER: 0.51

This problem falls under the category of 'Binomial Distribution' which is given by equation below:

$$P_n(x) = C(n,x)p^x q^{n-x}$$

n = # of grand slam tournaments.

x = # of tournament successes.

q = Failure probability.

p = Success probability.

According to the given scenario:

$n = 4$ $x = 2,3,4$ $p = 0.40$ $q = 0.60$

$$P_4(2) = C(4,2)0.4^2 0.6^{4-2} = 0.34 = 34\%$$

$$P_4(3) = C(4,3)0.4^3 0.6^{4-3} = 0.15 = 15\%$$

$$P_4(4) = C(4,4)0.4^4 0.6^{4-4} = 0.025 = 2.5\%$$

$$P_T = P_4(2) + P_4(3) + P_4(4) = 0.34 + 0.15 + 0.025 = 0.51$$

Therefore, tennis player has 51% chance of winning 2 to 4 grand slam tournaments out of 4.

2.3 e) CORRECT ANSWER : 0.0228

This problem falls under the category of 'Gaussian distribution'.

According to the problem statement $x = 700, \mu = 740, \sigma = 20$.

Since, $\mu \neq 0$ & $\sigma \neq 1$ this distribution should be standardized as shown below:

$$Z = \frac{x - \mu}{\sigma} = \frac{700 - 740}{20} = -2$$

Note that, $Z < -2$ is the same as $Z > 2$.

According to the unit normal distribution table given in NCEES® FE Reference Handbook:

$$P(Z > 2) = R(2) = 0.0228$$

Helpful tip – Learn how to use normal distribution table given in NCEES® FE Reference Handbook.

2.3 f) CORRECT ANSWER : 0.1359

According to the problem statement $x_1 = 12 \quad x_2 = 14 \quad \mu = 10, \sigma = 2$.

Since, $\mu \neq 0$ & $\sigma \neq 1$ this distribution should be standardized as shown below:

$$Z_1 = \frac{12 - 10}{2} = \frac{2}{2} = 1$$

$$Z_2 = \frac{14 - 10}{2} = \frac{4}{2} = 2$$

$$Z_1 \leq Z \leq Z_2$$

$$P(Z_1 \leq Z \leq Z_2) = F(2) - F(1) = 0.9772 - 0.8413 = 0.1359$$

2.3 g) CORRECT ANSWER : 0.0013

According to the problem statement $x = 2, \mu = 8, \sigma = 2$.

Since, $\mu \neq 0$ & $\sigma \neq 1$ this distribution needs to be standardized as shown below:

$$Z = \frac{2 - 8}{2} = \frac{-6}{2} = -3$$

Using the unit normal distribution table, we are interested in finding $P(-\infty \leq Z \leq -3)$.

Although such probability does not exist in the table, it is equal to $P(3 \leq Z \leq \infty)$ because of symmetry.

$$P(3 \leq Z \leq \infty) = R(3) = 0.0013 = 0.13\%$$

2.3 h) CORRECT ANSWER : 0.1587

According to the problem statement $x = 10$, $\mu = 8$, $\sigma = 2$.

Since, $\mu \neq 0$ & $\sigma \neq 1$ this distribution needs to be standardized as shown below:

$$Z = \frac{10 - 8}{2} = \frac{2}{2} = 1$$

Using the unit normal distribution table, we are interested in finding $P(1 \leq Z \leq \infty)$.

$$P(1 \leq Z \leq \infty) = R(1) = 0.1587 = 15.87\%$$

2.3 i) CORRECT ANSWER : 0.1359

According to the problem statement $x_1 = 4$, $x_2 = 6$, $\mu = 8$, $\sigma = 2$.

Since, $\mu \neq 0$ & $\sigma \neq 1$ this distribution needs to be standardized as shown below:

$$Z_1 = \frac{4 - 8}{2} = -\frac{4}{2} = -2 \quad Z_2 = \frac{6 - 8}{2} = -\frac{2}{2} = -1$$

Using the unit normal distribution table, we are interested in finding $P(-2 \leq Z \leq -1)$.

Although such probability does not exist in the table, it is equal to $P(1 \leq Z \leq 2)$ because of symmetry.

$$P(1 \leq Z \leq 2) = R(1) - R(2) = 0.1587 - 0.0228 = 0.1359 = 13.59\%$$

2.4 Expected values - Solutions

Consult NCEES® FE Reference Handbook – Pages 65 - 66 for reference

2.4 a) CORRECT ANSWER: 3.18

This problem falls under the category of 'Expected Values'.

According to the formula given in NCEES® FE Reference Handbook:

$$E[X] = \sum_{k=1}^{n} x_k f(x_k) = x_1 f(x_1) + x_2 f(x_2) + x_3 f(x_3)$$

$$E[X] = (2)\left(\frac{1}{33}\right)(3 \times 2 + 2) + (3)\left(\frac{1}{33}\right)(3 \times 3 + 2) + (4)\left(\frac{1}{33}\right)(3 \times 4 + 2) = 3.18$$

Helpful tip – Review probability density function, cumulative distribution function and expected values formulas given in NCEES® FE Reference Handbook.

2.4 b) CORRECT ANSWER: 0.63

This problem falls under the category of 'Expected Values'.

According to the formula given in NCEES® FE Reference Handbook:

$$\sigma^2 = V[X] = \sum_{k=1}^{n}(x_k - \mu)^2 f(x_k) = (x_1 - \mu)^2 f(x_1) + (x_2 - \mu)^2 f(x_2) + (x_3 - \mu)^2 f(x_3)$$

$$\mu = E[X] = 3.18$$

$$\sigma^2 = V[X] = \frac{1}{33}[(2 - 3.18)^2(3 \times 2 + 2) + (3 - 3.18)^2(3 \times 3 + 2) + (4 - 3.18)^2(3 \times 4 + 2)] = 0.63$$

2.4 c) CORRECT ANSWER: 5.5%

This problem falls under the category of 'Expected Values'.

Let X be the 'expected performance of fund'. According to the formula given in NCEES® FE Reference Handbook:

$$E[X] = \sum_{k=1}^{n} x_k f(x_k) = (-5\%)(0.10) + (0)(0.20) + (5\%)(0.30) + (10\%)(0.30) + (15\%)(0.10) = 5.5\%$$

2.4 d) CORRECT ANSWER : 5/6

This problem falls under the category of 'Expected Values'.

According to the formula given in NCEES® FE Reference Handbook:

$$E[X] = \int_{-\infty}^{\infty} x f(x)dx = \int_{0}^{1} x(4x - 1)dx$$

$$E[X] = \int_{0}^{1} (4x^2 - x)dx = \frac{1}{3}4x^3 - \frac{1}{2}x^2]_0^1 = \left[\left(\frac{4}{3} - \frac{1}{2}\right) - 0\right] = \frac{5}{6} = 0.83$$

Therefore, expected amount of study time spent by student in doing assignment is 0.83 or 83%.

2.4 e) CORRECT ANSWER : 2

This problem falls under the category of 'Expected Values'.

According to the formula given in NCEES® FE Reference Handbook:

$$E[X] = \int_{-\infty}^{\infty} xf(x)dx = \int_{1}^{\infty} x(2x^{-3})dx$$

$$E[X] = \int_{1}^{\infty} 2x^{-2}dx$$

$$E[X] = \frac{2}{(-2+1)}x^{-2+1}]_{1}^{\infty}$$

$$E[X] = -2x^{-1}]_{1}^{\infty}$$

$$E[X] = -\frac{2}{\infty} - \left(-\frac{2}{1}\right)$$

$$E[X] = [0 - (-2)]$$

$$E[X] = 2$$

Therefore, expected number of traffic violations per driver are 2.

2.4 f) CORRECT ANSWER : 1

The total area under probability density function and probability mass function is always equal to 1.

Chapter # 3 – Ethics and Professional Practice
3.1 Codes of Ethics & NCEES® Model Law and Rules - Solutions

Consult NCEES® FE Reference Handbook – Pages 4 - 11 for reference

3.1 a) CORRECT ANSWER - C

This problem falls under the category of 'Code of Ethics'.

According to the rule A3 of Model Rules Section 240.15, Rule of Professional Conduct:

"Licensees shall notify their employer or client and such other authority as may be appropriate when their professional judgment is overruled under circumstances in which the health, safety, or welfare of the public is endangered."

Therefore, junior engineer shall escalate her concerns to a higher level.

3.1 b) CORRECT ANSWER - D

This problem falls under the category of 'Code of Ethics'.

According to the rule B1 of Model Rules Section 240.15, Rule of Professional Conduct:

"Licensees shall undertake assignments only when qualified by education or experience in the specific technical fields of engineering or surveying involved."

John should review assignment requirements and his skills with the new supervisor and then decide accordingly.

3.1 c) CORRECT ANSWER - D

This problem falls under the category of 'Code of Ethics'.

According to the rule B2 of Model Rules Section 240.15, Rule of Professional Conduct:

"Licensees shall not affix their signatures or seals to any plans or documents dealing with subject matter in which they lack competence, nor to any such plan or document not prepared under their responsible charge."

Therefore, Sarah should not sign and seal these documents because they were not prepared under her responsible charge and she may not have sufficient time to review them.

3.1 d) CORRECT ANSWER - D

According to rule A4 of Model Rules Section 240.15, Rule of Professional Conduct:

"Licensees shall, to the best of their knowledge, include all relevant and pertinent information in an objective and truthful manner within all professional documents, statements, and testimony."

Therefore, professional engineer should include all relevant details in his recommendation and act in the client's best interest.

3.1 e) CORRECT ANSWER - C

This problem falls under the category of 'Code of Ethics'.

According to the rule B9 of Model Rules Section 240.15, Rule of Professional Conduct:

"Licensees shall not use confidential information received in the course of their assignments as a means

of making personal profit without the consent of the party from whom the information was obtained."

Therefore, Mark should first obtain consent from client prior to using their unique design on other projects.

3.1 f) CORRECT ANSWER – C3

This problem falls under the category of 'Code of Ethics'.

Obligation to respect fellow licensees is discussed in rule C3 of Model Rules Section 240.15, Rule of Professional Conduct.

3.1 g) CORRECT ANSWER – C

This problem falls under the category of 'Code of Ethics'.

Engineers both licensed and non-licensed are expected to conduct themselves professionally.

Ethical problems are not always straight forward.

Engineers possess special knowledge which is not common in public domain like other professions.

It is the responsibility of engineers to educate themselves about ethical practices.

3.1 h) CORRECT ANSWER – A, D

According to the Model Law, Section 110.20 'Definitions' only Professional Engineer and Professional Engineer, Retired are duly licensed by the board as professional engineers. Engineers and engineering interns cannot use the title of Professional Engineer until they are duly licensed by the board.

3.1 i) CORRECT ANSWER – B

According to the Model Law, Section 130.10 'General Requirements for Licensure' 2(3)(b), an applicant with a PhD. in engineering acceptable to the board and who has passed the FE exam requires 2 years of progressive engineering experience to meet experience requirements for PE licensure

3.1 j) CORRECT ANSWER – D

According to the Model Law, Sections 150.10, 150.30 and 160.70, boards can take disciplinary actions on valid grounds against licensed engineers/interns, unlicensed individuals and firms holding certificates of authorization.

3.2 Intellectual Property - Solutions

Consult NCEES® FE Reference Handbook – Pages 11 -12 for reference

3.2 a) CORRECT ANSWER - A

This problem falls under the category of 'Intellectual Property'.

According to the definitions of trademark, patent, copyright, and industrial design provided in NCEES® FE Reference Handbook, trademark is the most applicable product for advertising agency under the given scenario.

3.2 b) CORRECT ANSWER - C

This problem falls under the category of 'Intellectual Property'.

According to the definitions of trademark, patent, copyright, and industrial design provided in NCEES® FE Reference Handbook, patent is the most applicable product for this manufacturer under given scenario.

3.2 c) CORRECT ANSWER - B

This problem falls under the category of 'Intellectual Property'.

According to the definitions of trademark, patent, copyright, and industrial design provided in NCEES® FE Reference Handbook, copyright is the most applicable product for the publisher under given scenario.

3.2 d) CORRECT ANSWER - D

This problem falls under the category of 'Intellectual Property'.

According to the definitions of trademark, patent, copyright, and industrial design provided in NCEES® FE Reference Handbook, industrial design is the most applicable product for packaging firm under given scenario.

3.2 e) CORRECT ANSWER – 1-F, 2-A, 3-B

Trademark – ™

Copyright – ©

Registered Trademark – ®

3.2 f) CORRECT ANSWER - C

This problem falls under the category of 'Intellectual Property'.

Stocks, bonds, and real estate are examples of tangible assets whereas software program is an example of intellectual property.

3.3 Safety - Solutions

Consult NCEES® FE Reference Handbook – Pages 13 - 33 for reference

3.3 a) CORRECT ANSWER - C

National Electrical Code NEC® is developed by the National Fire Protection Association NFPA® and it is adopted across the U.S. as a benchmark for safe electrical design, installation, and inspection.

3.3 b) CORRECT ANSWER - B

NFPA® 70E is the 'Standard for Electrical Safety in the Workplace'. It addresses electrical safety-related work practices, safety-related maintenance requirements and procedures.

3.3 c) CORRECT ANSWER - B

According to the risk equation provided in NCEES® FE Reference Handbook: Risk = Hazard x Probability. Therefore, a scenario involving high degree of hazard and probability presents the highest risk.

3.3 d) CORRECT ANSWER - D

Reduction in the magnitude of transient overvoltage by means of grounding mitigates insulation damage which improves overall equipment reliability.

Grounding provides a path of low resistance to current which reduces the probability of current passing through an individual's body if an accidental contact is made by the individual with live equipment.

Protective devices (circuit breakers, fuses) can operate faster on a grounded system as compared to an ungrounded system which allows them to clear the fault and isolate faulty equipment quickly.

3.3 e) CORRECT ANSWER : 17mA – 99mA

Current as low as 17mA – 99mA can cause death due to extreme pain, respiratory arrest, severe muscular contractions, and inability of the victim to break electrical contact.

3.3 f) CORRECT ANSWER : 4

NFPA 70E® 'Standard for Electrical Safety in the Workplace' 2018 Table 130.7(C)(15)(c) divides arc flash PPE into 4 categories based on arc flash incident energy levels as shown below:

Category 1 = Arc-rated clothing, minimum arc rating of 4 cal/cm^2.

Category 2 = Arc-rated clothing, minimum arc rating of 8 cal/cm^2.

Category 3 = Arc-rated clothing, minimum arc rating of 25 cal/cm^2.

Category 4 = Arc-rated clothing, minimum arc rating of 40 cal/cm^2.

3.3 g) CORRECT ANSWER - D

SDS must contain 16 sections in a set order as noted in NCEES® FE Reference Handbook.

Chapter # 4 – Engineering Economics
4.1 Time value of money - Solutions

Consult NCEES® FE Reference Handbook – Page 230 for reference

4.1 a) CORRECT ANSWER: $241, 157

$i\% = 12\%$ $P = \$25,000,$ $n = 20\ years$ $F = ?$

$$F = \$25,000 \times \left(\frac{F}{P}, 12\%, 20\ years\right) = \$25,000 \times 9.6463 = \$241,157$$

Therefore, the future worth of given investment will be $241,157.

4.1 b) CORRECT ANSWER : $231, 225

$i\% = 4\%$ $F = \$750,000,$ $n = 30\ years$ $P = ?$

$$P = \$750,000 \times \left(\frac{P}{F}, 4\%, 30\ years\right)$$

$$P = \$750,000 \times 0.3083 = \$231,225$$

Therefore, the present worth of retirement fund is $231,225.

4.1 c) CORRECT ANSWER - B

Uniform Series Compound Amount factor converts an annuity to a future amount.

4.1 d) CORRECT ANSWER - A

Capital recovery factor converts a present value to an annuity.

4.1 e) CORRECT ANSWER: $17,440

$i\% = 6\%$ $P = \$200,000$ $n = 20\ years$ $A = ?$

$$A = \$200,000 \times \left(\frac{A}{P}, 6\%, 20\ years\right)$$

$$A = \$200,000 \times 0.0872 = \$17,440$$

Therefore, expected yearly payment of given annuity is $17,440.

4.1 f) CORRECT ANSWER: $392,724

$i\% = 8\%$ $A = \$40,000$ $n = 20\ years$ $P = ?$

$$P = \$40,000 \times \left(\frac{P}{A}, 8\%, 20\ years\right)$$

$$P = \$40,000 \times 9.8181 = \$392,724$$

Therefore, Amanda needs to have $392,724 saved today to purchase annuity described in the problem.

213
Copyrighted Material © 2020

4.1 g) CORRECT ANSWER: $1,699,248

$i\% = 8\%$ $A = \$15,000$ $n = 30\ years$ $F = ?$

$$F = \$15,000 \times \left(\frac{F}{A}, 8\%, 30\ years\right)$$

$$F = \$15,000 \times 113.282 = \$1,699,248$$

Therefore, the expected future worth of this investment is $1,699,248.

4.1 h) CORRECT ANSWER: 10.47%

$r = 10\%$ $m = 12$ $i_e = ?$

$$i_e = \left(1 + \frac{r}{m}\right)^m = \left(1 + \frac{0.1}{12}\right)^{12} - 1 = 0.1047 = 10.47\%$$

Therefore, the annual effective interest rate is 10.47%.

4.1 i) CORRECT ANSWER: $251,416

Cash flow presented in this problem can be expressed as the sum of uniform series present worth and uniform gradient present worth shown below:

$$P = \$40,000 \times \left(\frac{P}{A}, 2\%, 6\right) + \$2000 \times \left(\frac{P}{G}, 2\%, 6\right)$$

$$P = \$40,000 \times 5.6014 + \$2000 \times (13.6801)$$

$$P = \$251,416$$

4.1 j) CORRECT ANSWER: $4878

Cash flow presented in this problem can be expressed as the sum of uniform series present worth and uniform gradient present worth as follows:

$$P = \$600 \times \left(\frac{P}{A}, 8\%, 6\right) + \$200 \times \left(\frac{P}{G}, 8\%, 6\right)$$

$$P = \$600 \times 4.6229 + \$200 \times 10.5233$$

$$P = \$4878$$

4.2 Cost estimation - Solutions

Consult NCEES® FE Reference Handbook – Pages 231 – 232 for reference

4.2 a) CORRECT ANSWER – D

Note that we are given inflation rate (f) in the problem statement hence it also needs to be taken into consideration. Inflation adjusted interest rate per interest period (d) can be calculated as shown below.

$$d = i + f + i \times f = 6\% + 4\% + (6\% \times 4\%) = 10.24\%$$

4.2 b) CORRECT ANSWER – Straight line

Straight line depreciation method results in same value decline each year.

4.2 c) CORRECT ANSWER: $250,000

This problem falls under the category of capitalized costs.

Capitalized costs can be calculated using the formula given below.

$$Capitalized\ Cost\ = P = \frac{A}{i} = \frac{\$20,000}{0.08} = \$250,000$$

4.2 d) CORRECT ANSWER: $4,000

This problem falls under the category of depreciation analysis using straight line method.

We can calculate accumulated depreciation using the formula shown below.

$$D_j = \frac{C - S_n}{n}$$

$$D_j = \frac{\$32,000 - \$2,000}{30} = \$1,000$$

Accumulated depreciation in year $4 = 4 \times \$1,000 = \$4,000$

4.2 e) CORRECT ANSWER: $2,968

This problem falls under the category of depreciation analysis using MACRS.

As per problem details, we need to use 10-year recovery period and following formula.

$$D_j = (factor)C$$

Accumulated depreciation in year $3 = \sum(factor)C$

Accumulated depreciation in year $3 = 10\% \times \$7,000 + 18\% \times \$7,000 + 14.4\% \times \$7,000$

Therefore, accumulated depreciation in year $3 = \$2968$

Helpful tip - Salvage value is not relevant in MACRS depreciation.

4.2 f) CORRECT ANSWER: $26,000

This problem falls under the category of depreciation analysis using MACRS.

As per problem details, we need to use 5-year recovery period with following formula:

$$D_j = (factor)C$$

Accumulated depreciation in year 2 $= \sum(factor)C$

Accumulated depreciation in year 2 $= 20\% \times \$50,000 + 32\% \times \$50,000$

Accumulated depreciation in year 2 $= \$26,000$

4.2 g) CORRECT ANSWER: $24,000

This problem falls under the category of depreciation analysis using MACRS.

Book value (BV) of the truck in year 2 can be calculated using following formula:

$$BV = C - \sum D_j$$

$BV = \$50,000 - \$26,000 = \$24,000$

4.2 h) SOLUTION

According to MACRS factors for recovery period of 5 years given in NCEES FE Reference Handbook, MACRS depreciation schedule can be developed as shown below.

Year	Current Depreciation	Accumulated Depreciation	Book Value
0			$50,000
1	$50,000 x 20% = $10000	$10,000	$50,000 - $10,000 = $40,000
2	$50,000 x 32% = $16000	$26,000	$50,000 - $26,000 = $24,000
3	$50,000 x 19.2% = $9600	$35,600	$50,000 - $35,600 = $14,400
4	$50,000 x 11.52% = $5760	$41,360	$50,000 - $41,360 = $8640
5	$50,000 x 11.52% = $5760	$47,120	$50,000 - $47,120 = $2880
6	$50,000 x 5.76% = $2880	$50,000	$50,000 - $50,000 = $0

4.3 Risk Identification and Analysis - Solutions

Consult NCEES® FE Reference Handbook – Pages 231 - 232 for reference

4.3 a) CORRECT ANSWER: 20,000

This problem falls under the category of break-even analysis.

Cost structure of production line A $= \$100,000 + \$5x$

Cost structure of production line B $= \$10x$

At break-even production point, the cost structure of both production lines will be same.

$\$100,000 + 5x = \$10x \rightarrow$ Solving for x results in 20,000 items.

4.3 b) CORRECT ANSWER – B, C

This problem falls under the category of break-even analysis.

At $x = 20,000$ both lines are equally economical.

For $x > 20,000$, production line A is more economical because it has lower variable cost.

For $x < 20,000$, production line B is more economical because it has no fixed cost.

4.3 c) CORRECT ANSWER: 2000

This problem falls under the category of break-even analysis.

Cost price of a chair $= \$50,000 + \$2x$

Selling price of a chair $= \$27x$

At break-even production point, chair sales will cover cost of production.

$\$50,000 + 2x = \$27x$

Solving for x results in 2000. Therefore, at least 2000 chairs need to be sold before any profit is made.

4.3 d) CORRECT ANSWER – Contractor A

This problem falls under the category of 'Benefit-Cost Analysis'.

We can compare given options by looking at the present worth of their costs. The one with lower cost is better.

$$P_{Contractor\ A} = \$20,000 + \$40,000 \times \left(\frac{P}{F}, 8\%, 6\right) = \$20,000 + \$40,000 \times 0.6302 = \$45,208$$

$$P_{Contractor\ B} = \$10,000 \times \left(\frac{P}{A}, 8\%, 6\right) = \$10,000 \times 4.6229 = \$46,229$$

Therefore, contractor A is offering a better price.

4.3 e) CORRECT ANSWER – Investment Option C

This problem falls under the category of 'Benefit-Cost Analysis'.

We can compare given options by looking at their future worth.

Option resulting in highest future worth should be recommended.

$$F_{Option\ A} = \$200,000$$

$$F_{Option\ B} = \$5,000 \times \left(\frac{F}{A}, 10\%, 10\right) + \$160,000 = \$5,000 \times 15.9374 + \$160,000 = \$239,687$$

$$F_{Option\ C} = \$100,000 \times \left(\frac{F}{P}, 10\%, 10\right) = \$100,000 \times 2.5937 = \$259,370$$

It can be observed that Option C offers the best return on investment.

4.3 f) CORRECT ANSWER – Project B

Project resulting in the highest expected value (EV) will be the best choice.

$$EV_{Project\ A} = 0.60 \times 20\% + 0.40 \times 10\% = 16\%$$

$$EV_{Project\ B} = 0.20 \times 10\% + 0.70 \times 20\% + 0.10 \times 5\% = 16.5\%$$

$$EV_{Project\ C} = 0.30 \times 25\% + 0.60 \times 10\% + 0.10 \times (-10\%) = 12.5\%$$

It can be observed that Project B results in the highest expected value.

Chapter # 5 – Properties of Electrical Materials
5.1 Electrical Properties - Solutions

Consult NCEES® FE Reference Handbook – Pages 95, 355 - 357 for reference

5.1 a) CORRECT ANSWER - D

Resistivity is related to resistance, area, and length through following equation:

$$\rho = \frac{RA}{l} \qquad A = \pi r^2 = \pi \left(\frac{2mm}{2}\right)^2 = 3.141 \times 10^{-6} m^2 \quad l = 100m \quad R = 5\Omega.$$

$$\rho = \frac{RA}{l} = \frac{(5\Omega)(3.141 \times 10^{-6} m^2)}{100m} = 1.57 \times 10^{-7} \Omega.m$$

5.1 b) CORRECT ANSWER - C

Resistivity can be calculated using the equation $\rho = RA/l$

According to problem statement, $\rho_A = 4\rho_B$. It implies that $\frac{R_A A_A}{l_A} = 4\frac{R_B A_B}{l_B}$

If $l_A = l_B$ and $A_B = \frac{1}{4}A_A$ then $\frac{R_A A_A}{l_A} = 4\frac{R_B (A_A)/4}{l_A} = \frac{R_B A_A}{l_A}$

Therefore, $R_A = R_B$ if cable lengths are equal and area of cable 'B' is one-fourth of cable 'A'.

5.1 c) CORRECT ANSWER - D

Capacitance of a parallel plate capacitor is given by equation $C = \varepsilon A/d$

It can be observed that: Decreasing d $\downarrow$, increases C $\uparrow$ whereas increasing ε $\uparrow$, increases C $\uparrow$.

Therefore, decreasing the distance between plates and increasing dielectric strength will increase capacitance.

5.1 d) CORRECT ANSWER - B

By referring to 'Properties of Materials' table given in Materials Science/Structure of Matter section of NCEES® Reference Handbook, it can be observed that low electrical resistivity typically corresponds to high heat conductivity.

5.1 e) CORRECT ANSWER: $0.015 \ H/m$

Magnetic permeability can be calculated using following equation.

$$H = \frac{B}{\mu} = \frac{I}{2\pi r} \rightarrow \ \mu = \frac{2\pi r B}{I}$$

According to the problem statement, $I = 100A \quad B = 0.5T \quad r = 50cm$

$$\mu = \frac{2\pi r B}{I} = \frac{2\pi (50cm)(0.5T)}{100A} = 0.015 \ H/m$$

5.1 f) CORRECT ANSWER - D

Photoelectric effect can take place in all forms of matter. This phenomenon results in emission of electrons from material's surface when it is exposed to electromagnetic radiation (light).

5.1 g) CORRECT ANSWER - B

$$d(i) = dq(t)/d(t) \rightarrow dq(t) = i(t) \times d(t) = 1mA \times 5s = 5mC$$

Electron charge $= 1.6022 \times 10^{-19}C$

Number of electrons $= 5mC/1.6022 \times 10^{-19}C = 3.12 \times 10^{16}$

5.1 h) CORRECT ANSWER - D

Energy stored in a capacitor is given by the equation $CV^2/2$

$$C = \frac{\varepsilon A}{d} = \frac{(8.85 \times 10^{-12} F/m)(1m^2)}{0.1m} = 8.85 \times 10^{-11} F$$

$$\frac{CV^2}{2} = \frac{(8.85 \times 10^{-11} F)(200V)^2}{2} = 1.77 \times 10^{-6} J$$

5.1 i) CORRECT ANSWER - A

Capacitance of a parallel plate capacitor can be calculated using following formula.

$$C = \frac{\varepsilon A}{d} = \frac{(8.85 \times 10^{-12} Fm^{-1})(0.02m^2)}{0.01m} = 1.77 \times 10^{-11} F$$

$$V_c = \frac{Q}{C} = \frac{400\mu C}{1.77 \times 10^{-11} F} = 22.6 \ 10^6 V$$

5.1 j) CORRECT ANSWER - B

The current-voltage relationship of a capacitor is given by following equation.

$$v_c(t) = v_c(0) + \frac{1}{C} \int_0^t i_c(\tau) \, d\tau$$

$$10V = 5V + \frac{i_c(t) \times t}{100 \times 10^{-6} F} \rightarrow i_c(180s) = \frac{(10V - 5V)(100 \times 10^{-6} F)}{180s}$$

$$i_c(3min) = 2.7 \ \mu A$$

5.1 k) CORRECT ANSWER - B

Energy stored in a capacitor is given by the equation $\frac{1}{2} Cv^2(t)$.

$$\frac{1}{2} Cv^2(t) = \frac{1}{2}(200 \times 10^{-6} \ F)(240 sin377t \ V)^2$$

$$\frac{1}{2} Cv^2(t) = 5.76 \ sin^2 \ 377t \ J$$

5.1 l) CORRECT ANSWER - B

The current-voltage relationship of a capacitor is given by following equation.

$$v_c(t) = v_c(0) + \frac{1}{C} \int_0^t i_c(\tau)\, d\tau \rightarrow v_c(t) - v_c(0) = \frac{1}{C} \int_0^t i_c(\tau)d\tau$$

$$10V = \frac{1}{100\mu F}\, i(5s)(5s) \rightarrow i(5s) = 0.2mA$$

5.1 m) CORRECT ANSWER : 0.5 μF

$1\mu F$ branch capacitors are in parallel. They will result in $1\mu F + 1\mu F = 2\mu F$.

$1\mu F,\ 2\mu F, 2\mu F$ will be in series with each other.

$$C_{eqv} = \frac{1}{\left(\frac{1}{1}\right) + \left(\frac{1}{2}\right) + \left(\frac{1}{2}\right)} = 0.5\mu F$$

Helpful tip – Capacitors add differently in series and parallel when compared to resistors and inductors.

5.1 n) CORRECT ANSWER - A

Inductance can be calculated using following formula.

$$L = \frac{N^2 \mu A}{l}$$

$$L = \frac{100^2 \times 4\pi \times 10^{-7} Hm^{-1} \times 0.1m^2}{1m} = 1.25mH$$

5.1 o) CORRECT ANSWER - B

Voltage-current relationship of an inductor is given by 'Faraday's Law' as shown below.

$$V = L\frac{di}{dt}$$

$$V = 5mH \times \frac{100mA}{2ms} = 0.25V$$

5.1 p) CORRECT ANSWER - D

Energy stored in an inductor can be calculated using the formula given below.

$Li^2/2$ where L = inductance and i = current passing through inductor.

According to the problem statement, $i(t) = t^2 \rightarrow i(10) = 10^2 = 100A, L = 100mH$

$$\frac{Li^2}{2} = \frac{100 \times 10^{-3}H \times (100A)^2}{2} = 500J$$

5.1 q) CORRECT ANSWER - B

Energy stored in an inductor can be calculated as using following equation:

Energy storage capacity of an inductor $= Li^2/2$

Inductance $L = N^2\mu A/l$

Therefore, energy storage capacity $= (N^2\mu Ai^2)/2l$

It can be observed that, energy storage capacity of an inductor can be increased by:

- Increasing the number of turns $'N'$ in an inductor.
- Increasing the cross-sectional area $'A'$ of inductor.
- Increasing the current passing through inductor $'i'$.
- Decreasing the length of inductor $'l'$.

5.1 r) CORRECT ANSWER : 4H

The equivalent inductance of 2H branch inductors can be calculated as follows:

$L_{2H} = (2H + 2H)||(2H + 2H)$

$L_{2H} = (4H)||(4H)$

$L_{2H} = 2H$

It can be observed that the 1H inductors are in series with the equivalent inductance calculated above.

$L_{eq} = 1H + L_{2H} + 1H$

$L_{eq} = 1H + 2H + 1H = 4\ H$

Helpful tip – Addition of inductance in series and parallel is like addition of resistance in series and parallel.

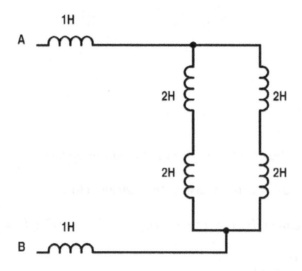

5.2 Thermal Properties - Solutions
Consult NCEES® FE Reference Handbook – Pages 104 - 105 for reference

5.2 a) CORRECT ANSWER - B

Bimetallic strips are fabricated using metals with different coefficients of thermal expansion.

5.2 b) CORRECT ANSWER - C

Thermal expansion coefficient can be calculated using following equation.

$$\alpha = \frac{\varepsilon}{\Delta T} = \frac{3 \times 10^{-3}}{7K} = 4.28 \times 10^{-4} \ K^{-1}$$

$T_{initial} = 296 \ K, \alpha = 4.28 \times 10^{-4} \ K^{-1}, \varepsilon_{req} = 6 \times 10^{-3}$

$$\Delta T = \frac{\varepsilon_{req}}{\alpha} = \frac{6 \times 10^{-3}}{4.28 \times 10^{-4} \ K^{-1}} = 14K$$

$T_{req} = T_{initial} + \Delta T = 296 \ K + 14 \ K = 310 \ K$

5.2 c) CORRECT ANSWER - B

Thermal expansion coefficient is given by following equation:

$$\alpha = \frac{\varepsilon}{\Delta T} \rightarrow \varepsilon = \alpha \times \Delta T = (1.2 \times 10^{-5} \ {}^0C^{-1}) \times (25 \ {}^0C) = 30 \times 10^{-5}$$

5.2 d) CORRECT ANSWER: $0.04 \ K^{-1}$

Resistance is related to temperature coefficient through following formula:

$$R = R_0 \left[1 + \alpha(T - T_0) \right]$$

According to the problem details:

$$2R_0 = R_0 \left[1 + \alpha(25) \right] \rightarrow \alpha = \frac{1}{25} = 0.04 \ K^{-1}$$

5.2 e) CORRECT ANSWER - D

$$\rho = \frac{RA}{l} \qquad \rho = \rho_0[1 + \alpha(T - T_o)]$$

Therefore, resistivity depends on resistance, area, length, and the temperature of given material.

5.2 f) CORRECT ANSWER - B

Heat capacity is directly proportional to the amount of material. Sample # 3 will have the highest heat capacity because it contains the largest amount of substance being tested. Sample # 1 has the least amount of substance therefore it will have the lowest heat capacity. Specific heat capacity of all three samples will be equal.

Chapter # 6 – Circuit Analysis
6.1 Kirchhoff's Laws – KCL, KVL - Solutions
Consult NCEES® FE Reference Handbook – Page 357 for reference

6.1 a) CORRECT ANSWER - B

Let us denote the voltage across $10k\Omega$ resistor as $V_{10k\Omega}$ (shown as V in the circuit). KCL can be written at $V_{10k\Omega}$ as follows:

$$\frac{V_{10k\Omega} - 0}{10k\Omega} + \frac{V_{10k\Omega} - 0}{4k\Omega} + \frac{V_{10k\Omega} - 0}{3k\Omega} + 10mA = 0$$

$$\frac{V_{10k\Omega}}{1463\Omega} = -10mA \rightarrow V_{10k\Omega} = -14.63V$$

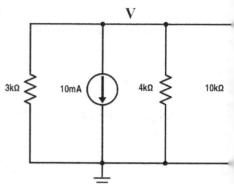

6.1 b) CORRECT ANSWER - D

Let us denote the voltage across 2 $k\Omega$ resistor as $V_{2k\Omega}$ (shown as V in the circuit). KCL can be written at $V_{2k\Omega}$ as follows:

$$10mA = I' + \frac{I'}{3} + \frac{V_{2k\Omega} - 0}{6k\Omega}$$

$$I' = \frac{V_{2k\Omega} - 0}{2\ k\Omega}$$

$$10mA = \frac{V_{2k\Omega}}{2k\Omega} + \frac{V_{2k\Omega}}{6k\Omega} + \frac{V_{2k\Omega}}{6k\Omega} \rightarrow V_{2k\Omega} = 12V$$

$$I' = \frac{V_{2k\Omega}}{2k\Omega} = \frac{12V}{2k\Omega} = 6\ mA$$

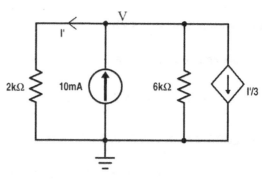

6.1 c) CORRECT ANSWER - B

$$R_{circuit} = (2\Omega + 4\Omega) + 4\Omega||(3\Omega + 2\Omega||2\Omega) = 8\Omega$$

$$I_{source} = \frac{V_{source}}{R_{circuit}} = \frac{10\ V}{8\ \Omega} = 1.25\ A$$

Current divider rule can be applied to calculate $I_{3\Omega}$.

$$I_X = \frac{R_T}{R_X + R_T} I_T$$

$$I_X = I_{3\Omega}\ ,\ R_T = 4\Omega\ ,\ R_X = 3\Omega + 2\ \Omega||2\ \Omega\ ,\ I_T = I_{source}$$

$$I_{3\Omega} = \frac{4\Omega}{3\Omega + 2\ \Omega||2\ \Omega + 4\Omega} 1.25A = 0.625A$$

$$V_{3\Omega} = I_{3\Omega} \times 3\Omega = 0.625A \times 3\Omega = 1.875\ V$$

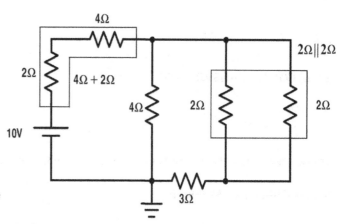

224

6.1 d) CORRECT ANSWER - D

We can use the principle of super-position to solve this circuit.

Let us first consider the 10A current source only.

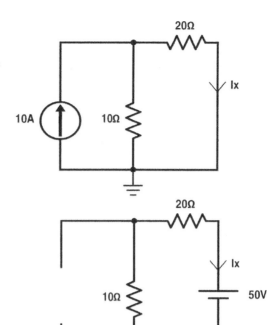

Using the current divider rule:

$$I_{x1} = \frac{R_T}{R_X + R_T} I_T = \frac{10\Omega}{20\Omega + 10\Omega} 10A = 3.33A$$

Let us now consider the 50V voltage source only.

KVL can be written as follows:

$$-50V = 30\Omega \times I_{x2}$$

$$I_{x2} = -1.66A$$

$$I_x = I_{x1} + I_{x2} = 1.66A \cong 1.7A$$

6.1 e) CORRECT ANSWER - A

The given circuit can be solved using current divider rule as shown below:

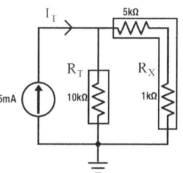

$$I_X = \frac{R_T}{R_X + R_T} I_T$$

$I_T = 5 \, mA$, $R_X = 6 \, k\Omega$ (since 1 $k\Omega$ and 5 $k\Omega$ are in series), $R_T = 10 \, k\Omega$

$$I_{1k\Omega} = \frac{10 \, k\Omega}{6 \, k\Omega + 10 \, k\Omega} 5 \, mA$$

$$I_{1k\Omega} = 3.125 \, mA$$

6.1 f) CORRECT ANSWER: 875 μA

We can solve this circuit using KCL.

Let us denote the voltage across 5 $k\Omega$ resistor as $V_{5k\Omega}$ (shown as V in the circuit diagram).

$$\frac{10 - V_{5k\Omega}}{10 \, k\Omega} + \frac{5 - V_{5k\Omega}}{2 \, k\Omega} = \frac{V_{5k\Omega} - 0}{5 \, k\Omega}$$

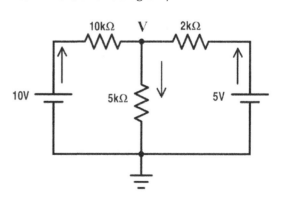

Multiply the above equation with $10k\Omega$ for simplification.

$$10 - V_{5k\Omega} + 5(5 - V_{5k\Omega}) = 2V_{5k\Omega} \rightarrow V_{5k\Omega} = 4.375V$$

$$I_{5k\Omega} = \frac{V_{5k\Omega}}{5k\Omega} = \frac{4.375 \, V}{5k\Omega}$$

$$I_{5k\Omega} = 875 \, \mu A$$

6.2 Series/Parallel Equivalent Circuits - Solutions

Consult NCEES® FE Reference Handbook – Page 357 for reference

6.2 a) CORRECT ANSWER - D

$R_{AB} = 5\ k\Omega || (10\ k\Omega + 2\ k\Omega || 1\ k\Omega)$

$2\ k\Omega || 1\ k\Omega = 0.66\ k\Omega$

$10\ k\Omega + 2\ k\Omega || 1\ k\Omega = 10.66\ k\Omega$

$R_{AB} = 5\ k\Omega || 10.66\ k\Omega = 3.4\ k\Omega$

Therefore, $R_{AB} \cong 3.4\ k\Omega$.

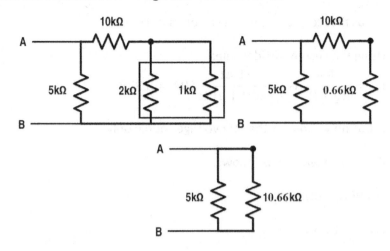

6.2 b) CORRECT ANSWER - A

$R_{AB} = 5\ k\Omega || 10\ k\Omega || (2\ k\Omega + 4\ k\Omega || 8\ k\Omega)$

$4\ k\Omega || 8\ k\Omega = 2.66\ k\Omega$

$2k\ \Omega + 4\ k\Omega || 8\ k\Omega = 2\ k\Omega + 2.66\ k\Omega = 4.66\ k\Omega$

$10\ k\Omega || (2\ k\Omega + 4\ k\Omega || 8\ k\Omega) = 10\ k\Omega || 4.66\ k\Omega = 3.178\ k\Omega$

$5\ k\Omega || 10\ k\Omega || (2\ k\Omega + 4\ k\Omega || 8\ k\Omega) = 5\ k\Omega || 3.178\ k\Omega \cong 2\ k\Omega$

Therefore, $R_{AB} \cong 2\ k\Omega$.

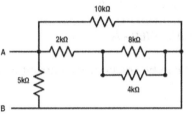
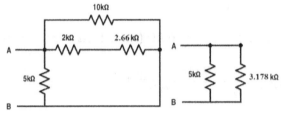

6.2 c) CORRECT ANSWER - B

$R_{AB} = 1\ k\Omega + 4\ k\Omega || (5\ k\Omega + 2\ k\Omega || 10\ k\Omega)$

$2\ k\Omega || 10\ k\Omega = 1.66\ k\Omega$

$5\ k\Omega + 2\ k\Omega || 10\ k\Omega = 5\ k\Omega + 1.66\ k\Omega = 6.66\ k\Omega$

$4\ k\Omega || (5\ k\Omega + 2\ k\Omega || 10\ k\Omega) = 4\ k\Omega || 6.66\ k\Omega = 2.50\ k\Omega$

$1k\Omega + 4k\Omega || (5k\Omega + 2k\Omega || 10k\Omega) = 1k\Omega + 2.5k\Omega = 3.50k\Omega$

Therefore, $R_{AB} = 3.50\ k\Omega$.

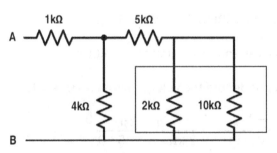
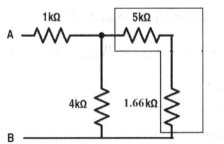

6.2 d) CORRECT ANSWER - C

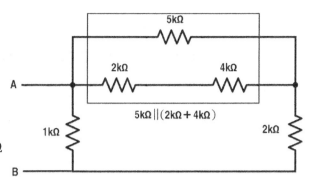

$R_{AB} = 1\ k\Omega||(5\ k\Omega||(2\ k\Omega + 4\ k\Omega) + 2\ k\Omega)$

$2\ k\Omega + 4\ k\Omega = 6\ k\Omega$

$6\ k\Omega||5\ k\Omega\ = 2.72\ k\Omega$

$5\ k\Omega||(2\ k\Omega + 4\ k\Omega) + 2\ k\Omega = 2.72k\Omega + 2k\Omega = 4.727\ k\Omega$

$R_{AB} = 1\ k\Omega||4.727\ k\Omega\ =\ 0.825\ k\Omega$

Therefore, $R_{AB} = 0.825\ k\Omega$.

6.2 e) CORRECT ANSWER : 6 $k\Omega$

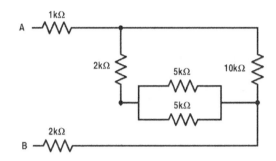

Given circuit can be simplified as shown on the right.

$R_{AB} = 1\ k\Omega + [2\ k\Omega + (5\ k\Omega||5\ k\Omega)]||10\ k\Omega + 2\ k\Omega$

$2\ k\Omega + (5\ k\Omega||5\ k\Omega) = 4.5\ k\Omega$

$[2\ k\Omega + (5\ k\Omega||5\ k\Omega)]||10\ k\Omega = 4.5\ k\Omega||10\ k\Omega\ =\ 3.1\ k\Omega$

$1\ k\Omega + [2\ k\Omega + (5\ k\Omega||5\ k\Omega)]||10\ k\Omega + 2\ k\Omega = 3.1\ k\Omega\ +\ 1\ k\Omega\ +\ 2\ k\Omega\ =\ 6.1\ k\Omega$

Therefore, $R_{AB} \cong 6\ k\Omega$.

6.3 Thevenin & Norton Theorem - Solutions

Consult NCEES® FE Reference Handbook – Pages 357 - 358 for reference

6.3 a) CORRECT ANSWER - B

V_{OC} is the voltage drop between terminals 'a' and 'b' as indicated in the problem description.

According to current divider rule, 5 mA current will be divided equally in each branch i.e. 2.5 mA

$$V_{OC} = 2\ k\Omega \times 2.5\ mA = 5\ V$$

6.3 b) CORRECT ANSWER: 1.5 $k\Omega$

R_{TH} is calculated by looking into the terminals 'a' and 'b'.

Current source is open-circuited as shown.

$$R_{TH} = 2\ k\Omega || (2\ k\Omega + 2\ k\Omega + 2\ k\Omega) = 1.5\ k\Omega$$

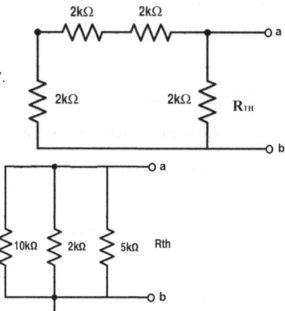

6.3 c) CORRECT ANSWER - A

R_{TH} is calculated by looking into terminals 'a' and 'b'.

Voltage sources need to be short-circuited.

$$R_{TH} = 10\ k\Omega || 2\ k\Omega || 5k\Omega = 1.25\ k\Omega$$

6.3 d) CORRECT ANSWER: 7.5mA

Apply Norton Theorem by shorting R_L with a wire to calculate I_{SC}

KCL can be written at V_X as follows:

$$\frac{10\ V - V_X}{2\ k\Omega} + \frac{10\ V - V_X}{2\ k\Omega} = \frac{V_X}{1\ k\Omega} \rightarrow V_X = 5\ V$$

$$I_{SC} = \frac{10\ V}{2\ k\Omega} + \frac{10\ V - V_X}{2\ k\Omega} = \frac{10\ V}{2\ k\Omega} + \frac{10\ V - 5V}{2\ k\Omega}$$

$$I_{SC} = 7.5\ mA$$

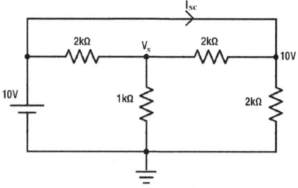

6.3 e) CORRECT ANSWER: 1 $k\Omega$

R_{eq} is calculated by looking into the circuit through R_L.

Voltage source needs to be short-circuited as shown.

$$R_{eq} = (2\ k\Omega || 1\ k\Omega + 2\ k\Omega) || 2\ k\Omega$$

$$R_{eq} = 1.142\ k\Omega \cong 1\ k\Omega$$

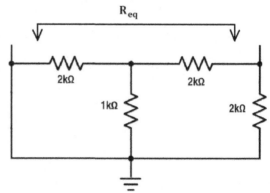

6.3 f) CORRECT ANSWER : 2A

Short circuit the terminals a-b as shown in the circuit diagram.

It can be observed that $I_{sc} = I_{12\Omega}$.

Moreover, 12Ω and 4Ω resistors are in parallel arrangement 12Ω||4Ω.

I_{sc} can be calculated using the current divider formula as shown below:

$$I_{sc} = \frac{4\Omega}{12\Omega + 4\Omega} 8A$$

$$I_{sc} = 2A$$

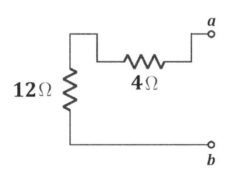

6.3 g) CORRECT ANSWER : 16 Ω

R_{eq} is calculated by open-circuiting the current source and looking into a-b.

It can be observed that the equivalent resistance is simply series arrangement of 12Ω and 4Ω resistors.

$$R_{eq} = 12\ \Omega + 4\ \Omega$$

$$R_{eq} = 16\ \Omega$$

6.3 h) CORRECT ANSWER : 32 V

Using source transformation, Thevenin equivalent voltage can be calculated as shown below:

$$V_{th} = I_{SC} \times R_{eq}$$

Since $I_{SC} = 2A$ and $R_{eq} = 32V$, we can substitute these values to calculate Thevenin equivalent voltage.

$$V_{th} = 2A \times 16\Omega = 32V$$

6.4 Waveform Analysis - Solutions

Consult NCEES® FE Reference Handbook – Pages 359 - 360 for reference

6.4 a) CORRECT ANSWER - C

For a full wave rectified sinusoidal signal, maximum and effective values are related as shown below.

$$X_{eff} = \frac{X_{max}}{\sqrt{2}} \quad X_{max} = \sqrt{2} \times X_{eff}$$

$$V_{max} = \sqrt{2} \times V_{eff} = \sqrt{2} \times 10\,V = 14.14\,V$$

6.4 b) CORRECT ANSWER - D

$$V_1 + V_2 = 10\cos(500t) + 15\cos(100t + 45°)$$

$$\cos(\alpha + \beta) = \cos(\alpha)\cos(\beta) - \sin(\alpha)\sin(\beta)$$

$$V_1 + V_2 = 10\cos(500t) + 15[\cos(100t)\cos(45) - \sin(100t)\sin(45)]$$

$$\cos(45°) = \sin(45°) = \frac{1}{\sqrt{2}}$$

$$V_1 + V_2 = 10\cos(500t) + \frac{15\cos(100t)}{\sqrt{2}} - \frac{15\sin(100t)}{\sqrt{2}}$$

$$V_1 + V_2 = 10\cos(500t) + 10.6\cos(100t) - 10.6\sin(100t)$$

6.4 c) CORRECT ANSWER - C

By comparing $100\cos(500t + 50°)$ with standard phasor representation $A\cos(\omega t + \vartheta)$ we can observe that:

$$\omega = 2\pi f = 500 \rightarrow f = \frac{500}{2\pi} = 79.5\,Hz$$

6.4 d) CORRECT ANSWER - B

For a half wave rectified sinusoidal signal, average value is given by following equation:

$$X_{ave} = \frac{X_{max}}{\pi} = \frac{15}{\pi} = 4.77$$

6.4 e) CORRECT ANSWER: 1A

Average value of the given periodic signal can be calculated as follows:

$$I_{ave} = \frac{1}{T}\int_0^T x(t)\,dt = \frac{1}{4}\int_0^4 x(t)\,dt$$

$$I_{ave} = \frac{1}{4}\left(\int_0^1 1\,dt + \int_1^2 2\,dt + \int_2^3 1\,dt + \int_3^4 0\,dt\right) = \frac{1}{4}(1 + 2 + 1 + 0) = \frac{4}{4} = 1A$$

6.4 f) CORRECT ANSWER – B

Time period of a periodic waveform can be calculated by finding time difference between occurrence of same points in the waveform. In the given problem, positive peak of sinusoidal waveform first appears at $t = 0s$ and then at $t = 5s$. Therefore, time-period of the given waveform is $5s - 0s = 5s$.

6.4 g) CORRECT ANSWER – B

Frequency of a periodic waveform can be calculated using following formula:

$$f = \frac{1}{T}$$

In the previous solution, time-period was calculated as $5s$.

$$f = \frac{1}{5} = 0.2Hz$$

6.4 h) CORRECT ANSWER – B

According to the problem statement:

$$i(t) = 40\sqrt{2}\cos(377t + 30°)\,A$$

Standard form of a sinusoidal waveform is given below:

$$i(t) = I_{max}\cos(\omega t + \theta)$$

$$I_{max} = 40\sqrt{2}\,A \quad \omega = 377rad/s \quad \theta = 30°$$

Therefore, peak current value $= 40\sqrt{2}\,A$

6.4 i) CORRECT ANSWER – C

As calculated earlier, $\omega = 377rad/s$.

$$\omega = 2\pi f = 377rad/s$$

$$f = \frac{377rad/s}{2\pi} = 60Hz$$

6.4 j) CORRECT ANSWER – A

RMS value of a full-wave rectified sinusoidal function can be calculated using following formula.

$$I_{RMS} = \frac{I_{max}}{\sqrt{2}}$$

$$I_{RMS} = \frac{40\sqrt{2}\,A}{\sqrt{2}} = 40A$$

6.5 Phasors - Solutions

Consult NCEES® FE Reference Handbook – Pages 360 - 361 for reference

6.5 a) CORRECT ANSWER - D

$v(t) = 100\sin(377t + 60°)$ requires conversion to standard cosine form as shown below.

$\sin(\vartheta) = \cos(\vartheta - 90°)$. Therefore, $v(t) = 100\cos(377t + 60° - 90°) = 100\cos(377t - 30°)$

$V_{rms} = \dfrac{V_{max}}{\sqrt{2}} = \dfrac{100}{\sqrt{2}} = 70.7\ V$

Phase angle is $\theta = -30°$.

Therefore, voltage phasor is 70.7/-30° V

$X_L = j\omega L = j \times 377 \times 100 \times 10^{-3}\Omega = j37.7\ \Omega = 37.7\underline{/90°}\Omega$

$I = \dfrac{V}{X_L} = 1.875\ A$

Phase angle is $\theta = -120°$

Therefore, current phasor $I = 1.875\underline{/-120°}A$.

6.5 b) CORRECT ANSWER - C

$v(t) = 212\cos(\omega t + 50°)\ V$

$V_{rms} = \dfrac{V_{max}}{\sqrt{2}} = 150V$

Phase angle is $\theta = 50°$.

Therefore, voltage phasor is 150$\underline{/50°}$ V.

6.5 c) CORRECT ANSWER - A

$v(t) = 212\sin(\omega t + 50°)$ requires conversion to standard cosine form as shown below.

$\sin(\vartheta) = \cos(\vartheta - 90°)$.

Therefore, $v(t) = 212\cos(377t + 50° - 90°)$

$v(t) = 212\cos(377t - 40°)$

$V_{rms} = \dfrac{V_{max}}{\sqrt{2}} = 150V$

Phase angle is $\theta = -40°$.

Therefore, voltage phasor is 150$\underline{/-40°}$ V.

6.5 d) CORRECT ANSWER - B

$$v(t) = 100 \cos(377t - 0°)$$

$$V_{rms} = \frac{V_{max}}{\sqrt{2}} = 70.7 \ V$$

Phase angle is $\theta = 0°$.

Therefore, voltage phasor is $70.7\underline{/0°}$ V.

$$Z = 500 - j100\Omega = 509.9\underline{/-11.4°}\Omega$$

$$I = \frac{V}{Z} = \frac{70.7V}{510\Omega} = 0.138A$$

Phase angle is $11.4°$.

Therefore, the current phasor is $I = 0.14\underline{/11.3°}A$.

6.5 e) CORRECT ANSWER - C

$v(t) = 100 \sin(377t + 100°)$ requires conversion to standard cosine form as shown below.

$$\sin(\vartheta) = \cos(\vartheta - 90°).$$

Therefore, $v(t) = 100\cos(377t + 100° - 90°) = 100\cos(377t + 10°)$

$$V_{rms} = V_{max}/\sqrt{2} = 70.7 \ V$$

Phase angle is $\theta = 10°$.

Therefore, voltage phasor is $70.7\underline{/10°}$ V.

$$X_C = 1/j\omega C = 0.0265\underline{/-90°} \ \Omega$$

$$I = \frac{V}{X_C} = 2665 \ A$$

Phase angle $\theta = 100°$

Therefore, current phasor is $I = 2665\underline{/100°}A$.

6.6 Impedance - Solutions

Consult NCEES® FE Reference Handbook – Page 361 for reference

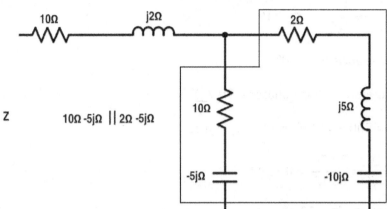

6.6 a) CORRECT ANSWER - A

$$Z_{eq} = 10 + j2\Omega + (10 - 5j\ \Omega)||(2 - 5j\Omega)$$

$$Z_{eq} = 10 + j2\Omega + \frac{540 - 770j}{244}$$

$$Z_{eq} = 10 + j2\Omega + (2.21 - 3.15j\Omega)$$

$$Z_{eq} \cong 12 - j\Omega$$

Helpful tip – Learn how to calculate Y, G, B.

6.6 b) CORRECT ANSWER - B

$$Z_{eq} = 10 - 5j\ \Omega\ ||\ 2 - 5j\ \Omega$$

$$Z_{eq} = \frac{540 - 770j}{244}$$

$$Z_{eq} = 2.21 - 3.15j\Omega$$

$$Z_{eq} \cong 2 - 3j\Omega$$

Helpful tip – Learn how to calculate Y, G, B.

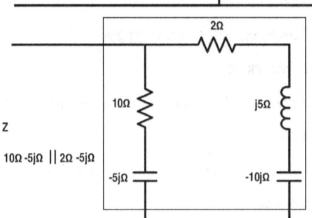

6.6 c) CORRECT ANSWER - B

$$Z_{eq} = R + X_C$$

$$X_C = \frac{1}{j\omega C} = \frac{1}{j377 \times 100 \times 10^{-9}} = -j26525\ \Omega$$

$$Z_{eq} = 50 - j26525\ \Omega$$

Helpful tip – Learn how to calculate Y, G, B.

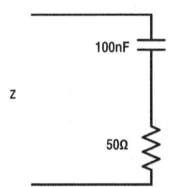

6.6 d) CORRECT ANSWER - C

$$Z_{eq} = (R + X_L)||X_C$$

$$X_L = j\omega L = j377 \times 2 \times 10^{-3} = j0.754\ \Omega$$

$$X_C = \frac{1}{j\omega C} = \frac{1}{j377 \times 100 \times 10^{-6}} = -j26.5\ \Omega$$

$$Z_{eq} = 10 + j0.754\ \Omega|| - j26.5\ \Omega$$

Helpful tip – Learn how to calculate Y, G, B.

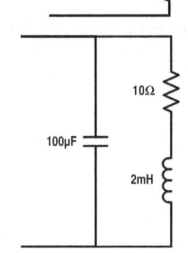

6.6 e) CORRECT ANSWER: $6.2 - 14j\,\Omega$

$Z = (5\,\Omega - j10\,\Omega) + (20\,\Omega)||(-j5\,\Omega)$

$Z = (5\,\Omega - j10\,\Omega) - \dfrac{100j\Omega}{20\Omega - 5j\Omega}$

$Z = (5\,\Omega - j10\,\Omega) - \dfrac{[(100\Omega j)(20\Omega + 5\Omega j)]}{[(20\Omega - 5\Omega j)(20\Omega + 5\Omega j)]}$

$Z = (5\,\Omega - j10\,\Omega) - \dfrac{[2000\Omega j - 500\Omega]}{[400\Omega + 25\Omega]}$

$Z = (5\,\Omega - j10\,\Omega) - \dfrac{[2000\Omega j - 500\Omega]}{[400\Omega + 25\Omega]}$

$Z = 5\Omega + \dfrac{500}{425}\Omega - 10j\Omega - \dfrac{2000}{425}j\Omega$

$Z = 6.176 - 14.47j\ \Omega$

$Z \cong 6.2 - 14j\Omega$

Helpful tip – Learn how to calculate Y - admittance, G - conductance, B - susceptance.

6.6 f) CORRECT ANSWER - D

Maximum power transfer occurs when $Z_{load} = Z^*_{Thevenin}$.

To calculate $Z_{Thevenin}$, open-circuit the current source and short-circuit the voltage source.

$Z_{Thevenin} = 10 - 5j + 2 + 6j$

$Z_{Thevenin} = 12 + j\ \Omega$

Therefore, for maximum power transfer $Z_{load} = Z^*_{Thevenin} = 12 - j\Omega$.

6.6 g) CORRECT ANSWER - A

Maximum power transfer occurs when $Z_{load} = Z^*_{Thevenin}$.

To calculate $Z_{Thevenin}$, open-circuit the current source.

$Z_{Thevenin} = 5 - j + 3j\ \Omega$

$Z_{Thevenin} = 5 + 2j\ \Omega$

Therefore, for maximum power transfer $Z_{load} = Z^*_{Thevenin} = 5 - 2j\Omega$

Chapter # 7 – Linear Systems
7.1 Frequency / transient response - Solutions

Consult NCEES® FE Reference Handbook – Pages 361 - 362 for reference

7.1 a) CORRECT ANSWER - C

Relevant formula for this problem is given below:

$$v_c(t) = v_c(0)e^{-\frac{t}{RC}} + V\left(1 - e^{-\frac{t}{RC}}\right) \quad v_c(0) = 20\,V$$

After switch changes position, $V = 0$ (external voltage source is not present).

$$t = 5 \times 60\,s = 300\,s$$

$$\tau = RC = 100s$$

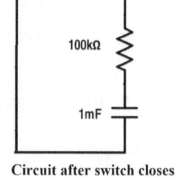

100kΩ

1mF

Circuit after switch closes

$$v_c(300s) = v_c(0)e^{-\frac{t}{RC}} + V\left(1 - e^{-\frac{t}{RC}}\right) \qquad R = 100\,k\Omega \quad C = 1\,mF$$

$$v_c(300s) = 20e^{-\frac{300}{100}}V = 0.995\,V \cong 1\,V$$

Helpful tip – Review and understand RC transient equations given in NCEES® FE Reference Handbook.

7.1 b) CORRECT ANSWER - B

Relevant formula for this problem is given below.

$$v_c(t) = v_c(0)e^{-\frac{t}{RC}} + V\left(1 - e^{-\frac{t}{RC}}\right) \quad v_c(0) = 10\,V$$

$$R = 10k\Omega \quad C = 200\mu F$$

$$RC = 2s$$

After switch changes position, $V = 0$ (external voltage source is not present).

$$v_c(t) = 10e^{-t/2}V$$

10kΩ   200µF

Circuit after switch opens

7.1 c) CORRECT ANSWER - D

Relevant formula for this problem is given below.

$$i(t) = i(0)e^{-\frac{Rt}{L}} + \frac{V}{R}\left(1 - e^{-\frac{Rt}{L}}\right)$$

$$i(0) = 0, V = 10\,V, R = 1\,k\Omega, L = 2\,mH \rightarrow \frac{R}{L} = 500000s$$

$$i(t) = 0.01\left(1 - e^{-500000t}\right)A$$

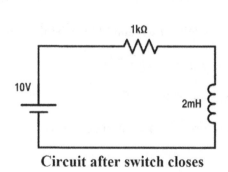

1kΩ

10V

2mH

Circuit after switch closes

Helpful tip – Review and understand RL transient equations given in NCEES® FE Reference Handbook.

7.1 d) CORRECT ANSWER - B

Relevant formula for this problem is given below.

$$i(t) = i(0)e^{-\frac{Rt}{L}} + \frac{V}{R}(1 - e^{-\frac{Rt}{L}})$$

Inductor can be replaced with a short wire because switch has been closed for a long time.

Current provided by the power source before switch opens at $t = 0$ is calculated as follows:

$$I = \frac{10\ V}{10\ \Omega + 5\ \Omega||10\ \Omega} == \frac{10\ V}{10\ \Omega + 3.33\ \Omega} = 0.75\ A$$

Voltage across $5\ \Omega||10\ \Omega$ before switch opens can be calculated as shown below:

$$v(0) = 0.75A \times 5\ \Omega||10\ \Omega = 2.5V$$

Current through inductor at $t = 0$ can be calculated using current divider rule.

$$i(0) = \frac{2.5\ V}{5\ \Omega} = 0.5\ A$$

According to the problem statement:

$$t = 10\tau \quad L = 1H \quad R = 15\Omega$$

$$\tau = \frac{L}{R} = 66.66\ ms$$

Note that $V = 0$ after switch opens.

$$i(10\tau) = i(0)e^{-\frac{Rt}{L}} + 0 = 22.6\ \mu A$$

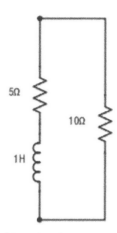

Circuit after switch opens

7.1 e) CORRECT ANSWER - C

Relevant formula for this problem is given below.

$$v_c(t) = v_c(0)e^{-\frac{t}{RC}} + V\left(1 - e^{-\frac{t}{RC}}\right)$$

$$v_c(0) = 10V$$

$$t = 5\tau = 5RC$$

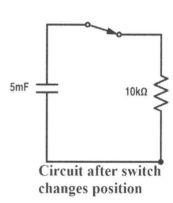

Circuit after switch changes position

After the switch changes position, $V = 0$ (external voltage source is not present).

$$v_c(5\tau) = 10e^{-5RC/RC} + 0\left(1 - e^{-\frac{5RC}{RC}}\right) = 10e^{-5} + 0$$

$$v_c(5\tau) = 67.3\ mV$$

7.2 Resonance - Solutions

Consult NCEES® FE Reference Handbook – Page 362 for reference

7.2 a) CORRECT ANSWER - D

The given circuit is an example of series resonance circuit for which relevant formula is given below.

$$\omega_o = \frac{1}{\sqrt{LC}}$$

$$\omega_o = \frac{1}{\sqrt{20mH \times 10\mu F}} = 2236 \; rad/s$$

7.2 b) CORRECT ANSWER - $5000 \; rad/s$

Bandwidth of a series resonance circuit can be calculated using formula given below.

$$BW = \frac{\omega_o}{Q}$$

$$BW = \frac{R}{L} = \frac{100\Omega}{20mH} = 5000 \; rad/s$$

7.2 c) CORRECT ANSWER - B

Maximum current occurs at resonant frequency because circuit impedance is lowest i.e. $Z = R$

$$I_{max} = \frac{120 \; V}{10 \; \Omega} = 12 \; A$$

7.2 d) CORRECT ANSWER: $3162 \; rad/s$

Resonant frequency can be calculated using following formula:

$$\omega_o = \frac{1}{\sqrt{LC}}$$

$$\omega_o = \frac{1}{\sqrt{10mH \times 10 \; \mu F}} = 3162 \; rad/s$$

7.2 e) CORRECT ANSWER : $316, 1 \; rad/s$

For a parallel resonant circuit, quality factor 'Q' can be calculated as shown below:

$$Q = \omega_o RC$$

$$\omega_o = \frac{1}{\sqrt{LC}} = \frac{1}{\sqrt{100 \times 10^{-3}H \times 100 \times 10^{-6}F}} = 316 \; rad/s$$

$$Q = 316 \; rad/s \times 10k\Omega \times 100\mu F = 316$$

$$BW = \frac{\omega_o}{Q} = 1 \; rad/s$$

7.2 f) CORRECT ANSWER : $3.16 \times 10^{-3}, 100000\ rad/s$

For a series resonant circuit, quality factor 'Q' can be calculated as shown below:

$$Q = \frac{\omega_o L}{R}$$

$$\omega_o = \frac{1}{\sqrt{LC}}$$

$$\omega_o = \frac{1}{\sqrt{100 \times 10^{-3}H \times 100 \times 10^{-6}F}} = 316\ rad/s$$

$$Q = \frac{316\ rad/s \times 100mH}{10k\Omega} = 3.16 \times 10^{-3}$$

$$BW = \frac{\omega_o}{Q} = \frac{316}{3.16 \times 10^{-3}} = 100,000\ rad/s$$

Helpful tip - It can be observed that high Q results in low BW and vice versa.

7.2 g) CORRECT ANSWER - B

For a parallel resonant circuit, quality factor 'Q' can be calculated as shown below:

$$Q = \frac{R}{\omega_o L}$$

$$\omega_o = \frac{1}{\sqrt{LC}} = 707\ rad/s$$

$$Q = \frac{10\Omega}{(20mH)(707\ rad.s^{-1})} = 0.707$$

Helpful tip – Q can be calculated using two different formulas.

7.2 h) CORRECT ANSWER: $1000\ rad/s$

Bandwidth of parallel resonance circuits can be calculated using formula given below.

$$BW = \frac{\omega_o}{Q}$$

$$BW = \frac{707}{0.707}rad/s$$

$$BW = 1000\ rad/s$$

7.3 Laplace Transform - Solutions

Consult NCEES® FE Reference Handbook – Page 56 for reference

7.3 a) CORRECT ANSWER - A

According to the Laplace transform pairs provided in NCEES® FE Reference Handbook:

$$\mathcal{L}[e^{-at}] = \frac{1}{s+a} \rightarrow \mathcal{L}[f(t)] = \frac{1}{s+b}$$

7.3 b) CORRECT ANSWER - B

$$f(t) = e^{-at} = e^{-a(t+1-1)} = e^{-a(t-1)}e^{-a} = e^{-(a)}[e^{-a(t-1)}u(t-1)]$$

According to the Laplace transform pairs provided in NCEES® FE Reference Handbook:

$$\mathcal{L}[f(t-\tau)u(t-\tau)] = e^{-\tau s}F(s) \qquad \mathcal{L}[e^{-at}] = \frac{1}{s+a}$$

It can be observed that in given case, $\tau = 1$.

$$\mathcal{L}[f(t)] = e^{-(a)}\frac{e^{-(s)}}{s+a} = \frac{e^{-(s+a)}}{s+a}$$

7.3 c) CORRECT ANSWER - C

$$f(t) = (t - 1 + 1)e^{-a(t-1+1)}u(t-1) = \left[(t-1)e^{-a(t-1)}u(t-1) + e^{-a(t-1)}u(t-1)\right]e^{-a}$$

According to the Laplace transform pairs provided in NCEES® FE Reference Handbook:

$$\mathcal{L}[f(t-\tau)u(t-\tau)] = e^{-\tau s}F(s) \quad \mathcal{L}(te^{-at}) = \frac{1}{(s+a)^2}$$

It can be observed that in the given case, $\tau = 1$.

$$\mathcal{L}[f(t)] = F(s) = e^{-(s+a)}\left(\frac{1}{(s+a)^2} + \frac{1}{s+a}\right)$$

7.3 d) CORRECT ANSWER - D

$$f(t) = \left[e^{-(t-3)} - e^{-3(t-3)}\right]u(t-3) = e^{-(t-3)}u(t-3) - e^{-3(t-3)}u(t-3)$$

As explained in previous solutions, Laplace transform of this function will be as follows:

$$\mathcal{L}[f(t)] = e^{-3s}\left(\frac{1}{s+1} - \frac{1}{s+3}\right)$$

7.3 e) CORRECT ANSWER - A

$$f(t) = te^{-at}\delta(t-2)$$

According to the sifting property of delta function $\int f(t)\delta(t-T)dt = f(T)$.

$$F(s) = (2)e^{-(2)a}e^{-(2)s} = 2e^{-2(a+s)}$$

7.3 f) CORRECT ANSWER - B

$$f(t) = tu(t) * \sin 4t$$

According to the Laplace transform table, convolution in time domain is equal to multiplication in s-domain.

$$\mathcal{L}[x(t) * h(t)] = X(s)H(s)$$

Let us assume that $x(t) = tu(t)$ and $h(t) = \sin 4t$.

According to the Laplace transform table:

$$\mathcal{L}[tu(t)] = \frac{1}{s^2} \rightarrow X(s) = \frac{1}{s^2}$$

$$\sin 4t = (1)\sin 4t = e^{-ot}\sin 4t \rightarrow \mathcal{L}[e^{-ot}\sin 4t] = \frac{4}{[(s+0)^2 + 4^2]} = \frac{4}{(s^2 + 16)} \rightarrow H(s) = \frac{4}{(s^2 + 16)}$$

$$\mathcal{L}[tu(t) * \sin 4t] = X(s)H(s) = \frac{1}{s^2}\frac{4}{s^2 + 16}$$

7.3 g) CORRECT ANSWER - D

$$F(s) = \frac{5}{(s+3) + (s+5)} = \frac{5}{(2s+8)} = \frac{5}{2(s+4)} = \frac{5}{2} \cdot \frac{1}{s+4}$$

According to the Laplace transform pairs provided in NCEES® FE Reference Handbook:

$$\mathcal{L}[e^{-at}] = \frac{1}{s+a} \rightarrow f(t) = \frac{5}{2}e^{-4t}$$

7.3 h) CORRECT ANSWER - C

$$F(s) = \frac{s+8}{(s+1)(s+7)}$$

$$\frac{s+8}{(s+1)(s+7)} = \frac{A}{s+1} + \frac{B}{s+7}$$

Multiply the entire equation by denominators $(s+1)(s+7)$.

$$s + 8 = A(s+7) + B(s+1)$$

$$\text{Let } s = -7, \quad 1 = B(-6), B = -\frac{1}{6} \qquad \text{Let } s = -1, \quad 7 = A(6), \quad A = 7/6$$

$$F(s) = \frac{7}{(6)(s+1)} - \frac{1}{(6)(s+7)} = \frac{1}{6}\left(\frac{7}{s+1} - \frac{1}{s+7}\right)$$

According to the Laplace transform pairs provided in NCEES® FE Reference Handbook:

$$\mathcal{L}[e^{-at}] = \frac{1}{s+a} \rightarrow f(t) = \frac{1}{6}(7e^{-t} - e^{-7t})$$

7.3 i) CORRECT ANSWER - A

$$F(s) = \frac{s^2 + 2s + 1}{(s + 2)(s + 3)(s)}$$

$$\frac{s^2 + 2s + 1}{(s + 2)(s + 3)(s)} = \frac{A}{s + 2} + \frac{B}{s + 3} + \frac{C}{s}$$

$$s^2 + 2s + 1 = A(s + 3)(s) + B(s + 2)(s) + C(s + 2)(s + 3)$$

$$\text{Let } s = 0, \quad 1 = C(2)(3), C = \frac{1}{6}$$

$$\text{Let } s = -2, \quad 4 - 4 + 1 = A(1)(-2), \quad A = -\frac{1}{2}$$

$$\text{Let } s = -3, \quad 9 - 6 + 1 = B(-1)(-3), \quad B = \frac{4}{3}$$

$$F(s) = \frac{-1}{2(s + 2)} + \frac{4}{3(s + 3)} + \frac{1}{6s}$$

According to the Laplace transform pairs provided in NCEES® FE Reference Handbook:

$$\mathcal{L}[e^{-at}] = \frac{1}{s + a} \quad \mathcal{L}[u(t)] = \frac{1}{s} \rightarrow f(t) = \frac{1}{6}u(t) - \frac{e^{-2t}}{2} + \frac{4e^{-3t}}{3}$$

7.3 j) CORRECT ANSWER - C

$$F(s) = \frac{s + 4}{(s^2)(s + 5)}$$

$$\frac{s + 4}{(s^2)(s + 5)} = \frac{A}{s} + \frac{B}{s^2} + \frac{C}{s + 5}$$

$$s + 4 = A(s)(s + 5) + B(s + 5) + C(s^2)$$

$$\text{Let } s^2 = 0, \quad 4 = B(5), B = \frac{4}{5}$$

$$\text{Let } s = -5, \quad -1 = C(25), \quad C = -\frac{1}{25}$$

Comparing the coefficients of $s^2 \rightarrow A + C = 0, A = -C, A = \frac{1}{25}$

$$F(s) = \frac{1}{25(s)} + \frac{4}{5(s^2)} - \frac{1}{25(s + 5)}$$

$$\mathcal{L}[e^{-at}] = \frac{1}{s + a} \quad \mathcal{L}[u(t)] = \frac{1}{s} \rightarrow f(t) = \frac{u(t)}{25} + \frac{4t}{5} - \frac{e^{-5t}}{25}$$

Helpful tip – Review partial fraction expansion for calculating inverse Laplace transforms.

7.4 Transfer Functions - Solutions

Consult NCEES® FE Reference Handbook – Pages 56, 361 - 362 for reference

7.4 a) CORRECT ANSWER: B, D

Transfer function is the ratio of an LTI system's output to its input in Laplace domain i.e. $H(s) = Y(s)/X(s)$

Initial conditions of the LTI system are assumed to be zero because in an LTI systems, output = 0 when input = 0. If initial conditions are non-zero, it is possible for output to be non-zero even when input is zero. Such a system can no longer be considered LTI.

7.4 b) CORRECT ANSWER: $2s + \dfrac{1}{s} - e^{-2s}$

Transfer function $H(s)$ of given function can be calculated as follows:

$$H(s) = \frac{Y(s)}{X(s)} \qquad Y(s) = \mathcal{L}[y(t)] \qquad X(s) = \mathcal{L}[x(t)]$$

$$y(t) = 2\frac{d}{dt}x(t) + \int_0^t x(t)dt - x(t-2)u(t-2)$$

$$\mathcal{L}[y(t)] = \mathcal{L}\left[2\frac{d}{dt}x(t) + \int_0^t x(t)dt - x(t-2)u(t-2)\right]$$

$$Y(s) = 2\mathcal{L}\left[\frac{d}{dt}x(t)\right] + \mathcal{L}\left[\int_0^t x(t)dt\right] - \mathcal{L}[x(t-2)u(t-2)]$$

$$Y(s) = 2sX(s) + \frac{1}{s}X(s) - e^{-2s}X(s)$$

$$Y(s) = X(s)\left(2s + \frac{1}{s} - e^{-2s}\right) \rightarrow \frac{Y(s)}{X(s)} = 2s + \frac{1}{s} - e^{-2s} \rightarrow H(s) = 2s + \frac{1}{s} - e^{-2s}$$

7.4 c) CORRECT ANSWER: $3e^{-t} - 2e^{-2t}$

Impulse response $h(t)$ can be calculated by taking inverse Laplace transform $h(t) = \mathcal{L}^{-1}H(s)$

$$H(s) = \frac{s+4}{s^2 + 3s + 2} = \frac{s+4}{(s+1)(s+2)} = \frac{A}{s+1} + \frac{B}{s+2}$$

$$s + 4 = A(s+2) + B(s+1) \rightarrow A = 3, B = -2$$

$$H(s) = \frac{3}{s+1} - \frac{2}{s+2}$$

$$h(t) = \mathcal{L}^{-1}[H(s)] = \mathcal{L}^{-1}\left(\frac{3}{s+1}\right) - \mathcal{L}^{-1}\left(\frac{2}{s+2}\right) = 3\mathcal{L}^{-1}\left(\frac{1}{s+1}\right) - 2\mathcal{L}^{-1}\left(\frac{1}{s+2}\right)$$

$$h(t) = 3e^{-t} - 2e^{-2t}$$

7.4 d) CORRECT ANSWER – D

Output impedance can be calculated as shown below:

$$Z_0 = (R + sL)|| \left(\frac{1}{sC} \right)$$

Total impedance can be calculated as shown below:

$$Z_T = R + (R + sL)|| \left(\frac{1}{sC} \right)$$

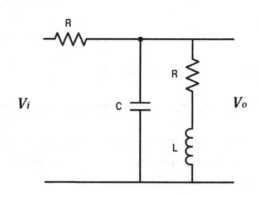

Voltage transfer function can be calculated as shown below:

$$\frac{V_0}{V_i} = \frac{Z_0}{Z_T} = \frac{(R + sL)|| \left(\frac{1}{sC} \right)}{R + (R + sL)|| \left(\frac{1}{sC} \right)}$$

7.4 e) CORRECT ANSWER – C

Output impedance can be calculated as shown below:

$$Z_0 = R + \frac{1}{sC}$$

Total impedance can be calculated as shown below:

$$Z_T = (R||sL) + \left(R + \frac{1}{sC} \right)$$

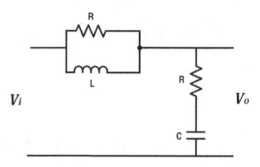

Voltage transfer function can be calculated as shown below:

$$\frac{V_0}{V_i} = \frac{Z_0}{Z_T} = \frac{R + \frac{1}{sC}}{(R||sL) + \left(R + \frac{1}{sC} \right)}$$

7.4 f) CORRECT ANSWER – D

Output impedance can be calculated as shown below:

$$Z_0 = R||sL|| \frac{1}{sC}$$

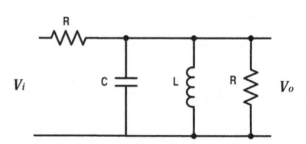

Total impedance can be calculated as shown below:

$$Z_T = R + R||sL|| \frac{1}{sC}$$

Voltage transfer function can be calculated as shown below:

$$\frac{V_0}{V_i} = \frac{Z_0}{Z_T} = \frac{R||sL|| \frac{1}{sC}}{R + R||sL|| \frac{1}{sC}}$$

Chapter # 8 – Signal Processing
8.1 Sampling - Solutions

Consult NCEES® FE Reference Handbook – Pages 225 and 376 for reference

8.1 a) CORRECT ANSWER - A

According to Nyquist Theorem, signal needs to be sampled at or above Nyquist rate for perfect reconstruction.

8.1 b) CORRECT ANSWER: 2000 Hz

The given signal is a summation of two $sinc$ functions $sinc(1000\pi t)$ and $sinc(2000\pi t)$.

$sinc(2000\pi t) = sinc[2\pi(1000)t]$ carries the highest frequency component.

According to Nyquist Theory, perfect reconstruction requires sampling rate to be $\geq$ 2 x highest frequency.

Therefore, required sampling rate shall be $\geq\ 2\ \times\ 1000\ Hz\ =\ 2000\ Hz.$

8.1 c) CORRECT ANSWER - C

According to the problem statement $x(t) = \cos(2\pi(1500)t + \theta)$.

Signal frequency $=\ 1500\ Hz$ and sampling frequency $=\ 2000\ Hz.$

Aliasing will occur because sampling frequency $<\ 2\ \times$ signal frequency.

8.1 d) CORRECT ANSWER - D

Alias frequency = |signal frequency – n x sampling frequency|

'n' is an integer that brings n x sampling frequency closest to signal frequency. In our case, n = 1 as shown below.

Alias frequency = |1500Hz – 1 x 2000Hz| = |– 500Hz| = 500 Hz.

Reconstructed signal frequency will be 500Hz with a negative phase angle (due to negative sign inside mod operator) as shown below.

$x'(t) = \cos(2\pi(500)t - \theta)$

$x'(t) = \cos(1000\pi t - \theta)$

8.1 e) CORRECT ANSWER - D

According to the problem statement $x(t) = \cos(2\pi(250)t + \theta)$.

Signal frequency $=\ 250\ Hz$ and sampling frequency $=\ 500\ Hz.$

Aliasing will not occur because sampling frequency $=\ 2\ \times\ 250\ Hz\ =\ 500\ Hz.$

8.1 f) CORRECT ANSWER - C

Alias frequency = |signal frequency − n x sampling frequency|.

'n' is an integer that brings n x sampling frequency closest to signal frequency.

In our case, n = 1 as shown below.

Alias frequency = |250Hz − 1 x 200Hz|= | 50Hz|= 50 Hz.

Reconstructed signal frequency will be 50Hz with a positive phase angle (due to positive sign inside mod operator) as shown below.

$$x'(t) = \cos(2\pi(50)t + \theta)$$

$$x'(t) = \cos(100\pi t + \theta)$$

8.1 g) CORRECT ANSWER - C

According to the problem statement $x(t) = \cos(2\pi(200)t + \theta)$.

Signal frequency = 200 Hz and sampling frequency = 300 Hz.

Aliasing will occur because sampling frequency < 2 x 200 Hz.

Alias frequency = |signal frequency − n x sampling frequency|.

'n' is an integer that brings n x sampling frequency closest to signal frequency. In our case, n = 1 as shown below.

Alias frequency = |signal frequency − n x sampling frequency|= |200 Hz − 1 x 300 Hz|= 100 Hz.

8.1 h) CORRECT ANSWER - C

Alias frequency = |signal frequency − n x sampling frequency|.

'n' is an integer that brings n x sampling frequency closest to signal frequency.

In our case, n = 1 as shown below.

Alias frequency = |200Hz − 1 x 150Hz|= | 50Hz|= 50 Hz.

Reconstructed signal frequency will be 50Hz with a positive phase angle (due to positive sign inside mod operator) as shown below.

$$x'(t) = \cos(2\pi(50)t + \theta).$$

$$x'(t) = \cos(100\pi t + \theta).$$

8.2 Analog Filters - Solutions

Consult NCEES® FE Reference Handbook – Pages 379 - 380 for reference

8.2 a) CORRECT ANSWER - D

Comparing the given transfer function to band-reject filter's transfer function given in NCEES® FE Reference Handbook confirms that it is an analog implementation of band-reject filter.

8.2 b) CORRECT ANSWER - C

Series RL circuit acts as a first-order low-pass filter and its cut-off frequency can be calculated as shown below:

$$\omega_c = \frac{R_s}{L} = \frac{2k\Omega}{2H} = 1000\ rad/s$$

8.2 c) CORRECT ANSWER - B

As noted above, series RL circuit acts as a first-order low-pass filter.

8.2 d) CORRECT ANSWER - A

Series RC circuit acts as a first-order high-pass filter and its cut-off frequency can be calculated as shown below:

$$\omega_c = \frac{1}{R_s C}$$

$$\omega_c = \frac{1}{(2k\Omega)(50\mu F)} = 10\ rad/s$$

8.2 e) CORRECT ANSWER - A

As noted above, series RC circuit acts as a first-order high-pass filter.

8.2 f) CORRECT ANSWER: $1000\ rad/s$

Series RLC circuit acts as a second-order band-pass filter and its bandwidth can be calculated as shown below:

$$BW = \frac{R_s}{L} = \frac{2k\Omega}{2H} = 1000\ rad/s$$

8.2 g) CORRECT ANSWER – Band-pass filter

As noted above, series RLC circuit acts as a second-order band-pass filter.

8.2 h) CORRECT ANSWER: B

Bandwidth of a second-order bandpass filter is given by following formula:

$$BW = \omega_U - \omega_L$$

$$\omega_L = \omega_U - BW$$

$$\omega_L = 1500\ rad/s - 1000\ rad/s = 500\ rad/s$$

8.3 Digital Filter, Z-transforms, Difference Equations - Solutions

Consult NCEES® FE Reference Handbook – Pages 369 - 371 for reference

8.3 a) CORRECT ANSWER - C

Z-transform is the equivalent of Laplace transform in difference equations. Laplace transforms solve differential equations. Discrete convolution provides zero state solution of a discrete linear time invariant system.

8.3 b) CORRECT ANSWER - B

$$x[n] = u[n] - u[n-5]$$

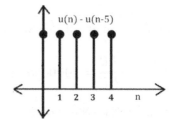

$$X[z] = \sum_{k=0}^{k=\infty} (u[k] - u[k-5])z^{-k} = \sum_{k=0}^{k=4} z^{-k} = 1 + z^{-1} + z^{-2} + z^{-3} + z^{-4}$$

8.3 c) CORRECT ANSWER - D

$$x[n] = 0.2^n u[n]$$

$$X[z] = \sum_{k=0}^{k=\infty} 0.2^k u[k] z^{-k} = \sum_{k=0}^{k=\infty} 0.2^k z^{-k} = \sum_{k=0}^{k=\infty} (0.2z^{-1})^k$$

According to the geometric series convergence formula:

$$\sum_{n=0}^{\infty} r^n = \frac{1}{1-r} \ for \ |r| < 1 \rightarrow X[z] = \sum_{k=0}^{k=\infty} 0.2^k z^{-k} = \frac{1}{1 - 0.2z^{-1}}$$

Note: This problem can also be solved used Z Transform table given in NCEES® FE Reference Handbook.

8.3 d) CORRECT ANSWER - A

$$x[n] = [2 \ 3 \ 1 \ 0 \ 5] \rightarrow x[0] = 2, x[1] = 3, x[2] = 1, x[3] = 0, x[4] = 5$$

$$X[z] = \sum_{k=-\infty}^{k=\infty} x[k]z^{-k} = \sum_{k=0}^{k=4} x[k]z^{-k} = x[0]z^{-0} + x[1]z^{-1} + x[2]z^{-2} + x[3]z^{-3} + x[4]z^{-4}$$

$$X[z] = 2z^{-0} + 3z^{-1} + z^{-2} + 5z^{-4} = 2 + 3z^{-1} + z^{-2} + 5z^{-4}$$

8.3 e) CORRECT ANSWER - B

$$x[n] = [2 \ 3 \ \breve{1} \ 0 \ 5] \rightarrow x[-2] = 2, x[-1] = 3, x[0] = 1, x[1] = 0, x[2] = 5$$

$$X[z] = \sum_{k=-\infty}^{k=\infty} x[k]z^{-k} = \sum_{k=-2}^{k=2} x[k]z^{-k} = x[-2]z^{-(-2)} + x[-1]z^{-(-1)} + x[0]z^0 + x[1]z^{-1} + x[2]z^{-2}$$

$$X[z] = 2z^2 + 3z^1 + z^0 + 5z^{-2} = 2z^2 + 3z + 1 + 5z^{-2}$$

8.3 f) CORRECT ANSWER - A

$x[n] = 5(0.75)^n u[n]$

$$X[z] = \sum_{k=0}^{k=\infty} 5(0.75)^k u[k] z^{-k} = 5 \sum_{k=0}^{k=\infty} (0.75z^{-1})^k = \frac{5}{1 - 0.75z^{-1}}$$

8.3 g) CORRECT ANSWER - B

$$X(z) = 4 + 2z^{-1} + 3z^{-3} + z^{-5} = 4z^0 + 2z^{-1} + 0z^{-2} + 3z^{-3} + 0z^{-4} + z^{-5}$$

$$X[z] = \sum_{k=-\infty}^{k=\infty} x[k] z^{-k} = \sum_{k=0}^{k=5} x[k] z^{-k} = x[0]z^0 + x[1]z^{-(1)} + x[2]z^{-(2)} + x[3]z^{-3} + x[4]z^{-4} + x[5]z^{-5}$$

$$x[n] = \{x[0], x[1], x[2], x[3], x[4], x[5]\} = \{4,2,0,3,0,1\}$$

8.3 h) CORRECT ANSWER - C

$$X(z) = \frac{z}{z - 0.5} = \frac{z}{z(1 - 0.5z^{-1})} = \frac{1}{1 - 0.5z^{-1}}$$

According to the z-transform pairs given in NCEES® FE Reference Handbook:

$$\beta^k \leftrightarrow \frac{1}{1 - \beta z^{-1}}$$

$$x[n] = (0.5)^n$$

8.3 i) CORRECT ANSWER - D

$$X(z) = \frac{5z + 2}{(z - 1)(z - 4)}$$

Inverse z-transform can be calculated using partial fraction expansion as shown below.

$$\frac{X(z)}{z} = \frac{5z + 2}{z(z - 1)(z - 4)} = \frac{C_1}{z} + \frac{C_2}{z - 1} + \frac{C_3}{z - 4}$$

$$5z + 2 = C_1(z - 1)(z - 4) + C_2(z)(z - 4) + C_3(z)(z - 1)$$

Let $z = 1$, $7 = C_2(-3) \rightarrow C_2 = -\frac{7}{3}$

Let $z = 4$, $22 = C_3(12) \rightarrow C_3 = \frac{11}{6}$

Let $z = 0$, $2 = C_1(-1)(-4) \rightarrow C_1 = \frac{1}{2}$

$$\frac{X(z)}{z} = \frac{1}{2z} - \frac{7}{3(z - 1)} + \frac{11}{6(z - 4)}$$

$$X(z) = \frac{1}{2} - \frac{7z}{3(z-1)} + \frac{11z}{6(z-4)}$$

$$X(z) = \frac{1}{2} - \frac{7z}{3z(1-z^{-1})} + \frac{11z}{6z(1-4z^{-1})}$$

$$x[n] = \frac{\delta[n]}{2} - \frac{7(1^n)}{3} + \frac{(11)(4^n)}{6}$$

8.3 j) CORRECT ANSWER - B

$$X(z) = \frac{(z-2)(z+1)}{(z-0.1)(z-0.2)}$$

$$\frac{X(z)}{z} = \frac{(z-2)(z+1)}{z(z-0.1)(z-0.2)} = \frac{C_1}{z} + \frac{C_2}{z-0.1} + \frac{C_3}{z-0.2}$$

$$(z-2)(z+1) = C_1(z-0.1)(z-0.2) + C_2(z)(z-0.2) + C_3(z)(z-0.1)$$

Let $z = 0.1$, $\quad -2.09 = C_2(-0.01) \rightarrow C_2 = 209$

Let $z = 0$, $\quad -2 = C_1(0-0.1)(0-0.2) \rightarrow C_1 = -100$

Let $z = 0.2$, $\quad -2.16 = C_3(0.2)(0.1) \rightarrow C_3 = -108$

$$\frac{X(z)}{z} = \frac{-100}{z} + \frac{209}{(z-0.1)} - \frac{108}{(z-0.2)} \quad \rightarrow \quad X(z) = -100 + \frac{209z}{(z-0.1)} - \frac{108z}{6(z-0.2)}$$

$$X(z) = -100 + \frac{209z}{(1-0.1z^{-1})} - \frac{108z}{z(1-0.2z^{-1})}$$

$$x[n] = -100\delta[n] + 209(0.1^n) - (108)(0.2^n)$$

8.3 k) CORRECT ANSWER - A

$$X(z) = \frac{(z+0.5)}{(z-0.1)(z+0.4)}$$

$$\frac{X(z)}{z} = \frac{(z+0.5)}{z(z-0.1)(z+0.4)} = \frac{C_1}{z} + \frac{C_2}{z-0.1} + \frac{C_3}{z+0.4}$$

$$(z+0.5) = C_1(z-0.1)(z+0.4) + C_2(z)(z+0.4) + C_3(z)(z-0.1)$$

Let $z = 0.1$, $\quad 0.6 = C_2(0.1)(0.5) \rightarrow C_2 = 12$

Let $z = -0.4$, $\quad 0.1 = C_3(-0.4)(-0.5) \rightarrow C_3 = \frac{1}{2}$

Let $z = 0$, $\quad 0.5 = C_1(-0.1)(0.4) \rightarrow C_1 = \frac{-25}{2}$

$$\frac{X(z)}{z} = \frac{-25}{2z} + \frac{12}{(z-0.1)} + \frac{1}{2(z+0.4)} \quad \rightarrow \quad X(z) = \frac{-25}{2} + \frac{12z}{(z-0.1)} + \frac{z}{2(z+0.4)}$$

$$X(z) = \frac{-25}{2} + \frac{12z}{z(1 - 0.1z^{-1})} + \frac{z}{2z(1 + 0.4z^{-1})}$$

$$x[n] = \frac{-25}{2}\delta[n] + 12(0.1)^n + \frac{(-0.4^n)}{2}$$

Helpful tip – Review partial fraction expansion for calculation of inverse Z-Transform.

8.3 l) CORRECT ANSWER: 4^n

$$y[n] + y[n-1] + 2y[n-2] = x[n] + x[n-1] + 2x[n-2]$$

$$Z[y[n] + y[n-1] + 2y[n-2]] = Z[x[n] + x[n-1] + 2x[n-2]]$$

$$Z[y[n]] + Z[y[n-1]] + 2Z[y[n-2]] = Z[x[n]] + Z[x[n-1]] + 2Z[x[n-2]]$$

$$Y(z) + z^{-1}Y(z) + 2z^{-2}Y(z) = X(z) + z^{-1}X(z) + 2z^{-2}X(z)$$

$$Y(z)(1 + z^{-1} + 2z^{-2}) = X(z)(1 + z^{-1} + 2z^{-2})$$

$$Y(z) = X(z) \rightarrow y[n] = x[n] = 4^n$$

8.3 m) CORRECT ANSWER: $(1 + 3z^{-1})/(1 + 2z^{-1})$

$$y[n] + 2y[n-1] = x[n] + 3x[n-1]$$

$$Z[y[n] + 2y[n-1]] = Z[x[n] + 3x[n-1]]$$

$$Z[y[n]] + 2Z[y[n-1]] = Z[x[n]] + 3Z[x[n-1]]$$

$$Y(z) + 2z^{-1}Y(z) = X(z) + 3z^{-1}X(z)$$

$$Y(z)(1 + 2z^{-1}) = X(z)(1 + 3z^{-1})$$

$$H(z) = \frac{Y(z)}{X(z)} = \frac{1 + 3z^{-1}}{1 + 2z^{-1}}$$

8.3 n) CORRECT ANSWER - A

Finite Impulse Response Filter (FIR) is non-recursive because it does not have a feedback loop (unity feedback).

8.3 o) CORRECT ANSWER - B

Infinite Impulse Response Filter (IIR) is recursive because it has a feedback loop.

8.3 p) CORRECT ANSWER - D

Sampling, A/D conversion and D/A conversion are important processes involved in digital filtering whereas phase modulation only applies to analog domain.

8.4 Continuous Time Convolution - Solutions

Consult NCEES® FE Reference Handbook – Page 370 for reference

8.4 a) CORRECT ANSWER - C

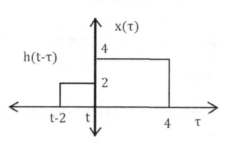

$y(t) = x(t) * h(t)$

It is easier to flip $h(t)$ into $h(-\tau)$.

<u>Region # 1</u> $y(t) = 0$ *for* $t < 0$ *no overlap*

<u>Region # 2</u> $y(t) = \int_0^t 8d\tau = 8t$ *for* $0 \le t \le 2$ *partial overlap*

<u>Region # 3</u> $y(t) = \int_{t-2}^t 8d\tau = 8t - 8(t-2) = 16$ *for* $2 < t \le 4$, *partial overlap*

<u>Region # 4</u> $y(t) = \int_{t-2}^4 8d\tau = 8(4 - t + 2) = 48 - 8t$ *for* $4 < t \le 6$, *partial overal*

<u>Region # 5</u> $y(t) = 0$ *for* $6 < t$, *no overlap*

8.4 b) CORRECT ANSWER - A

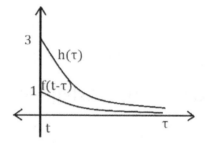

$y(t) = f(t) * h(t)$

It is easier to flip $f(t)$ into $f(-\tau)$.

<u>Region # 1</u> $y(t) = \int_0^\infty e^{(t-\tau)}3e^{(-\tau)}d\tau = \dfrac{3e^{(t)}}{2}$ *for* $t < 0$

<u>Region # 2</u> $y(t) = \int_t^\infty e^{(t-\tau)}3e^{(-\tau)}d\tau = \dfrac{3e^{(-t)}}{2}$ *for* $0 \le t$

8.4 c) CORRECT ANSWER - D

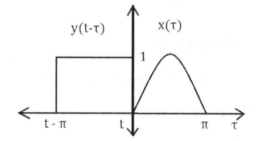

$f(t) = x(t) * y(t)$

It is easier to flip $y(t)$ into $y(-\tau)$.

<u>Region # 1</u> $f(t) = 0$ *for* $t < 0$ *no overlap*

<u>Region # 2</u> $f(t) = \int_0^t \sin(\tau)d\tau = 1 - \cos(t)$ *for* $0 < t \le \pi$ *partial overlap*

<u>Region # 3</u> $f(t) = \int_{t-\pi}^\pi \sin(\tau)\, d\tau = 1 - \cos(t)$ *for* $\pi < t \le 2\pi$, *partial overlap*

<u>Region # 4</u> $f(t) = 0$ *for* $\pi < t$, *no overlap*

8.4 d) CORRECT ANSWER - C

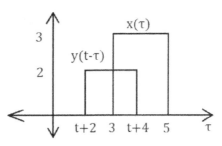

Let $f(t) = x(t) * y(t)$

It is easier to flip $y(t)$ into $y(-\tau)$.

Region # 1 $f(t) = 0$ _for_ $t < -1$ _no overlap_

Region # 2 $f(t) = \int_{3}^{t+4} (2)(3)d\tau = 6(t + 4 - 3) = 6(t + 1)$ _for_ $-1 \le t < 1$ _partial overlap_

Region # 3 $f(t) = \int_{t+2}^{5} 6d\tau = 6(5 - t - 2) = 6(3 - t)$ _for_ $1 \le t < 3$ _partial overlap_

Region # 4 $f(t) = 0$ _for_ $3 \le t$, _no overlap_

8.4 e) CORRECT ANSWER - C

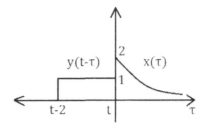

Let $f(t) = x(t) * y(t)$

It is easier to flip $y(t)$ into $y(-\tau)$.

Region # 1 $f(t) = 0$ _for_ $t < 0$ _no overlap_

Region # 2 $f(t) = \int_{0}^{t} 2e^{-\tau}d\tau = 2 - 2e^{-t}$ _for_ $0 \le t < 2$ _partial overlap_

Region # 3 $f(t) = \int_{t-2}^{t} 2e^{-\tau}d\tau = 2(e^{-t+2} - e^{-t})$ _for_ $t \ge 2$

8.5 Discrete Time Convolution - Solutions

Consult NCEES® FE Reference Handbook – Page 370 for reference

8.5 a) CORRECT ANSWER - B

$f[n] = x[n] * y[n] = \sum_{k=-\infty}^{k=\infty} x[k]y[n-k].$

It is easier to flip $y[n]$ into $y[-k]$.

For $n < 0$,   _there is no overlap_

For $n = 0$, $f[0] = 2.0 = 0$

For $n = 1$, $f[1] = 2.2 + 2.0 = 4$

For $n = 2$, $f[2] = 2.3 + 2.2 + 2.0 = 4 + 6 = 10$

For $n = 3$, $f[3] = 2.2 + 2.3 + 2.2 = 14$

For $n = 4$, $f[4] = 2.3 + 2.2 = 10$

For $n = 5$, $f[5] = 2.2 = 4$

For $n = 6$, $f[6] = 0$

Therefore, $f[n] = [0\ 4\ 10\ 14\ 10\ 4\ 0]$

8.5 b) CORRECT ANSWER - C

$f[n] = x[n] * y[n] = \sum_{k=-\infty}^{k=\infty} x[k]y[n-k].$

It is easier to flip $y[n]$ into $y[-k]$.

For $n < 0$ _there is no overlap_

For $n = 0$, $f[0] = 0$

For $n = 1$, $f[1] = 1.1 + 2.0 = 1$

For $n = 2$, $f[2] = 1.2 + 2.1 + 1.0 = 4$

For $n = 3$, $f[3] = 1.3 + 2.2 + 1.1 = 8$

For $n = 4$, $f[4] = 1.0 + 2.3 + 1.2 = 8$

For $n = 5$, $f[5] = 1.3 = 3$

For $n = 6$, $f[6] = 0$

Therefore, $f[n] = [0\ 1\ 4\ 8\ 8\ 3\ 0]$

8.5 c) CORRECT ANSWER - B

Zero input solution is found using characteristic polynomial roots.

Zero state response is the output of a system to a specific input when system has zero initial conditions and it is found using D-T convolution.

8.5 d) SOLUTION

$$x[n] = u[n] - u[n-5]$$

$$y[n] = 0.2^n u[n]$$

$$x[n] * y[n] = \sum_{k=-\infty}^{k=\infty} x[k]y[n-k]$$

$$x[n] * y[n] = \sum_{k=-\infty}^{k=\infty} (u[k] - u[k-5])(0.2^{n-k}u[n-k])$$

$$x[n] * y[n] = \sum_{k=-\infty}^{k=\infty} u[k](0.2^{n-k}u[n-k]) - \sum_{k=-\infty}^{k=\infty} u[k-5](0.2^{n-k}u[n-k])$$

$$x[n] * y[n] = \sum_{k=0}^{k=n} 0.2^{n-k} - \sum_{k=5}^{k=n} 0.2^{n-k}$$

$$x[n] * y[n] = 0.2^n \left(\sum_{k=0}^{k=n} 0.2^{-k} - \sum_{k=5}^{k=n} 0.2^{-k} \right)$$

8.5 e) SOLUTION

$$x[n] = u[n-2]$$

$$y[n] = 0.4^n u[n]$$

$$x[n] * y[n] = \sum_{k=-\infty}^{k=\infty} x[k]y[n-k]$$

$$x[n] * y[n] = \sum_{k=-\infty}^{k=\infty} x[k-2]0.4^{n-k}u[n-k]$$

$$x[n] * y[n] = \sum_{k=2}^{k=n} 0.4^{n-k}$$

$$x[n] * y[n] = 0.4^n \sum_{k=2}^{k=n} 0.4^{-k}$$

Chapter # 9 – Electronics
9.1 Semiconductor materials - Solutions

Consult NCEES® FE Reference Handbook – Pages 382 - 383 for reference

9.1 a) CORRECT ANSWER - A

According to the periodic table found in NCEES® FE Reference Handbook, Antimony is a group V element. Members of this group have 5 valance electrons which makes them suitable for n-type doping.

9.1 b) CORRECT ANSWER - D

According to the periodic table found in NCEES® FE Reference Handbook, Boron is a group III element. Members of this group have 3 valance electrons which makes them suitable for p-type doping.

9.1 c) CORRECT ANSWER - B

According to the formula given in NCEES® FE Reference Handbook, conductivity of a semiconductor is given by:

$$\sigma = q\left(n\mu_n + p\mu_p\right)$$

$$n = p = 2 \times 10^{10} m^{-3}, \quad q = 1.6 \times 10^{-19} C, \quad \mu_n = 0.20 m^2 V^{-1} s^{-1}, \quad \mu_p = 0.10 m^2 V^{-1} s^{-1}$$

$$\sigma = (1.6 \times 10^{-19})[(2 \times 10^{10})(0.20) + (2 \times 10^{10})(0.10)] = 9.61 \times 10^{-10} \, S.m^{-1}$$

9.1 d) CORRECT ANSWER: 0.634V

According to the formula given in NCEES® FE Reference Handbook, built-in potential of p-n junction is given by:

$$V_0 = \left(\frac{kT}{q}\right)\left(\ln \frac{N_a N_d}{n_i^2}\right) = (0.026)\left(\ln \frac{(2 \times 10^{15})(2 \times 10^{15})}{(1 \times 10^{10})^2}\right) = 0.634 \, V$$

9.1 e) CORRECT ANSWER - C

Insulators have large gap between valence and conduction bands which prevents free movement of electrons.

9.1 f) CORRECT ANSWER - A

The average velocity at which electrons move under the influence of an electrical field is called the drift velocity. Drift velocity results in drift current. It is directly proportional to the applied electrical field.

9.1 g) CORRECT ANSWER – C

Diffusion current is caused by the difference in charge concentration between different regions. This forms the basis of semiconductor doping.

9.1 h) CORRECT ANSWER – Group III

Group III elements of periodic table have 3 electrons in their outer orbit which allows them to form 3 covalent bonds with Si or Ge atoms. It creates a hole which makes them p-type doping agents. Boron and Aluminum are examples of p-type doping agents.

9.2 Diodes and Thyristors - Solutions

Consult NCEES® FE Reference Handbook – Page 385 for reference

9.2 a) CORRECT ANSWER - A

Let us first assume that both D1 and D2 are ON

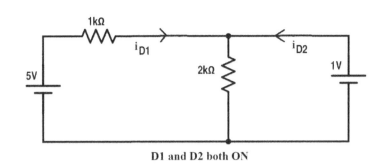

$$i_{D1} = \frac{5\,V - 1\,V}{1\,k\Omega} = 4\,mA$$

$$i_{D1} + i_{D2} = \frac{(1\,V)}{2\,k\Omega} = 0.5\,mA$$

D1 and D2 both ON

$$i_{D2} = 0.5\,mA - i_{D1} = 0.5\,mA - 3\,mA = -2.5\,mA$$

$i_{D2}<0$, result is not consistent with the assumption.

Let us now assume that D1 is ON and D2 is OFF.

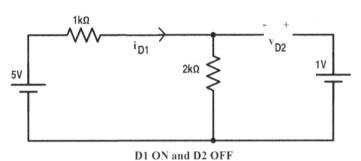

$$i_{D1} = \frac{5\,V}{3\,k\Omega} = 1.66\,mA$$

D1 ON and D2 OFF

$$v_{D2} = 1\,V - 1.66\,mA \times 2\,k\Omega$$

$$v_{D2} = -2.33\,V < 0$$

Since $i_{D1}>0$ and $v_{D2}<0$, the results are consistent with the assumptions.

9.2 b) CORRECT ANSWER: 0.66mA

The given circuit can be rearranged into a Thevenin equivalent circuit as shown below.

$$R_{th1} = 1\,k\Omega || 2\,k\Omega = 0.66\,k\Omega$$

$$V_{OC1} = 2\left(\frac{2}{3}\right) = 1.33\,V$$

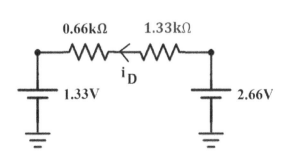

Similarly, $R_{th2} = 4\,k\Omega || 2\,k\Omega = 1.33\,k\Omega$

$$V_{OC2} = 4\left(\frac{4}{6}\right) = 2.66\,V$$

Let us assume that diode is "ON" i.e. forward biased.

$$i_D = \frac{2.66\,V - 1.33\,V}{1.33\,k\Omega + 0.66\,k\Omega} = 0.66\,mA$$

Since $i_D > 0$, Diode is ON.

Therefore, diode Q point is (0V, 0.66 mA)

Note that voltage drop across diode is assumed 0V since ideal diode model is being considered.

9.2 c) CORRECT ANSWER: 0.13 mA

Let us assume that diode is "ON" i.e. forward biased.

$$i_D = \frac{10\ V - 8V - 0.7V}{10\ k\Omega}$$

$$i_D = 0.13\ mA$$

Since diode is ON (because $i_D > 0$), our assumption is correct.

9.2 d) SOLUTION

Let us first assume that both D1 and D2 are ON.

$$i_{D1} = \frac{(5 - 0.7)\ V - (10 - 0.7)V}{2\ k\Omega}$$

$$i_{D1} = -2.5\ mA$$

Since $i_{D1} < 0$, this result is not consistent with the assumption.

Let us now assume that D1 is OFF and D2 is ON.

$$i_{D2} = \frac{(10V - 0.7V) - (-3\ V)}{5\ k\Omega}$$

$$i_{D2} = 2.46\ mA$$

$$V_{D1} = 5\ V - (10V - 0.7V)$$

$$V_{D1} = -4.3\ V < 0$$

Since $i_{D2} > 0$ and $V_{D1} < 0.7V$ this result is consistent with assumptions.

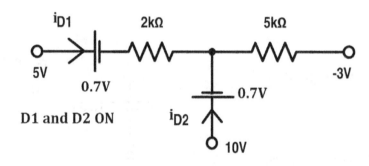

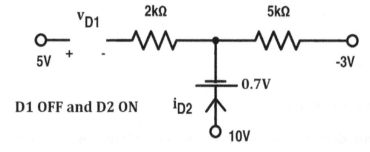

9.2 e) CORRECT ANSWER: 400Ω

Zener diode will maintain $V_Z = 2V$ across it if current passing through the diode $I_Z \geq 15mA$.

KCL can be written at the node connecting Zener diode, 500Ω resistor and R as follows:

$$\frac{12V - V_Z}{500\Omega} = I_Z + \frac{V_Z}{R} \rightarrow \frac{12V - 2V}{500\Omega} - \frac{2V}{R} = I_Z$$

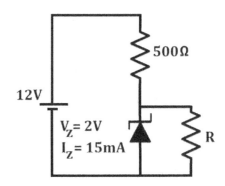

Since we require $I_Z \geq 15mA$ for Zener diode to maintain 2V across R.

$$0.02 - \frac{2V}{R} \geq 15mA \rightarrow R \geq 400\Omega$$

Therefore, $R_{min} = 400\Omega$ for Zener diode to maintain 2V across it.

9.2 f) CORRECT ANSWER: $2mA$

It can be observed that Zener diodes are connected in series. Both diodes will be operating in reverse biased mode with $V_Z = 4V$ across each one of them.

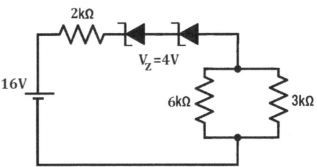

$$I = \frac{16V - V_Z - V_Z}{2\ k\Omega + 6k\Omega||3k\Omega}$$

$$I = \frac{16V - 4V - 4V}{2\ k\Omega + 2\ k\Omega} = 2mA$$

Therefore, $I = 2mA$ will flow through this circuit.

Note – Voltage drop across diodes adds in series.

9.2 g) CORRECT ANSWER: 1.4V

According to Shockley's equation given in NCEES® FE Reference Handbook:

$$i_D = I_S \left[e^{\frac{V_D}{\eta V_T}} - 1 \right]$$

$$V_D = \eta V_T \ln \left(1 + \frac{i_D}{I_S} \right)$$

$$V_T \approx 0.026V \ @ \ T = 300K$$

$$V_D = 2 \times 0.026 \times \ln \left(1 + \frac{50 \times 10^{-6}}{10^{-16}} \right) = 1.4V$$

9.2 h) CORRECT ANSWER: 114V

Average DC output voltage of a single-phase half-wave controlled rectifier can be calculated as follows:

$$V_{avg} = \frac{V_{max}}{2\pi} (1 + \cos\alpha) = \frac{480}{2\pi} (1 + \cos 60°) = 114V$$

Note: This formula is not provided in NCEES® FE Reference Handbook but it is commonly used for rectifiers.

9.2 i) CORRECT ANSWER: 152V

Average DC output voltage of a single-phase full-wave center-tap rectifier with an RL inductive load can be calculated as follows:

$$V_{avg} = \frac{2V_{max}}{\pi}(\cos\alpha) = \frac{2 \times 480}{\pi}(\cos 60°) = 152V$$

Note: This formula is not provided in NCEES® FE Reference Handbook but it is commonly used for rectifiers.

9.2 j) SOLUTION

BJTs and MOSFETs can be used as fully controllable switches by means of biasing.

Thyristors are semi-controllable switches whereas diodes are uncontrollable.

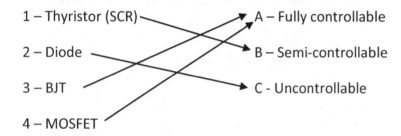

Semiconductor Devices

1 – Thyristor (SCR)

2 – Diode

3 – BJT

4 – MOSFET

Controllability

A – Fully controllable

B – Semi-controllable

C - Uncontrollable

Helpful tip – Review basic design, theory, and application of abovementioned semiconductor devices.

9.2 k) CORRECT ANSWER - B

According to the problem statement, we have a single-phase half-wave rectifier circuit with a resistive load of 5Ω and firing angle 45° as shown below. Thyristor is an electronic switch and works as explained below.

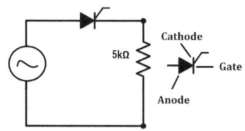

- It turns ON/starts conducting if gate current (pulse) is applied when Anode-Cathode is forward biased.
- It turns OFF when Anode-Cathode becomes reverse biased or anode current falls below threshold.

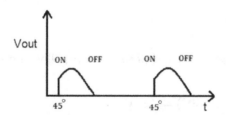

Thyristor will turn on at 45° firing angle and it will stay on until voltage polarity changes as shown above.

9.3 Bipolar Junction Transistors (BJTs) - Solutions

Consult NCEES® FE Reference Handbook – Page 386 for reference

9.3 a) CORRECT ANSWER - C

To analyze a BJT circuit we must assume a state of operation, enforce conditions, and then verify assumptions.

Let us assume that transistor is operating in the active region.

In active region: $V_{be} = 0.7\ V \quad I_b > 0mA \quad V_{ce} > 0.7V$

Base-emitter KVL can be written as shown below:

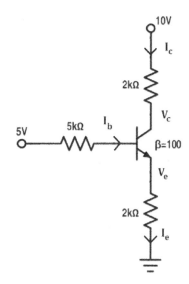

$$5V - (5k\Omega)(I_b) - V_{be} - (2k\Omega)(I_e) = 0$$

$$5V - (5k\Omega)(I_b) - 0.7V - (2k\Omega)(101I_b) = 0$$

$$I_b = 20.77\ \mu A \quad I_c = \beta I_b = (100)(20.77\ \mu A) = 2.07\ mA$$

KCL can be written at the collector as shown below:

$$\frac{10V - V_c}{2\ k\Omega} = I_c$$

$$V_c = 10\ V - (2\ k\Omega)(2.07\ mA) = 5.86\ V$$

KCL can be written at the emitter as shown below:

$$\frac{V_e - 0}{2\ k\Omega} = I_e$$

$$V_e = (2\ k\Omega)(2.09\ mA) = 4.18\ V$$

$$V_{ce} = V_c - V_e = 5.86\ V - 4.18\ V = 1.68\ V$$

Our assumptions are correct because $V_{ce} > 0.7\ V$, $I_b > 0mA$.

Therefore, transistor is operating in active mode.

9.3 b) CORRECT ANSWER - D

To analyze a BJT circuit we must assume a state of operation, enforce conditions, and then verify assumptions.

Let us assume that transistor is operating in the active region.

In the active region: $V_{be} = 0.7\ V \quad I_b > 0mA \quad V_{ce} > 0.7V$

Base-emitter KVL can be written as shown below:

$$3V - V_{be} - (2k\Omega)(I_e) = 0 \rightarrow I_e = \frac{3V - 0.7V}{(2k\Omega)} = 1.15\ mA$$

$$I_e = (\beta + 1)I_b = 101\ I_b \rightarrow I_b = 1.13 \times 10^{-5}A$$

$$I_c = \beta I_b = 1.138 \ mA$$

KCL can be written at collector as shown below:

$$\frac{7V - V_c}{3k\Omega} = I_c$$

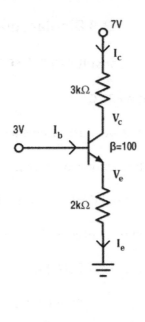

$$V_c = 7V - (3 \ k\Omega)(1.138 \ mA) = 3.58 \ V$$

$$V_{be} = V_b - V_e = 3V - V_e = 0.7V \rightarrow V_e = 2.3V$$

$$V_{ce} = V_c - V_e = 3.6 \ V - 2.3 \ V = 1.3 \ V$$

Our assumptions are correct because $V_{ce} > 0.7 \ V$, $I_b > 0mA$.

Therefore, transistor is operating in the active region.

9.3 c) CORRECT ANSWER – Cut-off

To analyze a BJT circuit we must assume a state of operation, enforce conditions, and then verify assumptions.

Let us assume that transistor is operating in the active region.

In active region: $V_{be} = 0.7 \ V \quad I_b > 0mA \quad V_{ce} > 0.7V$

Base-emitter KVL can be written as shown below:

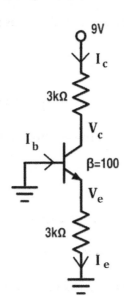

$$0 - V_{be} - (3k\Omega)(I_e) = 0$$

$$I_e = \frac{0 - 0.7V}{3k\Omega} = -0.233 \ mA$$

$$I_e = (\beta + 1)I_b$$

$$I_b = \frac{I_e}{(\beta + 1)} = -0.0023 \ mA$$

Transistor is operating in the cut-off region because $I_b < 0$.

$$I_b = I_c = I_e = 0.$$

9.3 d) CORRECT ANSWER - A

The given circuit can be simplified using Thevenin theorem.

$$R_{th} = 20 \ k\Omega || 10 \ k\Omega = 6.66 \ k\Omega$$

V_{th} can be calculated using the voltage divider rule as shown below.

$$V_{th} = 10V \left(\frac{10k\Omega}{30k\Omega}\right) = 3.33 \ V$$

Let us assume that transistor is operating in the active region.

In active region: $V_{be} = 0.7 \ V \quad I_b > 0mA \quad V_{ce} > 0.7V$

Base-emitter KVL can be written as shown below:

$$3.3V - (6.6k\Omega)(I_b) - V_{be} - (1k\Omega)(I_e) = 0$$

$$3.3V - (6.6k\Omega)(I_b) - 0.7V - (1k\Omega)(101\ I_b) = 0$$

$$I_b = 2.44 \times 10^{-5}A$$

$$I_c = \beta I b = (100)(2.44 \times 10^{-5}A) = 2.44\ mA$$

$$I_e = 101\ I_b = 2.46\ mA$$

KCL can be written at the collector as shown below:

$$\frac{10\ V - V_c}{2\ k\Omega} = I_c$$

$$V_c = 10\ V - (2\ k\Omega)(2.44\ mA) = 5.12\ V$$

KCL can be written at the emitter as shown below:

$$\frac{V_e - 0}{1\ k\Omega} = I_e$$

$$V_e = (1\ k\Omega)(I_e) = 2.46V$$

$$V_{ce} = V_c - V_e = 5.12\ V - 2.46\ V = 2.66\ V > 0.7\ V$$

Our assumptions are correct because $V_{ce} > 0.7\ V$, $I_b > 0mA$.

Therefore, transistor is operating in the active region.

9.3 e) CORRECT ANSWER: $3.23\ mA, 5.17V$

Let us assume that transistor is operating in the active region.

In active region: $V_{eb} = 0.7\ V$ $I_b > 0mA$ $V_{ec} > 0.7V$

Emitter - base KVL can be written as shown below:

$$5V - (1k\Omega)(I_e) - V_{eb} - (2k\Omega)(I_b) - 1V = 0$$

$$4V - (1k\Omega)(101I_b) - 0.7V - (2k\Omega)(I_b) = 0$$

$$I_b = 32.03\ \mu A$$

$$I_c = \beta I b = 3.2\ mA$$

$$I_e = 3.23\ mA$$

KCL can be written at the emitter as shown below:

$$\frac{5V - V_e}{1\ k\Omega} = I_e$$

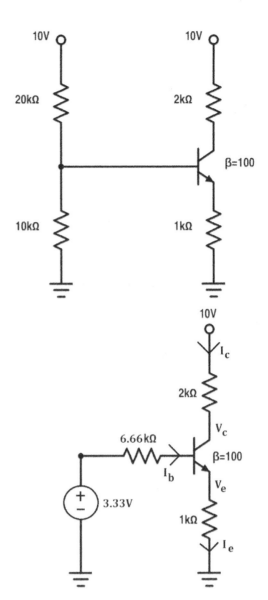

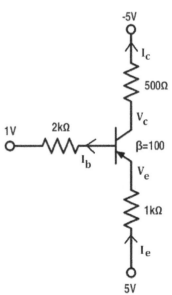

$V_e = 5V - (1 \, k\Omega)(3.23mA) = 1.77 \, V$

KCL can be written at the collector as shown below:

$$\frac{V_c - (-5V)}{500 \, \Omega} = I_c = 3.2 \, mA$$

$V_c = (3.2mA)(500 \, \Omega) - 5V = -3.4V$

$V_{ec} = V_e - V_c = 1.77 \, V - (-3.4 \, V) = 5.17V > 0.7 \, V$

Our assumptions are correct because $V_{ec} > 0.7 \, V$, $I_b > 0mA$.

Therefore, transistor is operating in active mode.

9.3 f) CORRECT ANSWER: $1.51 \, mA, 2V$

To analyze a BJT circuit we must assume a state of operation, enforce conditions, and then verify assumptions.

Let us assume that the transistor is operating in the active region.

In the active region: $V_{eb} = 0.7 \, V \quad I_b > 0mA \quad V_{ec} > 0.7V$

Emitter - base KVL can be written as shown below:

$5V - V_{eb} - (20k\Omega)(I_b) - 4V = 0$

$1V - 0.7V - (20k\Omega)(I_b) = 0$

$I_b = \dfrac{0.3V}{20k\Omega} = 1.5 \times 10^{-5}A$

$I_c = \beta I_b = 1.5 \, mA$

$I_e = 1.51 \, mA$

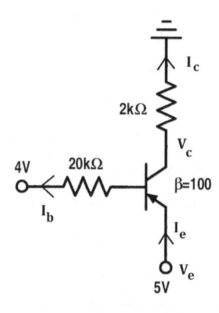

KCL can be written at the collector as shown below:

$$\frac{Vc - (0V)}{2 \, k\Omega} = I_c = 1.50 \, mA$$

$V_c = (I_c)(2 \, k\Omega) = 3 \, V$

$V_{ec} = V_e - V_c = 5 \, V - (3 \, V) = 2 \, V > 0.7 \, V$

Our assumptions are correct because $V_{ec} > 0.7 \, V$, $I_b > 0mA$

Therefore, transistor is operating in the active region.

9.3 g) CORRECT ANSWER: $2.83\ mA, 3.05V$

To analyze a BJT circuit we assume a state of operation, enforce conditions, and then verify assumptions.

Let us assume that the transistor is operating in the active region.

In active region: $V_{eb} = 0.7\ V \quad I_b > 0mA \quad V_{ec} > 0.7V$

Emitter - Base KVL can be written as shown below:

$10V = (5k\Omega)(I_e) + V_{eb} + (5k\Omega)(I_b) - 5V = 0$

$I_e = (\beta + 1)I_b = 101I_b$

$14.3V = (5k\Omega)101I_b + (5k\Omega)(I_b)$

$I_b = \dfrac{14.3V}{5k\Omega + 505k\Omega} = 28.03\mu A$

$I_c = \beta I_b = 2.803\ mA$

$I_c = \alpha I_e$

$I_e = \dfrac{I_c}{\alpha} = I_c \dfrac{(\beta + 1)}{\beta}$

$I_e = 2.803mA \dfrac{(100 + 1)}{100} = 2.83mA$

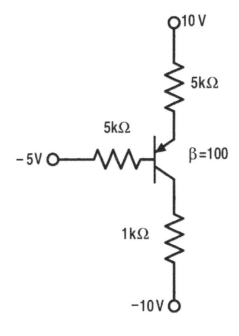

Emitter – Collector KVL can be written as shown below:

$10V = 5k\Omega \times I_e + V_{ec} + 1k\Omega \times I_c - 10V$

$V_{ec} = 3.05V > 0.7\ V$

Our assumptions are correct because $V_{ec} > 0.7\ V$, $I_b > 0mA$

Therefore, transistor is operating in the active region.

9.4 a) CORRECT ANSWER: 110Ω

Let us assume that the transistor is operating in the saturation region.

Gate-Source KVL can be written as shown below:

$$v_{gs} + (R_S)(i_d) = 0$$

$$R_S = \frac{-v_{gs}}{i_d}$$

In saturation region, drain current is given as follows:

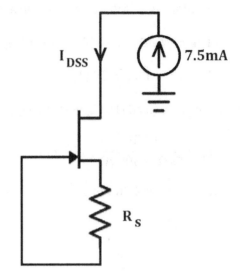

$$i_d = I_{DSS}\left(1 - \frac{v_{gs}}{V_p}\right)^2$$

$$1 - \frac{v_{gs}}{V_p} = \sqrt{\frac{i_d}{I_{DSS}}} = \sqrt{\frac{5mA}{7.5mA}} = 0.816$$

$$v_{gs} = (1 - 0.816)(V_p) = (0.1835)(-3V) = -0.55V$$

$$R_S = \frac{-(-0.55V)}{5mA} = 110\Omega$$

9.4 b) CORRECT ANSWER: 1mS

Transconductance of a JFET in saturation region can be calculated using following formula:

$$g_m = \frac{2\sqrt{I_{DSS}I_D}}{|V_p|}$$

Maximum value of transconductance is reached when $I_{DSS} = I_D$.

$$g_m = \frac{2\sqrt{I_{DSS}I_{DSS}}}{|V_p|} = \frac{2\sqrt{(I_{DSS})^2}}{|V_p|} = \frac{2I_{DSS}}{|V_p|}$$

According to the problem statement:

$$I_{DSS} = 2mA \quad V_p = -4V$$

$$|V_p| = |-4V| = 4V$$

$$g_m = \frac{2I_{DSS}}{|V_p|} = \frac{(2)(2mA)}{4V} = 1mS$$

9.4 c) CORRECT ANSWER - B

The given circuit can be simplified using Thevenin theorem.

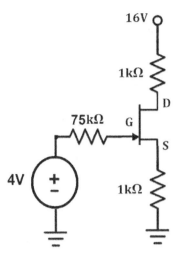

$R_{th} = 300 \, k\Omega || 100 \, k\Omega = 75 \, k\Omega$

$V_{th} = 16V \left(\dfrac{100k\Omega}{100k\Omega + 300k\Omega} \right) = 4 \, V$

Let us assume that the transistor is operating in the saturation region.

$v_g = 4 \, V, \quad i_g = 0 \, A$

Gate-Source KVL can be written as follows:

$4V - i_g \times 75 \, k\Omega - v_{gs} - 1 \, k\Omega \times i_D = 0$

$i_D = \dfrac{4V - v_{gs}}{1k\Omega}$

In saturation region, drain current can be calculated as follows:

$i_d = I_{DSS} \left(1 - \dfrac{v_{gs}}{V_p} \right)^2$

$\dfrac{4V - v_{gs}}{1k\Omega} = I_{DSS} \left(1 - \dfrac{v_{gs}}{V_p} \right)^2$

$\left(4V - v_{gs} \right) = 1k\Omega \times 10mA \left(1 - \dfrac{v_{gs}}{V_p} \right)^2 = 10 \left(1 - \dfrac{v_{gs}}{V_p} \right)^2 = 10 \left(1 + \dfrac{v_{gs}}{5} \right)^2$

$4V - v_{gs} = \dfrac{10}{25} \left(5 + v_{gs} \right)^2 \rightarrow 100V - 25v_{gs} = 10 \left(25 + v_{gs}^2 + 10v_{gs} \right) = 250 + 10v_{gs}^2 + 100v_{gs}$

$10v_{gs}^2 + 125v_{gs} + 150 = 0$

Dividing entire equation by 5 results in: $2v_{gs}^2 + 25v_{gs} + 30 = 0$

Quadratic formula can be used to solve this equation as shown below:

$v_{gs} = \dfrac{-25 \pm \sqrt{25^2 - 4(2)(30)}}{2 \times 2} = \dfrac{-25 \pm \sqrt{385}}{4} = \dfrac{-25 \pm 19.62}{4} = -11.2V, -1.35V$

v_{gs} must be $> V_p$ for saturation. Therefore, $v_{gs} = -1.35V$.

$i_D = \dfrac{4V - v_{gs}}{1k\Omega} = \dfrac{4V + 1.35V}{1k\Omega} = 5.35mA$

$i_D = \dfrac{16V - v_D}{1k\Omega} = 5.35mA \rightarrow v_D = 10.65V$

$v_{gd} = v_g - v_d = 4V - 10.65V = -6.65V < V_p$. Therefore, the transistor is operating in saturation region.

9.4 d) CORRECT ANSWER: 2.92mS

Transconductance of a JFET in saturation region can be calculated using following formula:

$$g_m = \frac{2\sqrt{I_{DSS}I_D}}{|V_p|}$$

According to the problem statement, $I_{DSS} = 10mA$, $V_p = -5V \rightarrow |V_p| = |-5V| = 5V$.

Drain current was calculated in last problem as $i_D = 5.35mA$.

$$g_m = \frac{2\sqrt{(10mA)(5.35mA)}}{5}$$

$$g_m = 2.92mS$$

9.5 MOSFETs - Solutions

Consult NCEES® FE Reference Handbook – Page 388 for reference

9.5 a) CORRECT ANSWER - D

To analyze a MOSFET circuit we assume a state of operation, enforce conditions, and then verify assumptions.

Let us assume that the transistor is operating in the saturation region.

Gate-Source KVL can be written as shown below:

$$0 - v_{gs} - (2k\Omega)(i_d) + 10V = 0 \rightarrow i_d = \frac{10V - v_{gs}}{2k\Omega}$$

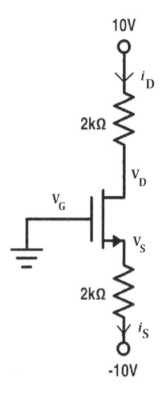

Drain-Source KVL can be written as shown below:

$$10V - (2k\Omega)(i_d) - v_{ds} - (2k\Omega)(i_d) + 10V = 0 \rightarrow v_{ds} = 20V - (4k\Omega)(i_d)$$

According to MOSFET's mathematical relationships: $i_d = K(v_{gs} - V_t)^2$

$$\frac{10V - v_{gs}}{2k\Omega} = K(v_{gs} - V_t)^2$$

Solving above given quadratic equations results in following values:

$$v_{gs} = 3.54\ V \ \ or \ \ v_{gs} = -2.54\ V$$

Since we assumed saturation, v_{gs} should be 3.54 V $\rightarrow$ $v_{gs} > V_t$

$$i_d = \frac{10V - v_{gs}}{2k\Omega} = \frac{10V - 3.54V}{2k\Omega} = 3.23\ mA$$

$$v_{ds} = 20V - (4k\Omega)(i_d) = 7.08\ V$$

$$v_{gs} = 3.54\ V > V_t \quad \quad v_{ds} = 7.08\ V > v_{gs} - V_t \ or \ v_{gd} < V_t$$

Our assumptions are correct because $v_{gs} > V_t$ and $v_{gd} < V_t$.
Therefore, the transistor is operating in saturation region.

9.5 b) CORRECT ANSWER - Triode

According to the details provided in problem statement:

$$v_g = 1\ V \quad v_s = 6\ V \quad v_d = 5\ V \quad i_g = 0 \quad V_t = -1V \rightarrow |V_t| = 1V$$

$$i_d = \frac{(5V - 0)}{5k\Omega} = 1\ mA$$

$$v_{sd} = v_s - v_d = 6V - 5V = 1\ V \quad \quad v_{sg} = v_s - v_g = 6V - 1V = 5V \rightarrow v_{sg} > |V_t|$$

$$v_{dg} = v_d - v_g = 5V - 1V = 4V > V_t$$

Since, $v_{sg} > |V_t|$ and $v_{dg} > |V_t|$ transistor is operating in triode region.

9.5 c) CORRECT ANSWER - B

The given circuit can be simplified using Thevenin theorem as shown below.

$R_{th} = 60 \ k\Omega || 40 \ k\Omega = 24 \ k\Omega$

$V_{th} = 4V \left(\dfrac{40k\Omega}{100k\Omega} \right) = 1.6 \ V$

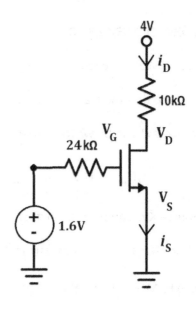

Let us assume that transistor is operating in the saturation region.

$v_g = 1.6 \ V, \quad i_g = 0 \ A, \quad v_s = 0 \ V$

$i_d = K \left(v_{gs} - V_t \right)^2 = 0.2mAV^{-2}(1.6V - 1V)^2 = 72 \ \mu A$

$\left(\dfrac{4V - v_d}{10k\Omega} \right) = 0.072 \ mA$

$v_d = 3.28 \ V, \qquad v_{ds} = 3.28V - 0V = 3.28V$

$v_{gs} = 1.6V > V_t$

$v_{gd} = 1.6V - 3.28V = -1.68 \ V < V_t$

Our assumptions are correct because $v_{gs} > V_t$ and $v_{gd} < V_t$.

Therefore, transistor is operating in the saturation region.

9.5 d) CORRECT ANSWER - C

The given circuit can be simplified using Thevenin theorem as shown below.

$R_{th} = 20 \ k\Omega || 20 \ k\Omega = 10 \ k\Omega$

$V_{th} = 4V \left(\dfrac{20k\Omega}{20k\Omega} \right) = 2 \ V$

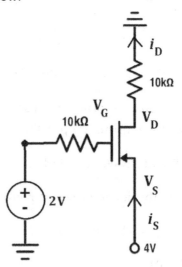

Let us assume that transistor is operating in the saturation region.

$v_g = V_{th} = 2 \ V, \quad i_g = 0, \quad v_{sg} = 4 \ V - 2 \ V = 2 \ V$

$i_d = K \left(v_{sg} - |V_{tp}| \right)^2 = 0.1mAV^{-2}(2V - |-1V|)^2 = 0.1 \ mA$

Source-Drain KVL can be written as follows:

$4V - v_{sd} - i_d \times 10k\Omega = 0 \quad \rightarrow \quad v_{sd} = 4V - i_d \times 10k\Omega = 3 \ V$

$v_{sg} = 2V > |V_{tp}|$

$v_{dg} = v_{sg} - v_{sd} = 2 \ V - 3 \ V = -1 \ V < |V_{tp}|$

Our assumptions are correct because $v_{sg} > V_t$ and $v_{dg} < |V_{tp}|$.

Therefore, transistor is operating in the saturation region.

9.5 e) CORRECT ANSWER: 0.44mA

The given circuit can be simplified using Thevenin theorem as shown below.

$R_{th} = 10 \ k\Omega || 20 \ k\Omega = 6.6 \ k\Omega$

$V_{th} = 4V \left(\dfrac{20k\Omega}{30k\Omega}\right) = 2.6 \ V$

To analyze a MOSFET circuit must assume a state of operation, enforce conditions, and then verify assumptions.

Let us assume that the transistor is operating in the saturation region.

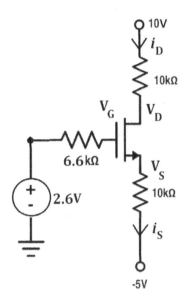

$v_g = V_{th} = 2.6 \ V$

For MOSFETs $i_{gs} = 0$ (always).

Gate-Source KVL can be written as shown below:

$2.6V - v_{gs} - (10k\Omega)(i_d) + 5V = 0$

$i_d = \dfrac{7.6V - v_{gs}}{10k\Omega} = K(v_{gs} - V_t)^2 = 0.1(v_{gs} - 1)^2$

Solving the above given quadratic equations results in following values:

$v_{gs} = 3.12 \ V \ or \ v_{gs} = -2.1 \ V$

Since we assumed the saturation region of operation in which $v_{gs} > V_t$.

This means that only $v_{gs} = 3.12 \ V$ is the applicable solution.

$i_d = 0.1mAV^{-2}(3.12V - 1V)^2$

$i_d = 0.44 \ mA$

$v_d = 10V - (10k\Omega)(i_d) = 5.6 \ V$

$v_{gs} = 3.12 \ V > V_t$

$v_{gd} = 2.6 \ V - 5.6 \ V = -3V < V_t$

Our assumptions are correct because $v_{gs} > V_t$ and $v_{gd} < V_t$.

Therefore, the transistor is operating in the saturation region.

9.5 f) CORRECT ANSWER - Saturation

It can be observed that $i_d = 25\mu A$ due to constant current source and $v_S = 0V$ because source is grounded.

$$v_{GS} = v_G - v_S = v_G - 0V = v_G$$

Let us assume that the transistor is operating in saturation region.

In saturation, drain current can be given by following equation:

$$i_d = K(v_{GS} - V_T)^2$$

$$25\mu A = (0.25mA/V^2)(v_G - 1)^2$$

$$(v_G - 1)^2 = 0.1$$

$$v_G = 1.31V \rightarrow v_{GS} = 1.31V - 0V = 1.31V$$

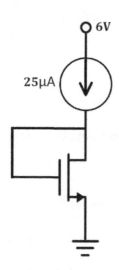

Since gate and drain are connected $v_G = v_D$

$v_{GD} = v_G - v_D = 0V < V_T$. Therefore, the transistor is operating in the saturation region.

9.5 g) CORRECT ANSWER: $5k\Omega, 3k\Omega$

Drain current can be calculated using following equation:

$$i_D = \frac{6V - v_D}{R_1} = 1mA$$

$$R_1 = \frac{6V - 1.2V}{1mA} = 5k\Omega$$

Let us assume that the transistor is operating in saturation region.

In saturation, drain current can be calculated by following equation:

$$i_d = K(v_{GS} - V_T)^2$$

$$1mA = (0.25mA/V^2)(v_{GS} - 1)^2$$

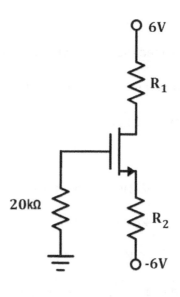

Solving for v_{GS} results in $v_{GS} = 3V$.

Since gate current $i_G = 0 \rightarrow v_G = 0V \rightarrow v_S = -3V$.

Following equation can be we written at the source node.

$$i_D = \frac{v_S - (-6V)}{R_2} = 1mA$$

$$R_2 = \frac{6V - 3V}{1mA} = 3k\Omega$$

Helpful tip – As an exercise, verify that the transistor is operating in the saturation region.

9.6 Operational Amplifier - Solutions

Consult NCEES® FE Reference Handbook – Page 381 - 382 for reference

9.6 a) CORRECT ANSWER: -5 V

According to NCEES® FE Reference Handbook, inverting amplifier gain is given by:

$$v_0 = -\frac{R_2}{R_1}v_a = -\frac{10k\Omega}{2k\Omega}(1V) = -5\,V$$

9.6 b) CORRECT ANSWER: 5 $k\Omega$

According to NCEES® FE Reference Handbook, non-inverting amplifier gain is given by:

$$v_0 = \left(1 + \frac{R_2}{R_1}\right)v_b = \left(1 + \frac{R}{1k\Omega}\right)2V = 12\,V \rightarrow R = 5\,k\Omega$$

9.6 c) CORRECT ANSWER: 2.5 V

According to NCEES® FE Reference Handbook, non-inverting amplifier gain is given by:

$$v_0 = -\frac{R_2}{R_1}v_a + \left(1 + \frac{R_2}{R_1}\right)v_b = -\frac{6k\Omega}{3k\Omega}1V + \left(1 + \frac{6k\Omega}{3k\Omega}\right)1.5V = 2.5\,V$$

9.6 d) CORRECT ANSWER: -35 V

We can solve this problem using principle of superposition as shown below:

Shorting the 6V power source results in following output.

$$\frac{3V - 0}{10\,k\Omega} = \frac{0 - v_{01}}{50\,k\Omega} \rightarrow \qquad v_{01} = -15\,V$$

Shorting the 3V power source results in following output.

$$\frac{6V - 0}{15\,k\Omega} = \frac{0 - v_{02}}{50\,k\Omega} \rightarrow \qquad v_{02} = -20\,V$$

$$v_0 = v_{01} + v_{02} = -15\,V - 20\,V$$

$$v_0 = -35\,V$$

9.6 e) CORRECT ANSWER: 0.5 V

According to NCEES® FE Reference Handbook, non-inverting amplifier gain is given by:

$$v_0 = -\frac{R_2}{R_1}v_a + \left(1 + \frac{R_2}{R_1}\right)v_b$$

$$v_0 = -\frac{5k\Omega}{10k\Omega}2V + \left(1 + \frac{5k\Omega}{10k\Omega}\right)1V$$

$$v_0 = 0.5\,V$$

9.6 f) CORRECT ANSWER: 4.3 V

According to NCEES® FE Reference Handbook, differential amplifier's operation is given by following equation:

$$\frac{i_{E1}}{i_{E2}} = \frac{e^{(v_{b1}-v_{b2})}}{V_T} \qquad i_{E1} + i_{E2} = I_{E-total}$$

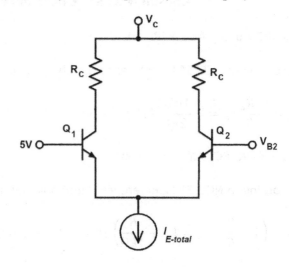

According to the problem statement:

$$i_{E1} = 2i_{E2} \quad V_T = 1V \quad v_{b1} = 5V$$

$$\frac{2i_{E2}}{i_{E2}} = \frac{e^{(5-v_{b2})}}{1}$$

$$2 = e^{(5-v_{b2})}$$

Taking the natural logarithm on both sides of the equation:

$$\ln 2 = \ln e^{(5-v_{b2})} = 5 - v_{b2}$$

Rearranging this equation in terms of v_{b2}.

$$v_{b2} = 5 - \ln 2 = 5 - 0.69 = 4.3V$$

9.6 g) SOLUTION

According to the problem statement:

$$I = 6mA \quad V_T = 1V \quad v_{b1} = 5V \quad v_{b2} = 4.3V$$

Emitter currents of BJT differential amplifiers can be calculated using the formulas provided in the NCEES® FE Reference Handbook as shown below.

$$i_{E1} = \frac{I}{1 + \dfrac{e^{(v_{b2}-v_{b1})}}{V_T}}$$

$$i_{E1} = \frac{6mA}{1 + \dfrac{e^{(4.3-5)}}{1}} = 4mA$$

Similarly, we can calculate i_{E2} as shown below:

$$i_{E1} = \frac{I}{1 + \dfrac{e^{(v_{b1}-v_{b2})}}{V_T}} = \frac{6mA}{1 + \dfrac{e^{(5-4.3)}}{1}} = 2mA$$

It can be observed that, $i_{E1} + i_{E2} = 4mA + 2mA = 6mA = I_{E-total}$

9.7 Power Electronics – Solutions

Consult NCEES® FE Reference Handbook – Page 384 for reference

9.7 a) CORRECT ANSWER - B

Chopper converts DC to DC i.e. constant DC to variable DC or variable DC to constant DC.

Inverter converts DC to AC with desired voltage and frequency.

Rectifier converts AC to DC.

Cyclo-converter changes given AC to AC with desired frequency and amplitude.

9.7 b) CORRECT ANSWER - C

Voltage conversion equation of a boost converter is given as follows:

$$V_{out} = \frac{V_{in}}{1-D} \qquad D = \frac{t_{ON}}{t_{ON}+t_{OFF}}$$

According to the problem statement:

$$V_{out} = 600VDC, \quad V_{in} = 150VDC, \quad t_{ON} = 10\mu s, \qquad t_{OFF} = ? \quad D = ?$$

$$D = 1 - \frac{V_{in}}{V_{out}} = 1 - \frac{150}{600} = 0.75$$

$$0.75 = \frac{10\mu s}{10\mu s + t_{OFF}} \rightarrow t_{OFF} = 3.33\mu s$$

$$T = t_{ON} + t_{OFF} = 10\mu s + 3.33\mu s = 13.33\mu s$$

$$f_{switching} = \frac{1}{T} = \frac{1}{13.33\mu s} = 75kHz$$

9.7 c) CORRECT ANSWER - C

Voltage conversion equation of a buck converter is given as follows:

$$V_{out} = V_{in} \times D = V_{in} \times \frac{1}{t_{ON}+t_{OFF}} \times t_{ON} = V_{in} \times \frac{1}{T} \times t_{ON} = V_{in} \times f \times t_{ON}$$

According to the problem statement:

$$V_{in} = 60VDC, \quad f = 500Hz, \quad t_{ON} = 1.5ms, \quad I_{out} = ?$$

$$V_{out} = 60VDC \times 500Hz \times 1.5ms = 45V$$

$$I_{out} = \frac{V_{out}}{R} = \frac{45V}{5\Omega} = 9A$$

9.7 d) CORRECT ANSWER - D

Voltage conversion equation of a buck-boost converter is given as follows:

$$V_{out} = V_{in} \times \left(-\frac{D}{1-D}\right)$$

According to the problem statement: $V_{in} = 60VDC$, $f = 500Hz$, $t_{ON} = 1.5ms$ $V_{out} =?$ $D = ?$

$$D = f \times t_{ON} = \frac{t_{ON}}{t_{ON} + t_{OFF}} = 0.75$$

$$V_{out} = V_{in} \times \left(-\frac{D}{1-D}\right) = 60 \times \left(-\frac{0.75}{1-0.75}\right) = -180VDC$$

9.7 e) CORRECT ANSWER - B

Average DC output voltage of a 6-pulse rectifier can be calculated using following equation:

$$V_{dc} = V_{rms} \times \frac{n\sqrt{2}}{\pi} \sin\frac{\pi}{n}$$

According to the problem statement: $V_{rms} = 600V$, $n = 6$.

$$V_{dc} = V_{rms} \times \frac{6\sqrt{2}}{\pi} \sin\frac{\pi}{6} = 810VDC$$

9.7 f) CORRECT ANSWER - C

Average DC output voltage of a 6-pulse rectifier can be calculated using following equation:

$$V_{dc} = V_{rms} \times \frac{n\sqrt{2}}{\pi} \sin\frac{\pi}{n}$$

According to the problem statement: $V_{rms} = 600V$, $n = 12$.

$$V_{dc} = V_{rms} \times \frac{12\sqrt{2}}{\pi} \sin\frac{\pi}{12} = 839VDC$$

9.7 g) CORRECT ANSWER: 183V

Average line-line RMS output voltage of a 3-phase VSI can be calculated using following equation:

$$V_{rms} = mV_{dc} \times \frac{1}{2} \sqrt{\frac{3}{2}}$$

$$V_{rms} = 0.5 \times 600 \times \frac{1}{2} \times \sqrt{\frac{3}{2}} = 183V$$

9.8 Instrumentation - Solutions

Consult NCEES® FE Reference Handbook – Pages 220 - 224 for reference

9.8 a) CORRECT ANSWER - C

Transducer converts a physical quantity/value into electrical signal. Microphone (voice), thermocouple (heat) and photodiode (light) convert different physical quantities into electrical signals.

9.8 b) CORRECT ANSWER - B

Resistance at a given temperature can be calculated using formula given below:

$$R_t = R_o[1 + \alpha(T - T_o)] = 200\Omega[1 + 0.0039°C^{-1}(15°C)] = 211 \ \Omega$$

9.8 c) CORRECT ANSWER: 5000 Ω

According to the problem statement, Wheatstone bridge is balanced. Therefore, unknown resistance can be calculated as shown below:

$$\frac{R_1}{R_2} = \frac{R_3}{R_x} \rightarrow R_x = \frac{R_2}{R_1}R_3 = \frac{1000 \ \Omega}{100 \ \Omega}500 \ \Omega = 5000 \ \Omega$$

9.8 d) CORRECT ANSWER: 200 Ω

ΔR of Wheatstone bridge can be calculated using formula given below:

$$\Delta V = \frac{\Delta R}{4(R)}V_{in}$$

$$\Delta R = \frac{\Delta V \times 4R}{V_{in}} = \frac{0.5 \ V \times 4000 \ \Omega}{10 \ V} = 200 \ \Omega$$

9.8 e) CORRECT ANSWER - C

Gauge Factor (GF) is given by the following equation which is provided in NCEES® FE Reference Handbook.

$$GF = \frac{\left(\frac{\Delta R}{R}\right)}{\frac{\Delta L}{L}} = \frac{\left(\frac{\Delta R}{R}\right)}{\varepsilon}$$

Rearranging this equation in terms of ΔR results in the following:

$$\Delta R = GF \times \varepsilon \times R = 1.5 \times 0.10 \times 100\Omega = 15\Omega$$

9.8 f) CORRECT ANSWER - B

Voltage across $10 \ k\Omega$ can be calculated as shown below:

$$V_{10k\Omega} = \frac{10 \ k\Omega||100 \ k\Omega}{10 \ k\Omega||100 \ k\Omega + 25 \ k\Omega||50 \ k\Omega + 20k\Omega}10V$$

$$V_{10k\Omega} = 1.986 \ V$$

9.8 g) CORRECT ANSWER - A

Voltage across $10\ k\Omega$ can be calculated as shown below:

$$V_{10k\Omega} = \frac{10\ k\Omega || 500\ k\Omega}{10\ k\Omega || 500\ k\Omega + 25\ k\Omega || 50\ k\Omega + 20 k\Omega}\ 10V$$

$$V_{10k\Omega} = 2.10\ V$$

9.8 h) CORRECT ANSWER - B

Actual current without ammeter can be calculated as shown below:

$$I_{actual} = \frac{10V}{2k\Omega + 1\ k\Omega || 1\ k\Omega} = \frac{10V}{2k\Omega + 0.5\ k\Omega} = 4\ mA$$

Current measured by ammeter is shown below:

$$I_{measured} = \frac{10V}{2k\Omega + 1\ k\Omega || 1\ k\Omega + 0.05 k\Omega} = 3.92\ mA$$

$$\%\ error = \frac{I_{actual} - I_{measured}}{I_{actual}} = \frac{4\ mA - 3.92\ mA}{4\ mA} = 2\%$$

Consult NCEES® FE Reference Handbook – Pages 363 – 368 for reference

10.1 a) CORRECT ANSWER : 592 W

$$S_{1\varphi} = V_{1\varphi} I_{1\varphi}^* = P + jQ.$$

$$V = 120V \quad Z_{line} = 2 + 2j\Omega \quad Z_{load} = 20 + 5j\Omega$$

$$I = \frac{V}{Z_{line} + Z_{load}} = \frac{120\,V}{(2 + 2j\Omega) + (20 + 5j\Omega)}$$

$$I = 5.19\underline{/-17.65^0}\,A$$

$$S_{1\varphi} = V_{1\varphi} I_{1\varphi}^* = (120\underline{/0^0})\,(5.19\underline{/17.65^0})VA$$

$$P = S\cos\theta = 622\,\cos 17.65^0 = 592\ W$$

10.1 b) CORRECT ANSWER - B

According to the problem statement:

$$V = 10\underline{/80^0}V \text{ and } Z = 5 + j\,\Omega = 5.09\underline{/11.3^0}\,\Omega.$$

$$I = V/Z = 1.96\underline{/68.7^0}\,A$$

10.1 c) CORRECT ANSWER - C

$$S_{1\varphi} = V_{1\varphi} I_{1\varphi}^*$$

$$Z = (5 + j\,\Omega)||(-2j\,\Omega)= 2\underline{/-67.3^0}\,\Omega$$

$$V_{1\varphi} = I_{1\varphi} \times Z =10\underline{/0}\,A \times 2\underline{/-67.3^0}\,\Omega =20\underline{/-67.3^0}\,V$$

$$S_{1\varphi} = V_{1\varphi} I_{1\varphi}^* = 200\underline{/-67.3^0}\,VA$$

10.1 d) CORRECT ANSWER : 9.19 W

$$S_{1\varphi} = V_{1\varphi} I_{1\varphi}^* = P + jQ.$$

$$Z = 10 + 5j - 2j\,\Omega = 10 + 3j\,\Omega = 10.4\underline{/16.7^0}\Omega \quad V=10\underline{/10^0}\,V$$

$$I = \frac{V}{Z} = 0.96\underline{/-6.7^0}A$$

$$S_{1\varphi} = V_{1\varphi} I_{1\varphi}^* = 9.6\underline{/16.7^0}\,VA$$

$$P = S\cos\theta = 9.57\,\cos 16.69^0 = 9.19\ W$$

10.1 e) CORRECT ANSWER - B

It can be observed that the voltage across 5Ω resistor is $5\underline{/0^0}$ V. Power absorbed by 5 Ω resistor can be calculated as shown below.

$$P = I^2R = \left(\frac{V}{R}\right)^2 R = \frac{V^2}{R} = \frac{5V^2}{5\Omega} = 5\ W$$

10.1 f) CORRECT ANSWER – C

Real power delivered by the source can be calculated using following formula:

$$P = V_{rms}I_{rms}\cos\theta$$

According to the problem statement:

$$v(t) = 120\sqrt{2}\cos(377t + 0^0)$$

$$V_{phasor} = \frac{120\sqrt{2}}{\sqrt{2}}\underline{/0^\circ}\ V = 120\underline{/0^\circ}\ V$$

$$V_{rms} = 120V$$

$$I_{phasor} = (120\underline{/0^\circ}\ V)/20\Omega = 6\underline{/0^\circ}\ A$$

$$I_{rms} = 6A \quad \cos\theta = \cos 0 = 1$$

$$P = 120V \times 6A \times 1 = 720W$$

10.1 g) CORRECT ANSWER – A

Real power delivered by the source can be calculated using following formula:

$$P = V_{rms}I_{rms}\cos\theta$$

According to the problem statement:

$$v(t) = 120\sqrt{2}\cos(377t + 0^0)$$

$$V_{phasor} = \frac{120\sqrt{2}}{\sqrt{2}}\underline{/0^\circ}\ V = 120\underline{/0^\circ}\ V$$

$$V_{rms} = 120V$$

$$X_L = j\omega L = j(377)(20 \times 10^{-3}) = 7.54\underline{/90^\circ}\ \Omega$$

$$I_{phasor} = (120\underline{/0^\circ}\ V)/7.54\underline{/90^\circ}\ \Omega = 15.9\underline{/-90^\circ}\ A$$

$$I_{rms} = 15.9A \quad \cos(-90^\circ) = 0$$

$$P = 120V \times 15.9A \times 0 = 0W$$

Inductors do not absorb real power.

10.1 h) CORRECT ANSWER – A

Real power delivered by the source can be calculated using following formula:

$$P = V_{rms}I_{rms}\cos\theta$$

According to the problem statement:

$$v(t) = 120\sqrt{2}\cos(377t + 0^0)$$

$$V_{phasor} = \frac{120\sqrt{2}}{\sqrt{2}}\underline{/0°}\ V = 120\underline{/0°}\ V$$

$$V_{rms} = 120V$$

$$X_C = -\frac{j}{\omega C} = -\frac{j}{(377)(300 \times 10^{-6})} = 8.84\underline{/-90°}\ \Omega$$

$$I_{phasor} = (120\underline{/0°}\ V)/8.84\underline{/-90°}\ \Omega = 13.5\underline{/90°}\ A$$

$$I_{rms} = 13.5A \quad \cos(90°) = 0$$

$$P = 120V \times 13.5A \times 0 = 0W.$$

Capacitors do not absorb real power.

10.2 a) CORRECT ANSWER - C

According to the problem statement, $V_{an} = 120\underline{/30^0}$ V.

In the given scenario, $V_{bn} = 120\underline{/30^0\text{-}120^0}$ V and $V_{cn} = 120\underline{/30^0\text{+}120^0}$ V

Line voltages lead phase voltages by 30^0 and they are also greater by a factor of $\sqrt{3}$.

$V_{ab} = \sqrt{3} \times 120\underline{/30^0\text{+}30^0}$ V= $208\underline{/60^0}$ V

$V_{bc} = 208\underline{/\text{-}60^0}$V and $V_{ca} = 208\underline{/180^0}$ V

10.2 b) CORRECT ANSWER - B

In a balanced 3φ-Y network, phase current can be calculated as shown below.

$$I_{an} = \frac{V_{an}}{Z_\varphi}$$

$V_{an} = 120\underline{/30^0}$ V

$Z_\varphi = 20 + 5j\ \Omega = 20.6\underline{/14^0}\ \Omega$

$I_{an} = 5.82\underline{/16^0}$A

10.2 c) CORRECT ANSWER - C

In a balanced 3φ-Y network, phase current equals line current.

$$I_{an} = \frac{V_{an}}{Z_\varphi + Z_l}$$

$$I_{an} = \frac{277 + 0j\ V}{(5 + 5j\Omega) + (1 + j\Omega)}$$

$I_{an} = I_l = 32.6\underline{/\text{-}45^0}$ A

10.2 d) CORRECT ANSWER - A

In a balanced 3φ-Y network, phase current and load voltage can be calculated as shown below.

$$I_{an} = \frac{V_{an}}{Z_{load} + Z_{line}}$$

$V_{an} = 120\underline{/60^0}$ V and $Z_{line} = 2 + j\Omega$ $Z_{load} = 10 + 10j\Omega$

$I_{an} = 7.4\underline{/18^0}$ A

$V_{load} = I_{an} \times Z_{load} = 104\underline{/63^0}$ V

10.2 e) CORRECT ANSWER - B

In a balanced 3ϕ-Y network, line current, voltage and impedance are related as shown below.

$$I_{an} = \frac{V_{an}}{Z_{load} + Z_{line}}$$

$$Z_{load} + Z_{line} = \frac{V_{an}}{I_{an}}$$

$$Z_{load} = \frac{V_{an}}{I_{an}} - Z_{line} = 23.4 + 1.75j \ \Omega = 23.5\underline{/4.5^0} \ \Omega$$

10.2 f) CORRECT ANSWER - B

$$Z_\Delta = 3Z_Y$$

$$Z_\Delta = 3(10 + 5j) \ \Omega = 30 + 15j \ \Omega$$

$$Z_\Delta = 33.54\angle 26.6^0 \Omega$$

$$I_\Delta^P = \frac{V_\Delta^P}{Z_\Delta}$$

$$I_\Delta^P = \frac{208\angle 30^0}{33.54\angle 26.6^0} = 6.20\angle 3.4^0 A$$

In a delta network, line current is larger than phase current by a factor of $\sqrt{3}$ and lags by 30^0.

$$I_\Delta^L = \sqrt{3} \times I_\Delta^P \angle \theta_p - 30^0$$

$$I_\Delta^L = \sqrt{3} \times 6.20\angle(3.4^0 - 30^0)A = 10.7\angle{-26.6^0}A$$

10.2 g) CORRECT ANSWER - D

It is important to note that impedance is connected in a Δ arrangement and source is Y connected.

$$V_{an} = 120\underline{/0^0}V$$

This problem can be solved easily by converting Z_Δ to Z_Y as shown below:

$$Z_\Delta = 10 + 2j \ \Omega$$

$$Z_\Delta = 3 \ Z_Y$$

$$Z_Y = \frac{10 + 2j \ \Omega}{3}$$

$$Z_Y = 3.4\underline{/11.3^0}\Omega$$

$$I_{an} = \frac{V_{an}}{Z_Y}$$

$$I_{an} = 35.3\underline{/-11.3^0} \ A$$

10.2 h) CORRECT ANSWER - A

It is important to note that the first load networks is Y-connected and the second load network is Δ-connected.

$$Z_{Y-1} = 10 + 5j \, \Omega$$

$$Z_{\Delta-2} = 6 + 9j \Omega$$

$$Z_{\Delta} = 3 \times Z_Y$$

$$Z_{Y-2} = \frac{Z_{\Delta-2}}{3} = 2 + 3j \, \Omega$$

$$Z_{eq-Y} = Z_{Y-1}||Z_{Y-2} = (10 + 5j)||(2 + 3j)\Omega$$

$$Z_{eq-Y} = 2.8\underline{/48°}\Omega$$

10.2 i) CORRECT ANSWER - C

Equivalent delta load can be calculated using this formula:

$$Z_{eq-\Delta} = 3 \times Z_{eq-Y} = 3 \times 2.8 = 8.4 \, \Omega$$

10.2 j) CORRECT ANSWER - D

3-ɸ complex power of a balanced system can be calculated using following formula.

$$S_{3p} = 3V_p I_p^*$$

$$I_{an} = \frac{V_{an}}{Z_{load}}$$

$$V_{an} = 120\underline{/0°}V \quad Z_{load} = 20\underline{/0°}\Omega$$

$I_{an} = 6\underline{/0°}$ A

$$S_{3p} = 3V_p I_p^* = 2160 \underline{/0°}VA$$

10.2 k) CORRECT ANSWER - C

Real power is related to voltage, current and power factor as shown below.

$$P = VI \cos\vartheta \rightarrow V = \frac{P}{I\cos\vartheta} = \frac{200kW}{(400A)(0.83)} = 602V$$

10.2 l) CORRECT ANSWER - A

Line losses are equal to the difference between power supplied by source and power consumed by load.

$$P_{load} = 100kW$$

$$P_{source} = VI \cos\vartheta = 600V \times 200A \times 0.85 = 102 \, kW$$

$$P_{loss} = P_{source} - P_{load} = 102kW - 100kW = 2 \, kW$$

10.2 m) CORRECT ANSWER - B

3-ϕ real power is related to voltage, current and power factor as shown below.

$$P_{3\phi} = 3V_\phi I_\phi \cos\vartheta$$

$$V_\phi = \frac{P_{3\phi}}{3I_\phi \cos\vartheta}$$

According to the problem statement:

$$P_{3\phi} = 125kW, \qquad I_\phi = I_L = 300A \qquad pf = 0.694$$

$$V_\phi = \frac{125kW}{3 \times 300A \times 0.694}$$

$$V_\phi = 200V$$

10.2 n) CORRECT ANSWER – D

Voltage between phase A and phase B can be calculated as shown below:

$$V_{AB} = V_A - V_B$$

$$V_{AB} = 208\underline{/0°}V - 208\underline{/-120°}V$$

$$V_{AB} = 208V - (208\cos(-120°) + j208\sin(-120°))$$

$$V_{AB} = 208V - \left(208(-0.5) + j208\frac{\sqrt{3}}{2}\right)$$

$$V_{AB} = 208V + 104V - j180V = 312 - j180$$

$$V_{AB} = 360\underline{/-30°}V = 208\sqrt{3}\underline{/-30°}V$$

It can be observed that $V_A - V_B$ is simply the line-line voltage of Y-network.

10.2 o) CORRECT ANSWER – C

Voltage between C and N can be calculated as shown below:

$$V_{CN} = V_C - V_N$$

$$V_{CN} = 208\underline{/120°}V - 0\underline{/0°}V$$

$$V_{CN} = 208\underline{/120°}V$$

It can be observed that $V_C - V_N$ is simply the line-neutral voltage of Y-network.

Helpful tip – Calculate the other phase and line voltages of given network.

10.3 Power Factor - Solutions

Consult NCEES® FE Reference Handbook – Pages 363 - 368 for reference

10.3 a) CORRECT ANSWER - D

Capacitance required to improve power factor angle from θ_1 to θ_2 can be calculated as follows.

$$C = \frac{P(\tan\vartheta_1 - \tan\vartheta_2)}{\omega V_{rms}^2}$$

Although this formula is not provided in NCEES® FE Reference Handbook, it can be derived from power triangle.

$\cos\vartheta_1 = 0.75, \quad \vartheta_1 = 41.4^0$

$\cos\vartheta_2 = 0.90, \quad \vartheta_2 = 25.8^0$

$$C = \frac{200kW(\tan41.4^0 - \tan25.8^0)}{(2\pi)(60Hz)(600V)^2} = 586\ \mu F$$

10.3 b) CORRECT ANSWER - B

Reactive power required to improve power factor angle from θ_1 to θ_2 can be calculated as follows.

$Q_c = P(\tan\vartheta_1 - \tan\vartheta_2)$

$\cos\vartheta_1 = 0.60, \quad \vartheta_1 = 53.1^0$

$\cos\vartheta_2 = 1.00, \quad \vartheta_2 = 0^0$

$Q_c = 100(\tan53.1^0 - \tan0^0) = 133.1\ kVAR$

10.3 c) CORRECT ANSWER: 0.98 lag

Capacitance required to improve power factor angle from θ_1 to θ_2 can be calculated as follows.

$$C = \frac{P(\tan\vartheta_1 - \tan\vartheta_2)}{\omega V_{rms}^2}$$

$\cos\vartheta_1 = 0.8, \quad \vartheta_1 = 36.86^0$

$C\omega V_{rms}^2 = P(\tan\vartheta_1 - \tan\vartheta_2)$

Power factor angle ϑ_2 can be calculated as follows:

$$\vartheta_2 = \tan^{-1}\left(\tan\vartheta_1 - \frac{C\omega V_{rms}^2}{P}\right) = 8.33^\circ$$

New power factor = $\cos(\vartheta_2) = 0.989$

It can be observed that the addition of a capacitor bank helped improve power factor from 0.80 to 0.989.

10.3 d) CORRECT ANSWER : 0.82 lag

$$S_1 = 75kVA\underline{/\cos^{-1}0.85}$$

$$P_1 = 75kVA \times pf_1 = 75kVA \times 0.85 = 63.75kW$$

$$Q_1 = 75kVA \times \sin(\cos^{-1}0.85) = 39.5kVAR$$

$$S_2 = 35kVA\underline{/\cos^{-1}0.75}$$

$$P_2 = 35kVA \times pf_2 = 35kVA \times 0.75 = 26.25kW$$

$$Q_2 = 35kVA \times \sin(\cos^{-1}0.75) = 23.1kVAR$$

$$S_{total} = S_1 + S_2 = 90kW + j62.65kVAR = 109.67kVA\underline{/34.84^0}$$

$$pf_{total} = \frac{P_{total}}{S_{total}} = \frac{90kW}{109kVA} = 0.82\ lagging$$

10.3 e) CORRECT ANSWER - D

Capacitance required to improve power factor angle from θ_1 to θ_2 can be calculated as follows.

$$C = \frac{P(\tan\vartheta_1 - \tan\vartheta_2)}{\omega V_{rms}^2}$$

$$\cos\vartheta_1 = 0.85$$

$$\vartheta_1 = \cos^{-1}0.85 = 31.78^0$$

$$\cos\vartheta_2 = 0.95$$

$$\vartheta_2 = \cos^{-1}0.95 = 18.19^0$$

$$P_{3\phi} = 375\ kW$$

$$P_{1\phi} = \frac{P_{3\phi}}{3} = \frac{375kW}{3} = 125\ kW$$

$$C_{1\phi} = \frac{125kW(\tan 31.87^0 - \tan 18.19^0)}{(2\pi)(60Hz)(120V)^2}$$

$$C_{1\phi} = 6.7\ mF \cong 7\ mF$$

10.4 a) CORRECT ANSWER - C

Voltage regulation can be calculated using formula given below.

$$V.R = \frac{V_{s,nl} - V_{s,fl}}{V_{s,fl}} = \frac{650\,V - 600\,V}{600\,V} = 8.33\%$$

10.4 b) CORRECT ANSWER - C

Ideal transformers are lossless. Therefore, for an ideal transformer the no-load voltage is equal to full load voltage and voltage regulation is zero.

10.4 c) CORRECT ANSWER : 7%

Voltage regulation can be calculated using formula given below.

$$V.R = \frac{V_{s,nl} - V_{s,fl}}{V_{s,fl}} = \frac{\frac{V_p}{a} - V_{s,fl}}{V_{s,fl}}$$

$$I_{s,rated} = \frac{10kVA}{400V} = 25\,A \quad pf = 0.85\ (\vartheta = 31.78^0)\ phase\ angle = -31.78^0$$

$$\frac{V_p}{a} = V_s + I_{s,rated}\left(R_{eq} + jX_{eq}\right) = 427.8\,V$$

$$V.R = \frac{\frac{V_p}{a} - V_{s,fl}}{V_{s,fl}} = \frac{427.8V - 400V}{400V} \times 100\% = 6.98\% \cong 7\%$$

10.4 d) CORRECT ANSWER - B

No-load voltage rating can be calculated using voltage regulation formula given below.

$$V.R = \frac{V_{s,nl} - V_{s,fl}}{V_{s,fl}}$$

$$0.05 = \frac{V_{s,nl} - 240\,V}{240\,V}$$

$$V_{s,nl} = 240\,V + 240\,V \times 0.05 = 252\,V$$

10.4 e) CORRECT ANSWER - B

Voltage regulation can be calculated using formula given below.

$$V.R = \frac{V_{s,nl} - V_{s,fl}}{V_{s,fl}}$$

In the case of leading power factor $V_{s,fl} > V_{s,nl}$. Therefore, $V.R < 0$.

10.4 f) CORRECT ANSWER - C

Voltage drop on feeder and branch circuits occur due to effective impedance of the cable which consists of resistance and reactance as shown below:

$$Z_{eff} = R \cos \vartheta + X \sin \vartheta$$

Note – Z_{eff} also depends on phase angle. Unity power factor will result in $Z_{eff} = R$.

Helpful tip – All voltage drop formulas are based on Ohm's law $V = IR$ but depending on accuracy requirements and circuit configuration, they can get complicated. Some of the commonly used voltage drop formulas are given below:

$$V_{drop,approx} = IR \cos \theta + IX \sin \theta$$

$$V_{drop-1\varphi} = 2I_{line}(R \cos \theta + X \sin \theta) = 2 \times V_{drop,approx}$$

$$V_{drop-3\varphi} = \sqrt{3}I_{line}(R \cos \theta + X \sin \theta) = \sqrt{3} \times V_{drop,approx}$$

$$V_{drop,exact} = V_s + I_{line}(R \cos \theta + X \sin \theta) - \sqrt{[V_s^2 - I_{line}(R \cos \theta + jX \sin \theta)^2}$$

These formulas can be found in IEEE® Std 141™ (Red Book).

10.4 g) CORRECT ANSWER - D

Total voltage drop (2-way) in a single-phase system with unity power factor and negligible circuit reactance can be calculated using following formula.

$$V_D = \frac{2LRI}{K \times 1000}$$

V_D = Voltage drop =?

L = One-way length of circuit (ft) = 500 ft

R = Conductor resistance (Ω/1000 ft) = 1.2 Ω/1000 ft

K = 1.0 for single-phase AC circuits

I = Load current = 20A

$$V_D = \frac{2(500)(1.2)(20)}{1 \times 1000} = 24V$$

Note - The voltage drop formula used in this problem is only valid for unity power factor loads where circuit reactance is negligible.

10.5 Transformers - Solutions

Consult NCEES® FE Reference Handbook – Pages 363 - 368 for reference

10.5 a) CORRECT ANSWER - B

$$V_s = I_s \times R_s = 1A \times 12\Omega = 12\ V$$

$$\frac{V_p}{V_s} = a = \frac{50}{1} \rightarrow \frac{V_p}{12V} = \frac{50}{1} \rightarrow V_p = 12V \times 50 = 600\ V$$

10.5 b) CORRECT ANSWER - A

Secondary current can be calculated using the formula given below:

$$S_\varphi = S_p = S_s = V_s I_s \rightarrow 15\ kVA = V_s\ I_s$$

$$I_s = \frac{15kVA}{120\ V} = 125\ A$$

10.5 c) CORRECT ANSWER: 4.16 A

Secondary current can be calculated using the formula given below:

$$I_s = \frac{S_\varphi}{V_s} = \frac{5\ kVA}{120\ V} = 41.6\ A \qquad \frac{I_s}{I_p} = a = \frac{10}{1} \rightarrow I_p = \frac{I_s}{a} = \frac{I_s}{10} = 4.16\ A$$

10.5 d) CORRECT ANSWER : 25000 Ω

Transformer primary and secondary impedances are related by formula shown below.

$$Z_p = a^2 Z_s = 50^2 \times 10\Omega = 25000\Omega$$

10.5 e) CORRECT ANSWER : 50 Ω

$$Z_p = a^2 Z_s \rightarrow Z_s = \frac{Z_p}{a^2}$$

$$Z_p = 10\ k\Omega || 10\ k\Omega = 5\ k\Omega \quad a = 10$$

$$Z_s = \frac{Z_p}{a^2} = \frac{Z_p}{10^2} = \frac{5\ k\Omega}{100} = 50\ \Omega$$

10.5 f) CORRECT ANSWER - D

The transformer connection shown in the problem statement represents a 'Wye-Wye' configuration.

10.5 g) CORRECT ANSWER - A

The transformer connection shown in the problem statement represents a 'Delta-Delta' configuration.

10.5 h) CORRECT ANSWER - C

The transformer connection shown in the problem statement represents a 'Wye-Delta' configuration.

10.6 Motors & Generators - Solutions

Consult NCEES® FE Reference Handbook – Pages 363 - 368 for reference

10.6 a) CORRECT ANSWER: C

AC motor poles can be calculated using the formula given below.

$$n_s = \frac{120f}{p} \rightarrow p = \frac{120f}{n_s} = \frac{(120)(60\ Hz)}{(1800\ rpm)} = 4$$

10.6 b) CORRECT ANSWER: C

Synchronous speed of AC motor can be calculated using the formula given below.

$$n_s = \frac{120f}{p} = \frac{(120)(60\ Hz)}{2} = 3600\ rpm$$

10.6 c) CORRECT ANSWER: B

$$n_s = \frac{120f}{p}$$

$$n_{s,50Hz} = \frac{120f}{p} = \frac{(120)(50\ Hz)}{4} = 1500\ rpm$$

$$n_{s,60Hz} = \frac{120f}{p} = \frac{(120\ V)(60\ Hz)}{2} = 3600\ rpm$$

$$n_{s,60Hz} - n_{s,50Hz} = 3600\ rpm - 1500\ rpm = 2100\ rpm$$

10.6 d) CORRECT ANSWER: 5.5%

$$n_s = \frac{120f}{p} = \frac{(120)(60)}{2} = 3600\ rpm \qquad n = 3400\ rpm$$

$$s = \frac{n_s - n}{n_s} = \frac{3600 - 3400}{3600} = 5.5\%$$

10.6 e) CORRECT ANSWER: D

$$n_s = \frac{120f}{p} = \frac{(120)(60)}{4} = 1800\ rpm$$

$$s = \frac{n_s - n}{n_s}$$

$$0.1 = \frac{1800 - n}{1800}$$

$$n = 1800 - 0.1 \times 1800 = 1620\ rpm$$

10.6 f) CORRECT ANSWER - B

Synchronous speed and slip of AC motor are given by following formula.

$$n_s = \frac{120f}{p} = \frac{(120)(60)}{2} = 3600 \; rpm$$

$$s = \frac{n_s - n_m}{n_s} \rightarrow 1.5 = \frac{3600 - n_m}{3600} \rightarrow n_m = n_s - n_s \times 1.5 = -1800 \; rpm$$

Since the direction of motor's rotation is opposite to the synchronous speed, motor is 'braking'.

10.6 g) CORRECT ANSWER - D

In the given scenario, slip is -0.5.

$$s = \frac{n_s - n_m}{n_s} \rightarrow -0.5 = \frac{3600 - n_m}{3600} \rightarrow n_m = n_s - n_s \times (-0.5) = 1.5n_s = 5400 \; rpm$$

Induction motor operates as generator when its slip becomes negative. In the given case, rotor is turning in the same direction as synchronous rotation at a higher speed, therefore motor is 'generating'.

10.6 h) CORRECT ANSWER - C

An induction motor acts as a generator when rotor is mechanically turned at speed greater than synchronous speed. As noted in the previous solution, slip also becomes negative in such scenarios.

10.6 i) CORRECT ANSWER - B

Armature voltage (E_a) of a generator can be calculated using following equation.

$$E_a = V_T + I_a(R_a + jX_L) = V_T + I_a(0 + jX_L) = V_T + jX_L I_a \; \text{(since } R = 0)$$

According to problem statement, line-line voltage is 480V.

$$V_T = \frac{480V}{\sqrt{3}} = 277V \underline{/0°}V$$

$$I_a = \frac{100kVA}{\sqrt{3} \times 480V} = 120.28A$$

$$pf = \cos^{-1}(0.90) = 25.84°$$

$$I_a = 120.28\underline{/-25.84°} \; A$$

$$X_L = 1j\Omega = 1\underline{/90°}\Omega$$

$$E_a = 277V\underline{/0°}V + j(120.28\underline{/-25.84°} \; A)(1\underline{/90°}\Omega) = 329.42 + j108.25 \; V$$

$$E_a = 347V/phase$$

10.6 j) CORRECT ANSWER - C

Synchronous generator's armature voltage is given by following equation:

$$E_a = V_T + I_a(R_a + jX_L)$$

In case of constant power factor, increasing armature current (I_a) will increase the voltage drop across jX_sI_a but E_A will remain unchanged because V_T will also reduce proportionately.

10.6 k) CORRECT ANSWER: 41.4kW

Efficiency of a machine is given by following equation:

$$\eta = \frac{P_{out}}{P_{in}}$$

$$P_{in} = \frac{P_{out}}{\eta} = \frac{(50 \times 746)W}{0.90} = 41.4kW$$

10.6 l) CORRECT ANSWER: 297Nm

Mechanical torque developed by machine can be calculated using following equation:

$$P_m = T\omega_m = T \times \left(\frac{2\pi}{60}\right) \times 1200$$

$$T = \frac{P_m}{\left(\frac{2\pi}{60}\right) \times 1200} = \frac{(50 \times 746)W}{125.6 \ rad/s} = 296.8Nm$$

10.6 m) CORRECT ANSWER: 173A

Electrical input power to DC motor's armature circuit is given by following equation:

$$P_{in} = V_T I_a$$ Armature current I_a can be calculated using following equation:

$$I_a = \frac{P_{in}}{V_T} = \frac{41.4kW}{240V} = 173A$$

10.6 n) CORRECT ANSWER: 215V

Internal voltage V_a of DC motor can be calculated using following equation:

$$P_m = V_a I_a$$

$$V_a = \frac{P_m}{I_a} = \frac{(50 \times 746)W}{173V} = 215V$$

10.6 o) CORRECT ANSWER: 0.14Ω

$$V_T = V_a + I_a R_a$$

$$R_a = \frac{V_T - V_a}{I_a} = \frac{240V - 215V}{173A} = 0.14\Omega$$

Chapter # 11 – Electromagnetics
11.1 Electrostatics - Solutions

Consult NCEES® FE Reference Handbook – Pages 355 - 356 for reference

11.1 a) CORRECT ANSWER - D

Electrostatic force between point charges can be calculated using the formula given below.

$$F = \frac{Q_1 Q_2}{4\pi\varepsilon r^2}$$

$$F = \frac{(5nC)(10nC)}{4\pi \times 8.85 \times 10^{-12} Fm^{-1} \times \left(\sqrt{5}\right)^2}$$

$$F = 90\ nN$$

11.1 b) CORRECT ANSWER - A

Electrostatic force between point charges can be calculated using formula given below.

$$F = \frac{Q_1 Q_2}{4\pi r^2 \varepsilon}$$

$$F = \frac{(10 \times 10^{-6} C)(100 \times 10^{-6} C)}{4\pi(0.01m)^2 \times (8.85 \times 10^{-12} Fm^{-1})}$$

$$F \cong 90\ kN$$

11.1 c) CORRECT ANSWER - C

Electric field intensity can be calculated as shown below.

$$\overline{E} = \frac{Q_1}{4\pi\varepsilon r^2}i + \frac{Q_2}{4\pi\varepsilon r^2}(-i)$$

$$\overline{E} = \frac{Q_1}{4\pi\varepsilon r^2}i - \frac{Q_2}{4\pi\varepsilon r^2}i$$

$$\overline{E} = \left(\frac{Q_1}{4\pi\varepsilon r^2} - \frac{Q_2}{4\pi\varepsilon r^2}\right)i$$

$$\overline{E} = \left(\frac{50nC}{4\pi\varepsilon\left(\sqrt{1}\right)^2} - \frac{-50nC}{4\pi\varepsilon\left(\sqrt{1}\right)^2}\right)i$$

$$|\overline{E}| = 900 V/m$$

Note that if both charges were of same polarity, the total electric field intensity would have been zero.

Electric field lines diverge from positive charges and the converge on to negative charges.

11.1 d) CORRECT ANSWER - B

Electric field intensity of a sheet charge with density ρ_s can be calculated as shown below.

$$\overline{E} = \frac{\rho_s}{2\varepsilon} k$$

We can use the principle of superposition as shown below.

$$\overline{E} = \frac{\rho_s}{2\varepsilon} k - \frac{\rho_s}{2\varepsilon}(-k)$$

$$\overline{E} = \frac{\rho_s}{\varepsilon} k$$

Note: If both electric plates were of same polarity, the total electric field intensity would have been zero.

11.1 e) CORRECT ANSWER - D

Electric field intensity of a line charge with density ρ can be calculated as shown below.

$$\overline{E} = \frac{\rho}{2\pi\varepsilon r} a_r$$

We can use the principle of superposition as shown below.

$$\overline{E} = \frac{2}{2\pi\varepsilon(0.5)} a_r + \frac{-1}{2\pi\varepsilon(0.5)}(-a_r) = 1.07 \times 10^{11}\ Vm^{-1}\ a_r$$

Helpful tip – Pay special attention to the direction of vectors while performing addition and subtraction.

11.1 f) CORRECT ANSWER - D

It is important to understand the difference between work, energy, and force.

Work done on a point charge in moving it from p1 to p2 in the presence of an electrical field is given by:

$$W_{12} = -Q \int_{p_1}^{p_2} E.\,dl = -Q_1 \int_{p_1}^{p_2} \frac{Q_2}{4\pi\varepsilon r_{21}^2} a_{r21}.\,dl = -Q_1 \frac{Q_2}{4\pi\varepsilon r_{21}^2} \int_{p_1}^{p_2} a_{r21}.\,dl = -Q_1 \frac{Q_2}{4\pi\varepsilon r_{21}^2} r_{21}$$

$$|W_{12}| = \frac{Q_1 Q_2}{4\pi\varepsilon r_{21}} \qquad r_{21} = \sqrt{(2-0)^2 + (0-0)^2 + (0-0)^2} = 2\ m$$

$$W_{12} = 9 \times 10^{-3} J$$

11.1 g) CORRECT ANSWER - B

Work and energy have same units of measurements.

Potential energy of given system is equal to the amount of work required to keep charges apart as shown below.

$$W_{12} = \frac{Q_1 Q_2}{4\pi\varepsilon r_{12}} \qquad r_{12} = \sqrt{(1-0)^2 + (0-1)^2 + (0-0)^2} = \sqrt{2}$$

$$W_{12} = 31.9\ mJ$$

11.1 h) CORRECT ANSWER - A

Potential energy of system 'A' can be calculated as $W_{12} = Q_1 Q_2 / 4\pi\varepsilon r_{12} = 45J$

Potential energy of system 'B' can be calculated as $W_{34} = Q_3 Q_4 / 4\pi\varepsilon r_{34} = 45J$

It can be observed that the potential energies of both systems are equal.

11.1 i) CORRECT ANSWER - D

The amount of work required to reduce spacing will be equal to the difference in system energy at 1m and 1cm.

System energy at 1m charge spacing can be calculated as $W_{12} = Q_1 Q_2 / 4\pi\varepsilon(1m) = 1.215 \times 10^{-6}J$

System energy at 1cm charge spacing can be calculated as $W_{12} = Q_1 Q_2 / 4\pi\varepsilon(1cm) = 1.215 \times 10^{-4}J$

The amount of work required is equal to energy difference between two systems.

$\Delta = (1.215 \times 10^{-4}J) - (1.215 \times 10^{-6}J) = 1.202 \times 10^{-4}J$

11.1 j) CORRECT ANSWER - B

Work done by an external agent in moving a charge Q from P1 to P2 in an electric field is given by:

$$W = -Q \int_{P1}^{P2} \mathbf{E}.\,d\mathbf{l}$$

Note that charge is moved along y-axis and electric field is along x-axis.

$$W = -Q \int_{P1}^{P2} 200\,Vm^{-1} \mathbf{a}_x.\,\mathbf{a}_y$$

Dot product of perpendicular vectors is always $0 \to \mathbf{a}_x.\,\mathbf{a}_y = 0$

Therefore, the work done on point charge is 0. $W = 0$

11.1 k) CORRECT ANSWER - A

Potential difference (V) can be calculated using the formula given below.

$$E = \frac{V}{d} \to V = E \times d$$

$V = 2000 Vm^{-1} \times 1m = 2000V$

11.1 l) CORRECT ANSWER - C

Potential difference (V) can be calculated using formula given below.

$$E = \frac{V}{d}$$

$V = E \times d = 1000 Vm^{-1} \times 200m = 200\,kV$

11.2 Magnetostatics - Solutions

Consult NCEES® FE Reference Handbook – Pages 355 - 356 for reference

11.2 a) CORRECT ANSWER - D

Force on a current carrying conductor in uniform magnetic field can be calculated using following equation.

$$\overline{F} = I\,\overline{L} \times \overline{B}$$

Since we are only interested in the magnitude of force, we can take modulus as shown below.

$$|F| = ILBsin\theta$$

$$|F| = 2A \times 2m \times 0.5T\ sin30^0 = 1\ N$$

11.2 b) CORRECT ANSWER : $5\mu J$

Energy stored (E) in a magnetic field can be calculated using following equation.

$$E = \frac{\mu H^2}{2} \times Vol$$

$$E = \frac{4\pi \times 10^{-7} Hm^{-1}}{2} \times (2Am^{-1})^2 \times 2m^3$$

$$E = 5\mu J$$

11.2 c) CORRECT ANSWER : 11.5^0

Force on a current-carrying conductor can be calculated using following formula:

$$F = IL \times B = ILBsin\alpha$$

$$\alpha = sin^{-1}\left(\frac{F}{ILB}\right)$$

$$\alpha = sin^{-1}\left(\frac{1 \times 10^{-6}N}{5A \times 0.1m \times 10 \times 10^{-6}}\right) = 11.5^0$$

11.2 d) CORRECT ANSWER - B

According to Faraday's Law, voltage induced in a coil can be calculated as shown below.

$$v = -N\frac{d\Phi}{dt}$$

$$v = -20\frac{1.4\ Wb}{2s}$$

$$v = -14\ V$$

Helpful tip – Review vector and integral form of Faraday's Law given in NCEES® FE Reference Handbook.

11.2 e) CORRECT ANSWER : 0.15 μV

According to Faraday's Law, voltage induced in a coil can be calculated as shown below.

$$v = L\frac{di}{dt} = \frac{N^2\mu A}{l}\frac{di}{dt} = \frac{(50)^2 \times 4\pi \times 10^{-7}Hm^{-1} \times 2cm^2}{20cm} \times \frac{100mA - 50mA}{1s} = 0.15\ \mu V$$

11.2 f) CORRECT ANSWER : 500 μT

Magnetic flux density can be calculated using Ampere's Law as shown below.

$$H = \frac{B}{\mu} \qquad \frac{B}{\mu}\oint dl = I_{enc}$$

$$I_{enc} = NI = (50)(1\ A) = 50\ A$$

$$\oint dl = 2\pi r = 2\pi(2\ cm) \qquad \text{circumference of torus}$$

$$B = \frac{\mu I_{enc}}{2\pi \times 2\ cm} = 500\ \mu T$$

11.2 g) CORRECT ANSWER : 0.4 μT

This problem can be solved using Ampere's Law and principle of superposition.

Magnetic flux density at point A due to first wire is given as:

$$B_1 = \frac{I\mu}{2\pi r} = 0.2\ \mu T$$

Magnetic flux density at point A due to second wire is given as:

$$B_2 = \frac{I\mu}{2\pi r} = 0.2\ \mu T$$

Adding the two magnetic fields result in $B_{net} = B_1 + B_2 = 0.4\ \mu T$

Note: In this case magnetic fields add due to current direction. If current were flowing in opposite direction, magnetic fields would have cancelled each other. Apply right hand rule to determine magnetic field direction.

11.2 h) CORRECT ANSWER : 100 kA

Current passing through wire can be calculated using Ampere's Law.

$$B = \frac{I\mu}{2\pi r}$$

$$I = \frac{2\pi r B}{\mu}$$

$$I = \frac{(2\pi)(0.2m)(0.1T)}{4\pi \times 10^{-7}H/m} = 100\ kA$$

Helpful tip – Review vector and integral form of Ampere's Law given in NCEES® FE Reference Handbook.

11.3 Electrodynamics – Maxwell's Equations - Solutions

Consult NCEES® FE Reference Handbook – Pages 59 – 60, 368 for reference

11.3 a) CORRECT ANSWER - D

Divergence of an electric field can be calculated using Del (∇) operator as shown below.

$$div\,\overline{E} = \nabla.\overline{E}$$

$$div\,\overline{E} = \left(\frac{d}{dx}i + \frac{d}{dy}j + \frac{d}{dz}k\right).(3xi + 2y^2j + xk)$$

$$div\,\overline{E} = \frac{d}{dx}3x + \frac{d}{dy}2y^2 + \frac{d}{dz}x$$

$$div\,\overline{E} = 3 + 4y$$

Helpful tip – Review vector operators i.e. gradient, curl and divergence given in NCEES® FE Reference Handbook.

11.3 b) CORRECT ANSWER - B

$$div\,\overline{D} = \nabla.\overline{D} = \left(\frac{d}{dx}i + \frac{d}{dy}j + \frac{d}{dz}k\right)(xyi + yzj + xz^2k)$$

$$div\,\overline{D} = \frac{d}{dx}xy + \frac{d}{dy}yz + \frac{d}{dz}xz^2 = y + z + 2xz$$

11.3 c) CORRECT ANSWER - C

According to Gauss' Law, electric flux over a closed surface can be calculated as shown below.

$$\varphi = \oint E.ds = \frac{Q_{enc}}{\varepsilon}$$

$$\varphi = \frac{+1\,nC - 2\,nC + 3\,nC + 1\,nC}{8.85 \times 10^{-12}\,C/Vm} = 339\,Vm$$

Helpful tip – Review vector and integral form of Gauss' Law given in NCEES® FE Reference Handbook.

11.3 d) CORRECT ANSWER - B

$$\varphi = \oint E.ds = \frac{Q_{enc}}{\varepsilon} = \frac{Q_1 + Q_2}{8.85 \times 10^{-12}C/Vm}$$

$$Q_1 = 3\mu\frac{C}{m^2} \times 4\pi\left(\frac{1}{100}\right)^2 = 3.76 \times 10^{-9}C$$

$$Q_2 = -5\mu\frac{C}{m^2} \times 4\pi\left(\frac{3}{100}\right)^2 = -56.5 \times 10^{-9}C$$

$$\varphi = -5963\,Vm$$

11.3 e) CORRECT ANSWER - C

We can calculate the value of "a" by taking divergence of magnetic field $\overline{B}$.

$$div\ \overline{B} = \nabla.\overline{B}$$

$$div\ \overline{B} = \left(\frac{d}{dx}i + \frac{d}{dy}j + \frac{d}{dz}k\right)(3axi + 2yj - 2zk)$$

$$div\ \overline{B} = \frac{d}{dx}3ax + \frac{d}{dy}2y - \frac{d}{dz}2z$$

$$div\ \overline{B} = 3a + 2 - 2 = 3a$$

In order for $\overline{B}$ to qualify as a magnetic field, $3a = 0 \rightarrow a = 0$

Helpful tip – Divergence of a magnetic field is always equal to zero.

11.3 f) CORRECT ANSWER - B

According to Maxwell's equations, divergence of a magnetic field is always equal to zero.

$$div\ \overline{A} = \nabla.\overline{A}$$

$$div\ \overline{A} = \frac{d}{dx}2x^2 + \frac{d}{dy}y + \frac{d}{dz}3z^2 = 4x + 1 + 6z$$

$$div\ \overline{B} = \nabla.\overline{B}$$

$$div\ \overline{B} = \frac{d}{dx}2y^2 + \frac{d}{dy}3x - \frac{d}{dz}2xy = 0$$

Divergence of $\overline{B}$ is zero. Therefore, $\overline{B}$ can be a magnetic field vector.

11.3 g) CORRECT ANSWER - B

The rate of change of magnetic field $\overline{B}$ is equal to the curl of electric field strength vector $\overline{E}$.

$$\nabla \times \overline{E} = -\frac{d}{dt}\overline{B}$$

$$\overline{E} = 2yzi + 3x^2yj + x^2y^2k$$

$$\frac{d}{dt}\overline{B} = -\left(\frac{dEz}{dy} - \frac{dEy}{dz}\right)i - \left(\frac{dEx}{dz} - \frac{dEz}{dx}\right)j - \left(\frac{dEy}{dx} - \frac{dEx}{dy}\right)k$$

$$\frac{d}{dt}\overline{B} = -2x^2yi - (2y - 2xy^2)j - (6xy - 2z)k$$

11.3 h) CORRECT ANSWER - C

The rate of change of magnetic field $\overline{B}$ is equal to the curl of electric field strength vector $\overline{E}$.

$$\nabla \times \overline{E} = -\frac{d}{dt}\overline{B}$$

$$\overline{B} = -\cos^2(3t)\,k$$

$$\nabla \times \overline{E} = -\frac{d}{dt}\overline{B}$$

$$\nabla \times \overline{E} = -\left(-\frac{d}{dt}\cos^2 3t\right)k$$

$$\nabla \times \overline{E} = \frac{d}{dt}\cos^2 3t\,k$$

$$\nabla \times \overline{E} = -6\cos(3t)\sin(3t)k$$

11.3 i) SOLUTION

Column A   **Column B**

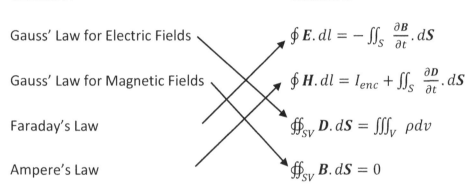

Gauss' Law for Electric Fields

Gauss' Law for Magnetic Fields

Faraday's Law

Ampere's Law

$$\oint E.\,dl = -\iint_S \frac{\partial B}{\partial t}.\,dS$$

$$\oint H.\,dl = I_{enc} + \iint_S \frac{\partial D}{\partial t}.\,dS$$

$$\oiint_{SV} D.\,dS = \iiint_V \rho dv$$

$$\oiint_{SV} B.\,dS = 0$$

11.3 j) CORRECT ANSWER - D

According to Maxwell's equation, divergence of a magnetic field is zero i.e. $\nabla.B = 0$. Therefore, the total magnetic flux emitting from a closed surface is also equal to zero. This is in contrast with the electric field. In the case of an electric field, net flux is directly proportional to the electric charge contained inside the object.

11.4 Electrodynamics - Wave Propagation - Solutions

Consult NCEES® FE Reference Handbook – Page 369 for reference

11.4 a) CORRECT ANSWER - B

$$\beta = \frac{2\pi}{\lambda} = \frac{2\pi}{20} = \frac{\pi}{10}$$

$$V(d) = V^+ e^{j\beta d} + V^- e^{-j\beta d}$$

$$V(100) = V^+ e^{j10\pi} + V^- e^{-j10\pi}$$

Helpful tip – Review transmission line voltage equation given in NCEES® FE Reference Handbook.

11.4 b) CORRECT ANSWER - C

$$\beta = \frac{2\pi}{\lambda} = \frac{2\pi}{20} = \frac{\pi}{10}$$

$$I(d) = I^+ e^{j\beta d} + I^- e^{-j\beta d}$$

$$I^+ = \frac{V^+}{Z_0} \qquad I^- = -\frac{V^-}{Z_0}$$

$$I(100) = \frac{1}{100}(V^+ e^{j10\pi} - V^- e^{-j10\pi})$$

Helpful tip – Review transmission line current equation given in NCEES® FE Reference Handbook.

11.4 c) CORRECT ANSWER – D

Comparing the given sinusoidal equation of magnetic field strength $H = 10\cos(10^8 t - 4z)\hat{a}_x \, A/m$ with the general equation of magnetic field $\boldsymbol{H} = H_o \cos(\omega t - \beta z)\boldsymbol{a}_x A/m$ shows that $\omega = 10^8 rad/s$ and $\beta = 4$.

$$\omega = 2\pi f \rightarrow f = \omega/2\pi \; Hz$$

$$f = \frac{10^8}{2\pi} Hz$$

11.4 d) CORRECT ANSWER – B

As observed in the previous solution, $\beta = 4$ for given electromagnetic wave.

According to the formula given in NCEES® FE Reference Handbook:

$$\beta = 2\pi/\lambda \rightarrow \lambda = 2\pi/\beta$$

$$\lambda = \frac{2\pi}{4} = \frac{\pi}{2} m$$

11.4 e) CORRECT ANSWER – D

Comparing the given sinusoidal equation of electric field intensity $E = 12\cos(2\times10^9 t - \beta z)\hat{a}_x \; A/m$ with the general equation of electric field $E = E_o\cos(\omega t - \beta z)a_x A/m$ shows that $\omega = 2\times10^9 \, rad/s$.

$$\omega = 2\pi f$$

$$f = \omega/2\pi \; Hz$$

$$f = \frac{2\times10^9}{2\pi} = \frac{10^9}{\pi} Hz$$

Time period is related to frequency through following equation:

$$T = \frac{1}{f} = \frac{\pi}{10^9} s$$

In one time-period, electromagnetic wave will cover a distance equal to its one complete wavelength λ.

50% of λ will be covered in T/2 time i.e. $\pi/(2\times10^9) \; s$

11.4 f) CORRECT ANSWER – A

According to the formula given in NCEES® FE Reference Handbook:

$$\lambda = \frac{U}{f}$$

As calculated in previous problem, $f = 10^9/\pi \; Hz$ and $U = 3\times10^8 m/s$ (speed of light).

$$\lambda = \frac{3\times10^8 m/s}{\dfrac{10^9}{\pi} Hz} = 0.3\pi \; m$$

11.5 Transmission Lines - Solutions

Consult NCEES® FE Reference Handbook – Page 369 for reference

11.5 a) CORRECT ANSWER: $0.5 \underline{/6.91^0}$

Reflection coefficient can be calculated using following formula.

$$\Gamma = \frac{Z_l - Z_o}{Z_l + Z_o}$$

$$\Gamma = \frac{\left((300 + 50j\ \Omega) - 100\ \Omega\right)}{(300 + 50j\ \Omega) + 100\ \Omega}$$

$$\Gamma = 0.5\ phase\ 6.91^0$$

Helpful tip – Review transmission line reflection coefficient equation given in NCEES® FE Reference Handbook.

11.5 b) CORRECT ANSWER - C

Reflection coefficient can be calculated using following formula.

$$\Gamma = \frac{Z_l - Z_o}{Z_l + Z_o} = \frac{(500 + 25j\ \Omega) - 50\ \Omega}{(500 + 25j\ \Omega) + 50\ \Omega}$$

$$\Gamma = 0.818\ phase\ 0.57^0$$

$$SWR = \frac{1 + |\Gamma|}{1 - |\Gamma|} = \frac{1 + 0.818}{1 - 0.818} = 10$$

Helpful tip – Review transmission line standing wave ratio equation given in NCEES® FE Reference Handbook.

11.5 c) CORRECT ANSWER - B

Reflection coefficient is given by following formula.

$$\Gamma = \frac{Z_l - Z_o}{Z_l + Z_o}$$

Characteristic impedance can be calculated using following formula.

$$Z_o = \sqrt{\frac{L}{C}} = 100\ \Omega$$

According to the problem statement, $\Gamma = 0.5$

$$0.5 = \frac{Z_l - Z_o}{Z_l + Z_o} = \frac{Z_l - 100}{Z_l + 100}$$

$$Z_l = 300\ \Omega$$

11.5 d) CORRECT ANSWER - D

$$\beta = \frac{2\pi}{\lambda} = \frac{2\pi}{10}$$

$$Z_{in}(d) = Z_o \frac{Z_l + jZ_o \tan(\beta d)}{Z_o + jZ_l \tan(\beta d)}$$

$$Z_o = 200\Omega \quad Z_l = 500\Omega$$

$$Z_{in}(100) = 200 \frac{500 + j200 \tan(\beta \times 100)}{200 + j500 \tan(\beta \times 100)}$$

$$\tan\left(\frac{2\pi}{10} \times 100\right) = 0$$

$$Z_{in}(100) = 200 \, \Omega \left(\frac{500\Omega}{200\Omega}\right) = 500\Omega$$

11.5 e) CORRECT ANSWER - D

Standing wave ratio can be calculated using following equation.

$$SWR = \frac{1 + |\Gamma|}{1 - |\Gamma|} = 2$$

$$\Gamma = \frac{1}{3}$$

Reflection coefficient can be calculated using following formula.

$$\Gamma = \frac{Z_l - Z_o}{Z_l + Z_o}$$

$$\frac{1}{3} = \frac{Z_l - 250 \, \Omega}{Z_l + 250 \, \Omega}$$

$$Z_l = 500\Omega$$

11.5 f) CORRECT ANSWER - B

Standing wave ratio can be calculated using following equation.

$$SWR = \frac{I_{max}}{I_{min}} = \frac{10A}{2A} = 5$$

$$SWR = \frac{1 + |\Gamma|}{1 - |\Gamma|}$$

$$|\Gamma| = \frac{S - 1}{S + 1} = \frac{5 - 1}{5 + 1} = \frac{4}{6} = \frac{2}{3}$$

Chapter # 12 – Control Systems
12.1 Block Diagrams - Solutions

Consult NCEES® FE Reference Handbook – Pages 226 - 227 for reference

12.1 a) CORRECT ANSWER - $\dfrac{G_1(s)G_2(s)}{1+H(s)G_1(s)G_2(s)}$

Let us define error $E(s)$ as $E(s) = R(s) - H(s)Y(s)$

$Y(s) = E(s)G_1(s)G_2(s) = \big(R(s) - H(s)Y(s)\big)G_1(s)G_2(s) = R(s)G_1(s)G_2(s) - H(s)Y(s)G_1(s)G_2(s)$

$Y(s) + H(s)Y(s)G_1(s)G_2(s) = R(s)G_1(s)G_2(s) \rightarrow Y(s)\big(1 + H(s)G_1(s)G_2(s)\big) = R(s)G_1(s)G_2(s)$

$$\frac{Y(s)}{R(s)} = \frac{G_1(s)G_2(s)}{1 + H(s)G_1(s)G_2(s)}$$

Note: Closed-loop transfer function can also be calculated using the classical negative feedback control system model relations given in NCEES® FE Reference Handbook.

12.1 b) CORRECT ANSWER - $H(s)G_1(s)G_2(s)$

As mentioned above, closed-loop transfer function of given control system can be given as follows.

$$\frac{Y(s)}{R(s)} = \frac{G_1(s)G_2(s)}{1 + H(s)G_1(s)G_2(s)}$$

The open-loop transfer function of this control system is $H(s)G_1(s)G_2(s)$.

12.1 c) CORRECT ANSWER - $\dfrac{(s+2)^2}{s(s+4)}$

Equivalent transfer function of control blocks arranged in parallel configuration can be calculated as follows:

$T = G_1(s) + G_2(s)$

$T = \dfrac{1}{s} + \dfrac{s+3}{s+4}$

$T = \dfrac{(s+4) + s(s+3)}{s(s+4)} = \dfrac{s+4+s^2+3s}{s(s+4)} = \dfrac{(s+2)^2}{s(s+4)}$

12.1 d) CORRECT ANSWER - $\dfrac{s+3}{s(s+4)}$

Equivalent transfer function of control blocks arranged in series configuration can be calculated as follows:

$T = G_1(s)G_2(s)$

$T = \left(\dfrac{1}{s}\right)\left(\dfrac{s+3}{s+4}\right) = \dfrac{s+3}{s(s+4)}$

12.1 e) CORRECT ANSWER - A

Let us define error $E(s)$ as $E(s) = R(s) - H(s)Y(s)$

$Y(s) = kE(s)G_1(s)$

$Y(s) = k\big(R(s) - Y(s)H(s)\big)G_1(s) \to Y(s) = kR(s)G_1(s) - kY(s)H(s)G_1(s)$

$Y(s) + kY(s)H(s)G_1(s) = kR(s)G_1(s) \to Y(s)\big(1 + kH(s)G_1(s)\big) = kR(s)G_1(s)$

$Y(s) = R(s)\dfrac{kG_1(s)}{1 + kG_1(s)H(s)}$

$\dfrac{Y(s)}{R(s)} = T(s) = \dfrac{kG_1(s)}{1 + kG_1(s)H(s)}$

12.1 f) CORRECT ANSWER - $Y(s) = \dfrac{R(s)G_1(s)G_2(s) - N(s)G_1(s)G_2(s) + L(s)G_2(s)}{1 + G_1(s)G_2(s)}$

Let us define error $E(s)$ as $E(s) = R(s) - \big(Y(s) + N(s)\big)$

$Y(s) = \big(E(s)G_1(s) + L(s)\big)G_2(s) = [R(s) - \big(Y(s) + N(s)\big)]G_1(s)G_2(s) + L(s)G_2(s)$

$Y(s) = R(s)G_1(s)G_2(s) - Y(s)G_1(s)G_2(s) - N(s)G_1(s)G_2(s) + L(s)G_2(s)$

$Y(s) + Y(s)G_1(s)G_2(s) = R(s)G_1(s)G_2(s) - N(s)G_1(s)G_2(s) + L(s)G_2(s)$

$Y(s) = \dfrac{R(s)G_1(s)G_2(s) - N(s)G_1(s)G_2(s) + L(s)G_2(s)}{1 + G_1(s)G_2(s)}$

12.1 g) CORRECT ANSWER - $\dfrac{G_4(s)(G_1(s) - G_2(s) + G_3(s))}{1 + G_4(s)(G_1(s) - G_2(s) + G_3(s))}$

Let us define error $E(s)$ as $E(s) = R(s) - Y(s)$

$Y(s) = E(s)\big(G_1(s) - G_2(s) + G_3(s)\big)G_4(s)$

$Y(s) = \big(R(s) - Y(s)\big)\big(G_1(s) - G_2(s) + G_3(s)\big)G_4(s)$

$Y(s) + Y(s)\big(G_4(s)\big(G_1(s) - G_2(s) + G_3(s)\big)\big) = R(s)G_4(s)\big(G_1(s) - G_2(s) + G_3(s)\big)$

$Y(s)\big(1 + G_4(s)\big(G_1(s) - G_2(s) + G_3(s)\big)\big) = R(s)G_4(s)\big(G_1(s) - G_2(s) + G_3(s)\big)$

$Y(s) = R(s)\dfrac{G_4(s)\big(G_1(s) - G_2(s) + G_3(s)\big)}{\big(1 + G_4(s)(G_1(s) - G_2(s) + G_3(s))\big)}$

$\dfrac{Y(s)}{R(s)} = T(s) = \dfrac{G_4(s)\big(G_1(s) - G_2(s) + G_3(s)\big)}{1 + G_4(s)(G_1(s) - G_2(s) + G_3(s))}$

12.1 h) CORRECT ANSWER - $\dfrac{G_1(s)G_2(s)+G_1(s)G_2(s)G_3(s)}{1+G_1(s)G_2(s)-H(s)+G_1(s)G_2(s)G_3(s)}$

Let us define error $E(s)$ as $E(s) = R(s) - Y(s)$

$$Y(s) = E(s)G_1(s)G_2(s) + H(s)Y(s) + E(s)G_1(s)G_2(s)G_3(s)$$

$$Y(s) = \big(R(s) - Y(s)\big)G_1(s)G_2(s) + H(s)Y(s) + \big(R(s) - Y(s)\big)G_1(s)G_2(s)G_3(s)$$

$$Y(s) = R(s)G_1(s)G_2(s) - Y(s)G_1(s)G_2(s) + H(s)Y(s) + R(s)G_1(s)G_2(s)G_3(s) - Y(s)G_1(s)G_2(s)G_3(s)$$

$$Y(s) + Y(s)G_1(s)G_2(s) - H(s)Y(s) + Y(s)G_1(s)G_2(s)G_3(s) = R(s)\big(G_1(s)G_2(s) + G_1(s)G_2(s)G_3(s)\big)$$

$$Y(s)\big(1 + G_1(s)G_2(s) - H(s) + G_1(s)G_2(s)G_3(s)\big) = R(s)\big(G_1(s)G_2(s) + G_1(s)G_2(s)G_3(s)\big)$$

$$Y(s) = R(s)\frac{G_1(s)G_2(s) + G_1(s)G_2(s)G_3(s)}{1 + G_1(s)G_2(s) - H(s) + G_1(s)G_2(s)G_3(s)}$$

$$\frac{Y(s)}{R(s)} = T(s) = \frac{G_1(s)G_2(s) + G_1(s)G_2(s)G_3(s)}{1 + G_1(s)G_2(s) - H(s) + G_1(s)G_2(s)G_3(s)}$$

12.2 Bode Plot - Solutions

Consult NCEES® FE Reference Handbook – Pages 373 - 374 for reference

12.2 a) CORRECT ANSWER - A

Slope of given Bode plot changes from 0 dB/decade to -20 dB/decade at $\omega = 10 \, rad/s$.

Therefore, a pole must exist at $\omega = 10 \, rad/s$.

Open-loop transfer function can be expressed as follows:

$$G(s) = \frac{K}{\left(\frac{s}{10} + 1\right)}$$

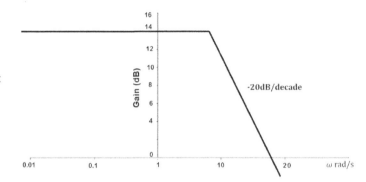

Constant term can be calculated as shown below:

$$|G(j\omega)|_{\omega=1} = 14dB.$$

$$20\log(K) = 14 \rightarrow K = 5$$

$$G(s) = \frac{K}{\left(\frac{s}{10} + 1\right)}$$

$$G(s) = \frac{5}{\left(\frac{s}{10} + 1\right)} = \frac{50}{s + 10}$$

12.2 b) CORRECT ANSWER - D

Slope (S) of given Bode plot can be calculated as shown below:

$$S = \frac{-20dB - 20dB}{10} = -40db/dec$$

This implies that there must be a second order pole at origin.

Open-loop transfer function can be expressed as follows:

$$G(s) = \frac{K}{s^2}$$

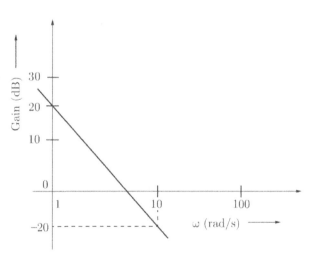

Constant term can be calculated as shown below:

$$|G(j\omega)|_{\omega=1} = 20dB.$$

$$20\log(K) = 20 \rightarrow K = 10$$

$$G(s) = \frac{10}{s^2}$$

12.2 c) CORRECT ANSWER - C

Slope of given Bode plot changes from 0 dB/decade to +20 dB/decade at $\omega = 10\ rad/s$.

Therefore, zero exists at $\omega = 10\ rad/s$.

Slope of given Bode plot changes from +20 dB/decade to 0 dB/decade at $\omega = 100\ rad/s$.

Therefore, a pole must exist at $\omega = 100\ rad/s$.

Open-loop transfer function can be expressed as follows:

$$G(s) = \frac{K\left(\frac{s}{10}+1\right)}{\left(\frac{s}{100}+1\right)}$$

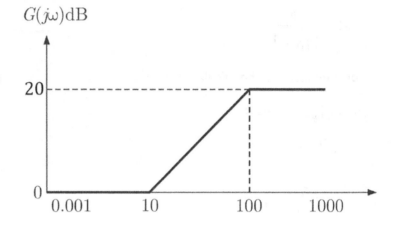

$$G(j\omega)\mathrm{dB}$$

Constant term can be calculated as shown below:

$$|G(j\omega)|_{\omega=1} = 0dB.$$

$$20\log(K) = 0 \rightarrow K = 1$$

$$G(s) = \frac{1\left(\frac{s}{10}+1\right)}{\left(\frac{s}{100}+1\right)} = \frac{\frac{s+10}{10}}{\frac{s+100}{100}} = \frac{10(s+10)}{s+100}$$

12.2 d) CORRECT ANSWER - $\dfrac{10\left(\frac{s}{0.1}+1\right)^2}{\left(\frac{s}{10}+1\right)\left(\frac{s}{100}+1\right)}$

Slope of given Bode plot changes from 0 dB/decade to +40 dB/decade at $\omega = 0.1\ rad/s$.

Therefore, two zeros must exist at $\omega = 0.1\ rad/s$.

Slope of given Bode plot changes from +40 dB/decade to +20 dB/decade at $\omega = 10\ rad/s$.

Therefore, a pole must exist at $\omega = 10\ rad/s$.

Slope of given Bode plot changes from +20 dB/decade to 0 dB/decade at $\omega = 100\ rad/s$.

Therefore, a pole must exist at $\omega = 100\ rad/s$.

Open-loop transfer function can be expressed as follows:

$$G(s) = \frac{K\left(\frac{s}{0.1}+1\right)^2}{\left(\frac{s}{10}+1\right)\left(\frac{s}{100}+1\right)}$$

Constant term can be calculated as: $20\log(K) = 20 \rightarrow K = 10$

$$G(s) = \frac{10\left(\frac{s}{0.1}+1\right)^2}{\left(\frac{s}{10}+1\right)\left(\frac{s}{100}+1\right)}$$

12.2 e) CORRECT ANSWER - D

Transfer function can be rearranged into standard form as shown below:

$$G(s) = \frac{1}{(4s + 100)} = \frac{1}{100\left(\frac{4s}{100} + 1\right)} = \frac{\frac{1}{100}}{\frac{s}{25} + 1}$$

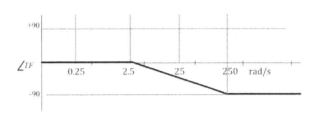

It can be observed that there is no phase shift at 2.5 rad/s, -45-degree phase angle at 25 rad/s and -90-degree phase angle at 250 rad/s. Poles that are not located at origin impact Bode log phase plot in this manner.

12.2 f) CORRECT ANSWER: $-60\ dB$

Transfer function can be rearranged into standard form as shown below:

$$H(s) = \frac{50(s + 2)}{(s + 100)(s + 1000)} = \frac{(50)(2)(s/2 + 1)}{100(s/100 + 1)1000(s/1000 + 1)} = \left(\frac{1}{1000}\right)\frac{\left(\frac{s}{2} + 1\right)}{\left(\frac{s}{100} + 1\right)\left(\frac{s}{1000} + 1\right)}$$

Transfer function has poles at $s = -100$, $s = -1000$ and a zero at $s = -2$.

Gain $= 20\log(1/1000) = -60\ dB$

12.2 g) CORRECT ANSWER : $20\ dB$

$$H(s) = \frac{100(s + 1)}{s(s + 10)} = \frac{100(s + 1)}{10s(s/10 + 1)} = (10)\frac{(s + 1)}{(s)\left(\frac{s}{10} + 1\right)}$$

Gain $= 20\log(10) = 20\ dB$

Transfer function has poles at $s = 0, s = -10$ and a zero at $s = -1$.

12.2 h) CORRECT ANSWER : $-33.9\ dB$

Transfer function can be rearranged in standard form as shown below:

$$H(s) = \frac{100s}{(s^2 + 150s + 5000)} = \frac{100s}{(s + 50)(s + 100)} = \frac{100s}{50(s/50 + 1)100(s/100 + 1)}$$

$$H(s) = \frac{1}{50}\frac{s}{\left(\frac{s}{50} + 1\right)\left(\frac{s}{100} + 1\right)}$$

Gain $= 20\log\left(\frac{1}{50}\right) = -33.9\ dB$. Transfer function has poles at $s = -50$, $s = -100$ and a zero at $s = 0$.

12.3 a) CORRECT ANSWER - B

The stability of a control system depends on the location of its poles.

12.3 b) CORRECT ANSWERS – A, C

Control system is considered stable if bounded-input results in bounded-output (BIBO). Control system is also considered stable if its poles are in the left half of s-plane.

12.3 c) CORRECT ANSWERS – C

A control system with non-repeated roots on imaginary axis is considered marginally stable. As poles approach origin, the stability of control system decreases.

12.3 d) CORRECT ANSWERS – B

A control system with repeated roots on imaginary axis is considered unstable.

12.3 e) CORRECT ANSWER - D

$PM = 180° + \angle G(j\omega_{0dB})$ ω_{0dB} is the frequency at which $|G(j\omega)| = 1$.

$$G(s) = \frac{1}{(s+1)^2} \rightarrow G(j\omega) = \frac{1}{(j\omega + 1)^2}$$

$$|G(j\omega)| = \frac{1}{\sqrt{(\omega^2 + 1)}^2} = \frac{1}{(\omega^2 + 1)}$$

$$|G(j\omega_{0dB})| = \frac{1}{(\omega_{0dB}^2 + 1)} = 1 \rightarrow \omega_{0dB} = 0$$

$$\angle G(j\omega_{0dB}) = -2\tan^{-1}\omega_{0dB} = -2(0) = 0$$

$$PM = 180° + \angle G(j\omega_{0dB}) = 180° + 0° = 180°$$

12.3 f) CORRECT ANSWER - B

$$GM = -20\log|G(j\omega_{180})|$$

$$G(s) = \frac{1}{(s+1)^4} \rightarrow \angle G(j\omega) = -4\tan^{-1}\omega$$

$$\angle G(j\omega_{180}) = -180^0 \rightarrow \angle G(j\omega_{180}) = -4\tan^{-1}\omega_{180} = -180^0 \rightarrow \omega_{180} = 1$$

$$G(s) = \frac{1}{(s+1)^4} \rightarrow |G(j\omega_{180})| = \frac{1}{\sqrt{(\omega_{180}^2 + 1)}^4} = \frac{1}{(1+1)^2} = \frac{1}{4}$$

$$GM = -20\log|G(j\omega_{180})| = -20\log\left(\frac{1}{4}\right) = 12dB$$

12.3 g) CORRECT ANSWER - $s^2 + 3s + 2 + ks = 0$

According to classical negative feedback control system diagram given in NCEES® FE Reference Handbook:

$$Y(s) = \frac{R(s)k\left(\dfrac{s}{(s+1)(s+2)}\right)}{1 + \dfrac{ks}{(s+1)(s+2)}}$$

$$Y(s) = \frac{R(s)ks}{s^2 + 3s + 2 + ks}$$

The closed loop characteristic equation is $s^2 + 3s + 2 + ks = 0$

12.3 h) CORRECT ANSWER: $-8/3$

The closed-loop characteristic equation is $2s^5 + 3s^4 + 7s^2 + s + 10 = 0$

Route Array can be developed using formula given in NCEES® FE Reference Handbook (version 9.5 and older).

s^5	2		2
s^4	3		7
s^3	$b_1 = \dfrac{3 \times 2 - 2 \times 7}{3} = -\dfrac{8}{3}$		

The given system is unstable because b_1 is negative.

Note – Although Route-Array formulas are not provided in latest NCEES® FE Reference Handbook, it is an important technique in the context of control system stability.

12.3 i) CORRECT ANSWER - B

The closed loop characteristic equation of given system is $2s^4 + 3s^3 + s^2 + s + 1 = 0$

Route Array can be developed using formula given in NCEES® FE Reference Handbook (version 9.5 and older).

s^4	2	1	1
s^3	3	1	0
s^2	$b_1 = \dfrac{3 - 2}{3} = \dfrac{1}{3}$	$b_2 = \dfrac{3 - 2 \times 0}{3} = 1$	-
s	$c_1 = \dfrac{\dfrac{1}{3} - 3 \times 1}{\dfrac{1}{3}} = -8$		-

The given system is unstable because c_1 is negative.

Note – Although Route-Array formulas are not provided in latest NCEES® FE Reference Handbook, it is an important technique in the context of control system stability.

12.3 j) CORRECT ANSWER : $0 < k < 5$

The closed loop characteristic equation of given system is $3s^3 + 5s^2 + (k+10)s + 5k = 0$

Routh Array can be developed using formula given in NCEES® FE Reference Handbook (version 9.5 and older).

s^3	3		k+10
s^2	5		5k
s	$b_1 = \dfrac{5(k+10) - 3 \times 5k}{5}$		
s^0	5k		

For the system to remain stable all entries in first column should have same sign (positive).

$$\frac{5(k+10) - 3 \times 5k}{5} > 0 \quad \rightarrow \quad k < 5$$

$$5k > 0 \rightarrow k > 0$$

By combining both conditions we obtain stability range as $0 < k < 5$

Note – Although Routh-Array formulas are not provided in latest NCEES® FE Reference Handbook, it is an important technique in the context of control system stability.

12.4 Controller performance - Solutions

Consult NCEES® FE Reference Handbook – Pages 227 - 229 for reference

12.4 a) CORRECT ANSWER : $20\left(1 - e^{-\frac{t}{2}}\right)$

According to NCEES® FE Reference Handbook, output $y(t)$ of a 1st order system can be expressed as follows:

$$y(t) = y_0 e^{-t/\tau} + KM\left(1 - e^{-\frac{t}{\tau}}\right)$$

According to the problem statement: $K = 4$, $\tau = 2$, $M = 5$, $y_0 = 0$.

$$y(t) = y_0 e^{-t/\tau} + KM\left(1 - e^{-\frac{t}{\tau}}\right) = (0)e^{-\frac{t}{2}} + (4)(5)\left(1 - e^{-\frac{t}{2}}\right) = 20\left(1 - e^{-\frac{t}{2}}\right)$$

12.4 b) CORRECT ANSWER : $4\left(1 - e^{-\frac{(t-3)}{2}}\right)$

According to NCEES® FE Reference Handbook, output $y(t)$ of 1st order system with delay is expressed as follows:

$$y(t) = y_0 e^{-(t-\theta)/\tau} + KM\left(1 - e^{-\frac{(t-\theta)}{\tau}}\right)$$

According to the problem statement: $\theta = 3$, $K = 4$, $\tau = 2$, $M = 1$, $y_0 = 0$.

$$y(t) = y_0 e^{-(t-\theta)/\tau} + KM\left(1 - e^{-\frac{(t-\theta)}{\tau}}\right) = (0)e^{-\frac{(t-3)}{2}} + (4)(1)\left(1 - e^{-\frac{(t-3)}{2}}\right) = 4\left(1 - e^{-\frac{(t-3)}{2}}\right)$$

12.4 c) CORRECT ANSWER : 2

By comparing the given transfer function with standard second-order control system model provided in NCEES® FE Reference Handbook (as shown below), we can observe following details:

$$\frac{Y(s)}{R(s)} = \frac{32}{s^2 + 4s + 16} \qquad\qquad \frac{Y(s)}{R(s)} = \frac{K\omega_n^2}{s^2 + 2\zeta\omega_n s + \omega_n^2}$$

$\omega_n^2 = 16 \rightarrow \omega_n = 4$

$K\omega_n^2 = 32 \rightarrow K(16) = 32 \rightarrow K = 2$

Therefore, steady-state gain $K = 2$.

12.4 d) CORRECT ANSWER : 0.50

Damping ratio can be calculated by observing that $2\zeta\omega_n s = 4s \rightarrow \zeta\omega_n = 2$

Since $\omega_n = 4 \rightarrow \zeta = 0.50$. Therefore, damping ratio is 0.50.

12.4 e) CORRECT ANSWER - A

Since $\zeta < 1$, given control system is considered underdamped.

12.4 f) CORRECT ANSWER : 0.90s

Peak-time can be calculated using following equation:

$$t_p = \frac{\pi}{\omega_n\sqrt{1-\zeta^2}} = \frac{\pi}{4\sqrt{1-(0.50)^2}} = 0.90s$$

12.4 g) CORRECT ANSWER : 1.16

Peak-output can be calculated using following equation:

$$M_p = 1 + e^{-\frac{\pi\zeta}{\sqrt{1-\zeta^2}}} = 1 + e^{-\frac{\pi(0.5)}{\sqrt{1-0.5^2}}} = 1.16$$

12.4 h) CORRECT ANSWER : 16.3%

The peak-overshoot (%OS) response can be calculated using following equation:

$$\%OS = 100e^{-\frac{\pi\zeta}{\sqrt{1-\zeta^2}}} = 100e^{-\frac{\pi(0.5)}{\sqrt{1-0.5^2}}} = 16.3\%$$

12.4 i) CORRECT ANSWER : 3.46 rad/s

The damped natural frequency ω_d can be calculated using following equation:

$$\omega_d = \omega_n\sqrt{1-\zeta^2} = 4\sqrt{1-(0.50)^2} = 3.46\,rad/s$$

12.4 j) CORRECT ANSWER : 2.82 rad/s

The damped resonant frequency ω_r can be calculated using following equation:

$$\omega_r = \omega_n\sqrt{1-2\zeta^2} = 4\sqrt{1-2(0.50)^2} = 2.82\,rad/s$$

12.4 k) CORRECT ANSWER : 3.62

The logarithmic decrement δ can be calculated using following equation:

$$\delta = 2\pi\zeta/\sqrt{1-\zeta^2} = 2\pi(0.5)/\sqrt{1-(0.5)^2} = 3.62$$

12.4 l) CORRECT ANSWER : 2s

2% settling time can be calculated using following equation:

$$T_s = 4/\zeta\omega_n = 4/(0.5 \times 4) = 2s$$

12.4 m) CORRECT ANSWER – 0.24

For a unity feedback system, steady-state error can be calculated using final value theorem as shown below:

$$e(\infty) = \lim_{s \to 0} sE(s) = \lim_{s \to 0} \frac{sR(s)}{1 + G(s)}$$

$$r(t) = 10u(t) \to R(s) = \frac{10}{s}$$

$$G(s) = \frac{(50)(s + 4)}{(s + 1)(s + 5)}$$

$$e(\infty) = \lim_{s \to 0} \frac{s \dfrac{10}{s}}{1 + \dfrac{(50)(s + 4)}{(s + 1)(s + 5)}}$$

$$e(\infty) = \lim_{s \to 0} \frac{10}{1 + \dfrac{(50)(s + 4)}{(s + 1)(s + 5)}} = \frac{10}{1 + \dfrac{(50)(0 + 4)}{(0 + 1)(0 + 5)}} = 0.24$$

Helpful tip – Understand steady-state error calculation formula and learn how to use it for different inputs.

12.4 n) CORRECT ANSWER - ∞

For a unity feedback system, steady-state error can be calculated using final value theorem as shown below:

$$e(\infty) = \lim_{s \to 0} sE(s) = \lim_{s \to 0} \frac{sR(s)}{1 + G(s)}$$

$$r(t) = 5t\, u(t) \to R(s) = \frac{5}{s^2}$$

$$G(s) = \frac{100s}{s^2 + 11s + 30}$$

$$e(\infty) = \lim_{s \to 0} \frac{s \dfrac{5}{s^2}}{1 + \dfrac{100s}{s^2 + 11s + 30}}$$

$$e(\infty) = \lim_{s \to 0} \frac{\dfrac{5}{s}}{1 + \dfrac{100s}{s^2 + 11s + 30}}$$

$$e(\infty) = \frac{\dfrac{5}{0}}{1 + \dfrac{100(0)}{0 + 11(0) + 30}} = \infty$$

Helpful tip – Refer to Laplace transform table for different $r(t) \leftrightarrow R(s)$ pairs.

12.4 o) CORRECT ANSWER - ∞

For a unity feedback system, steady state-error can be calculated using final value theorem as shown below:

$$e(\infty) = \lim_{s \to 0} sE(s) = \lim_{s \to 0} \frac{sR(s)}{1 + G(s)}$$

$$r(t) = 10t^2 u(t) \to R(s) = \frac{20}{s^3}$$

$$G(s) = \frac{s}{s^2 + 100s + 10}$$

$$e(\infty) = \lim_{s \to 0} \frac{s\frac{20}{s^3}}{1 + \frac{s}{s^2 + 100s + 10}} = \lim_{s \to 0} \frac{\frac{20}{s^2}}{1 + \frac{s}{s^2 + 100s + 10}} = \frac{\frac{20}{0}}{1 + \frac{0}{0 + 100(0) + 10}} = \infty$$

12.4 p) CORRECT ANSWER - ∞

For a unity feedback system, steady-state error can be calculated using final value theorem as shown below:

$$e(\infty) = \lim_{s \to 0} sE(s) = \lim_{s \to 0} \frac{sR(s)}{1 + G(s)}$$

$$r(t) = 2t\, u(t) \to R(s) = \frac{2}{s^2}$$

$$G(s) = \frac{1}{(s + 2)(s + 3)}$$

$$e(\infty) = \lim_{s \to 0} \frac{s\frac{2}{s^2}}{1 + \frac{1}{(s + 2)(s + 3)}} = \lim_{s \to 0} \frac{\frac{2}{s}}{1 + \frac{1}{(s + 2)(s + 3)}} = \frac{\frac{2}{0}}{1 + \frac{1}{(0 + 2)(0 + 3)}} = \infty$$

12.4 q) CORRECT ANSWER – 0.11

For a unity feedback system, steady-state error can be calculated using final value theorem as shown below:

$$e(\infty) = \lim_{s \to 0} sE(s) = \lim_{s \to 0} \frac{sR(s)}{1 + G(s)}$$

$$r(t) = 3u(t) \to R(s) = \frac{3}{s}$$

$$G(s) = \frac{10(s + 5)}{(s + 1)(s + 2)}$$

$$e(\infty) = \lim_{s \to 0} \frac{s\frac{3}{s}}{1 + \frac{10(s + 5)}{(s + 1)(s + 2)}} = \lim_{s \to 0} \frac{3}{1 + \frac{10(s + 5)}{(s + 1)(s + 2)}} = \frac{3}{1 + \frac{10(0 + 5)}{(0 + 1)(0 + 2)}} = 0.115$$

Chapter # 13 – Communications
13.1 – Communication Theory - Solutions

Consult NCEES® FE Reference Handbook – Page 372 for reference

13.1 a) CORRECT ANSWER - C

Unit step function starting at $t = t_0$ (time shifting) with amplitude $= A$ (amplitude scaling) is $Au(t - t_0)$.

Therefore, given unit step function can be represented as $2u(t - 4)$.

13.1 b) CORRECT ANSWER: $u(t - 3)$

$$u(3t - 9) = u\big(3(t - 3)\big)$$

Time scaling does not affect unit step function because $u(ct) = u(t)$ where c is a constant.

Therefore, $u\big(3(t - 3)\big) = u(t - 3)$.

13.1 c) CORRECT ANSWER - D

Rectangular pulse centered at $t = t_0$ (time shifting) with amplitude $= A$ (amplitude scaling) and time period τ is given as $A\prod\left(\frac{t-t_0}{\tau}\right)$. Therefore, the rectangular pulse given in problem statement can be represented as follows:

$$2\prod\left(\frac{t - 4}{\frac{1}{3}}\right) = 2\prod\big(3(t - 4)\big)$$

13.1 d) CORRECT ANSWER - B

Triangular pulse centered at $t = t_0$ (time shifting) with amplitude $= A$ (amplitude scaling) and $\tau = 2$ is given as $A\Lambda\left(\frac{t-t_0}{\tau}\right)$. Therefore, the triangular pulse given in problem statement can be represented as follows:

$$5\Lambda\left(\frac{t - (-1)}{2}\right) = 5\Lambda\left(\frac{t + 1}{2}\right)$$

13.1 e) CORRECT ANSWER : $\frac{1}{3}\delta(t)$

Time scaling property of unit impulse function can be expressed as follows:

$$\delta(ct) = \frac{1}{|c|}\delta(t)$$

In the given case, constant $c = -3$.

$$\delta(-3t) = \frac{1}{|-3|}\delta(t) = \frac{1}{3}\delta(t)$$

13.1 f) CORRECT ANSWER : D

$f(4t)$ will compress the time-period of $f(t)$ by a factor of 4. Conversely, $f(t/4)$ will expand the time-period of $f(t)$ by a factor of 4.

13.1 g) CORRECT ANSWER - A

A given function is considered even if $x(-t) = x(t)$.

$$f(t) = t^5 \sin 3t$$

$$f(-t) = (-t)^5 \sin(-3t)$$

$$f(-t) = (-t^5)(-\sin 3t)$$

$$f(-t) = t^5 \sin 3t$$

Since $f(t) = t^5 \sin 3t = f(-t)$, $t^5 \sin 3t$ is considered an even function.

13.1 h) CORRECT ANSWER - B

A given function is considered odd if $x(-t) = -x(t)$.

$$f(t) = \sin 3t$$

$$f(-t) = \sin(-3t)$$

$$f(-t) = -\sin 3t$$

Since $f(t) = \sin 3t = -f(t)$, $\sin 3t$ is considered an odd function.

Helpful tip – Validate that $t^2 + \sin 3t$ is neither even nor odd.

13.1 i) CORRECT ANSWER: 18J

According to Parseval's Theorem, the total energy contained in a finite signal $x(t)$ can be calculated as follows:

$$E = \int_{-\infty}^{\infty} |x(t)|^2 dt$$

In the given scenario, $x(t)$ is a rectangular pulse which has an amplitude of 3, centered at 2 and a time-period of 2. Therefore, it is a finite signal which exists from $t = 1$ to $t = 3$ as shown below.

$$E = \int_{1}^{3} 3^2 dt$$

$$E = 9t]_1^3 = 9(3 - 1)$$

$$E = 18 \, Joules$$

Helpful tip – Sketch the given rectangular pulse to confirm its limits of integration.

13.2 Amplitude Modulation - Solutions

Consult NCEES® FE Reference Handbook – Page 375 for reference

13.2 a) CORRECT ANSWER : 7V

According to the problem statement, maximum amplitude of AM wave is 12V and minimum amplitude is 2V.

$$A_c + A_m = 12V$$

$$A_c - A_m = 2V$$

In the above equations, A_c represents carrier wave amplitude and A_m represents message wave amplitude.

Adding both equations result in $2A_c = 14V \rightarrow A_c = 7V$.

13.2 b) CORRECT ANSWER : 5V

As shown in the previous solution, $A_c = 7V$. We can substitute this value in following equation to calculate A_m.

$$A_c + A_m = 12V \rightarrow A_m = 12V - A_c$$

$$A_m = 12V - 7V = 5V$$

13.2 c) CORRECT ANSWER : 0.71

Modulation index (m) of given AM wave can be calculated as shown below:

$$m = \frac{A_m}{A_c} = \frac{5V}{7V} = 0.71$$

13.2 d) CORRECT ANSWER : 0.80

According to the problem statement, AM wave is given by following equation:

$$x(t) = 50(1 + 0.8 \cos 400\pi t) \cos(100000\pi t)$$

We can compare this equation with standard form of AM wave to extract useful details:

$$x(t) = A'_c(1 + am_n(t)) \cos(2\pi f_c t) \text{ where } a = \text{modulation index}, f_c = \text{carrier frequency.}$$

Therefore, modulation index of given AM wave is 0.80.

13.2 e) CORRECT ANSWER : 200Hz

$$x(t) = 50(1 + 0.8 \cos 400\pi t) \cos(100000\pi t) = 50(1 + 0.8 \cos 2(200)\pi t) \cos(2(50000)\pi t)$$

$f_m = \text{message/modulating frequency} = 200Hz$.

13.2 f) CORRECT ANSWER : 50,000Hz

$$x(t) = 50(1 + 0.8 \cos 400\pi t) \cos(100000\pi t) = 50(1 + 0.8 \cos 2(200)\pi t) \cos(2(50000)\pi t)$$

$f_c = \text{carrier frequency} = 50,000Hz$.

13.2 g) CORRECT ANSWER - D

As per NCEES® FE Reference Handbook, Costas loop can be used for detecting Double-Side Modulation (DSB).

13.2 h) CORRECT ANSWER - C

Modulation index can be calculated using following formula: $m = A_m/A_c$

Message signal $m(t) = 5\sin2\pi(1000t)$

Carrier signal $c(t) = 50\sin2\pi(4000t)$

$A_m = 5, \qquad A_c = 50$

$m = \dfrac{5}{50} = 0.1 = 10\%$

13.2 i) CORRECT ANSWER: 15.2%

Efficiency of an amplitude modulated wave can be calculated using following formula:

$$\eta = \frac{a^2 < m_n^2(t) >}{1 + a^2 < m_n^2(t) >}$$

According to the problem statement:

$a = 0.60 \qquad < m_n^2(t) > = 0.5$

$$\eta = \frac{a^2 < m_n^2(t) >}{1 + a^2 < m_n^2(t) >}$$

$$\eta = \frac{0.6^2 \times 0.5}{1 + 0.6^2 \times 0.5}$$

$\eta = 0.152 = 15.2\%$

13.2 j) CORRECT ANSWER: 84.7%

Based on the efficiency calculations in previous problem, 15.2% transmitted power contains message whereas the remaining 84.7% contains the carrier.

13.2 k) CORRECT ANSWER - A

Amplitude modulation results in variation of carrier wave's amplitude by signal wave.

Helpful tip – Learn how to identify different forms of modulation graphically.

13.3 Angle Modulation - Solutions

Consult NCEES® FE Reference Handbook – Pages 375 - 376 for reference

13.3 a) CORRECT ANSWER: 3.18

According to NCEES® FE Reference Handbook, frequency-deviation ratio can be calculated as follows:

$$D = \frac{k_F \max|m(t)|}{2\pi W}$$

According to the problem statement, $k_F \max|m(t)| = 100kHz, \ W = 5kHz \rightarrow 2\pi W = 10\pi kHz$

$$D = \frac{100kHz}{10\pi kHz} = 3.18$$

13.3 b) CORRECT ANSWER: 41.8kHz

According to NCEES® FE Reference Handbook, 98% power bandwidth of a FM wave with $D > 1$ can be calculated using following formula:

$B = 2(D + 1)W$. As calculated in previous problem, $D = 3.18 > 1$ and $W = 5kHz$.

Therefore, $B = 2(3.18 + 1)(5kHz) = 41.8kHz$

13.3 c) CORRECT ANSWER - B

According to the problem statement, analog modulated wave is given by following equation:

$x(t) = 20\cos(2000\pi t + 5\sin(20\pi t))$ and original message signal is $10\pi\cos(20\pi t)$.

According to NCEES® FE Reference Handbook, the general form of frequency modulated (FM) wave is as follows:

$$x_{FM}(t) = A_c \cos\left(2\pi f_c t + \int_{-\infty}^{t} m(t)dt\right)$$

It can be observed that given wave contains a sine term within brackets which is an integral of cosine. and the original message is a cosine function.

Therefore, $x(t)$ is frequency modulated i.e. message signal is modulating the frequency.

13.3 d) CORRECT ANSWER: 1000Hz, 10Hz

According to the problem statement, analog modulated wave is given by following equation:

$x(t) = 20\cos(2\pi(1000)t + 5\sin(2\pi(10)t))$ and original message signal is $10\pi\cos(20\pi t)$.

It can be observed that $f_c = 1000Hz$ and $f_m = 10Hz$.

13.3 e) CORRECT ANSWER: C

According to the problem statement, analog modulated wave is given by following equation:

$x(t) = 20 \cos(2000\pi t + 10\pi \cos(20\pi t))$ and original message signal is $10\pi \cos(20\pi t)$.

According to NCEES® FE Reference Handbook, the general form of phase modulated (PM) wave is as follows:

$$x_{PM}(t) = A_c \cos\left(2\pi f_c t + k_p m(t)\right)$$

It can be observed that $x(t)$ contains a cosine term within brackets which is same as the original message.

Therefore, $x(t)$ is phase modulated i.e. message signal is modulating the phase.

13.3 f) CORRECT ANSWER: $2000\pi t + 10\pi \cos(20\pi t)$

According to the problem statement, analog modulated wave is given by following equation:

$x(t) = 20 \cos(2000\pi t + 10\pi \cos(20\pi t))$ and original message signal is $10\pi \cos(20\pi t)$.

According to NCEES® FE Reference Handbook, the general form of frequency modulated (FM) wave is as follows:

$$x_{FM}(t) = A_c \cos\left(2\pi f_c t + \varphi(t)\right)$$

It can be observed that $\varphi(t) = 10\pi \cos(20\pi t)$.

Instantaneous phase $\varphi_i(t) = 2\pi f_c t + \varphi(t) = 2000\pi t + 10\pi \cos(20\pi t)$.

Therefore, $x(t)$ is phase modulated i.e. message signal is modulating the phase.

13.3 g) CORRECT ANSWER: $2000\pi - 200\pi^2 \sin 20\pi t$

Instantaneous frequency can be calculated as shown below:

$$\omega_i = \frac{d}{dt}\varphi_i(t)$$

$$\omega_i = \frac{d}{dt}(2000\pi t + 10\pi \cos(20\pi t)) = \frac{d}{dt}2000\pi t + \frac{d}{dt}10\pi \cos(20\pi t)$$

$$\omega_i = 2000\pi - (10\pi)(20\pi)\sin 20\pi t = 2000\pi - 200\pi^2 \sin 20\pi t$$

13.3 h) CORRECT ANSWER: $-200\pi^2 \sin 20\pi t$

Frequency deviation can be calculated as shown below:

$$\Delta\omega = \frac{d}{dt}\varphi(t)$$

$$\Delta\omega = \frac{d}{dt}10\pi \cos(20\pi t) = -200\pi^2 \sin 20\pi t$$

13.3 i) CORRECT ANSWER - D

According to NCEES® FE Reference Handbook, 98% power bandwidth can be calculated using following formula:

$$B = 2(D + 1)W$$

According to the problem statement:

$$D = 1.25 > 1 \quad W = 10kHz$$

$$B = 2(D + 1)W$$

$$B = 2(1.25 + 1) \times 10000Hz$$

$$B = 45000 \ Hz$$

Helpful tip – Review angle modulation formulas given in NCEES® FE Reference Handbook.

13.3 j) CORRECT ANSWER - B

As per NCEES® FE Reference Handbook, phase-lock loop can be used to demodulate angle modulated signals.

13.3 k) CORRECT ANSWER - B

Frequency modulation results in variation of carrier wave's frequency by signal wave.

13.3 l) CORRECT ANSWER - C

Phase modulation results in variation of carrier wave's phase by signal wave. Note that phase and frequency modulation are very similar. They are collectively called as angle modulation.

13.3 m) CORRECT ANSWER - D

According to NCEES® FE Reference Handbook, 98% power bandwidth can be calculated using following formula:

$$B = 2W$$

According to the problem statement:

$$D = 0.1 < 1 \quad W = 10kHz$$

$$B = 2W$$

$$B = 2 \times 10 \ kHz$$

$$B = 20 \ kHz$$

13.4 Fourier Transform - Solutions

Consult NCEES® FE Reference Handbook – Pages 52 – 55, 372 - 373 for reference

13.4 a) CORRECT ANSWER: $40 \sin c(8f)$

The given function is a rectangular pulse centered at $t = 0$, amplitude of 5 and duration of 8 i.e. $5\Pi\left(\frac{t}{8}\right)$

Fourier transform can be calculated using pairs given in NCEES® FE Reference Handbook as shown below.

$$5\Pi\left(\frac{t}{8}\right) \xleftarrow{\quad Fourier\ Transform \quad} 5(8\sin c(8f)) = 40 \sin c(8f)$$

13.4 b) CORRECT ANSWER: $12 \sin c(4f)e^{-4j\pi f}$

The given function is a rectangular pulse centered at $t = 2$, amplitude of 3 and duration of 4 i.e. $3\Pi\left(\frac{t-2}{4}\right)$

Fourier transform time shifting property needs to be used as shown below.

$$3\Pi\left(\frac{t-2}{4}\right) \xleftarrow{\quad Fourier\ Transform \quad} 3(4\sin c(4f))e^{-j2\pi f(2)} = 12 \sin c(4f)e^{-4j\pi f}$$

13.4 c) CORRECT ANSWER - C

Fourier transform's modulation property needs to be used in the given case as shown below.

$$\Pi\left(\frac{t}{6}\right) \xleftarrow{\quad Fourier\ Transform \quad} 6\sin c(6f)$$

$$\cos(2\pi(300)t)\,\Pi\left(\frac{t}{6}\right) \xleftarrow{\quad Fourier\ Transform \quad} 3\sin c\big(6(f-300)\big) + 3\sin c(6(f+300))$$

13.4 d) CORRECT ANSWER - D

Fourier transform can be calculated using pairs given in NCEES® FE Reference Handbook as shown below.

$$e^{-5t}u(t) \xleftarrow{\quad Fourier\ Transform \quad} \frac{1}{5 + j2\pi f}$$

$$\cos(2\pi(20)t)e^{-5t}u(t) \xleftarrow{\quad Fourier\ Transform \quad} \frac{1}{2}\left(\frac{1}{5 + j2\pi(f + 20)} + \frac{1}{5 + j2\pi(f - 20)}\right)$$

13.4 e) CORRECT ANSWER : $8 \sin c(2f)e^{-(4\pi jf)}$

Fourier transform can be calculated using pairs given in NCEES® FE Reference Handbook as shown below.

$$4\Pi\left(\frac{t-2}{2}\right) \xleftarrow{\quad Fourier\ Transform \quad} 4(2\sin c(2f))e^{-(4\pi jf)}$$

Helpful tip – Learn how to use Fourier transform table given in NCEES® FE Reference Handbook.

13.5 Digital Communications - Solutions

Consult NCEES® FE Reference Handbook – Pages 377 and 379 for reference

13.5 a) CORRECT ANSWER: 128

Quantization levels can be calculated using following formula.

$q = 2^n$ where 'q' is the quantization levels and 'n' is the number of bits.

According to the problem statement: $n = 7$

$q = 2^7 = 128$ levels

Helpful tip – Review PCM and PAM formulas given in NCEES® FE Reference Handbook.

13.5 b) CORRECT ANSWER - D

Minimum bandwidth for PCM message transmission can be calculated using following formula.

$B = 2W \log_2 q$

$q = 2^n = 2^8 = 256$

$B = (2)(100Hz) \log_2 256$

$B = 1600\ Hz$

13.5 c) CORRECT ANSWER - B

According to the Nyquist sampling theorem, $f_s \geq 2W$

$f_{s,min} = 2W$

$f_{s,min} = 2 \times 15\ kHz$

$f_{s,min} = 30\ kHz$

13.5 d) CORRECT ANSWER - C

Time spacing between adjacent samples can be calculated using following formula.

$T_s = \dfrac{1}{f_s}$

$T_s = \dfrac{1}{30\ kHz}$

$T_s = 33.3\ \mu s$

13.5 e) CORRECT ANSWER : $34.5 kbps$

According to the 'Shannon Channel Capacity' formula provided in NCEES® FE Reference Handbook:

$$C = BW \log_2\left(1 + \frac{S}{N}\right)$$

As noted under 'Decibels and Bode Plots' heading of NCEES® FE Reference Handbook, dB equation for ratio between two powers (such as signal and noise) is $dB = 10 \log_{10} P_1/P_2$.

According to the problem statement:

$$\frac{S}{N} = 10 dB$$

$$10 \log_{10} S/N = 10 \rightarrow \frac{S}{N} = 10$$

$$C = BW \log_2\left(1 + \frac{S}{N}\right) = 10,000 \log_2(1 + 10) = 10,000 \times 3.459 = 34.5 kbps$$

13.5 f) CORRECT ANSWER : $11.7 dB$

According to the 'Shannon Channel Capacity' formula provided in NCEES® FE Reference Handbook:

$$C = BW \log_2\left(1 + \frac{S}{N}\right) \rightarrow 100,000 = 25,000 \log_2\left(1 + \frac{S}{N}\right)$$

$$\log_2\left(1 + \frac{S}{N}\right) = 4 \rightarrow 1 + \frac{S}{N} = 2^4$$

$$\frac{S}{N} = 2^4 - 1 = 15$$

$$10 \log_{10} S/N = 10 \log_{10} 15 = 11.7 dB$$

13.5 g) CORRECT ANSWER : 11

According to the Cyclical Redundancy Code (CRC) equation provided in NCEES® FE Reference Handbook:

$$E(x) = \frac{T(x)}{G(x)} = \frac{101011}{111}$$

It is important to note that this division is performed using modulo-2 arithmetic with XOR operation.

Refer to 'Logic Operators and Boolean Algebra' section of NCEES® FE Reference Handbook for XOR truth table.

XOR operation is performed at each step instead of subtraction as shown on next page.

Moreover, since the length of generator code is 3, we need to append 3 − 1 = 2 zeroes at the end of data frame.

This will result in 10101100.

```
  10101100
⊕111
  01001100
 ⊕111
   0111100
  ⊕111
    000100
     ⊕111
      011
```

Therefore, remainder $E = 11$ needs to be appended in place of the two zeroes that we added to T earlier.

13.5 h) CORRECT ANSWER : 10101111

According to the Cyclical Redundancy Code (CRC) equation provided in NCEES® FE Reference Handbook, the transmitted code is $T(x) + E(x)$.

As noted in previous solution, $E(x) = 11$ shall be appended in place of the two zeros that were added to $T(x)$.

Therefore, transmitted code is 10101111.

Helpful tip – Confirm that 10101111/11 = 0 using modulo-2 arithmetic. This will imply an error-free transmission.

13.5 i) SOLUTION

Odd-parity bit is added to the data frame to ensure that total number of 1s in the data frame remain odd.

Data Frame	Odd Parity Bit (0/1)
0000	1 (# of 1s after adding odd parity bit = 1 which is odd)
1000	0 (# of 1s after adding odd parity bit = 1 which is odd)
0111	0 (# of 1s after adding odd parity bit = 3 which is odd)

13.5 j) SOLUTION

Even-parity bit is added to the data frame to ensure that total number of 1s in the data frame remain odd.

Data Frame	Even Parity Bit (0/1)
0000	0 (# of 1s after adding even parity bit = 0 which is even)
1000	1 (# of 1s after adding even parity bit = 2 which is even)
0111	1 (# of 1s after adding even parity bit = 4 which is even)

13.6 Multiplexing - Solutions

13.6 a) CORRECT ANSWER - A

Time Division Multiplexing (TDM) is an example of digital multiplexing.

13.6 b) CORRECT ANSWER - C

N channels require at least N-1 guard bands. Therefore 3 channels will require at least 2 guard bands.

$$BW_{min} = BW_{Ch\,1} + Guard\,Band + BW_{Ch\,2} + Guard\,Band + BW_{Ch\,3}$$

$$BW_{min} = 50kHz + 5kHz + 100kHz + 5kHz + 50kHz$$

$$BW_{min} = 210kHz$$

13.6 c) CORRECT ANSWER - C

Since the system can multiplex 1 byte/channel, each frame will carry 1 byte/channel. There are 5 channels. Therefore, frame size will be: $5 \times 1\,byte = 5\,bytes$

13.6 d) CORRECT ANSWER : 400 bps

Since each channel is sending 10 bytes/second and each frame must carry 1 byte/channel, the frame rate must be 10 frame/second. As calculated in the previous problem, minimum frame size is 5 bytes. Bit rate can be calculated as follows:

$$10\,frame/second \times 5\,bytes/frame = 50\,bytes\,/second = 400\,bits\,/\,second = 400\,bps.$$

13.6 e) CORRECT ANSWER - B

Frame is taking 1 bit from each channel; therefore frame size is 3 bits. There are 50000 frames/second and 3 bits per frame. Therefore, total number of bits/second = 50000 frames/second x 3 bits/frame = 150000 bps.

Bit duration = 1 / 150000 = 6.66μs.

13.6 f) CORRECT ANSWER : 20 μs

There are 50000 frames per second. Frame duration $= 1/50000 = 20\,\mu s$

13.6 g) CORRECT ANSWER: 15kHz

Nyquist sampling rate of $x_1(t) = f_{s1} = 2 \times BW_1 = 2 \times 4kHz = 8kHz$

Nyquist sampling rate of $x_2(t) = f_{s2} = 2 \times BW_2 = 2 \times 2kHz = 4kHz$

Nyquist sampling rate of $x_3(t) = f_{s3} = 2 \times BW_3 = 2 \times 1kHz = 2kHz$

Nyquist sampling rate of $x_4(t) = f_{s4} = 2 \times BW_4 = 2 \times 0.5kHz = 1kHz$

Overall sampling rate required for perfect reconstruction $= f_{s1} + f_{s2} + f_{s3} + f_{s4} = 15kHz$

Chapter # 14 – Computer Networks
14.1 Routing & Switching - Solutions

Consult NCEES® FE Reference Handbook – Pages 392 - 407 for reference

14.1 a) CORRECT ANSWER - Routing

Routing is the process of finding efficient paths between nodes based on their addresses.

14.1 b) CORRECT ANSWER - D

Router maintains routing table and forwarding table.

14.1 c) CORRECT ANSWER - Network

Network layer performs node management functions such as routing, addressing and traffic control.

Helpful tip – Review OSI Model and TCP/IP Model layers given in NCEES® FE Reference Handbook.

14.1 d) CORRECT ANSWER – Data Link

Network switch typically operates in data link layer.

It can also perform routing functionality in the network layer, if upgraded.

14.1 e) CORRECT ANSWER – C

Network Interface Card (NIC) establishes computer's unique hardware media access control (MAC) address.

14.1 f) CORRECT ANSWER – A

Router has access to IP datagram and can use IP address for optimal routing of data packets.

14.1 g) SOLUTION

It can be observed that only two nodes are directly connected to A and this results in two branches.

Therefore, to visit the first branch (nodes B, D and F), the next hop from A must be to node B.

Similarly, to visit the second branch (nodes C, E, H and I), the next hop from A must be to node C.

Destination Node	Next Hop
B	B
C	C
D	B
E	C
F	B

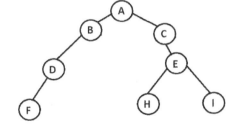

14.2 Network Topologies / Types / Models - Solutions

Consult NCEES® FE Reference Handbook – Pages 392 - 407 for reference

14.2 a) CORRECT ANSWER – Application layer

Application layer will run http and email.

Helpful tip – Review OSI Model and TCP/IP Model layers given in NCEES® FE Reference Handbook.

14.2 b) CORRECT ANSWER – A

Session layer is responsible for managing user interactions only.

14.2 c) CORRECT ANSWER - C

A single break in connection can disrupt an entire network in the implementation of ring topology.

14.2 d) CORRECT ANSWER - D

Local Area Networks (LAN) can be implemented using any one of the suggested implementations.

14.2 e) CORRECT ANSWER - A

Asynchronous Transfer Mode (ATM) LAN is an example of star topology.

14.2 f) CORRECT ANSWER - B

Local Area Network (LAN) can cover small areas (office, hospital etc.).

Wide Area Network (WAN) can cover large geographical regions (states, countries etc.).

Metropolitan Area Network (MAN) can cover municipalities.

Personal Area Network (PAN) can cover distance within range of a person (typically few feet).

14.2 g) CORRECT ANSWER: 406

Number of links required in a full mesh network is equal to $n(n-1)/2$ where $n =$ number of nodes.

In the given case, $n = 29 \rightarrow n(n-1)/2 = (29)(28)/2 = 406$.

Therefore, 406 links are required to implement a fully-connected mesh network of 29 nodes.

14.2 h) CORRECT ANSWER: 28

Number of input/output ports required on each node in a fully-connected mesh network can be found using $(n-1)$ where $n =$ number of nodes.

In the given case, $n = 29 \rightarrow (n-1) = 28$

Therefore, 28 ports are required on each node to implement a fully-connected mesh network of 29 nodes.

14.2 i) CORRECT ANSWER: C

Tree topology is also known as hierarchical topology. It is a hybrid of star and bus topologies and share many of their features. For example, each layer in tree topology acts like a bus topology and tree topology also contains a central node like star topology.

Helpful tip – Understand advantages and disadvantages of bus, star, ring, tree and mesh topologies.

14.2 j) CORRECT ANSWER: D

Mesh topology is the most complicated network configuration to implement due to large amount of cabling. As noted earlier, $n(n-1)/2$ links are required to implement a fully connected mesh network. The number of links grow exponentially.

In comparison, number of links required for implementation of a star network are equal to n and the number of links required for implementation of a bus network are equal to $n-1$.

14.2 k) CORRECT ANSWER: B

Ring topology is generally used to create a wide area network (WAN) which spans large geographical regions extending up to countries and continents. Bus topology is rarely used in modern computer networks. Star topology is primarily used for high speed LAN. Mesh topology is used to interconnect LANs in a WAN.

14.2 l) CORRECT ANSWER: D

OSI Model's presentation layer is responsible for managing the syntax and semantics of message which includes encryption/decryption (security), compression/decompression, encoding/decoding (translation) etc.

14.2 m) CORRECT ANSWER: C

Data link layer performs physical addressing by adding header to packet frames which defines the address of next node in the route. Some of the other responsibilities of data link layer include framing, flow control, error control and media access control.

Helpful tip – Review functions and features of all OSI Model Layers and TCP/IP Layers.

14.2 n) CORRECT ANSWER: C

Encapsulation is the process of building protocol data unit as the data passes from upper layer (application) to lower layer (physical). Headers (and sometimes trailers) are added by different protocols during this process.

The reverse process of encapsulation is called decapsulation.

14.3 Internet Protocol Addressing: IPv4/IPv6 - Solutions

Consult NCEES® FE Reference Handbook – Pages 394 - 400 for reference

14.3 a) CORRECT ANSWER - D

Identification, flag, and fragment offset fields of IPv4 header are responsible for fragmentation of IPv4 datagram. Fragmentation is the process of dividing an IP datagram into smaller chunks called fragments during its transmission. Identification field makes sure that whenever an IP packet is fragmented during transmission, all fragments will contain same identification number to identify the original IP datagram. Flag field tells the network device (router) if an IP packet needs to be fragmented or not. Fragment offset helps in determining the correct position of the fragment in the original IP packet.

14.3 b) CORRECT ANSWER - D

Least significant bit of 'Flags' field corresponds to bit # 2 which is called More Fragments (MF). It is set (=1) for all fragments except the last fragment because the IP datagram must end after the last fragment and more fragments are not required after it.

14.3 c) CORRECT ANSWER - D

IPv4's 'Time To Live' (TTL) field is also known as 'Hop Limit' or 'Hop Counter' in IPv6. It tells the network how many routers this packet can visit before being discarded. If TTL = 20, it means that given IP datagram can visit 20 routers before being dropped. Every time an IP datagram visits a router, TTL is decremented. This is done by design to prevent the packet from indefinitely looping in a network.

14.3 d) CORRECT ANSWER - D

Internet Header Length (IHL) field is used to specify the size of IPv4 header. It is multiplied by 32 bits to determine the actual header length.

According to the problem statement: $1000_2 = 8_{10}$

$$8 \times 32 \ bits = 256 \ bits = \frac{256}{8} = 32 \ bytes$$

Therefore, header length of this IPv4 datagram is 32 bytes.

14.3 e) CORRECT ANSWER - C

In the previous problem, header length was calculated as 32 bytes. Minimum header size of IPv4 datagram is 20 bytes (0 bytes used for Options field). This means that the given IPv4 header uses 12 bytes for Options field.

14.3 f) CORRECT ANSWER - C

Fragment offset field identifies the exact position of fragment in the original IPv4 datagram. It is measured in 8-byte blocks. In the given case, 200 x 8 = 1600 Bytes. It means that 1600 Bytes of data has already arrived ahead of this fragment.

14.3 g) CORRECT ANSWER - D

IPv6 header length is of fixed size i.e. 40 bytes.

14.3 h) CORRECT ANSWER - C

IPv6's 'Hop Limit' field is the same as IPv4's 'Time To Live' field.

14.3 i) CORRECT ANSWER - C

According to the problem statement, IPv6 address in expanded form is given below:

2A1F:0000:0000:0011:0000:0000:0000:2100

We can use following provisions to abbreviate IPv6 address:

1. Leading zeroes can be dropped. This is applicable to $0011 \rightarrow 11$.
2. Consecutive groups of zeroes can be replaced with double colon :: We have the choice of converting two groups of 0000s or three groups of 0000s. Converting two groups of zeroes to :: will result in 2A1F::11:0:0:0:2100. Converting three groups of 0000s to :: will result in 2A1F:0:0:11::2100 which is a more abbreviated form.

Therefore, the most abbreviated form of given IPv6 address is 2A1F:0:0:11::2100.

Note: Option D is not valid because we can use double colon :: only once.

14.3 j) CORRECT ANSWER - C

According to the problem statement, IPv6 address in abbreviated form is given below:

B:C8::15:0:AC

IPv6 address must contain 8 groups of 4 hexadecimal digits separated by colons. Double colons can be expanded into sets of zeroes (to complete 8 groups) and leading zeroes can be added for address expansion.

$$B \rightarrow 000B, C8 \rightarrow 00C8, :: \rightarrow 0000:0000:0000, 0 \rightarrow 0000, AC \rightarrow 00AC$$

Therefore, the expanded form of given IPv6 address is 000B:00C8:0000:0000:0000:0015:0000:00AC.

14.4 Protocols: TCP/UDP/ICMP - Solutions

Consult NCEES® FE Reference Handbook – Pages 400 - 404 for reference

14.4 a) CORRECT ANSWER - B

Protocol data unit is called a 'Segment' in TCP, 'Datagram' in UDP and IP, 'Frame' in Data Link Layer and 'Bit' in Physical Layer.

14.4 b) CORRECT ANSWER - D

UDP is a connectionless and unreliable protocol with a very low overhead. Unlike TCP, UDP does not use acknowledgment mechanism.
Helpful tip – Understand the key features of TCP and UDP.

14.4 c) CORRECT ANSWER - C

TCP header consists of minimum 20 bytes and maximum 60 bytes. Options field in TCP has 0 – 40 bytes range.
Helpful tip – Understand the TCP header fields and their applications.

14.4 d) CORRECT ANSWER - B

TCP establishes connection between a client and a server through a three-way handshake as explained below:
Step # 1 – Client sends a request segment to server with SYN bit set to 1. This segment does not contain any payload, it just contains the TCP header.
Step # 2 – After receiving the request segment, server responds by sending a reply segment. TCP header of reply segment contains SYN and ACK bits that are set to 1.
Step # 3 – After receiving reply segment from server, client sends an acknowledgment with ACK bit set to 1. Three-way acknowledgment forms an important part of TCP's reliability mechanism.
Helpful tip – Understand TCP's four-way handshake for termination of a full-duplex connection.

14.4 e) CORRECT ANSWER - D

Telnet (remote access), SMTP (email) and http (web browsing) require high degree of reliability offered by TCP.

14.4 f) CORRECT ANSWER - D

Internet control message protocol (ICMP) is designed to compensate for the lack of error-control and management query mechanisms in Internet Protocol (IP). ICMP messages can be broadly categorized into error-reporting and query messages.

14.4 g) CORRECT ANSWER - C

ICMP error messages are only reported back to the source to reduce unnecessary traffic and avoid network congestion. Sending such messages to intermediate routers would reduce overall network performance.

14.4 h) CORRECT ANSWER - D

According to partial list of ICMP type and code values for IPv4 given in NCEES® FE Reference Handbook, ICMP 'Type 3 = Destination Unreachable' and ICMP 'Code 4 = Fragmentation Needed and DF set' are most applicable.

14.5 Network Security: Intrusion Detection/Prevention and Encryption - Solutions

Consult NCEES® FE Reference Handbook – Pages 413 - 416 for reference

14.5 a) CORRECT ANSWER - A

Encryption helps in keeping data secret while it is in transit, but it does not provide overall network security. To make network more secure, an electronic security guard is required in the form of a firewall. Firewalls protect network from unauthorized traffic by performing user authentication and implementing access control.

14.5 b) CORRECT ANSWER - A

Packet filtering firewalls allow/block information packets by inspecting IP and TCP header fields which are compared against a set of rules. These rules dictate whether traffic can be allowed in/out of certain IP addresses, protocols, port numbers etc.

Helpful tip – Review stateful packet filters, stateless packet filters, application level gateway firewall, circuit level gateway firewall.

14.5 c) CORRECT ANSWER - A

Signature-based IDS works on the basis of previously known and documented list of malicious patterns (signatures). Observed events are compared with signatures to respond to a threat.

14.5 d) CORRECT ANSWER - D

Anomaly-based IDS works by establishing a baseline of acceptable network activities. They continuously review the current state of network traffic and devices to compare them against the baseline to detect patterns that may be malicious. Baseline values can be established using parameters such as unusual traffic patterns (spikes or sags), time-of-day usage of network devices, very high computer power consumption, activity level of a user which does not match acceptable profile. The disadvantage of anomaly-based IDS is that they can be fooled by an intruder who carefully blends in by increasing the activity level gradually.

14.5 e) CORRECT ANSWER - D

Nmap is a network mapper which is widely used for exploring a network and conducting security audits. The given command nmap 192.1.2.3 will scan IP 192.1.2.3 and reveal its ports, services, and domain names.

Helpful tip – Develop familiarity with nmap commands.

14.5 f) CORRECT ANSWER - B

F flag is used for conducting a fast scan.

Helpful tip – Develop familiarity with nmap flags.

14.5 g) CORRECT ANSWER - B

RSA public-key cryptosystem based digital signatures allow senders to use private key in order to digitally sign a message/document as $s = m^d (mod\ n)$ that can be verified by receiver using sender's public key 'e'.

14.5 h) CORRECT ANSWER - C

According to the problem statement: $p = 7$, $q = 9$, $e = 11$, $d =?$

$n = p \times q = 7 \times 9 = 63$ $t = LCM(p - 1, q - 1) = LCM(6, 8) = 24$

$e * d = 1 \ (mod \ t)$

$$d = \frac{1 + k \times t}{e}$$

k is a real number and it is chosen so that it will result in an integer value of d.

$$d = \frac{1 + 5 \times 24}{11} = \frac{121}{11} = 11$$

Therefore, Alpha's private key must be 11.

14.5 i) CORRECT ANSWER - 8

In RSA public-key cryptosystem, cyphertext c can be calculated using following equation: $c = m^e (mod \ n)$

According to the problem statement and the results of previous solution:

$m = 8$, $n = 77$.

$c = 8^{11} (mod \ 77) = 8$

Helpful tip – Decrypt the cyphertext and retrieve original message using $m = c^d (mod \ n)$

14.5 j) CORRECT ANSWER - B

Public-key cryptosystems use public keys for encryption which allows anyone to encrypt and send messages. However, messages can only be decoded by the intended recipient with correct secret/private key.

14.5 k) CORRECT ANSWER: 4

According to the problems statement: $g = 3$, $p = 5$.

Let $\alpha_{private-key} = x = 1$, $\beta_{private-key} = y = 2$.

We can calculate public key of each party using following formula:

$\alpha_{public-key} = g^x (mod \ p) = 3^1 (mod \ 5) = 3$ $\beta_{public-key} = g^y (mod \ p) = 3^2 (mod \ 5) = 4$

α and β will exchange their public keys. These keys will be used each other to establish a common private key.

Secret key obtained by $\alpha = \beta_{public-key}{}^x (mod \ p) = 4^1 (mod \ 5) = 4$

Secret key obtained by $\beta = \alpha_{public-key}{}^y (mod \ p) = 3^2 (mod \ 5) = 4$

It can be observed that both parties have obtained a common secret key without exchanging it publicly.

Helpful tip – Decrypt the cyphertext and retrieve original message using $m = c^d (mod \ n)$

14.5 l) SOLUTION

To create a control flow diagram, we first need to identify code segments that qualify as nodes (i.e. statements) and edges that demonstrate control flow from one node to another node.

Let us denote nodes alphabetically.

Control flow diagram can be created as shown below:

int sumCalculator (int x) {

int count = 0; // **Node A**

int sum = 0; // **Node B**

while (count < x) { // **Node C**

sum = sum + count; // **Node D**

count++; } // **Node E**

return sum;} // **Node F**

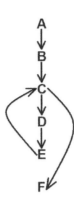

It can be observed that there are 6 nodes and 6 edges.

14.5 m) CORRECT ANSWER: B

McCabe's cyclomatic complexity number can be found using following formula:

$c = e - n + 2$

$c = $ McCabe's cyclomatic complexity

$n = $ # of nodes = 2

$e = $ # of edges = 2

$c = 6 - 6 + 2 = 2$

Therefore, McCabe's cyclomatic complexity number for given algorithm is 2.

Typically, algorithms/codes with $c > 15$ are considered very complex.

Chapter # 15 – Digital Systems
15.1 Number Systems - Solutions

Consult NCEES® FE Reference Handbook – Page 389 for reference

15.1 a) CORRECT ANSWER: 100010101101_2

Number system conversion can be efficiently performed using calculators.

$8AD_{HEX} = 100010101101_2$

15.1 b) CORRECT ANSWER: 1111000011_2

Number system conversion can be efficiently performed using calculators.

$963_{10} = 1111000011_2$

15.1 c) CORRECT ANSWER - D

$2A_{16} = 2 \times 16^1 + A \times 16^0 = 2 \times 16 + 10 \times 1 = 32 + 10 = 42_{10}$

$101010_2 = 1 \times 2^5 + 0 \times 2^4 + 1 \times 2^3 + 0 \times 2^2 + 1 \times 2^1 + 0 \times 2^0 = 32 + 0 + 8 + 0 + 2 + 0 = 42_{10}$

$52_8 = 5 \times 8^1 + 2 \times 8^0 = 40 + 2 = 42_{10}$

15.1 d) CORRECT ANSWER: 0101_2

(+2) 0010_2

(+3) 0011_2

(+5) 0101_2 Note that given numbers are unsigned (MSB of positive numbers is always 0).

15.1 e) CORRECT ANSWER: 1001_2

The given binary numbers are negative because MSB is 1.

$1101_2 = - (0010)_2 = - (2)_{10}$

$1011_2 = - (0100)_2 = - (4)_{10}$

$\quad\quad 1101_2 \quad (-2)_{10}$

$\quad +1011_2 \quad (-4)_{10}$

$\quad 1 \quad 1000$

carry $\quad\quad 1$

$\quad\quad 1001_2 \quad (-6)_{10}$ Note that carry is added in 1's complement.

15.1 f) CORRECT ANSWER: 0000_2

2's complement addition can be performed as shown below.

1011_2 (-5)

$+0101_2$ (+5)

1   0000   = 0000_2

Ignore carry   Note that carry is ignored in 2's complement.

15.1 g) CORRECT ANSWER: 0011_2

2's complement addition can be performed as shown below.

1110_2 (-2)

$+0101_2$ (+5)

1   0011   (+3)   = 0011_2

Ignore carry   Note that carry is ignored in 2's complement.

15.1 h) CORRECT ANSWER - D

2's complement numbers can be converted into decimal numbers by flipping all the bits and adding 1. The resulting binary number is converted into decimal and a negative sign is added to obtain the final answer.

Flipping all the bits results in: $1010_2 \rightarrow 0101_2$ and $111010_2 \rightarrow 000101_2$

Adding 1 results in: $0101_2 + 0001_2 = 0110_2 = 6_{10}$ and $111010_2 + 000001_2 = 000110_2 = 6_{10}$

Adding negative sign to the result obtained in last step confirms that given 2's complement numbers are -6_{10}.

15.1 i) CORRECT ANSWER - D

It can be observed that -11_{10} and 101111_2 do not form a correct pair of decimal and 2's complement representation. Flipping all the bits results in: $101111_2 \rightarrow 010000_2$. Adding 1 results in: $010000_2 + 000001_2 = 010001_2 = 17_{10}$. Adding a negative sign to the result obtained in last step confirms that given 2's complement number is -17_{10} which is not equal to -11_{10}.

Helpful tip – Validate the remaining pairs by converting 2's complement numbers into decimal equivalents.

15.1 j) CORRECT ANSWER - B

It can be observed that -16_{10} and 110010_2 do not form a correct pair of decimal and 2's complement representation. Flipping all the bits results in: $110010_2 \rightarrow 001101_2 = 13$. Adding a negative sign to the result obtained in last step confirms that given 1's complement number is -13_{10} which is not equal to -16_{10}.

Helpful tip – Validate the remaining pairs by converting 1's complement numbers into decimal equivalents.

15.2 Boolean Logic - Solutions

Consult NCEES® FE Reference Handbook – Page 390 for reference

15.2 a) CORRECT ANSWER - D

Applying De Morgan's theorem to given logical function results in:

$$\overline{A + BC\overline{D} + (\overline{E} + \overline{F})} = (\overline{A})(\overline{BC\overline{D}})\,(\overline{\overline{E} + \overline{F}}) = (\overline{A})(\overline{B} + \overline{C} + D)(E)(F)$$

Helpful tip – Review De Morgan's theorem given in NCEES® FE Reference Handbook.

15.2 b) CORRECT ANSWER - A

Applying De Morgan's theorem to given logical function results in:

$$\overline{(ABC)(D + E\overline{F})} = \overline{(ABC)} + \overline{(D + E\overline{F})} = \overline{A} + \overline{B} + \overline{C} + \overline{D}(\overline{E} + F)$$

15.2 c) CORRECT ANSWER - B

Applying De Morgan's theorem to given logical function results in:

$$A\overline{B} + A\overline{(BC)} + B\overline{(A + C)} = A\overline{B} + A(\overline{B} + \overline{C}) + B\,\overline{A}\,\overline{C}$$
$$A\overline{B} + A\overline{(BC)} + B\overline{(A + C)} = A\overline{B} + A\overline{B} + A\overline{C} + \overline{A}\,\overline{C}B$$
$$A\overline{B} + A\overline{(BC)} + B\overline{(A + C)} = A\overline{B} + A\overline{C} + \overline{A}\,\overline{C}B$$
$$A\overline{B} + A\overline{(BC)} + B\overline{(A + C)} = A\overline{B} + \overline{C}(A + \overline{A}B)$$

According to Redundancy Law: $A + \overline{A}B = A + B$

$$A\overline{B} + A\overline{(BC)} + B\overline{(A + C)} = A\overline{B} + \overline{C}(A + B)$$

15.2 d) CORRECT ANSWER - B

$$AB + B(A + C) + C(A + B) = AB + AB + BC + AC + BC$$

According to Idempotent Law: $AB + AB = AB$ $\quad\quad BC + BC = BC$

$$AB + B(A + C) + C(A + B) = AB + BC + AC$$

15.2 e) CORRECT ANSWER - C

$$(A + B)(A + B + C) = A + AB + AC + AB + B + BC$$

According to Idempotent Law: $AB + AB = AB$

$$(A + B)(A + B + C) = A + AB + AC + B + BC$$
$$(A + B)(A + B + C) = A(1 + B) + AC + B(1 + C)$$

According to Identity Law: $(1 + B) = 1$.

$$(A + B)(A + B + C) = A + B + AC = A(1 + C) + B = A + B$$

15.2 f) CORRECT ANSWER - B

$$A\overline{C} + \overline{A}C = A(\overline{A\overline{B} + \overline{A}B}) + \overline{A}(A\overline{B} + \overline{A}B) = A\left[\overline{(A\overline{B})}\,\overline{(\overline{A}B)}\right] + \overline{A}A\overline{B} + \overline{A}\,\overline{A}B$$

$$A\overline{C} + \overline{A}C = A(\overline{A} + B)(A + \overline{B}) + 0 + \overline{A}B = A(\overline{A}A + \overline{A}\,\overline{B} + AB + B\overline{B}) + \overline{A}B$$

$$A\overline{C} + \overline{A}C = A(0 + \overline{A}\,\overline{B} + AB + 0) + \overline{A}B = A\overline{A}\,\overline{B} + AAB + \overline{A}B = 0 + AB + \overline{A}B = B(1) = B$$

15.3 Logic gates and circuits - Solutions

Consult NCEES® FE Reference Handbook – Page 390 for reference

15.3 a) CORRECT ANSWER - B

$(AB)\,XOR\,(CD) = AB\,\overline{(CD)} + \overline{(AB)}\,CD$

$(AB)\,XOR\,(CD) = AB\,(\overline{C} + \overline{D}) + CD\,(\overline{A} + \overline{B})$

$(AB)\,XOR\,(CD) = AB\overline{C} + AB\overline{D} + \overline{A}CD + \overline{B}CD$

Helpful tip – Review logical operations and gates given in NCEES® FE Reference Handbook.

15.3 b) CORRECT ANSWER - C

$\overline{(A\overline{B})(\overline{A}B)} = \overline{(A\overline{B})} + \overline{(\overline{A}B)}$

$\overline{(A\overline{B})(\overline{A}B)} = \overline{A} + B + A + \overline{B} = (\overline{A} + A) + (B + \overline{B}) = 1 + 1 = 1$

$\overline{(A\overline{B})(\overline{A}B)} = 1$

15.3 c) CORRECT ANSWER - A

$\overline{A\overline{B}\,\overline{C}} + C = (\overline{A} + B + C) + C$

According to Idempotent Law: $C + C = C$

$\overline{A\overline{B}\,\overline{C}} + C = \overline{A} + B + C$

15.3 d) CORRECT ANSWER - C

$(\overline{A})(\overline{B})(C) = \overline{A}\,\overline{B}\,C$

15.3 e) CORRECT ANSWER - B

$\overline{(\overline{A}\,\overline{B})(A + B)} = \overline{A\overline{A}\,\overline{B} + \overline{A}\,\overline{B}B}$

$\overline{(\overline{A}\,\overline{B})(A + B)} = \overline{0 + 0}$

$\overline{(\overline{A}\,\overline{B})(A + B)} = 1$

15.3 f) CORRECT ANSWER - C

It can be observed from the truth table of XOR function given in NCEES® FE Reference Handbook that XOR always results in a high output (1) whenever input contains odd number of ones. Therefore, XOR can be used to detect odd number of 1s.

Helpful tip – Create a truth table of XNOR and confirm that it can be used to detect even number of 1s.

Copyrighted Material © 2020

15.4 Logic minimization – K-Maps/SOP/POS - Solutions

Consult NCEES® FE Reference Handbook – Pages 391 - 392 for reference

15.4 a) CORRECT ANSWER – B

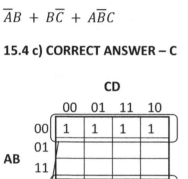

$$\overline{A}B + B\overline{C} + A\overline{B}C$$

15.4 b) CORRECT ANSWER - D

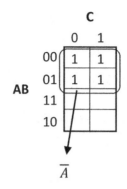

$$\overline{A}$$

15.4 c) CORRECT ANSWER – C

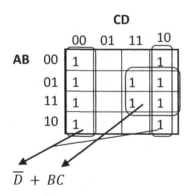

$$\overline{B}$$

15.4 d) CORRECT ANSWER - A

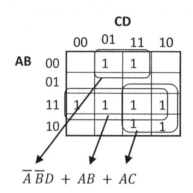

$$\overline{A}\,\overline{B}D + AB + AC$$

15.4 e) CORRECT ANSWER – C

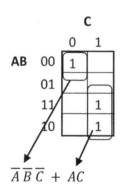

$$\overline{D} + BC$$

15.4 f) CORRECT ANSWER - C

$$\overline{A}\,\overline{B}\,\overline{C} + AC$$

Helpful tip – Review rules related to logic minimization and function simplification related to K-Maps.

15.5 – Sequential Circuits - Flip Flops and Counters - Solutions

Consult NCEES® FE Reference Handbook – Page 391 for reference

15.5 a) CORRECT ANSWER - C

Input 101 to flip-flop # 1 appears as 010 at its complement output $\overline{Q}$. This complement output $\overline{Q}$ of flip-flop # 1 acts as input for flip-flop # 2. This input 010 appears as output Q of flip-flop # 2.

15.5 b) CORRECT ANSWER - B

Comparing the input /output relationship of given circuit with SR flip-flop truth table shows that it is an implementation of SR flip-flop. Refer to the truth table given in NCEES® FE Reference Handbook.

15.5 c) CORRECT ANSWER - C

Comparing the input/output relationship of given circuit with D flip-flop truth table shows that it is an implementation of D flip-flop. Refer to the truth table given in NCEES® FE Reference Handbook.

15.5 d) CORRECT ANSWER - A

Comparing the input/output relationship of given circuit with JK flip-flop truth table shows that it is an implementation of JK flip-flop. Refer to the truth table given in NCEES® FE Reference Handbook.

15.5 e) CORRECT ANSWER - B

D flip-flop input 001 appears as 001 and 110 at its outputs Q_1 and $\overline{Q_1}$ respectively.

D flip-flop's output Q_1 serves as set input (S) for SR flip-flop.

D flip-flop's output $\overline{Q_1}$ serves as reset input (R) for SR flip-flop.

Following truth table summarizes input and output relationship between the two flip-flops.

D Flip-Flop		SR Flip-Flop		
Q_1	$\overline{Q_1}$	$S = Q_1$	$R = \overline{Q_1}$	Q_2
0	1	0	1	0
0	1	0	1	0
1	0	1	0	1

Therefore, SR flip-flop output Q_2 will be 001.

Helpful tip - Refer to D flip-flop and SR flip-flop truth table to confirm above mentioned results.

15.5 f) CORRECT ANSWER - B

The given logic circuit is an implementation of the Johnson counter. Note that clock is applied simultaneously to all flip-flops. Initially, $Q_1 = Q_2 = Q_3 = 0$. It is important to keep track of inputs values residing at each flip-flop before every clock cycle. Before the first clock cycle, $\bar{Q}_3 = 1$ will serve as input to flip-flop # 1, $Q_1 = 0$ will serve as input to flip-flop # 2 and $Q_2 = 0$ will be input to flip-flop # 3. Therefore, when the first clock cycle arrives, $\bar{Q}_3 = 1$ will be loaded to flip-flop # 1 and its output will change from 0 to 1, $Q_1 = 0$ will be loaded flip-flop # 2 and its output will remain 0. Similarly, $Q_2 = 0$ will be loaded to flip-flop # 3 and its output will also remain unchanged as 0. Using this approach, output transitions can be summarized as shown below.

Clock cycle	Q3	Q2	Q1
0	0	0	0
1	0	0	1
2	0	1	1
3	1	1	1

15.5 g) CORRECT ANSWER - D

The given logic circuit is an implementation of a 4-bit asynchronous down counter. Flip-flops are 'positive edge triggered' i.e. outputs will change on a rising clock edge only. Transition from 0 to 1 is considered a rising edge. Initial output states are 1111. The rising edge of input clock pulse will cause the output Q_0 to become 0, and the next clock pulse will make Q_0 output return to logic 1. As Q_0 becomes high, it makes $Q_1 = 0$ low because $\overline{Q_1} = 0$ was sitting at second flip flop's input waiting for a positive edge trigger. The next (third) clock pulse will cause Q_0 to become low (because $Q_0 = 0$ was sitting at first flip flop's input waiting for the positive edge trigger), now both Q_0 and Q_1 will be low. Using this approach, output transitions can be summarized as shown below.
Note - One transition in Q_1 is requiring two transitions in Q_0.
Helpful tip – Investigate why Q_2 and Q_1 have not changed states within 3 clock cycles?

Clock cycle	Q3	Q2	Q1	Q0
0	1	1	1	1
1	1	1	1	0
2	1	1	0	1
3	1	1	0	0

15.5 h) CORRECT ANSWER - A

The given logic circuit is an implementation of a 2-bit synchronous up counter. It is important to note that the current value of Q_0 serves as input for J_1, K_1 in the next clock cycle. Initial states are $Q_1 Q_0 = 00$.
1st clock cycle – Flip-flop # 1 output Q_1 will not change because $Q_0 = J_1 = K_1 = 0$ (output does not toggle).
Flip-flop # 0 output Q_0 will change from 0 to 1 because $J_0 = K_0 = 1$ (toggles the output).
2nd clock cycle – Flip-flop # 1 output Q_1 will change from 0 to 1 because $Q_0 = J_1 = K_1 = 1$ (toggles the output).
Flip-flop # 0 output Q_0 will change from 1 to 0 because $J_0 = K_0 = 1$ (toggles the output).
3rd clock cycle – Flip-flop # 1 output Q_1 will not change because $Q_0 = J_1 = K_1 = 0$.
Flip-flop # 0 output Q_0 will change from 0 to 1 because $J_0 = K_0 = 1$ (toggles the output).

Clock cycle	Q_1	Q_0
Initial state	0	0
1	0	1
2	1	0
3	1	1

15.6 – Combinational circuits - Solutions

Consult NCEES® FE Reference Handbook – Page 391 for reference

15.6 a) CORRECT ANSWER - D

Decoder, encoder, and multiplexer are examples of combinational circuits. Flip-flops are sequential circuits.

15.6 b) CORRECT ANSWER - C

A decoder with n inputs has 2^n outputs. For example, a decoder with 2 inputs will have 4 outputs which results in a 2-to-4 decoder. Similarly, a decoder with 3 inputs will have 8 outputs which results in a 3-to-8 decoder.

15.6 c) SOLUTION

Truth table of a 2-to-4 decoder is given below.

E	A	B	y_3	y_2	y_1	y_0
0	X	X	0	0	0	0
1	0	0	0	0	0	1
1	0	1	0	0	1	0
1	1	0	0	1	0	0
1	1	1	1	0	0	0

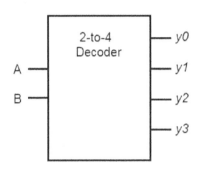

15.6 d) SOLUTION

$$y_0 = \bar{A}\bar{B}E, \qquad y_1 = \bar{A}BE, \qquad y_2 = A\bar{B}E, \qquad y_3 = ABE$$

Column A	Column B
y_0	ABE
y_1	$A\bar{B}E$
y_2	$\bar{A}BE$
y_3	$\bar{A}\bar{B}E$

15.6 e) SOLUTION

Truth table of a 3-to-8 decoder is given below.

E	A	B	C	y_7	y_6	y_5	y_4	y_3	y_2	y_1	y_0
0	X	X	X	0	0	0	0	0	0	0	0
1	0	0	0	0	0	0	0	0	0	0	1
1	0	0	1	0	0	0	0	0	0	1	0
1	0	1	0	0	0	0	0	0	1	0	0
1	0	1	1	0	0	0	0	1	0	0	0
1	1	0	0	0	0	0	1	0	0	0	0
1	1	0	1	0	0	1	0	0	0	0	0
1	1	1	0	0	1	0	0	0	0	0	0
1	1	1	1	1	0	0	0	0	0	0	0

15.6 f) SOLUTION

$$y_0 = \bar{A}\bar{B}\bar{C}E, \qquad y_1 = \bar{A}\bar{B}CE, \qquad y_2 = \bar{A}B\bar{C}E, \qquad y_7 = ABCE$$

Column A	Column B
y_0	$ABCE$
y_1	$\bar{A}\bar{B}\bar{C}E$
y_2	$\bar{A}\bar{B}\bar{C}E$
y_7	$\bar{A}\bar{B}CE$

15.6 g) CORRECT ANSWER: $E(\bar{A}\bar{B}C + \bar{A}BC + A\bar{B}\bar{C})$

$$X = \sum m(1,3,4) = \bar{A}\bar{B}CE + \bar{A}BCE + A\bar{B}\bar{C}E = E(\bar{A}\bar{B}C + \bar{A}BC + A\bar{B}\bar{C})$$

15.6 h) CORRECT ANSWER: $E(A\bar{B}C + AB\bar{C} + ABC)$

$$Y = \sum m(5,6,7) = A\bar{B}CE + AB\bar{C}E + ABCE = E(A\bar{B}C + AB\bar{C} + ABC)$$

15.6 i) CORRECT ANSWER - B

A multiplex (MUX) with n selection lines will have 1 output and 2^n inputs. For example, MUX with 2 selection lines will have 4 inputs and 1 output. Similarly, MUX with 3 selection lines has 8 inputs and 1 output.

15.6 j) CORRECT ANSWER - A

$[2^4 \times 1]$ MUX will have 16 inputs, 4 selection lines and one output.

15.6 k) SOLUTION

Truth table of a $[4 \times 1]$ MUX is given below.

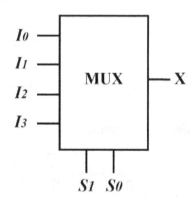

E	S_1	S_0	X
0	X	X	0
1	0	0	I_0
1	0	1	I_1
1	1	0	I_2
1	1	1	I_3

15.6 l) CORRECT ANSWER - C

The output X can be represented in terms of inputs, selection lines and enable as follows:

$$X = I_0 + I_1 + I_2 + I_3$$

$$X = E[\bar{S}_1\bar{S}_0 I_0 + \bar{S}_1 S_0 I_1 + S_1\bar{S}_0 I_2 + S_1 S_0 I_3]$$

15.6 m) SOLUTION

Truth table of a $[8 \times 1]$ MUX is given below.

E	S_2	S_1	S_0	X
0	X	X	X	0
1	0	0	0	I_0
1	0	0	1	I_1
1	0	1	0	I_2
1	0	1	1	I_3
1	1	0	0	I_4
1	1	0	1	I_5
1	1	1	0	I_6
1	1	1	1	I_7

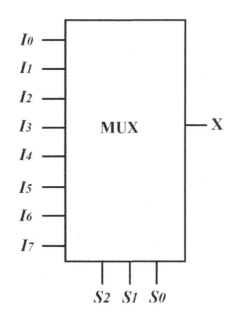

15.6 n) CORRECT ANSWER – C

$$f = I_0 + I_1 + I_2 + I_3$$

$$f = E[\bar{S_1}\bar{S_0}I_0 + \bar{S_1}S_0I_1 + S_1\bar{S_0}I_2 + S_1S_0I_3]$$

Substitute $E = 1,\ S_1 = X, S_0 = Y,\ I_0 = Z,\ I_1 = I_2 = I_3 = 1$

$$f = \bar{X}\bar{Y}Z + \bar{X}Y(1) + X\bar{Y}(1) + XY(1)$$

$$f = \bar{X}(\bar{Y}Z + Y) + X(\bar{Y} + Y)$$

According to Boolean algebra's redundancy law: $\bar{Y}Z + Y = Y + Z$

According to Boolean algebra's complement law: $\bar{Y} + Y = 1$

$$f = \bar{X}(Y + Z) + X(1)$$

$$f = \bar{X}Y + \bar{X}Z + X$$

$$f = \bar{X}Y + X + \bar{X}Z$$

According to Boolean algebra's redundancy law: $\bar{X}Y + X = X + Y$

$$f = X + Y + \bar{X}Z$$

$$f = \bar{X}Z + X + Y$$

According to Boolean algebra's redundancy law: $\bar{X}Z + X = X + Z$

$$f = X + Y + Z$$

15.7 – Programmable Logic Devices/Gate Array - Solutions

15.7 a) SOLUTION

Programmable Array Logic (PAL), Programmable Logic Array (PLA) and ROM fall under the category of programmable logic devices (PLDs). The main difference between these devices lies in programmability of their AND-plane and OR-plane.

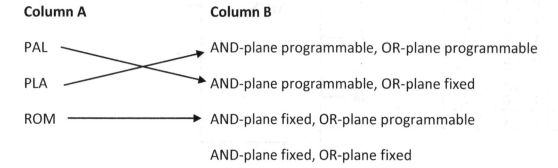

Column A

Column B

PAL

AND-plane programmable, OR-plane programmable

PLA

AND-plane programmable, OR-plane fixed

ROM

AND-plane fixed, OR-plane programmable

AND-plane fixed, OR-plane fixed

15.7 b) CORRECT ANSWER - B

It can be observed that given programmable logic device has a programmable AND-plane and a programmable OR-plane. Therefore, it is an example of a PLA.

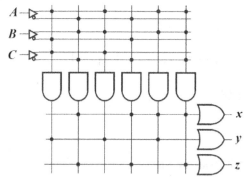

15.7 c) CORRECT ANSWER - C

It can be observed that output x is the sum of the output of 2nd, 4th, 5th and 6th AND gates (starting from left).

$$x = \bar{A}B\bar{C} + \bar{A}\bar{B}\bar{C} + AB + AB\bar{C}$$

15.7 d) CORRECT ANSWER - B

It can be observed that output y is the sum of the output of 1st, 3rd and 5th AND gates (starting from left).

$$y = A\bar{B}C + ABC + AB$$

15.7 e) CORRECT ANSWER - A

It can be observed that output z is the sum of the output of 2nd, 4th and 6th AND gates (starting from left).

$$z = \bar{A}B\bar{C} + \bar{A}\bar{B}\bar{C} + AB\bar{C}$$

15.7 f) CORRECT ANSWER - A

It can be observed that given programmable logic device has a programmable AND-plane and a fixed OR-plane. Therefore, it is an example of a PAL.

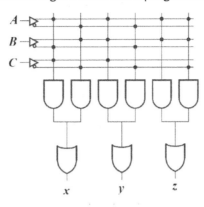

15.7 g) CORRECT ANSWER - C

It can be observed that x is the sum of the output of 1st and 2nd AND gates (starting from left).

$$x = A\bar{B}C + \bar{A}B\bar{C}$$

15.7 h) CORRECT ANSWER - B

It can be observed that y is the sum of the output of 3rd and 4th AND gates (starting from left).

$$y = ABC + \bar{A}\bar{B}\bar{C}$$

15.7 i) CORRECT ANSWER - A

It can be observed that z is the sum of the output of 5th and 6th AND gates (starting from left).

$$z = AB + AB\bar{C}$$

15.8 State Machine Design - Solutions

Consult NCEES® FE Reference Handbook – Page 34 for reference

15.8 a) CORRECT ANSWER - C

According to the state diagram, if present state is C and w = 0, system will transition to state A and output will be 1. Similarly, if present state is C and w = 1 system will transition to state B and output will be 1.

Helpful tip – Learn how to navigate from state table to state diagram and vice versa.

15.8 b) CORRECT ANSWER - D

The table given below summarizes transitions from initial state A if input = 111.

Current State, Input	Next State	Output
A, 1	B	0
B, 1	B	1
B, 1	B	1

15.8 c) CORRECT ANSWER - C

The table given below summarizes the transitions from initial state A if inputs = 000.

Current State, Input	Next State	Output
A, 0	C	0
C, 0	A	1
A, 0	C	0

15.8 d) CORRECT ANSWER - A

According to the state diagram, if present state is C and ab = 00 system will stay in state C and output will be 0.

Similarly, if present state is C and input ab = 01 system will transition to state D and output will be 0.

15.8 e) CORRECT ANSWER - D

The output expression for 'z' as a function of y_2y_1 can be found using k-map as shown below.

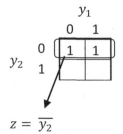

$$z = \overline{y_2}$$

4

352
Copyrighted Material © 2020

15.9 – Timing - Solutions

15.9 a) CORRECT ANSWER - B

For a logical circuit with positive edge-triggered clock, propagation delay is equal to the time difference between 50% mark of clock's triggering edge and 50% mark of output's changing state.

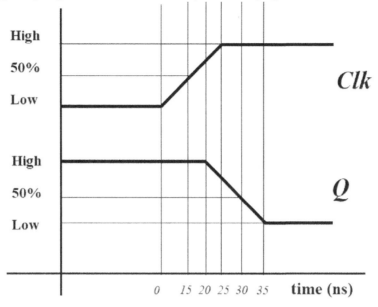

It can be observed that 50% mark of clock's triggering edge is at 15ns. 50% mark of output's changing state is at 30ns. Therefore, propagation delay $= 30ns - 15ns = 15ns$

15.9 b) CORRECT ANSWER - B

An input change that causes the output to unintentionally change from 1 to 0 to 1 when the output was originally expected to stay constant as 1, is called a 'Static-1 hazard'.

Note: Timing hazards are caused by propagation delays.

15.9 c) CORRECT ANSWER - C

An input change that causes the output to unintentionally change from 0 to 1 to 0 when the output was originally expected to stay constant as 0, is called a 'Static-0 hazard'.

15.9 d) CORRECT ANSWER - A

An input change that causes the output to unintentionally change from 0 to 1 to 0 to 1 or 1 to 0 to 1 to 0 when the output was expected to change just once as 0 to 1 or 1 to 0 is called a 'Dynamic hazard'.

15.9 e) CORRECT ANSWER - D

Racing condition can be observed in a JK Flip-Flop when clock signal is high and J = K = 1.

15.9 f) CORRECT ANSWER - C

Racing condition of JK Flip-Flop can be addressed by implementing a Master-Slave JK Flip-Flop.

Chapter # 16 – Computer Systems
16.1 Microprocessors - Solutions

Consult NCEES® FE Reference Handbook – Page 409 for reference

16.1 a) CORRECT ANSWER - B

Program counter register – contains the address of next instruction to be executed.
Stack pointer register – contains the address of last executed instruction.
Instruction pointer register – contains the address of the current instruction being executed.
Accumulator register – contains the results of arithmetic and logic operations.

16.1 b) CORRECT ANSWER - A

Program counter register – contains the address of next instruction to be executed.
Stack pointer register – contains the address of last executed instruction.
Instruction pointer register – contains the address of the current instruction being executed.
Accumulator register – contains the results of arithmetic and logic operations.

16.1 c) CORRECT ANSWER - A

Microprocessor – A single integrated circuit (IC) that accepts and executes code instructions for data processing data and controlling associated computer circuitry. It is basically a CPU on a programmable electronic chip. Examples include: Intel® 4004, Intel® 8008 and Intel® 8086.

Microcomputer – An interconnected group of integrated circuits (ICs), input/outputs and memory systems used for data processing and other applications. It is basically an assembly of microprocessors. Examples include Mark-8, Altair 880 etc.

Microcontroller – An integrated system of a single integrated circuit containing microprocessors, input/output devices and memory systems. Microcontrollers can be considered miniature computers designed to control small features of a large system. Examples include building automation, robotics, lighting controls, toys etc.

16.1 d) CORRECT ANSWER - B

RISC stands for "Reduced Instruction Set Computer". It uses a set of very simple but highly optimized set of instructions. This results in a reduction in the number of cycles per instruction and higher power efficiency. RISC is used in many portable devices such as music players, hand-held game consoles etc.

Helpful tip – Review CISC "Complex Instruction Set Computer" and compare it with RISC.

16.1 e) CORRECT ANSWER - B

ADD R5, #6 is an example of immediate addressing mode because in the case of immediate addressing mode, the constant (operand) data on which the action is performed is stored as part of the instruction. The range of constant data that can be used for immediate addressing is restricted by address field instruction size.

Op-Code	Operand

...ii add the constant 6 to register R5.

16.1 g) CORRECT ANSWER - D

LOAD R4, (R5) is an example of register indirect addressing mode because in the case of register indirect addressing mode, a register is used to hold effective address of the data (operand) on which an action is to be performed by the given instruction. This makes it possible to access large address spaces.

16.1 h) CORRECT ANSWER – D

LOAD R4, (R5) loads the content stored at memory location pointed by register R5 into register R4.

16.1 i) SOLUTION

Column A	Column B

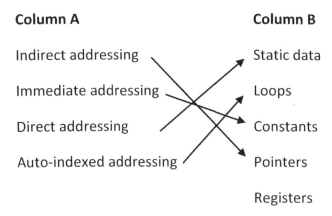

Indirect addressing — Pointers
Immediate addressing — Constants
Direct addressing — Static data
Auto-indexed addressing — Loops

Registers

16.1 j) CORRECT ANSWER – D

Option A is incorrect because multithreading allows simultaneous execution of multiple threads within a process. Thread is a subset of a process.

Option B is incorrect because single-core processors use time-division multiplexing to provide multithreading.

Option C is incorrect because multicore processors can provide true multithreading without multiplexing.

16.2 – Memory Technology & Systems - Solut...

Consult NCEES® FE Reference Handbook – Page 409 for reference

16.2 a) CORRECT ANSWER - D

Cassette tapes, CDs, DVDs, and hard disks are examples of sequential access storage devices. Flash memory is an example of a random-access storage device.

16.2 b) CORRECT ANSWER: 8×2^{30} bits

Giga in binary $= 2^{30}$ and $Byte = 8$. Therefore, $1\ Giga\ Byte = 8 \times 2^{30}\ bits$

Helpful tip – Review binary prefixes and unit conversions.

16.2 c) CORRECT ANSWER - C

Cache memory has low capacity and very high speed. It stores frequently used data for ready access.

16.2 d) CORRECT ANSWER - C

DVD is a secondary memory storage device. It is non-volatile and cannot be directly accessed by computer. Primary memory systems are volatile and can be accessed directly.

Helpful tip – Understand the difference between primary memory storage and secondary memory storage.

16.2 e) CORRECT ANSWER - A

PROM – Programmable Read-Only Memory can be programmed only once. EPROM – Erasable Programmable Read-Only Memory can be erased using ultra-violet light. EEPROM – Electrically Erasable Programmable Read-Only Memory can be erased electrically.

Helpful tip – Learn the difference between various types of ROMs.

16.2 f) CORRECT ANSWER - B

Bit = 1 digit, Byte = 8 digits, and Nibble = 4 digits.

Word can vary as 16/32/64 bits depending on system architecture.

16.2 g) CORRECT ANSWER: 18

Total number of address bits required for cache memory is determined by the size of main memory.

$256KB = 2^{18} bytes \rightarrow \log_2 2^{18} = 18\ bits$

16.2 h) CORRECT ANSWER: 9

Block offset bits are determined by the block size. According to problem statement, block size is 512 bytes. Therefore, block offset bits can be calculated as follows:

$\log_2 512 = \log_2 2^9 = 9\ bits$

16.2 i) CORRECT ANSWER: 6

Index bits are determined by the number of sets (S) which can be calculated as shown below.

$C = S * A * B$ where C = cache size = 32KB, A = 1 for direct mapped cache, B = block size = 512B, S = ?

$$S = \frac{C}{A * B} = \frac{32KB}{1 * 512B} = \frac{2^5 \times 2^{10}}{2^9} = 2^6$$

$\log_2 S = \log_2 2^6 = 6 \; bits$

16.2 j) CORRECT ANSWER: 3

According to NCEES® FE Reference Handbook, total number of tag bits can be calculated as follows:

tag bits = # address bits - # index bits - # block offset bits = 18 – 6 – 9 = 3

16.2 k) CORRECT ANSWER - A

Replacement policy is not required for direct mapping because new memory block from main memory simply overrides the existing cache memory block in the event of a collision. Replacement policy is required for fully associative and n-way set associative mapping techniques because main memory blocks can be placed in more than one location of cache memory.

Helpful tip – Review replacement policies LRU, MRU, LIFO, FIFO etc. for n-way set associative and fully associative mapping.

16.2 l) CORRECT ANSWER: 18

Total number of address bits required for cache memory address are determined by the size of main memory.

$256KB = 2^{18} bytes \rightarrow \log_2 2^{18} = 18 \; bits$

16.2 m) CORRECT ANSWER: 9

Total number of block offset bits is determined by block size. According to the problem statement, block size is 512 bytes. Therefore, block offset bits can be calculated as follows:

$\log_2 512 = \log_2 2^9 = 9 \; bits$

16.2 n) CORRECT ANSWER: 0

Fully-associative mapping does not require index bits because main memory block can go anywhere in the cache. Therefore, 0 bits are required for index field.

16.2 o) CORRECT ANSWER: 9

According to NCEES® FE Reference Handbook, total number of tag bits can be calculated as follows:

tag bits = # address bits - # index bits - # block offset bits = 18 – 0 – 9 = 9

16.2 p) CORRECT ANSWER: 9

Total number of block offset bits is determined by block size. According to the problem statement, block size is 512 bytes. Therefore, block offset bits can be calculated as follows:

$\log_2 512 = \log_2 2^9 = 9 \; bits$

16.2 q) CORRECT ANSWER: 16

Total number of sets (S) can be calculated using following formula.

$C = S * A * B$ where C = cache size = 32KB, $A = 4$, B = block size = 512B, $S = ?$

$$S = \frac{C}{A * B} = \frac{32KB}{4 * 512B} = \frac{2^5 \times 2^{10}}{2^2 \times 2^9} = 2^4 = 16$$

16.2 r) CORRECT ANSWER: 4

Total number of index bits is determined by number of sets (S) which can be calculated as shown below.

$$\log_2 S = \log_2 2^4 = 4 \; bits$$

16.2 s) CORRECT ANSWER: 5

According to NCEES® FE Reference Handbook, the total number of tag bits can be calculated as follows:

tag bits = # address bits - # index bits - # block offset bits = $18 - 4 - 9 = 5$

16.2 t) CORRECT ANSWER - D

Average memory access time (AMAT) can be calculated using following formula:

AMAT = hit-time + miss-rate x miss penalty = 5ns + (100%-90%) x 200ns

AMAT = 5ns + 10% x 200ns = 25ns

16.3 – Architecture & Interfacing - Solutions

Consult NCEES® FE Reference Handbook – Page 409 for reference

16.3 a) CORRECT ANSWER - B

RAM – Random Access Memory (RAM) is a type of computer storage memory. Typically, it is volatile, and BIOS is loaded into RAM only after computer boots. ROM – Read Only Memory (ROM) is a type of computer storage memory. It is non-volatile and BIOS is generally stored in ROM which is used to boot the computer.
USB – It is typically used as secondary memory storage device for portable data storage options.

16.3 b) CORRECT ANSWER - B

Encryption is a data conversion process which prevents unauthorized personnel from accessing. Encoding is a data transformation process which involves changing data format for another system. Hashing transforms a string into shorter fixed length value representing original string. Decoding is the opposite of encoding and converts encoded data to its original format.

16.3 c) CORRECT ANSWER - D

Computer architecture describes the logical and functional design of a computer system including its instruction sets, registers, addressing mode etc. It deals with high level issues. Computer organization describes the structure and connection of various components within a computer system and deals with low level issues.

16.3 d) CORRECT ANSWER - D

Central Processing Unit (CPU) is responsible for decoding and executing instructions. It consists of Arithmetic Logic Unit (ALU), Control Unit (CU) and Register Array/Set. ALU performs arithmetic and logic operations such as ADD, subtract, AND, OR etc. Control Unit co-ordinates operations between ALU, memory and I/O devices. Registers are storage devices that are used for extremely fast (but very small) memory access.

16.3 e) CORRECT ANSWER - D

Bus provides communication path between CPU and its peripheral devices. They can be broadly classified as:
1) Address bus – allows CPU to address memory locations. It is unidirectional and only carries address.
2) Data bus – Bidirectional bus that carries data/instructions between CPU and peripheral devices
3) Control bus – Bidirectional bus that carries primary command/control and timing signals.

16.3 f) CORRECT ANSWER - B

The width of a data bus determines the amount of data that can be transferred per unit time. A wider data bus will be able to transfer more data per unit time which results in a higher computer speed. Overall system performance also depends on several other factors.

16.3 g) CORRECT ANSWER - B

Von Neumann/Princeton architecture comprises of a main memory which is used to store both data and instruction. Control unit communicates with this memory using a single pathway which is known as Von Neumann bottleneck. In comparison, Harvard architecture consists of dedicated pathways for data and instruction. Both computer architectures are used in modern computer design.

Chapter # 17 – Software Engineering
17.1 – Algorithms – Complexity/Big-O - Solutions
Consult NCEES® FE Reference Handbook – Page 412 for reference

17.1 a) CORRECT ANSWER: 7

Values at the end of loop # 1 are as follows: y = 1, x = 1, z = 7

Values at the end of loop # 2 are as follows: y = 2, x = 3, z = 4

Values at the end of loop # 3 are as follows: y = 3, x = 5, z = 1

Values at the end of loop # 4 are as follows: y = 4, x = 7, z = -2

z < 0 at the end of loop # 4 therefore program will not run loop # 5 and values at the end of loop # 4 are final.

17.1 b) CORRECT ANSWER: 2^9

Values at the end of loop # 1 are as follows: N = 2^1 + 1 = 3, temp = 2^1

Values at the end of loop # 2 are as follows: N = 2^3 + 1 = 9, value = 2^3

Values at the end of loop # 3 are as follows: N = 2^9 + 1 > 100, value = 2^9

N > 100 at the end of loop # 3 therefore program will not run loop # 4 and values at the end of loop # 3 are final.

17.1 c) CORRECT ANSWER - C

The dominant term in $60 + 0.005n^3 + 0.01n$ is $0.005n^3$. This term will grow fastest and determine the overall processing time of the algorithm as n becomes very large. Therefore, for the given algorithm Big-O is $O(n^3)$.

Note: The constant 0.005 is ignored due to coefficient rule for Big-O calculation.

17.1 d) CORRECT ANSWER - C

The dominant term in $0.5n + 15n^2 + 20n \log_2 n$ is $15n^2$. This term will grow fastest and determine the overall processing time of this algorithm as n becomes very large. Therefore, for the given algorithm Big-O is $O(n^2)$.

Note: The constant 15 is ignored due to coefficient rule for Big-O calculation.

17.1 e) CORRECT ANSWER - A

Option A is an incorrect representation of Big-O's rule of sums. The correct representation of Big-O's rule of sums is provided in Option C. Option B is a correct representation of Big-O's rule of products. Option D is a correct representation of Big-O's scaling/coefficient rule.

17.1 f) CORRECT ANSWER - B

The dominant (and only) term in algorithm X's processing time equation is $0.2n^2 \log_{10} n$.

Big-O expression for algorithm X is $O(n^2 \log_{10} n)$.

The dominant (and only) term in algorithm Y's processing time equation is $10n^2$.

Big-O expression for algorithm Y is $O(n^2)$.

Algorithm Y is more efficient for very large values of n because $O(n^2) < O(n^2 \log_{10} n)$.

17.1 g) CORRECT ANSWER: 10^{50}

To calculate n_o we need to find n for which: Run-time of algorithm X $\leq$ Run-time of algorithm Y.

$$0.2n^2 \log_{10} n_o \leq 10{n_o}^2$$

$$\log_{10} n_o \leq 50$$

$$n_o \leq 10^{50}$$

Therefore, if problem size $n_o \leq 10^{50}$, algorithm X will perform better than Y.

17.1 h) CORRECT ANSWER - B

Worst-case time complexity of the nested loops with counters 'i' and 'j' is $O(n^2)$.

The worst-case time complexity of loop with counter 'k' is $O(n)$.

Overall time complexity of this code fragment can be calculated by using the rule of sums as shown below:

$$O(x + y) = O\big(\max(O(x), O(y))\big)$$

$$O(x + y) = O\big(\max(O(n^2), O(n))\big)$$

$$O(x + y) = O(n^2).$$

17.1 i) CORRECT ANSWER - B

2^n grows faster than n^2 for large values of n.

Therefore, $O(2^n) > O(n^2)$.

17.2 a) CORRECT ANSWER - C

1st pass of bubble sort will involve following steps:

4 is compared with 0. Since 4 > 0, swap the items.

4	0	3	1	7

4 is compared with 3. Since 4 > 3, swap the items.

0	4	3	1	7

4 is compared with 1. Since 4 > 1, swap the items.

0	3	4	1	7

4 is compared with 7. Since 4 < 7, swapping not required.

0	3	1	4	7

2nd pass of bubble sort will involve following steps:

0 is compared with 3. Since 0 < 3, swapping not required.

0	3	1	4	7

3 is compared with 1. Since 3 > 1, swap the items.

0	3	1	4	7

3 is compared with 4. Since 3 < 4, swapping not required.

0	1	3	4	7

After two passes of bubble sort, the array will be:

0	1	3	4	7

Notice that in the 1st pass, n – 1 comparisons were made whereas n – 2 comparisons were made in second pass.

17.2 b) CORRECT ANSWER - C

Total number of passes required to sort an unsorted array of 'n' items using bubble sort = n – 1. Total number of comparisons required by bubble sort $= (n)(n-1)/2 = (7)(6)/2 = 21$

17.2 c) CORRECT ANSWER - B

Best case time complexity of bubble sort is $O(n)$. This is possible when the list is already sorted. Bubble sort will only run for 1 pass, perform n – 1 comparisons and zero swaps. $O(n)$ means that the algorithm will still have to travel through the entire list of 'n' items.

17.2 d) CORRECT ANSWER: 7

Insertion sort requires n – 1 passes to completely sort a list of 'n' items. Therefore, 8 – 1 = 7 passes will be required to sort an unsorted array of 8 items using insertion sort.

17.2 e) CORRECT ANSWER - A

Key = 15 is in its correct location with respect to (w.r.t) 10.

10	15	5	13

Key = 5 needs to be inserted in its correct location w.r.t 10, 15.

10	15	5	13

Key = 13 needs to be inserted in its correct location w.r.t 5, 10, 15.

5	10	15	13

Once 13 is inserted in its correct location, sorting will be complete.

5	10	13	15

17.2 f) CORRECT ANSWER - D

The final step of merge sort requires combining two sorted sub-arrays into a single larger array. To achieve this, we need enough space to hold the merged result. Since the two sub-arrays have a total of 'n' items, we need an additional $O(n)$ space.

17.2 g) CORRECT ANSWER - D

Merge sort requires same number of steps to be executed for each scenario. Therefore, its time complexity is identical in each case i.e. $O(n \log n)$.

17.2 h) CORRECT ANSWER - A

Since both sub-arrays a[ ] and b[ ] are already sorted, we will compare first items of each sub-array and place the smaller of the two items at the front of final merged array c[ ] as shown below.

14	46	60	64		31	33	76	82

14							

The next comparison will be made between 46 from 1st sub-array and 31 in the 2nd sub-array. Since 31 < 46, 31 will be inserted next to 14 in the merged array. This process will be repeated until the entire merged list is complete and all the items from two sub-arrays have been inserted in correct locations.

Helpful tip – Complete necessary comparisons and insert all items from sub-arrays into merged array.

17.2 i) CORRECT ANSWER - D

Selecting the first or last items of a given list/array as a pivot for quick sort is very easy to implement. However, if the list is sorted or partially sorted, quick sort's performance will reduce to $O(n^2)$ with this pivot selection. Most items will end up in either left sub-array or right sub-array due to which the true advantage of quick sort i.e. divide-and-conquer will not be utilized.

Median-of-three is relatively simple to code but slightly slower than just selecting the first or last element. It offers a greater chance to achieve $O(n \log n)$ performance but a list/array can still be constructed to result in $O(n^2)$ performance as a worst-case scenario.

Random selection is more complicated to implement because of the overhead involved in the form of random number generator. It offers the best chance to achieve $O(n \log n)$ performance because it is very difficult to come up with a worst-case array arrangement that can result in $O(n^2)$ performance.

17.2 j) CORRECT ANSWER: 43

Median-of-three is calculated by selecting the median from the first (43), middle (17) and last (73) array elements.

Median {43, 17, 73}. It can be observed that in {43, 17, 73}, $17 \leq 43 \leq 73$. Therefore, median-of-three for given array is 43. As discussed in the previous solution, median-of-three results in a better Big-O performance than selecting first or last array element as pivot.

17.2 k) CORRECT ANSWER - C

In Option C, all items to the left of 4 are < 4 and all items to the right of 4 are > 4. This means that pivot has probably been inserted in its correct location using quick sort. In quick sort, two pointers (left and right) are used as shown below. Both pointers are moved towards the middle of the array in a stepwise manner. Left pointer searches for items > Pivot and right pointer searches for items < Pivot.

3	9	8	10	2	11	4
L-Pointer					R-Pointer	Pivot

Initially, left pointer = 3 < Pivot. We need to advance the left pointer until we find an item > Pivot.

3	9	8	10	2	11	4
	L-Pointer				R-Pointer	Pivot

Left pointer = 9 > Pivot. This entry needs to be swapped with a right pointer item < Pivot.
Right pointer = 11 > Pivot. We need to advance the right pointer until we find an item < Pivot.

3	9	8	10	2	11	4
	L-Pointer			R-Pointer		Pivot

Right pointer = 2 < Pivot, now we can swap left pointer item with right pointer item as shown below.

3	2	8	10	9	11	4
	L-Pointer			R-Pointer		Pivot

Left pointer = 2 < Pivot. We need to advance the left pointer until we find an item > Pivot.

3	2	8	10	9	11	4
		L-Pointer		R-Pointer		Pivot

Left pointer = 8 > Pivot. This entry needs to be swapped with a right pointer item < Pivot.
Right pointer = 9 > Pivot. We need to advance the right pointer until we find an item < Pivot.

3	2	8	10	9	11	4
		L-Pointer	R-Pointer			Pivot

Right pointer = 10 > Pivot. We need to advance the right point until we find an item < Pivot.

3	2	8	10	9	11	4
		L-Pointer R-Pointer				Pivot

Right pointer = 8 > Pivot. We need to advance the right point until we find an item < Pivot.

3	2	8	10	9	11	4
	R-Pointer	L-Pointer				Pivot

Since right pointer has crossed left pointer, we can be sure that all the items smaller than pivot are correctly inserted before left pointer. We can simply insert the pivot in its correct location by swapping it with left pointer item. Now, our pivot 4 has been inserted in its correct location using quick sort.

3	2	4	10	9	11	8

Helpful tip – Continue sorting this array using quick sort until it is completely sorted.

17.2 l) CORRECT ANSWER - C

Array Index	0	1	2	3	4
	5	10	15	25	105

We can apply binary search algorithm as shown below:

1st recursion:

Low index (L)= 0, High index = 4, Middle index (M) = L + (H − L)/2 = 0 + (4 − 0)/2 = 2
Index 2 item = 15, 15 < 105. Now L = M + 1 = 2 + 1 = 3

2nd recursion:

L = 3, H = 4, M = L + (H − L)/2 = 3 + (4 − 3)/2 = 3 + 0 = 3   Note: ½ = 0.5 but in the integer form 0.5 = 0
Index 3 item = 25, 25 < 105. Now L = M + 1 = 3 + 1 = 4

3rd recursion:

L = 4, H = 4, M = L + (H − L)/2 = 4 + (4 − 4)/2 = 4 + 0 = 4
Index 4 item = 105 = search key.

Therefore, we require 3 recursions to find 105 using binary search on the given array.

Helpful tip – Understand binary search algorithm's formulas for calculation of low, middle, and high indices.

17.2 m) CORRECT ANSWER – A

Hash table can be constructed using array entries and hash function as shown below.

Array Item	Hash Function	Index
20	20 % 8 = 4	4
10	10 % 8 = 2	2
16	16 % 8 = 0	0
14	14 % 8 = 6	6
15	15 % 8 = 7	7
17	17 % 8 = 1	1

Note: % represents modulus operator which returns the remainder of division. Therefore, hash table for given array and hash function can be represented as follows:

Index	0	1	2	3	4	5	6	7
	16	17	10		20		14	15

Helpful tip – Although in this problem, each array item has been successfully hashed to a unique index, it is possible that in another scenario two or more items might hash to same index. In such cases, a collision resolution technique is used to address loss of data. Some of the common resolution techniques include linear probing, quadrative probing, plus-3 probing and chaining.

17.3 a) CORRECT ANSWER - C

The array given in problem statement can be represented as follows:

Array Index	0	1	2	3	4	5
	11	9	15	16	21	3

It is important to note that the counter $'i'$ will reach a maximum value of 3 before exiting the loop. Therefore, only the array items at index 0, 1, 2 and 3 will get printed i.e. 11, 9, 15 and 16.

17.3 b) CORRECT ANSWER - C

Linked list is a data structure that organizes items sequentially. To count the total number of items in a linked list, it is necessary to traverse through the entire list until a node is found for which next pointer is null. Key performance parameters of linked list are summarized in the table given below.

Performance Parameter	Worst-case Scenario Performance
Space complexity	$O(n)$
Insertion at the beginning	$O(1)$
Insertion at the end	$O(1)$
Insertion within the list	$O(n)$
Deletion	$O(n)$
Search	$O(n)$
Traversal/Counting	$O(n)$

Linked list's main advantage is its flexibility with respect to its size. Unlike arrays, there is no need to declare linked list's size in advance because it can dynamically grow and shrink during run-time.

17.3 c) CORRECT ANSWER - D

The function given in problem statement adds a new node at the beginning of the linked list as follows:
// Reference to head of the list is provided along with data of integer type to the function
struct node * function (struct node * head, int data) {
// A new node 'temp' is declared within the function and memory is allocated to it
struct node * temp = (struct node*) malloc (size(struct node));
// Data field of 'temp' will hold input data
temp -> data = data;
// next of 'temp' is made to point to head
temp -> next = head;
// 'temp' is returned as the new head pointer
return (temp); }
This function will be called in the main ( ) body as follows:
head = function (head, 10); where 10 is an arbitrary integer data for the new node.
Helpful tip – Understand pseudo code of other linked list functions such as insertion at end/beginning, deletion.

17.3 d) CORRECT ANSWER - C

Linked list node contains data and a link to the next node as shown below.

17.3 e) CORRECT ANSWER - A

The process of adding data to a stack is called 'Push' operation. Stack stores data as last-in, first-out (LIFO) order. A pile of plates on a table is an example of a stack. The plate that is placed last on this pile is removed first. 'Pop' function removes the item from top of the stack. 'Top' function views the item on the top of stack without removing it. Key performance parameters of stack are summarized in the table given below.

Performance Parameter	Worst-case Scenario Performance
Space complexity	$O(n)$
Push	$O(1)$
Pop	$O(1)$
Peek/Top	$O(1)$

17.3 f) CORRECT ANSWER - C

The function given in problem statement displays the item at the top of stack. It is called 'Top' or 'Peek'. When this function is called in the main ( ) body of the program it will display the data contained in the data field of top most node of the stack.
Note: Stacks can be implemented using array as well as linked list. Review and understand implementation of other important stack operations including Push, Pop, Search, Traversal, Min, Max etc.

17.3 g) CORRECT ANSWER - D

Sequence of popped values is 8, 10 as explained below.

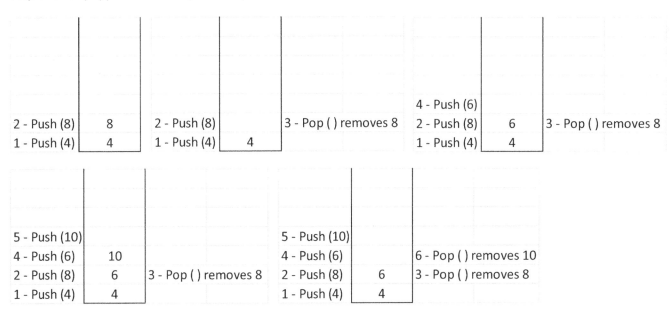

17.3 h) CORRECT ANSWER - D

As explained in the previous solution, after performing Push (4), Push (8), Pop ( ), Push (6), Push (10) and Pop ( ) operations, the stack will look as follows:

5 - Push (10)		
4 - Push (6)		6 - Pop ( ) removes 10
2 - Push (8)	6	3 - Pop ( ) removes 8
1 - Push (4)	4	

17.3 i) CORRECT ANSWER - B

Dequeue ( ) operation (deletion) is being performed by given function. It is printing the data value of item at the front of the queue and discarding reference to this item by making the front pointer to point to the item after the printed item.

Note: Also review and understand pseudo code of Enqueue ( ), Peek ( ) and Display ( ) functions.

17.3 j) CORRECT ANSWER - B

Enqueue ( ) operation on this queue will be performed as follows:

5 will be inserted at the front of queue followed by 6, 3, 1 and 9.

Dequeue ( ) operation on this queue will be performed as follows:

5 will be dequeued followed by 6, 3, 1, and 9.

It can be observed that a queue follows first-in, first-out (FIFO) order of operation.

17.4 a) CORRECT ANSWER - C

Tree is a non-linear data structure that organizes data hierarchically. Information is stored in nodes. First node of a tree is called the root. Every node links to zero or more child nodes. For all nodes other than root node, there is one parent node. Degree of a node is defined as the number of its children. Depth of a node is defined as the length of path from roots to the node (each node has a unique path to root). Height of a tree is defined as the maximum depth of any node within the tree.

17.4 b) CORRECT ANSWER - D

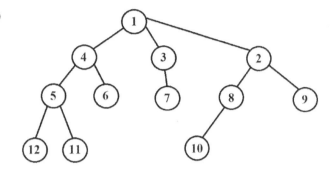

12, 11 and 10 are the deepest nodes in given tree with a depth of 3. Therefore, height of this tree is 3.

17.4 c) CORRECT ANSWER - A

Depth of root node is always equal to 0.

17.4 d) CORRECT ANSWER - C

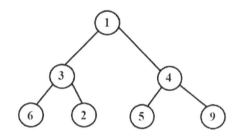

According to in-order tree traversal algorithm, we are required to traverse left sub-tree, then visit the current (root) node and finally traverse the right sub-tree at the end. Therefore, in-order tree traversal of given binary tree will be as follows: 6, 3, 2, 1, 5, 4 and 9.

17.4 e) CORRECT ANSWER - B

According to pre-order tree traversal algorithm, we are required to visit the current (root) node, then traverse left sub-tree and finally traverse the right sub-tree at the end. Therefore, pre-order tree traversal of given binary tree will be as follows: 1, 3, 6, 2, 4, 5 and 9.

17.4 f) CORRECT ANSWER - A

According to post-order tree traversal algorithm, we are required to traverse left sub-tree, then right sub-tree and finally visit the current (root) node. Therefore, post-order tree traversal of given binary tree will be as follows: 6, 2, 3, 5, 9, 4 and 1.

17.4 g) CORRECT ANSWER - D

Graphs allow arbitrary relationships between any two vertices (nodes). Tree is a special (structured) type of graph. A graph 'G' is defined as G = (V, E) where V is the set of all vertices and E is the set of all edges.

A graph can be represented as adjacency matrix, adjacency list or an incidence matrix.

Adjacency matrix – Represents graph in the form of a n x n matrix where n is the number of vertices.
Adjacency list – Represents graph in the form of a n x 1 array of pointers where each element points to a linked list of edges that are found on vertices.
Incidence matrix – Represents n x m matrix where n is the number of vertices and m is the number of edges.

17.4 h) CORRECT ANSWER: 4 x 4

Since there are 4 vertices, we require a 4 x 4 adjacency matrix as shown below. Matrix entries for adjacent vertices are set to 1. For example, A – C = 1, C – A = 1 but A – B = 0.

	A	B	C	D
A	0	0	1	0
B	0	0	0	1
C	1	0	0	1
D	0	1	1	0

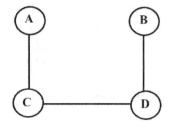

17.4 i) CORRECT ANSWER: 6

As explained in previous solution, there are 6 non-zero entries in the adjacency matrix of given graph.

17.4 j) CORRECT ANSWER - B

Breadth first search (BFS) algorithm is used for traversing a graph (and sometimes trees). It requires visiting all the unvisited nodes adjacent to starting node. This process is repeated for each visited node as shown in the figure on right.

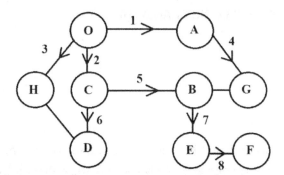

17.4 k) CORRECT ANSWER – A, D

Depth first search (DFS) algorithm is used for traversing a graph (and sometimes trees). It requires visiting one unvisited adjacent node and traversing down one path as deep as possible before backtracking to the last visited node and repeating the process until all nodes have been visited. There are two possible solutions to this problem as shown in the diagram. The underlined traversal sequence represents Option A and the one without underline represents Option D.

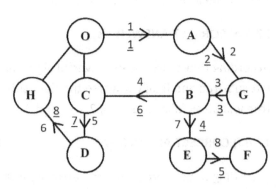

370

17.5 – Software design methods/implementation/testing - Solutions
Consult NCEES® FE Reference Handbook – Pages 412 – 413 for reference

17.5 a) CORRECT ANSWER - Fragile

Rigid – A software design that is difficult to change.
Fragile – A software design that is prone to breaking in multiple places whenever a change is made.
Portable – A software design that ca n be used in different environments.
Immobile – A software design that is difficult to reuse for different projects.

17.5 b) CORRECT ANSWER - A

Static software testing involves verification using program code reviews, walk-throughs and inspections.

17.5 c) CORRECT ANSWER – White box

Glass box/White box testing involves detailed investigation of code's internal logic and structure. Internal details of the code are made available to the tester so that tester can investigate if any section of the code is non-compliant with performance requirements. White-box testing is in-depth detailed. But it can be time consuming and costly.

17.5 d) CORRECT ANSWER – Black box

Black-box testing does not require tester to have any knowledge of code's internal structure. Tester does not have access to source code. Tester simply provides a set of inputs and compares the outputs with a pre-established set of expected results to determine whether the software is meeting performance requirements or not. Black-box testing does not require highly skilled testers and it can be completed quickly. However, it provides limited coverage and requires good test cases to be effective.

17.5 e) CORRECT ANSWER – C

Unit-testing involves dynamically executing units of codes to verify their individual performance. It helps in isolating code sections and demonstrating their functionality. However, unit testing cannot catch the problems that may result from interaction of different code sections i.e. problems residing at the boundaries.
Helpful tip – Also review the procedure involved in system-testing, integration testing and user acceptance testing. Understand the difference between dynamic and static testing.

17.5 f) CORRECT ANSWER – C

Waterfall model is a linear/sequential process of software development which consists of predetermined phases and milestones. It is managed by means of milestone reviews, baselines, and version controls. Some of the key steps involved in waterfall model include specification development, software design, implementation, and testing. Being a one-pass software development model, it has the advantage of being simple, easy to implement and manage. However, its rigidity does not allow major scope changes during execution and it is not suitable for complex projects.
Helpful tip – Also review iterative model, V-model, and code-and-fix model.

17.5 g) CORRECT ANSWER – B

The algorithm represented by flow chart in this problem calculates and prints average of 'n' inputs.

FE Electrical and Computer Exam Preparation

Fundamentals of Engineering (FE) Electrical and Computer – Practice Exam # 1

Fundamentals of Engineering (FE) Electrical and Computer – Practice Exam # 2

Fundamentals of Engineering (FE) Electrical and Computer – Practice Exam # 3

On-demand FE Electrical and Computer Exam Preparation Course

containing 150+ lectures with detailed explanations and step-by-step solutions

PE Electrical and Computer – Power Exam Preparation

Study Guide for PE Electrical and Computer – Power Exam

On-demand PE Power Exam Preparation Course

containing 100+ lectures based on the latest exam specification

Visit **www.studyforfe.com** for more details.

Made in the USA
Monee, IL
24 May 2025

18090714R00208